Listening to the Jar Flies

Listening to the Jar Flies

Growing Up in Wheaton and Rocky Comfort

Jimmy R. Lewis

LISTENING TO THE JAR FLIES
GROWING UP IN WHEATON AND ROCKY COMFORT

iUniverse books may be ordered through booksellers or by contacting:

iUniverse
1663 Liberty Drive
Bloomington, IN 47403
www.iuniverse.com
1-800-Authors (1-800-288-4677)

Because of the dynamic nature of the Internet, any web addresses or links contained in this book may have changed since publication and may no longer be valid. The views expressed in this work are solely those of the author and do not necessarily reflect the views of the publisher, and the publisher hereby disclaims any responsibility for them.

Any people depicted in stock imagery provided by Thinkstock are models, and such images are being used for illustrative purposes only.
Certain stock imagery © Thinkstock.

ISBN: 978-1-4917-6664-4 (sc)
ISBN: 978-1-4917-6665-1 (e)

Library of Congress Control Number: 2015907354

Print information available on the last page.

iUniverse rev. date: 06/15/2015

To my daughters, Angela Lewis Isaacs and Shannon Lewis Vigil; their husbands, Seth Isaacs and Donald Vigil; and my grandchildren, Stella and Cyrus Isaacs and Lila Ray Vigil, so they will know more about life in the Missouri Ozarks.

Contents

Preface

This book began as my spring tonic—a cup of sassafras tea for my spirit. Nearly every year in the early spring, after the sap started to run in the Ozark hills of southwest Missouri where I grew up, my mother would grab a shovel, and we would walk to the patch of sassafras trees in the field south of our barn and dig until we exposed the orange roots. Then we would cut small chunks of the root ends, take them home, and boil them. The result was sassafras tea. The old-timers said sassafras tea was a spring tonic that thinned the blood, cleared the winter cobwebs, and prepared the body for the hard work of the summer to come.

In the spring of 1996, as I was recuperating from surgery in Fair Oaks, California, I was eighteen hundred miles and forty years removed from the old sassafras patch, but I needed an elixir. My body was healing, but I needed a tonic to boost my morale. Sitting on my patio in the spring sun, I decided to take a look at the notes I had scribbled the previous summer before delivering a short talk about my recollections of my hometown of Wheaton, Missouri. The occasion had been a reunion of all the Wheaton High School classes of the 1950s. I had taken the Wheaton High alums—who by then were scattered from Alaska to Florida—on a memory walk down the three blocks of Main Street as it was in the 1940s and '50s.

Wheaton was, and still is, just a dot on a map—population 393 in 1940, the year after I was born, and 394 in 1950 when I was eleven. Apparently, no one had died, and someone had had a baby during that decade. Just two and a half miles to the southwest of Wheaton is another relic of my childhood, Rocky Comfort, a town that is an even smaller, but much older, dot on the map. Rocky, as the locals call it, was established in the 1850s near the headwaters of Indian Creek. By 1900, it was a thriving town of several hundred persons and businesses, including grocery stores, a grain mill, a bank, a drugstore, a lumberyard, a post office, cafés, and more.

Then in 1907, a small railroad company, the Missouri and North Arkansas (M&NA), laid the tracks for a new rail line that eventually connected Neosho and Joplin, Missouri, to small towns in Arkansas, including Eureka Springs, Harrison, and Helena. Instead of going through the two pioneer towns of Stella and Rocky Comfort, Missouri, the M&NA decided to bypass those two towns and build a depot in a wheat field two and a half miles to the northeast of Rocky Comfort. The depot became Wheaton.

It was the beginning of Rocky's slow decline. Over the next four decades, a number of Rocky's merchants and a prominent physician reestablished themselves in Wheaton. Rocky's numbers shrank to 284 in 1940 and then to 230 in 1950. I doubt that there are even one hundred persons living there now, and most of the businesses are gone. Wheaton, on the other hand, became a bustling little town and a source of decades-long irritation for lots of locals who remained loyal to Rocky. By 2012, Wheaton's population had ballooned to 695.

As I was growing up, I had a foot in both communities. My family's farm was located three miles west of Wheaton, where I went to school from seventh grade through high school after six years at a one-room country school called Oshkosh. When I looked to the east from our front yard, I could see Wheaton's water tower. When I looked to the southeast, I could see the redbrick Rocky Comfort school building.

I went to church at Rocky Comfort, where I regularly caught up on Rocky news from my best friend, Dan Shewmake, because that's where he went to school. When the rural Oshkosh School District was split into three parts after my sixth grade year, our farm became part of the Wheaton Consolidated School District, so during junior high and high school, I kept Dan informed on news in Wheaton.

For years, after graduating from Wheaton High and finishing my formal education at the University of Missouri, I regaled friends and colleagues with stories about the colorful persons, young and old, whom I had known in both communities. But I'd never tried to write about those very practical, often comical, but extremely wise people of those two communities who had shaped and enriched my life. In that spring of 1996, I decided it was time.

I began to write—not hurriedly as I did on a typewriter and then a computer keyboard during the nearly quarter century that I was a newspaper reporter in St. Louis and Sacramento, or later when I had staff jobs on Capitol Hill, for the California State Legislature, the California State Treasurer, and the State Building & Construction Trades Council of California. Instead, I wrote slowly in longhand, with a pen, on a yellow legal tablet as I sat in my backyard.

At first, I was content to write only from memory, but after talking with friends who had grown up in both the Wheaton and Rocky Comfort communities, I began to accumulate a much wider range of stories about the folks we knew as kids—some who were my grandparents' age and long since departed; some who were my parents' age, many of whom also had gone on; and others of my own generation who had pushed the envelope of achievement well beyond what might have been expected of someone from a small town that was off the beaten path.

Then something happened that made me determined to expand the scope of my stories.

Some 250 graduates of Wheaton High during the 1950s gathered for a reunion on Saturday, September 3, 2005. They agreed to a proposal presented by 1954 Wheaton High graduate Jon Paden to purchase and preserve a set of microfilm of all available copies of the weekly *Wheaton Journal*, a newspaper that reported news in the Wheaton area and its surrounding farm communities, including Rocky Comfort. By the end of the day, support sufficient to purchase microfilm from the State Historical Society of Missouri had been pledged by the assembled graduates.

In February 2006, the Wheaton graduates of the 1950s donated a set of *Journal* microfilm to the Barry-Lawrence Regional Library in Cassville, the county seat of Barry County where Wheaton is located.[1] Now copies of the *Journal* are available on DVD for editions that start in 1919 and continue, with a few gaps, through the paper's closure in 2005.

I suddenly had a trove of information about the people who had lived in and near those two little towns when I was a boy. In 2007, my cousin Ralph Lamberson and his wife, Betty, who was a Wheaton High classmate of mine, compiled a book of Wheaton's history, *Wheaton Echoes*, that also was a valuable resource. Some information was also found in the *Cassville Democrat*, books, and various websites.

As a result of the new information that became available, there are three types of stories in this book—the ones that come purely from my memory; the ones that combine my memory with articles in the *Wheaton Journal*, the *Cassville Democrat*, and *Wheaton Echoes*; and the ones that come from historical research into events around Wheaton and Rocky Comfort that occurred before I was born.

ABOVE: Missouri state map   BELOW: Southwest Missouri, home of Wheaton & Rocky Comfort

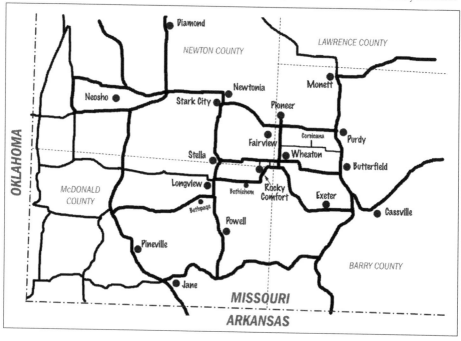

Introduction

From time to time—and exactly when is never predictable—the memories of our childhoods open the doors of our consciousness without knocking. Sometimes they barge in wearing heavy work shoes, yelling for attention: a sudden vision of "Uncle" Newt Kelly— long since gone on to his eternal reward—spitting tobacco juice to the side of the wagon, snapping the reins and cursing in machine-gun bursts to encourage more effort out of a pair of small mules as they strain to pull a great load of gravel out of Indian Creek.

Sometimes those memories just waft in through open windows in our minds, insinuating themselves at first like the faint scent of our mothers' lilac perfume until their sweetness overwhelms all other thought: Sitting on Granddad and Grandma's back porch in the twilight of a warm summer day ... watching Granddad fit his high-top leather work shoe over an iron shoe last so he can pound down a tack that had poked through the sole ... drinking in the smell of the honeysuckle growing on the garden fence near the locust tree where jar flies pierce the heavy evening air with sounds like a grindstone on metal.

The bad memories—the ones that still wound us to the core of our souls—often gather slowly like the white, puffy cumulus clouds that are so pretty in the morning but which pile together in the afternoon until they take the shape of an anvil that God pounds with his hammer, sending lightning and hail and wind and rain: my cousin Bill Slinkard killed on a road deep in the hill country of northern Arkansas when a waterlogged tree fell on his milk truck ...

Bill Haynes, when he was a Wheaton High junior, shaking with great sobs while leaning on the casket of Thelma Smith, the high-school English teacher.

But the mental storms, like the thunderstorms that strike the Ozarks with unpredictable irregularity, soon blow over, replaced by blue skies of remembered humor: "Uncle" John Robinson, our neighbor, who—at my dad's deadpan suggestion—employed a unique method of taking the squeal out of his radio ... Palo Stewart, deep in the hills, cooling his food in a way that wouldn't have earned the Good Housekeeping Seal ... Brock Cantrell handling his brother Arch's departure from this walk of life the old-fashioned way.

Some memories are neither fair nor foul, but vivid nevertheless. Like the metallic, grinding song of the jar flies, those memories also can't be ignored: Wheaton on a Saturday afternoon when the town was full of farm families ... men in bib overalls and women in print dresses made from feed sacks ... the screaming and shouting of the crowd when the Rocky Comfort Greyhounds played the Wheaton Bulldogs in a basketball game ... Wheaton barber Bryan Wolfenbarger chain-smoking cigarettes while he cut your hair ... Luther Cartwright, blue chambray shirt and bib overalls crisp and pressed, with one leg of his overalls neatly folded and pinned behind the stump of his amputated leg, moving down Wheaton's Main Street sidewalk faster than most people could walk ... Delmont "Democrat" Carter, in his striped overalls and engineer's cap, sauntering out to his gravity-fed gas pumps as he rolled a cigarette with one hand and whisked a match across the bib of his overalls to light up as he pumped gas into Granddad's '36 Chevy with his other hand.

Those are but a few of the recollections that have invaded my thoughts with increasing frequency as I have lurched from late middle age into early old age. One day, it occurred to me that it would be a shame, in a culture bombarded with homogenized, electronically delivered sights and sounds and factoids of dubious worth, to let a period of such rich experiences slip into the dark void of unrecorded history like, as the Apostle James noted, "a vapour, that appeareth for a little time, and then vanisheth away."

I have just two wishes for those of you who read what I have written: that the stories spark your own precious memories and that they inspire you to pass those memories on to your friends and loved ones so that a hundred years from now, someone will be telling the story about your "uncle" Newt Kelly, savoring your mother's biscuits and gravy and declaring in his unique vernacular, "That's mighty good doughgod."

1

Around Wheaton, the Way It Was

Our neighbor Argyl Haynes used to say that if any of his eleven children squealed a tire within thirty miles of Wheaton, he would hear about it the next morning. Argyl was right. Just about every father in the farm country around Wheaton and Rocky Comfort, Missouri, during the 1940s and '50s could have said the same thing with no fear of being contradicted.

Those of us who came of age during those years probably were among the last to have surrogate parents up and down every street, every country road, every creek bank and hollow from the flatlands north of Wheaton to the hill country south of Wheaton and Rocky (we almost never called it "Rocky Comfort"). Burn rubber, steal a watermelon, park with your girlfriend along some country road, and chances are, someone would just casually mention it to your dad or mom the next day.

Everyone in those rural communities knew almost everyone else—in detail. Our farm was a half mile west of the Haynes' farm, and I can still remember the names of the Haynes kids in the order in which they were born: Claude, Frieda, Melvin, Bill, Joyce, Darril, Carolyn, Wesley, Wylene, Veva Jean, and Gary. Joyce and I were classmates all the way from first through twelfth grades. And despite the fact that nearly all the Haynes boys were great basketball players, with Melvin and Bill enjoying basketball success for small college teams, I still contend that Joyce was the best rebounder. I never could root her out of position when I played basketball with the Haynes family in their backyard.

Nearly everyone had a pretty good idea of whether a family was well-off, poor, or dirt-poor. There were no other financial categories that I knew of, and the only point of difference was each person's definition of "well-off." But there weren't many in that category, so that particular difference didn't generate a lot of controversy.

The community also had a collective opinion about whether your family members were generally smart, slow of wit, honest, ornery, or ambitious. Just about everybody knew whether your mother was a good housekeeper, canned her vegetables, and was a good cook.

Your neighbors, friends, and acquaintances knew what kind of a pickup truck or car your family drove. The result was that people were identified by their vehicles, just as they had been identified by their horses in previous generations: "Here comes ol' George's blue Ford coupe" or "I saw Charlie's green Chevy pickup parked at her house last night." People who lived along the most used roads—like the one between Wheaton and Stella, where we lived—could tell you if their neighbor two miles down the road had gone to town that day.

I learned to drive our Ford tractor at age eight, standing up on the footrests to step on the brakes when I had to stop. A hand lever near the steering wheel controlled the gas. An early task that perfected driving skills consisted of steering an old 1941 Ford pickup between hay bales in the field as men heaved bales into the truck bed, where the stackers piled them as high as was safe. I was so short I needed to scoot down in the seat and stretch to reach the clutch and brake pedals. There was no need to reach the accelerator, because the truck moved forward in low gear at exactly the right speed for the haulers to throw on the bales and the stacker on the truck to keep his balance.

On the farm, there were always chickens to feed, hogs to slop, and cows to milk, to say nothing of field work on the tractor—plowing, working ground, and drilling in the seeds in the spring; cutting hay, baling it, and harvesting grain in the summer—an endless cycle of work.

Growing up on a dairy farm where Dad and I milked about fifty cows morning and night until I graduated from Wheaton High, I thought the "town kids"—sons and daughters of the merchants and businessmen and women (yes, Wheaton had some businesswomen)—had one distinct advantage: freedom from farm chores.

But the truth was—the town kids also had their own kinds of chores. Most of the boys who lived in the metropolis of Wheaton with its nearly four hundred souls had a steer or a heifer or a pig on someone's nearby farm that they cared for as a Future Farmers of America (FFA) project. Town boys also delivered newspapers, bagged groceries, swept out and cleaned up for various Wheaton merchants, and, in general, stayed busy.

From the time that I was very small, a trip to Wheaton with Dad or Granddad was a treat. I never went with my mother or grandmother, because they never learned to drive a car. Wheaton's Main Street was wide, flat, and paved, but most of the little town's side streets remained unpaved until I was in high school. In rainy weather, Main Street offered relief from the rutted roads outside of town that left cars, pickups, and big trucks alike splattered and coated with mud in rainy weather. During dry spells, it was enjoyable to drive down Main Street, because it was free of the dust stirred up by every moving vehicle on the unpaved country roads.

Despite a population that fell just shy of four hundred during World War II and the postwar years, flatland farmers to the west and northwest, farmers from the rolling Shoal Creek country to the east, and hill country farmers from the south and southwest came to Wheaton in droves on Saturdays.

During the first two decades after World War II, Wheaton's merchants were gamblers and scramblers who were willing to purchase and operate almost any type of business that sold whatever they knew local farm families either needed or could be persuaded to buy.

Folks who weren't too particular about fashion and those who were willing to wait a few days for parts for pumps or milking machines or radios could get along by trading only in Wheaton. But occasionally, they needed to make purchases in the larger towns of Cassville, the Barry County seat fifteen miles to the southeast; Monett, twenty miles to the northeast; or Neosho, twenty-five miles to the northwest. Joplin, fifty miles to the northwest, and Springfield, sixty-five miles to the northeast, offered the more sophisticated and affluent persons even more choices for all kinds of goods and services.

Wheaton's businesses frequently changed ownership. One small grocery store on Main Street changed hands more often than Zsa Zsa Gabor changed husbands. At the end of the war in 1945, Frazier-Daniels & Brattin Grocery and Market was owned by veteran Wheaton merchant Joe Frazier and two younger men, Floyd Daniels and Leonard Brattin. Then, in May 1946, Horace H. Stacy of nearby Purdy, and a partner, Raleigh Sallee, bought the grocery, which was renamed the Stacy & Sallee Food Market.

Seven months later, Joe Frazier became manager of a rival grocery store, the Farmers Exchange, a block to the west. Leonard, his wife, Ila, and daughter, Modena, moved to Yakima, Washington, where Leonard got a job in a grocery store and meat market. When Leonard and family came back to Wheaton for a visit in September 1946, *Wheaton Journal* editor Wally Fox talked with Leonard, who gave Wally a glowing description of his Yakima job. Wally reported that Leonard's Yakima job was "right down his alley." But ten months later, in July 1947, Leonard came back to Wheaton and decided to stay. He and Floyd, who reportedly "had been taking a rest," repurchased their old store, which then became Daniels & Brattin Food Market, according to an article in the July 10, 1947, edition of the *Journal*. Floyd and Leonard went back to work in the store they had owned fourteen months earlier.

There were two reasons I liked to go with my folks to Daniels & Brattin's grocery. The first was that it had color pictures of World War II fighter planes and bombers high on each wall, and I prided myself on being able to identify every plane. The second reason was that Darrell Cantrell, the father of my future classmate, James Cantrell, clerked there. Almost every time I went into the store, Darrell would tease me by telling me that I was "just uglier than a mud fence." At ages seven and eight, I thought that was about the funniest line I'd ever heard and was disappointed when Darrell didn't say it when I walked into the store.

Darrell, who was occasionally called Shorty because he wouldn't have been the center on a basketball team, had bad teeth and was forced to have all of them pulled a few months after Floyd and Leonard repurchased the store.

It was getting close to Christmas 1947. Darrell, who was eating a lot of soup and soft foods while his gums healed, was expectantly waiting for his new false teeth to arrive in the mail so he could enjoy a great Christmas feast. On Christmas Eve, a small package arrived, just the right size to contain a set of dentures. Darrell tore it open.

Yup, it was dentures, all right—made of paraffin and candy corn. Wally's story in the *Journal* reported:

PRACTICAL CHRISTMAS GIFT

Darrell Cantrell, who is employed at the Daniels & Brattin Food Market, received a practical and very useful Christmas gift Wednesday morning. When he received the package he was so anxious to see what he had received that he opened it up a day early.

The package contained a set of false teeth made out of paraffin and teeth made from yellow candy. As Darrell has been without teeth for some time he says the present will come in handy when he goes to eat his Christmas dinner. The dentist who made his teeth failed to include his name so Darrell is at a loss as to who to thank.[2]

The word soon leaked that the sender was Leonard, who loved practical jokes.

Four years later, in September 1951, Floyd Daniels had a spell of bad health, which set off a flurry of ownership changes for the little grocery. Floyd and Leonard sold the store to two Wheaton area couples, Mr. and Mrs. Ralph Dickson and Mr. and Mrs. Roscoe "Pos" McKinley. The last two lines of the article announcing the store's new ownership quoted some of Leonard's Ozark wit:

> Mr. Brattin has made no announcement as to his future plans. He says, now that he is out of business, when he meets anyone and speaks to them, he really means it.[3]

Wheaton's merchants were versatile. Previously, Ralph had operated Dickson's D-X service station, and then he sold it and took a job as janitor and bus driver for the Wheaton School District. The Dicksons and McKinleys operated the little grocery for eight months, selling it to Tom and Ava Stewart in May 1952. Tom and Ava owned it for less than a month, selling it in June of '52 to Earl Hooten. Earl had formerly operated a poultry dressing plant in Cassville.

From mid-1952 until April 1959, the store was known as Hooten's Grocery & Meat Market. Earl then sold it to another former Wheaton merchant, Don Linebarger. Don owned it for two days. Then Leonard Brattin bought it again, announcing plans to redecorate and remodel the interior of the store and carry a complete line of groceries, meats, and fresh produce.

It didn't work out that way. In less than a week in April 1959, there was another twist of ownership and plans. Leonard changed his mind again. He sold the grocery back to Don Linebarger. Leonard then announced plans to partner with Price Naramore, who had just sold the rival IGA grocery, to open a new lumberyard and building supply store on the highway south of town.

In baseball, one of the most famous double play combinations of the early 1900s was Chicago Cubs shortstop Joe Tinker to second baseman Johnny Evers to first baseman Frank Chance.[4] If the ownership of the small grocery had been recorded like a baseball scorecard between 1945 and 1959, it would have read Frazier-Daniels & Brattin, to Stacy & Sallee, to Daniels & Brattin, to Dickson & McKinley, to Stewart, to Hooten, to Linebarger, to Brattin, to Linebarger. That would make even the neatest scorekeeper's card unreadable. To be sure of the ownership, customers needed to be loyal readers of the *Wheaton Journal.*

The strange thing was—I never heard any of the store's many owners admit they lost money on a single one of these deals.

There were always at least two other places where farm families could buy groceries in Wheaton during the '40s and '50s. The stores I remember best were the IGA store and the Farmers Exchange, which was the Missouri Farmers Association (MFA) co-op store.

The IGA also changed hands several times. As World War II ended, Jay Fithian, who later lost a leg due to medical complications after he fell off the roof of an army barracks at nearby Camp Crowder while he was salvaging lumber, operated the IGA. Later, Don Linebarger, Horace Stacy, Price and Carolyn Naramore, Warren Cullers, and Dale Boyer were added to the list of owners.

The IGA store, when it was owned by the Naramores and Carolyn's brother-in-law Warren Cullers, became Wheaton's first supermarket, with shopping carts and a checkout counter. But at the Farmers Exchange, a clerk took a customer's grocery list, collected the items, and packed the groceries in a box or paper sack while the customer watched or sometimes held the sack. No running a shopping cart down the aisle at the Exchange. If you needed cattle feed or chicken feed, you could buy it on the feed-room side of the store. If you had a flock of laying hens, you could sell your eggs at the Exchange—just as you could at the little grocery a block to the east that changed hands so often.

On the south side of Main, between the Exchange and Doc McCall's Bank of Wheaton, was Roy Killion and Floyd "Fat" Flora's hardware store. The tables and bins at the hardware held every kind of nut, bolt, cog, sprocket, spring, or fixture known to the human race in addition to a pocketknives, kerosene lanterns, plumbing supplies, hand tools, insect spray, and a gazillion other items.

During those early postwar years, folks could buy building materials from E. L. Thomas's lumberyard or from the Calhoon-Putnam Lumber Company, managed by Gordon Kenney. Occasionally, Gordon, a reasonable but businesslike man, had to chase several of my future classmates out of the sand piles and stacks of lumber at Calhoon-Putnam's.

Movies at the Cozy Theatre were even more fun than playing at the lumberyard. Several guys told me they first put their arm around a girl in the Cozy Theatre and kept it there until their arms went to sleep. After they had worked up the courage to hug their date, they didn't want to remove their arm until the movie was over. In 1946, admission was a dime for a kid and a quarter for an adult. By 1950, admission was still a dime for children, but the price had shot all the way to thirty cents for an adult.

We could get our shoes repaired at Jerry's Shoe Shop, operated by Jerry Guiles, a thrifty guy with a buck. A full line of women's or men's apparel was available between 1940 and 1960 at Chenoweth's or Rowland's or Wiseman's or Dorothy's clothing stores.

On our farm west of town, our nearest neighbors were Roy and Virgie Robinson. Roy, always chewing on an unlit cigar, operated Wheaton Maytag—an appliance store that also was a radio and TV repair shop—on the south side of Main.

Floyd and Anna Lea Lamberson Hughes (my cousin) owned Wheaton Sundries, the drugstore where kids went to buy a fountain Coke, talk to their pals or girlfriend, buy toilet water for their mother's birthday, play the pinball machine, or park themselves in front of the funny-book stand and see how many they could read without buying one. Floyd and Ann kept a wide assortment of comic books, from *Archie's Pal Jughead* to *Frontline Combat, Two-Fisted Tales,* and *Bugs Bunny*—thus satisfying the most sophisticated comic-book readers.

Tom and Ava Stewart ran the locker plant for frozen foods for several years, followed by Don Linebarger, Pos McKinley and his wife, and Barney Bates. The locker plant was a great place to cool off for about five minutes on a hot summer afternoon. Any longer than that and customers risked frostbite as they retrieved their frozen hamburger or peaches from their family's personal locker.

Barney also had operated a store that sold electrical supplies, hardware, and home furnishings. Later, Barney ran a jewelry and watch repair store. It seemed that around Wheaton, if you could run one kind of a store, you could run any of 'em. And your job description could change quickly.

When Don Linebarger sold the locker plant in 1954, the last paragraph of the *Journal* article said:

> Mr. Linebarger, who has operated the locker plant for the past four years, reports that he has made no plans for the future. He was ordained a Baptist minister some time ago and is Pastor of the Stella Baptist Church at present.[5]

Several people I knew disputed Don's statement about his future plans. They concluded that because of his ordination, Don was making plans for his far distant future in the great beyond.

In the middle of town was the weekly *Wheaton Journal*. Wally Fox, cousin of my best friend Dan Shewmake's mother, Hessie, was reporter, editor, ad salesman, and print-shop boss of the *Journal*. At his side and able to do just about everything Wally did was his very able wife, Bessie.

Just north of the *Journal* was the blacksmith shop where the town's two blacksmiths, Port Potts and Clarence Rodgers, shoed horses until Port was injured and Clarence left Wheaton as the decade of the '40s ended. By then, John Deere, Ford, Massey-Harris, Case, Oliver, and Farmall tractors had largely replaced the great teams of workhorses that had been the beasts of burden on Ozark farms since the area was settled by pioneers a hundred years earlier.

Bolted to the back of the blacksmith shop, next door to Virgil and Winnie Paden's home, were a basketball goal and an ash-covered outdoor court that was the scene of fierce pickup basketball games nearly every Saturday afternoon, except in the heat of the summertime. I remember wiping sweat from my face and going home grimy from the games played on that court where we probably breathed in enough heavy metal from the forge ash that today we would be labeled toxic.

On the east end of town, near the railroad tracks, was Allman's grain elevator, mill, and feed store where farmers sold their grain or had it ground into livestock feed. Stratton Allman was the manager. His father, Herman, had been manager of the Neosho Milling Company's grain-milling operation from the 1920s until August 1939, when he purchased the milling company's interest in the business and it became Allman Produce and Feed. Allman's was a sight to behold, especially in the summer when lines of trucks loaded with wheat, oats, and barley queued up to sell their harvest or have it ground into feed for their cattle, hogs, horses, or other livestock.

If Wheaton had a Rat Pack like Frank Sinatra's, Stratton Allman was its handsome leader. Strat was born in 1919, and during the late 1930s, before he married Mary Kathleen McNabb, the M&A was running a fast, gasoline-powered, streamlined passenger car known locally as the Blue Goose. Everyone around Wheaton knew the Blue Goose schedule and generally when the slower, steam-powered freight trains would chug into Wheaton.

During his single days, the story goes, Strat and some of the local young men about town discovered that if they let some of the air out of an automobile's tires, a car would stay on the railroad tracks without a need for steering it. Another advantage, for the purposes of Strat and his pals, was that prewar cars, with manual transmissions, usually kept moving in lower gears without the need for a foot on the accelerator.

So Strat and a few of his pals enjoyed putting their cars on the M&A tracks at Wheaton and taking the rails seven or eight miles into the countryside southeast of town to a spot where they could turn around and return. With a date, this "hands-free driving" offered more freedom than a drive-in movie. Wonderful way to enjoy an evening with a girlfriend—until one night when several of Strat's friends got an idea.[6]

They got a big piece of plywood, sawed it into the shape of the front of the Blue Goose, and painted it in the Blue Goose colors of blue and silver gray. They sawed a circle in the plywood where the sleek passenger coach's headlight was positioned, got a spotlight and an air horn capable of emitting a blast that could wake the dead, and waited until Strat and his date headed down the tracks.

The pranksters raced ahead on the road until they got to a place a few miles southeast of Wheaton where they could stop and scramble up the railroad embankment with their plywood Blue Goose dummy, the spotlight, and the air horn.

When Strat's car—with Strat and his date in the backseat—got in sight, the tricksters turned on the light and made a few blasts with the air horn. At first, Strat and his date were too preoccupied with other things to notice, but when they realized that they were about to be smashed by the Blue Goose, Strat jumped into the front seat, jerked his car off the tracks, and plunged down a steep embankment into some brush. Fortunately, the car didn't turn over, and there was only minor damage to the car and no visible damage to Strat and his date.

Chester O. "Buck" Higgs, the father of my classmate, Betty, and her brother, Joe, told me the story many years later. Buck laughed so much that it was hard for him to finish the story. He strongly implied, without actually saying so, that he just might have had something to do with the prank.

Strat was equally good at telling stories. When customers went to the mill to buy feed or get their grain ground, they could count on either Strat or another guy hanging out there to tell them something that would make them laugh.

One of the best stories involved one of Wheaton's up-and-coming young businessmen of the 1950s, Junior Bixler. Junior had been to Texas and came home with a pair of expensive alligator cowboy boots, which he bragged about when he came to Allman's mill. A few days later, he brought the boots in, packed in their original box.

He carefully placed one on the counter and put a sign on it that he would sell the boots for $300—a tidy sum in those days. He didn't say why he wanted to sell them.

They were Strat's size, and after a few days, he decided to buy the boots. A few more days passed before Strat put the boots back on the counter with a sign that he'd sell them for $300. Leo Holmes—who operated a trucking service called the Gateway Express—wanted the boots but didn't want to pay $300 for them. Leo knew that Strat and Kathleen were doing some landscaping around their place and needed a load of dirt. So he offered Strat a load of dirt in return for the boots. Strat accepted.

But when Leo delivered the dirt, he accidentally drove over a newly constructed septic tank in Strat and Kathleen's backyard, caved it in, and had to dump the dirt in the middle of the yard. There was never a consensus on whether it was an accident or not, but it was probably poetic justice. It seems that the boots were perfectly crafted and of excellent quality, but they both were for the left foot. Not a single one of the boots' series of owners ever admitted the truth, at least not until long afterward. No one knows what happened to the fancy footwear. As news reporters often are told when they ask about the location of the president during a national crisis, the boots ended up in an "undisclosed location."

Another Wheaton merchant who was in various businesses in the 1940s and '50s was Henry Lombard. Just after World War II, Henry operated Lombard Garage just south of the east end of Main Street. Later, at the same location, he operated Lombard Produce & Feed. For years, he also ran a fleet of chicken trucks. I was a few grades behind two of his boys, Carrol and Bob. Bob stayed in Wheaton, married my classmate, Sharon Kay Stewart, and operated an insurance office at the east end of Main for many years. He also served as mayor and fire chief and to this day is one of the town's spark plugs.

Wheaton had other great places of business in the '40s and '50s. In Bryan's Barber Shop, Bryan Wolfenbarger, the bald-headed barber; his sidekick, George Hussey; and at times, George's brother,

Everett, could give you a white sidewall flattop—all waxed up and with a brushing of talcum powder around your ears—in the time it took them to chain-smoke three or four cigarettes that engulfed your head in a blue haze. Any worry about secondhand smoke in those days? Nah!

If a customer got a regular cut, he walked out smelling of either red or blue alcohol-laced "fu-fu juice" that announced his fresh haircut even before he came around the corner. I was eighteen years old before I discovered that my hair actually had a little wave in it because Bryan, George, and Everett had kept my hair cut so short over the years.

As we sat in one of the three barber chairs in Bryan's shop, we could look at huge calendars on the opposite wall above the row of wooden chairs that were bolted to the floor. The calendars had reproductions of color paintings of dogs sitting at a table playing cards. Bryan's Barber Shop is long gone, but I'm told those calendars are collectors' items now.

Depending on who was in the shop waiting for a haircut, Bryan's customers often could hear some of the juiciest gossip about stuff going on in the area—things that only the menfolk could talk about. I remember hearing one fellow describing his, shall we say, romantic experiences in Japan while he was getting some R&R during the Korean War. It was an education for a young sprout like me.

And during basketball season, barbershop patrons would be guaranteed to get a postmortem of the latest Wheaton Bulldogs' game. How many points did Mac Smith or Melvin Haynes or J. C. Duncan or Jon Paden or Jack Higgs or Bill Haynes or Robert Higgs or Dewey Brattin or John Howerton or, over the years, lots of other players get? Did you see that slick pass that James Leslie Royer made to Mel Haynes under the basket to ice the game in the last few seconds?

The next-best place for basketball commentary and analysis was the MZ-Dee Café, owned by my great-aunt Marie Lamberson and her partners—Zelma Dickson and Dee McCullah. The MZ-Dee Café would give you the best cup of coffee and the biggest plate of roast beef or meatloaf and mashed potatoes and green beans for miles around. The best item on the menu at the MZ-Dee, however, was local gossip and current events. It was here that you went to find out who had cattle for sale, who was stepping out on his wife, who was looking for boys with strong backs to buck bales during hay harvest, or who had been seen going in or coming out of the back door of Walter McAtee's liquor store.

I still can see Walter, a quiet man with slicked-back gray hair, sitting on the concrete steps of the most peculiar business in Wheaton. Mac's Liquor, on the north side of the east end of Main Street, was a viable business virtually my entire childhood. And yet, in all those years, I'll wager I could count on one hand the number of people I ever saw going in and out of the front door.

There were only a couple of explanations for Mr. McAtee's ability to stay in business with no visible customers in that town in the middle of the Bible Belt. One obvious answer is that lots of people used the back door by the base of the town water tower behind the old jail. The less obvious answer, which I discovered when I was a teenager, is that Mr. McAtee delivered, discreetly, to his best customers around town after dark.

When I was a small boy, Wheaton had two physicians—Doc McCall and Doc Ellison—and boyee, were they ever a study in contrasting personalities.

Dr. Otis Sheridan McCall, also the town banker, was the epitome of whatever establishment Wheaton had at the time. He was bald and portly and taught Sunday school at the Methodist church.

Dr. John Ellison was handsome, sharp tongued, an owner of prize bird dogs, and a collector of Native American arrowheads and pipes. He absolutely didn't give a tinker's damn as to how he was viewed by the community.

Later on, Drs. Jim Holmes, Elburn Smith, and Fred Clark treated the ailments of the local residents, but McCall and Ellison are more vividly etched in my memory.

There were three and sometimes four churches in Wheaton when I was a boy—the Baptist church on Highway 86, the Church of

Christ on the highway about three blocks north of Main, and the Methodist church in the heart of town. For a while, there also was "Little Charley" Keeling's Full Gospel Mission church at the east end of town across the street from the Calhoon-Putnam Company.[7]

The Polish folks, most of whom were Catholics and lived northeast of Wheaton, had to drive to a Catholic church at Pulaskifield eight miles to the north. The closest Jewish people were in Joplin and Springfield.

My family worshiped at the Church of Christ in Rocky, two and a half miles southwest of Wheaton. Not everyone around Wheaton and Rocky attended church in those postwar years, but everyone in the community knew precisely who did, who didn't, and which church each person believed offered the surest path to the pearly gates.

The bottom line was that the young people who grew up around those little towns during the postwar years were pretty good kids because they were watched so closely that they couldn't get away with much, or pretty clever kids because they managed to get away with mischief in spite of having "parents" everywhere they went.

2

Feed Room Manners

Most people—including Emily Post, the reigning queen of etiquette in the 1940s and '50s—wouldn't have considered the feed room of the Farmers Exchange in Wheaton, Missouri, a likely place for a lesson in manners. But on almost any Saturday afternoon during those years, a kid could learn something about politeness, courtesy, and civility by hanging around the feed room of the MFA Farmers Exchange—pronounced *ex*-change, with emphasis on the "ex."[8]

Lombard Produce and Feed, Allman's Produce and Feed, Schrader Hatchery, and a few others sold livestock feed over the years, but the Exchange was the *only* place in town that sold feed and groceries at the same location.

For a while, W. T. Baker managed the Exchange, followed by Joe Frazier. But I remember James Woods the most clearly. He was businesslike, fair, and polite to the farmers who used his feed room as a place to loaf and gossip and catch up on cattle and commodity prices posted on the chalkboard high on the back wall. Nearby, a radio was always tuned to station KWTO—Keep Watching the Ozarks—in Springfield, Missouri, because the station offered periodic reports on livestock prices at Springfield's stockyards and commodity prices in Chicago.

There were several ways to enter the Exchange's feed room. You could walk in directly from the sidewalk on the south side of Main Street. Before you ambled in, you might want to stop and peer through the dusty plate-glass windows of the storefront to see if there was anybody inside whom you wanted to gab with. Another entryway was through the double doors between the Exchange's grocery store and the feed room. If you entered from the grocery store, the first thing you saw in the feed room was a large coal-fed stove, always fired up in the wintertime.

The third way into the feed area was from the loading dock that faced the alley at the back of the Exchange. Customers who had a truck and needed to buy a lot of feed could drive through the alley behind the bank, go past the hardware store, and back up to the loading dock.

There was, by today's standards, an incredible civility in that old feed room—a place that smelled of molasses-laced cattle feed, dry bran, cottonseed meal, chicken mash, and pipe tobacco. In the summertime, ceiling fans turned overhead to stir the air and mix the competing smells. Most of the feed came in burlap sacks, with a couple of exceptions. Ground corn and chicken mash came in white cotton bags, and chicken pellets came in colorful cotton print sacks.

By unspoken custom, the feed room was generally considered a man's hangout—a place where men in bib overalls and blue chambray work shirts and a few in jeans or khaki twill pants gathered and sat or leaned on the feed sacks. Almost all the men wore high-top leather work shoes and a hat or a cap. In the summer, straw hats or billed caps were the usual headgear, and in the winter, felt hats were more common—always with sweat stains that showed through on the outside. Some men preferred striped shop caps like the railroaders wore.

Feed-room denizens would fire up their pipes or roll cigarettes or cut a plug of tobacco and take a chaw. Then they'd talk about the weather and the price of cattle and oats and corn, about their Farmall or Ford or John Deere or Massey-Harris tractors, and—in the summer—how their hay baler had broken down and they still had lespedeza or oat hay to bale. They'd talk about their "five-gallon" Guernsey or Jersey cow in the days when five gallons was a lot of milk for a cow to produce in one day. Or they'd talk about their best bird dog or coonhound. Lots of farmers still hunted, treed, and shot raccoons for sport.

If the feed-room loafers didn't smoke or chew, they whittled. Lots of men carried a whittling stick, and with pocketknives honed sharp enough to shave the stubble off their faces, they'd take out their stick and, as they gabbed, casually shave slices as thin as paper that curled into tiny ringlets. There was sort of an unspoken competition that involved who had the sharpest knife and the skill to shave off the thinnest curl from his whittling stick.

In the wintertime, if you were a kid, you were sometimes called on to go throw some coal into the stove and stoke the fire with an iron poker. On such occasions, it was advisable to *pour* the coal from the coal hod into the stove, because etiquette dictated that the men who were chewing tobacco either spit into the spittoons or into the coal hod, whichever was closer and easier to hit. So any unwary boys who reached barehanded into the coal hod for chunks of coal might be in for a nasty surprise.

If there was a hint of a scandal in the community, only the roughest of the men ever used a four-letter word to describe it in the feed room, and even slightly off-color stories—like the ones commonly exchanged among men and women in casual office conversations these days—usually were spoken in very low tones to make sure they weren't overheard by anyone randomly walking in to place a feed order.

Often, while a man loafed in the feed room, his wife or daughter or mother or grandmother would be in the adjoining grocery store stocking up on staples for the week. The Exchange's grocery clerks— men or women—always had a pencil tucked behind one ear and usually wore a full-length white apron.

The clerk—I remember Aud Lamberson's wife, Pearl, in particular—took your list and a cardboard box and went to the shelves to fetch your Oxydol or Duz washing powder, your Fletcher's

Castoria or Black Draught laxative, your Kix or Post Toasties or Grape Nuts or Pep breakfast cereal, your Morton's salt and your Pillsbury flour. If you were thrifty, you didn't need Crisco shortening, because most farm women saved meat grease in a can at home. Pearl, a tall, sturdy woman who kept her hair pinned carefully on top of her head, could easily handle a large, heavy cardboard box loaded with groceries.

During World War II and for a year or so afterward, butter was rationed. Oleomargarine, a concoction of vegetable oils, was the butter substitute. Oleo, as it was referred to, was cream colored, so it came with a little package of orange dye that had to be kneaded into it to make it look more like real butter.[9] Sometimes, a box of Mother's Oats—the brand that came with a dish inside—would be on the grocery list. A few slices of yellow cheddar cheese were a treat, especially if your mother bought a fresh box of Sunshine Krispy crackers to go with the cheese.

The clerk brought the box of groceries back to the counter and tallied up how much the lady of the house owed after subtracting the total that she was paid for the eggs—from her little flock of laying hens—she had sold to the Exchange that day. Then she might tell the clerk she needed a sack or two of chicken feed, and would he or she please add that to the bill? After the bill was paid, a carryout boy would take the box of groceries to the customer's old Ford pickup, the prewar Chevy car, or maybe the GMC flatbed truck.

Once the groceries were purchased, the mistress of the household often would hurry to find her mother or daughter or a neighbor lady, and they'd stroll into the feed room together. A woman almost never entered the feed room alone.

That was when the casual atmosphere abruptly changed for the men. Seeing the ladies coming down the center aisle between the stacks of feed sacks, the men stopped their conversations in midsentence. The ones sitting on sacks rose to their feet. Hats and caps were doffed, and greetings to the ladies were offered.

"How'd do, Miz Haynes?" if you were acquainted but didn't

know her too well. "How're you, Geneva?" if you were good friends. "Afternoon, Miz Ralston, Miz Hughes, Miz Lamberson."

As the women made their way to the stacks of print chicken feed sacks, the men would begin to talk again, but in quieter tones, respectful of the women looking over the selection to see if any new print patterns had arrived that week.

In those days, despite the fact that farm families' income improved a bit just after World War II, most people who lived around Wheaton had no money to spare, and farm women did everything they could to make ends meet. Most of them made their dresses, curtains, tablecloths, dish towels, aprons—and occasionally even underwear—from the cotton print feed sacks that had been the idea of a marketing genius in Kansas City, Missouri, in the early 1930s.

Richard Peek, vice president for the Percy Kent Bag Company, realized that farm families used sacks for many of their household needs, and he wanted to energize the lagging sales the Depression had brought. So Mr. Peek's company began producing cotton feed sacks in colorful flower prints. His idea was such a success that later he would be called "the Hattie Carnegie" of sack fashions.[10]

The Staley Feed Company in Kansas City is believed to be the first company to test Peek's idea. Staley sent a trial carload shipment to the Crescent Feed and Flour Company in Springfield, Missouri, and the feed flew out the door. Farm women were hungry for something pretty and immediately began to buy patterns and sew all sorts of clothing and household items.[11]

The women around Wheaton were no different. Every man gathered in the feed room of the Exchange on those long-ago Saturday afternoons were acutely aware that their women were plenty serious about going home with just the right print for Sissy's new dress or that they might need one more feed sack of the same print to finish a matching set of curtains for the back window in the kitchen. The men also remembered the day when *they* were sent to find a particular print pattern, and they overlooked it because they were in a hurry or because it was on the bottom of a six-foot pile of sacks. That was *not* a pleasant thing to explain, especially when the neighbor lady turned up with the requested print a couple of days later because *her* husband had searched a little harder.

So it was partly out of old-fashioned courtesy, partly out of respect, and partly out of mutual self-protection that the men lowered their conversation and kept a wary eye on the ladies until they selected the sack with the pattern they wanted. If one of the ladies spied a new pattern on a sack that was in the middle of the pile, a couple of the men would walk over and throw the sacks above it off the pile, which allowed her to have a better look. This was done with a minimum of words and always in a way that didn't interfere with the loading operations of the feed-room employees.

During my entire childhood, I don't remember hearing a man complain about how many sacks he had to move for women who came searching for just the right feed sack print; nor do I remember any man ever being impolite to a woman in the feed room.

It's often said that the best teaching is by example, and for a boy who grew up around Wheaton, the feed room at the Exchange was a place where you learned manners and other practical lessons: always doff your hat and speak politely to the ladies, stay out of their way until they need help, don't tell off-color stories while womenfolk are within earshot, don't complain when you're helping them, and don't reach into the coal hod with your bare hand.

3

The Ride with Ol' Mack

One day in the summer of 1951, the summer I turned twelve, I talked my mother into letting me walk three miles to my closest friend Dan Shewmake's house. It was a big deal. I'd never walked all the way to Dan's. The Korean War was raging, and I was dressed for battle, at least as dressed as several purchases at an army surplus store in Joplin allowed me to be.

On my head, I wore an army helmet liner, which real soldiers wore under the metal pot that was the heavy part of the headwear. But it looked like a helmet. Hooked to the thick army surplus belt around my waist was an army canteen full of water and a snap-shut pouch that contained medical items in case I was wounded in battle. Crisscrossed under one arm and over the opposite shoulder was an army ammunition belt that I had filled with as many BBs for my Red Ryder Daisy Air Rifle as I could afford on my allowance of seventy-five cents a week. I would have preferred an M1 rifle, but that couldn't be arranged.

I knew that when I got to Dan's, he would be similarly equipped—actually even more ready for battle than I—because his parents had sprung for a pair of combat boots that more or less fit his twelve-year-old feet. I was very envious of those boots, but of course I was determined not to let him know it.

Dan and I were soldiers that summer, partly because the Korean War was in the news every day and partly because we knew and admired someone who might soon be involved in the fighting—Dan's older brother, Dick. Dick had been drafted from his school-teaching job at nearby Cassville, Missouri, and sent to boot camp at Camp Chaffee near Fort Smith, Arkansas.

I walked east from our farm along the dusty dirt road toward Wheaton for about a mile and a half until I got to the Gaston Corner. I never knew why it was called the Gaston Corner, but that was what Granddad Lamberson always called it, and I reasoned that he had been around long enough to know. At the Gaston Corner, I turned south on a narrower dirt road toward the Rocky Comfort Cemetery, about a mile away. By this time, I was getting hot, and my sweat had slicked the leather suspension straps inside my helmet liner, causing the pot to slide down my forehead and over my eyes. I remember unhooking my canteen and taking a swig of water. A little sweat couldn't bother a soldier on the march. Only an occasional car or pickup passed by on that hot summer afternoon, kicking up a cloud of dust that turned to grit in my teeth. I walked by Elsie Bufford's and Elliot Roller's place and down the hill toward the cemetery. I passed Melvin and Opal Tichenor's house, then Curt Long's, Uncle Awk (his real name was Oscar) and Aunt Virgie Davidson's, the cemetery, and the Prosperity Baptist Church. Then I trudged east, up the hill toward Highway 44. I was about half a mile from Dan's when a big flatbed truck pulled over and stopped just ahead of me.

After I wiped the sweat off my glasses, I recognized the driver. It was Ol' Mack Harader. I always called him "Ol' Mack," because it just seemed to fit. I found out later that he would have been only fifty-three years old that summer, but to my young eyes, he seemed quite a bit older.

Sometimes Mack hauled cattle to the Springfield stockyards for my dad, and he had been to our farm several times to load cattle. I figured Mack, who was no more than six feet tall, weighed at least three hundred pounds. Mack mostly wore faded blue bib overalls. He probably wore overalls, I thought, because overalls were about the only work clothes that would comfortably accommodate his belly. Partly because of his weight and partly because it was his nature, Mack never seemed to be in a hurry, and he never seemed to get upset.

I heard a raspy voice holler, "Need a ride?"

"Well, I'm just goin' up to the Shewmakes there," I said, pointing toward Dan's place, which was in sight up the road a piece.

"That's all right. It's pretty hot out there, especially with that helmet on, I imagine," Ol' Mack said. "Hop in, and I'll drop you off."

So I climbed in. And there we sat, Mack wearing a striped engineer's cap—his belly, behind his overalls, brushing the steering wheel—and me, a ninety-eight-pound kid in glasses, wearing a big old soldier's helmet liner with all kinds of army gear hanging off him. Mack just grinned and ground the gearshift and asked me what kind of BB gun I had. I told him it was a *gen-u-ine* Daisy Air Rifle made at the factory at Springdale, Arkansas.

In a minute or less, he pulled the old truck over to the side of the highway in front of the Shewmake house and stopped to let me out. I remember that he told me to be careful crossing the road.

Summoning up as much adult dignity as a twelve-year-old with most of his head hidden under an army pot could muster, I said, "Much obliged," as was the custom of men in the Missouri Ozarks if someone had done them a favor.

As I walked across the highway, I heard Ol' Mack chuckle a little, no doubt getting a kick out of watching the skinny kid with the BB gun walking toward the front lines.

"We'll see ye," he said.

I survived the battle that day and saw Mack quite a bit over the next several months when he hauled cattle for Dad. Then one day the next spring, Dad came home and said Mack had collapsed of a stroke. That hit me pretty hard. I really liked Mack, because he was good-natured and took time to notice kids and be kind to them.

His misfortune hit the Wheaton community pretty hard too. Mack was acquainted with just about everyone who lived within twenty or thirty miles of Wheaton. In addition to farming and trucking, he had been a helper at Wheaton's Pogue Funeral Home for twenty-five years.

On May 8, 1952, a headline on the front page of the weekly *Wheaton Journal* said:

MACK HARADER
SUFFERS STROKE

Mack Harader is a patient in the Cardwell Hospital at present and is in a serious condition from a stroke of paralysis.

Mr. Harader became sick Tuesday night and suffered the stroke Wednesday morning. He was taken to the hospital about 12:30 Wednesday afternoon.

His entire right side is paralyzed. He appears to be slightly improved at present and is able to talk some. If he continues to improve for the next twenty-four hours there is hopes that he will recover from the stroke.

The spring of 1952 had not been a good one for either Mack or his married son, James Lee Harader, who lived about halfway between Wheaton and our farm.

On April 7, exactly a month before Mack's stroke, he and James Lee had been loading logs several miles west of Wheaton in the rural community of Wanda when a heavy walnut log rolled off Mack's truck while James Lee was loosening a chain. Much of James Lee's body was safely under the truck, except for his head and his left side where the log struck him. The impact cut his head, dislocated his shoulder, and fractured his collarbone and pelvis.

James Lee managed to crawl a short distance, but he couldn't walk, and Mack couldn't lift him into the cab of the big truck. So Mack had to leave him on the ground, drive to Wanda to find someone with a car to help him load James Lee, and drive him three miles to the hospital at Stella. Mack found a schoolteacher, a woman who, with difficulty, helped Mack wrestle James Lee into her car and drove him to the hospital. James Lee recuperated from the accident, but when Mack suffered his stroke, my dad always said it might not have happened if the fright and exertion from James Lee's accident hadn't taken a heavy toll on Mack.[12]

Over the next two years, lots of people, including me, prayed for Mack and rooted for him in many ways. Marvin McCullah, a local farmer and heavy equipment operator, gave Mack's family a winch that helped them hoist Mack out of bed and move him into different positions. *Wheaton Journal* editor Wally Fox reported on Mack's condition from time to time, listing the names of people who had visited him the previous week—articles no one would be likely to find in a metropolitan newspaper unless the report was about a celebrity.

MACK HARADER REMAINS ABOUT THE SAME read a headline on April 15, just eight days after his stroke. MACK HARADER IMPROVED SOME read another headline on June 26. There were other short stories reporting on Mack's condition over the next two years.

Then on April 15, 1954, Wally ran a front-page article with a photo of Mack celebrating his fifty-sixth birthday in bed, surrounded by the eighty-nine birthday cards he had received.

ENJOYS BIRTHDAY IN BED

Above is a picture of Mack Harader which was made by Rev. Sherman Ragsdale, who operates a home studio. The picture was made in the Harader home in the east part of town on March 28, Mack's 56th birthday anniversary. In the background is shown a number of birthday cards sent him for the occasion. He received a total of 89 cards.

Mr. Harader suffered a stroke of paralysis May 7, 1952, which left his left side completely paralyzed. He is cheerful and enjoys company and can be put in a car and make a rather long trip without tiring him too much.

A person never knows what the future holds for them. In the case of Mr. Harader, he was apparently in good health and prior to the stroke it never entered his mind that he would suddenly be left an invalid, probably for the remainder of his life.

Needless to say, his faithful wife deserves a lot of praise for caring for her husband, even though her health is not too good.

Mack's visitors the past week were Noah Bixler, R.W. Powell, Mrs. Leslie Corn and children, Mrs. Carl Kirk and granddaughter, Rev. and Mrs. Vernie Cantrell, Mr. and Mrs. Wilber Ray and children, Mr. and Mrs. James Harader and children, Mr. and Mrs. Clifford Logan and Don Pogue of the U.S. Army.

As a teenager by then, I read the headline and probably took it too literally. I remember asking my parents if they thought Mack actually enjoyed celebrating his birthday in bed, but they said it was better to be cheerful that he was alive rather than dwelling on the "in bed" part. (I also noted that the birthday story said his left side was paralyzed, but actually both legs and his entire right side were paralyzed.)

About a month later, it occurred to someone that if Mack had an Autoette—a three-wheeled, two-seated, battery-powered vehicle that he could steer with his good left hand—then maybe he could get out of his house just to the east of Wheaton and drive down the road a quarter of a mile or so to Main Street.

James Lee and Mack's son-in-law, Wilbur Ray, drove Mack to Joplin, the nearest place where Autoettes were sold, and let him take one for a test drive. Lo and behold, the old truck driver handled it just fine. The problem was that it cost $650, and in 1954, neither Mack nor his relatives nor anyone in Wheaton had $650 just lying on the dresser to spend. So Mack's friends, meaning just about everyone in the Wheaton community, formed a committee to solicit donations to raise enough money to buy an Autoette. Under a *Journal* headline, AN

APPEAL TO THE PUBLIC in the May 13, 1954, edition, the committee explained its mission.

I don't know who suggested the committee membership, but my folks said they were just exactly the right people to raise the money. First thing they did was get God involved by naming to the committee the three preachers for the three main churches in town: the Reverend Lee Marshall of the Wheaton Baptist Church; the Reverend Sherman Ragsdale, pastor of the Wheaton Methodist Church; and Bruce Veteto, minister of the Church of Christ. Rounding out the committee were Wheaton's mayor, W. H. "Bill" Stone, who owned the Barnes-Stone Chevrolet dealership; my great-uncle Earl Lamberson, the town's postmaster; Earl Hooten, proprietor of Hooten's Finer Foods; and Leslie Phillips, the assistant postmaster. There wasn't a soul in a twenty-mile radius who didn't know and trust all of the committee members.

Leslie, the good-natured and well-liked assistant postmaster who had survived serious injuries in World War II when his B26 bomber had been forced to crash-land in England, would collect the money, keep track of the contributions, and report them every week to Wally Fox at the *Journal*. Although Wally wasn't a committee member, he made the *Journal* an important part of the fund-raising effort by promising to publish the names of the donors each week.

Wally may have been a country editor, raised deep in the hills of McDonald County, but he had an innate understanding of human nature, and he knew that just about everyone liked to see his name in the paper, especially if it was connected with an act of kindness. The *Journal* articles that followed over the summer never listed the amount anyone gave, providing only the contributors' names. In other words, if you gave fifty cents, your name would be in next Thursday's *Journal* right along with someone who gave fifty dollars.

The committee-signed kickoff article invited everyone to contribute, "even though the amount of their individual contribution may be small," the article said. "In line with that thought, we should remember Jesus' comment relative to the Widow's Mite: Mark

12:41-44 and Luke 21:1-4," the article continued, no doubt reflecting the influence of the three preachers.[13]

Wally's story said the Autoette would remain the property of the community so that "if at a future time Mack has no further use of it, it will be available for some other unfortunate victim of life's misfortune." The committee closed its appeal by writing: "Folks, regardless of where you live, will you consider favorably this most worthy cause and make life a bit more bright for Mack Harader."[14]

In week number one, the committee raised $58, contributed by sixteen people, which averages a widow's mite over $3.60 apiece. Next week's headline reported $112 in the fund, donated by an additional fifteen persons plus the Pioneer Community Club. By July 8, there was $419.27 in the fund.

Then on August 5, when the *Journal* listed sixty-seven individuals, twelve businesses, and the Wheaton Community Club as contributors, the $650 was in hand, and the Autoette was ordered. In the last paragraph of the article, the committee thanked everyone who had "contributed in any way in bringing this project to a successful conclusion, and in closing may we use God's admonition to Moses to be passed on to the children of Israel: The Lord bless thee; the Lord make His face shine upon thee and be gracious unto thee; the Lord lift up his countenance upon thee and give thee peace." It was signed, "The Committee."[15]

But the work and the contributions weren't quite done. Mack needed some alterations in his house before he could use the Autoette. A window had to be removed, a ramp built, and a large door purchased and installed. Mack's family, assisted by his many friends, completed the tasks. The ramp allowed Mack to drive the Autoette in and out of his house, and a ramp also was built to the east door of the Wheaton Methodist Church so that he could attend services without having to be helped off the machine.

Mack enjoyed his Autoette and drove it to Wheaton's Main Street several times. But his condition never really improved, and on January 15, 1959, he died. He was sixty years old and had been severely disabled for nearly seven years. His obituary said what everyone in the community already knew:

"He bore his affliction with patience, but often expressed his willingness and readiness to go to be at peaceful rest beyond and was not afraid of death. Mack was a kind father and a loving husband. He always knew friends whenever he met them, and was a good neighbor, always trying to do something to help someone along life's way."[16]

I was away in college when Mack Harader died, but I never will forget three things about him—how he brought out the best in his community, his gravelly laugh, and how he stopped one hot summer day and gave a ride to a skinny twelve-year-old boy wearing an army helmet and carrying a BB gun.

4

Wheaton on Saturday

"You goin' to the drawing today?" was a question Grandma Lamberson nearly always asked my mother and me if we saw her on Saturday mornings in the 1940s and '50s. That was because the drawing was a big deal in Wheaton on Saturdays, beginning in 1932 and ending in April 1956 when I was a high school junior.[17]

I don't know who came up with the idea for a drawing to give away merchant-donated money, but on January 14, 1937, a *Wheaton Journal* article announced that the total amount to be given away *that* year was $1,000—nearly double the $520 given away in 1933:

WHEATON MERCHANTS TO GIVE AWAY $1,000 THIS YEAR

Wheaton merchants and individuals interested in the town and community will give away absolutely free one thousand dollars during the next 50 Saturdays of this year. The money will be given away at the rate of $20 each Saturday, ten dollars at 10 a.m. and 3 p.m. to persons who do their shopping in Wheaton.

These days, ten bucks might not seem like much, but Wheaton merchants knew that it was a lot of money to dirt-poor farmers in southwest Missouri during the Depression. The possibility of winning ten dollars at 10:00 a.m. or 3:00 p.m. would encourage farm families—who came to town on Saturday, anyway—to stay a little longer. Maybe they would spend a bit more of their hard-earned cash. The idea worked. The people I talked with years later agreed that Saturday's crowds grew, lured by the Depression-era incentive of winning money.

Joe Frazier's Grocery & Produce ran an ad in the February 4, 1937, issue of the *Journal* that showed just how far ten dollars would go. For $2.16, you could buy everything listed in the Frazier ad.

Our Every Day Prices

In spite of higher prices you will find many items at our store at the old price.

Flour, 24 lbs	-	-	-	70 cents
Oranges, 2 for-	-	-	-	5 cents
Mixed candy, 2 lbs-		-	-	15 cents
Beans, split, per lb-		-	-	4 cents
Tomatoes, 3 cans	-	-	-	25 cents
Cocoa, 2 lb. can	-	-	-	15 cents
Onions, per pound-		-	-	3 cents
Sorghum, per gallon		-	-	70 cents
Candy—all kinds of bars	-		-	4 cents
Toilet soap, large bar		-	-	5 cents

"Quick Sales and Small Profits"—JOE FRAZIER GRO. & PRO.

Years later, when I was helping my mother clean out Grandma and Granddad Lamberson's house after their deaths, I found several small ledger books listing how much Grandma was paid for her weekly egg sales and how much my grandparents spent on groceries and other small necessities in Wheaton during the 1930s. Many of the transactions were in cents, not dollars and cents, and it was rare that the weekly sales of eggs or the purchase of groceries involved more than five or six dollars.

Except for the *Journal* item announcing the drawing, I can't remember the use of the term *shopping* ever being used around Wheaton during the 1940s or '50s. People went to town to do their *trading*, and actual trading occurred. Many farmers ran a tab in the grocery and feed stores. They brought in cream, eggs, and occasionally live chickens and traded their value for groceries, livestock feed, seed, and other necessities. An ad by Joe Frazier Grocery & Produce in the February 17, 1937, *Journal* urged farm families to sell their commodities at Frazier's store:

We Have It
What?

Spear Brand Feeds: Egg Mash; Egg Pellets; Pig and Hog Fattener and Dairy Feed. The Best You Can Buy For the Money.

Lettuce Sowing Time

We have just opened up a new case of Northup Kings garden seed of all kinds.

Bring us your Chickens, Eggs and Cream.
We do the best for our customers.
"Quick Sales and Small Profits"
JOE FRAZIER GRO. & PRO.

A few of the more prosperous farmers had begun to buy tractors by 1937, but teams of workhorses still pulled most of the farm machinery—plows, harrows, hay rakes, binders, drills, wagons, and many other heavy implements. Horses, not tractors, were the focus of an ad for the Wheaton Hardware store on February 17, 1937:

Harness, Collars & Lines

Spring work calls for new harness, new collars, new lines and many other repair parts. You will find a nice line of this merchandise on display in our store at money saving prices.

Butt breeching harness with a price range of	**$30.00 to $60.00**
Horse collars	**$1.25 to $4.50**

Let Us Show You Our Offerings
Wheaton Hdwe. Co.

Financial perils weren't the only hazards facing families trying to scratch out a living from the land in southwest Missouri. Daily living, especially in the hill country to the south of Wheaton, was perilous in more ways than just their nearly empty pocketbooks. The day the drawing was announced in January 1937, the *Journal* carried a story about the demise of "a fine mule" that was bitten on the ankle by either a copperhead or a rattlesnake on a farm in the hill country near Lanagan, twenty-five miles southwest of Wheaton. On the same page was an article about a woman from the same area whose missing dog returned, apparently rabid, and bit her several times on her hand and leg. She escaped harm only because she was wearing heavy pants and work gloves, and the bites didn't break the skin.

An article in the February 4, 1937, edition of the *Journal* related that Wheaton's school had been closed the previous week because nearly 50 percent of the students and several of the teachers were absent due to colds and flu. Three new cases of scarlet fever were reported in one home south of town.

Although the 350 residents of Wheaton had electricity in 1937, many farms surrounding the little town did not. Most farmhouses in southwest Missouri were lit with kerosene lamps until sometime in 1940 when the Rural Electrification Administration (REA) began to build power lines deeper into the sparsely populated countryside.

When I was born in July 1939, more than seven years after the drawing began, conditions around Wheaton hadn't changed much. In a letter my dad wrote me on my birthday when I was in the navy, he described living conditions in 1939 on the rented farm three miles west of Wheaton where he and my mother lived:

> Twenty-two years since I paid Dr. Cardwell the last $10 and brought you and Mother home. We had saved money for months to pay for you.
>
> The day you were born we cooked breakfast on a wood-burning stove. A.E. Elkins (Wheaton merchant) had secured the agency for some newfangled gas to cook with called butane, but at the time we never hoped to use it. We pumped water by hand and carried it in a bucket to the house. Our lights were kerosene lamps, though thanks to FDR (President Franklin D. Roosevelt) and the REA (Rural Electrification Administration) we secured lights the next year. I washed your first diapers in a little hand powered washing machine and boiled them in a big kettle over an open fire.

In the summer of 1939, when I was an infant, Dad wrote that he and another young man, Harold Barnett, cut two hundred acres of grain with a binder pulled by an old iron-wheeled tractor.[18] Some farmers, Dad's letter said, were beginning to put rubber tires on tractors, "but rubber tires were considered a luxury. We hauled the bundled grain to a thrashing machine with horse-drawn wagons.[19]

"I remember going to Bryan's ... and getting a haircut the day after you arrived. Haircuts were 25 cents those days," Dad recalled. "I also remember telling Ern Shewmake about you. He was interested because Daniel Waldo was due before long."

Bryan Wolfenbarger's barbershop in Wheaton was a place where men often traded news and gossip. At the shop that day, Dad saw Ern

Shewmake, whose wife, Hessie, would give birth to Daniel Waldo Shewmake in October 1939. Dan would become my best friend, and a few years later, Ern would become Dad's first cattle-trading partner.

Dad's letter also recalled the run-up to World War II as isolationism gave way to military mobilization. Then came the surprise Japanese attack on the United States' naval base at Pearl Harbor on December 7, 1941. Wheaton and all the surrounding rural communities, like all other parts of the country, pitched headlong into the war effort. Young men and young women volunteered and were drafted into military service, and farmers raised crops and livestock to help feed millions of soldiers, sailors, aviators, and defense workers.

My dad was thirty-two years old when the war started. The local draft board kept giving him deferments, because farmers were considered vital to the war effort, he was married with a child, and was on the upper end of the age scale in the draft.

One day, when I was four or five years old, Dad, Mom, and I were driving to our farm from Wheaton. We stopped at our mailbox at the end of the lane that led to our house, and Dad pulled out a letter from the draft board. Before he opened it, he said that it probably would be his orders to report for duty. I wasn't old enough to understand all the implications, but I knew that it would mean he would have to leave, and it scared me. But it wasn't his call to report for duty, and his deferment lasted until the end of the war in the summer of 1945.

During the four tough war years, everything from sugar to gasoline to tires was rationed, and no new household appliances, cars, or trucks were made. We didn't own a car, but we did have a tractor during the war—a green John Deere two-cycle "poppin' John." We made it through the war by borrowing Granddad and Grandma's old Model A Ford when we had to go somewhere. They lived at the end of our little lane that ran a quarter of a mile south of the Wheaton-to-Stella road. Our house was about half that distance down the lane, so it was easy to borrow the car, although I think Mom was embarrassed that we had to ask that favor of her parents so often. When gasoline rationing was lifted in the summer of 1945,

Dad bought us a car and began to make a few bucks buying and selling prewar cars.

Wheaton began to come back to life. On Saturdays, especially for several hours in the afternoon before the 3:00 p.m. drawing, farm families and returning veterans—hungry for new products and a chance to win some money—flooded into Wheaton in greater numbers than ever. The signs on Highway 86 to the north and south of town said the population was 393 after the 1940 census, but it would be safe to say that around 3:00 p.m. on many Saturdays, that number doubled and sometimes tripled.

I often went to town with Granddad Lamberson during those early postwar years. Earnest William Lamberson—Earn to his friends and family—was five foot seven, never weighed more than 140 pounds, had whiskers that felt like toothbrush bristles, and was tough as nails. Before he went to town, he always shed his dirty overalls, scraped his stubble off with a straight razor, and slipped into a clean pair of blue bib overalls and a freshly ironed blue chambray shirt buttoned at the neck. In the summer, he usually wore a wide-brimmed straw hat to protect his face from the sun.

Lots of times when he needed to gas up his 1930 Model A Ford—and later, his '36 Chevy—we started our Saturday afternoons by going to Democrat Carter's Phillips 66 station. Democrat, of course, wasn't his real name. I always guessed that he got his nickname because he was a strong Democrat, but I don't remember ever asking. His real name was Calvin Delmont Carter, but most people shortened his nickname to Dimmer.

Dimmer was about Granddad's age—born in the 1880s. He was thin, stood ramrod straight and stone faced, and always wore striped bib overalls and a matching striped engineer's cap. His station on Highway 86 was a little building that rose to a sharp peak with gray flagstone rock siding. When we'd drive up, Dimmer would saunter out and ask how much gas we wanted.

"Fill her up," was Granddad's standard answer. Gasoline prices between 1945 and 1950 ranged somewhere between fifteen and twenty cents per gallon, so less than two dollars' worth would fill up the Model A's ten-gallon tank.[20]

Then an amazing ritual began. With his right hand, Dimmer would begin to work the handles on the side of the old gravity-flow pumps back and forth to start the gas flowing up into the glass tank at the top. And as he did that, he'd reach with his left hand into the pocket of his bib overalls, extract a packet of OCB cigarette papers, slide a paper out with his fingers, and tuck the packet back into his bib pocket. By then, he was pumping gas with his right hand. Then, holding the cigarette paper just so with his left hand, he'd use it to pull from his bib pocket a Bull Durham tobacco pouch and spread the pouch open with a couple of fingers. Somehow, without spilling even a shred of tobacco, he'd pour the exact amount for a cigarette into the paper he held in the same hand, magically use his fingers to roll a smoke, give it a swift lick to seal it, bite the Bull Durham pouch strings, pull it closed with his teeth, tuck the pouch back into the bib pocket of his overalls, reach into the lower pocket of his overalls, pull out a wooden kitchen match, strike it across the bib of his overalls, and light up—all the while pumping Granddad's gas with his other hand.

I remember wondering if we would someday be blasted all the way to Fairview in a ball of fire as Dimmer lit up while he was pumping gas. Obviously, we never were, but by the time I was old enough to drive a car, I remember thinking that it was sheer luck that Dimmer hadn't blown himself and some unlucky customer into the next county.

If anyone bought more than a dollar's worth of gas at Dimmer's station, he'd give them a pack of cigarettes. If they didn't smoke, he'd give them a package of chewing gum. Granddad smoked Wings or Chesterfield cigarettes during World War II, but by the time I was in grade school, he had switched to a pipe, so at Dimmer's station, I'd usually end up with a pack of gum.

As a kid, there were comments about Dimmer that puzzled me. It was a local legend that Dimmer was very tight with his money, which didn't square with his giving away cigarettes and chewing gum. But there was another story that jibed with Dimmer's being a little miserly.

According to that story, Dimmer had paid for a new 1939 Ford coupe with dimes he had socked away. A Ford coupe cost about $750 in 1939, which would have meant that Dimmer had squirreled away 7,500 dimes. I never got the answer to the puzzle of how, or whether, he actually saved that many dimes.

Much later, I found out that Dimmer had an ornery streak. Rebecca and Herman "Butch" Allman and their playmates, Sally and Jane Minnehan and Billy Stone, lived near Dimmer and his wife, Pruda, on the west end of town. Occasionally, a stray baseball, softball, or even a basketball belonging to one of them would land near a drain in front of Dimmer's station. If it had been raining, the balls sometimes would wash past Dimmer's property and could be retrieved, Butch said. If they stopped on Dimmer's property, he would snatch them up, lock the balls in a glass case inside the station, and sell them to his filling-station patrons. The kids' fathers—Stratton Allman, who ran Wheaton's grain mill and feed store; Joe Minnehan, vice president and later president of the Bank of Wheaton; and Bill Stone, of Barnes and Stone Chevrolet—occasionally would confront Dimmer and plead for him to return the balls. No dice. Dimmer would never return them, arguing that once the offending orbs were on his property, they were his to be sold. Maybe he did accumulate 7,500 dimes.[21]

But I was oblivious to Dimmer's ball poaching on those Saturday outings with Granddad. When we were at Dimmer's station, Granddad sometimes would nod that it was okay to go inside and fetch a bottle of pop—maybe a Grapette or a Dad's Root Beer or an Orange Crush—from a cooler where customers opened the lid and reached down into the icy water to pull out a bottle. One day as I was fishing around in the bottom of the cooler where the coldest bottles were, I came up with a bottle of real beer, discovering that Dimmer kept his private refreshment there. Even though many of the teetotalers in that Bible Belt community were scandalized by his fondness for the devil's brew, I didn't care if Dimmer drank beer. When I left his station with either a soda pop or a package of gum—or both—Saturday afternoons with Granddad were off to a good start.

We'd leave Dimmer's, drive south on Highway 86, and turn left on Main Street.

Wheaton on Saturday didn't have quite as much action as New York's Times Square, but there was enough activity to keep a country kid entertained. Rusty, dusty Ford and Chevy pickups and beat-up flatbed GMC and International Harvester trucks mixed with a lot of Ford, Chevy, and Plymouth automobiles parked diagonally on both sides of Main and for a block or two on the cross streets. Mercury, Dodge, and Studebaker cars were rare. Pontiacs, Oldsmobiles, Buicks, and Cadillacs were even scarcer and were regarded status symbols.

A convertible drew a crowd. Often, a gaggle of men would be walking around a ragtop, leaning in to get a closer look at the dashboard, steering wheel, gearshift, and seat covers as they speculated on how fast "she" would go and how slick the paint job was. Even as a small boy, I understood that the men talked about cars the way they talked about good-lookin' women.

Between 1945 and 1950, lots of prewar cars—boxy 1930s-vintage Fords and Chevys with running boards and some that could be cranked if the starter balked—were common sights. Occasionally, a sporty coupe with a rumble seat rolled into town. Ah, the rumble seats. Not long after the war, my dad traded for a 1936 Ford coupe with a rumble seat. I remember the day Dad and Mom took the seat in the cab while Granddad and I enjoyed the wind in our faces as we rode in the rumble seat all the way to Joplin—a great fifty-mile ride.

Smack in the middle of Wheaton, at the intersection of Main and Reasor, all vehicles on Main Street had to jog either to the right or the left to avoid the old town well and its manually operated pump that was protected by a sturdy three- or four-foot concrete wall. Later, the well was plugged, and the pump was replaced by a flagpole, but the barrier at the intersection remained. At the east end of Main Street sat a concrete horse trough that had watered the four-legged "vehicles" farmers had driven to town just a few years earlier.

It was an unspoken rule, but sometimes on Saturdays when parking got very scarce, drivers just started parking parallel, single file, in the middle of Main Street. If the line of cars strayed too close to one side of the street or the other, anyone parked diagonally at the curb had a hard time backing out. The only remedy was to find the owner of the offending vehicle—if you recognized the vehicle and knew who the owner was—and ask him to move it. If you didn't know who owned it, you just had to wait until the owner decided to leave, which led to a lot of grumbling from the driver who was penned in.

Trotting randomly through the crowds on the sidewalks were always a few town dogs that stopped from time to time, sniffing a potpourri of odors, including car and truck tires, in case one smelled good enough to pee on.

On the streets during crowded Saturdays, squeaky-clean boys with well-gooped burrs or flattops yelled and ran and played with boys who sported haircuts obviously administered at home by their moms or dads or some other family member who wasn't afraid to use scissors and comb. The boys with home cuts, I noticed, often also wore faded bib overalls. Most of the other boys wore jeans. I didn't have anything against bib overalls, and I sometimes wore them to Oshkosh, the one-room country school west of town that I attended until seventh grade. Overalls were just a way of guessing where a boy might live if I didn't know him.

There were three standard uniforms for the men. Some wore blue chambray work shirts, bib overalls, and high-top work shoes. Others favored matching gray or khaki twill shirts and trousers, and low-top leather shoes. A few other guys wore jeans and either low-top shoes or cowboy boots. Fewer people were riding horses after the war, and boots were favored more by auctioneers, cattle traders, and others who enjoyed strutting their stuff a bit.

Regardless of attire, men on Saturday afternoons leaned on the fenders of cars and pickups parked on Main Street. Some supported themselves by putting their backs against the front walls of shops as they puffed pipes or cigarettes or spat from great chaws of tobacco that swelled their cheeks. Depending on the weather over the last few weeks, they talked about the rain, the drought, the hail, the wind, or the prices of hay and grain and milk and cattle. Occasionally, the men would remove their wide-brimmed straw hats or their striped shop caps or baseball caps and mop the sweat that had accumulated on their brows, revealing a strip of white forehead above a brown and weathered face.

The town women were more likely to wear store-bought dresses, more makeup than farm women, and more earrings or other jewelry. When I was very young, women in jeans hadn't yet made it to Wheaton's fashion world, but by the time I was in high school, women's jeans had made a breakthrough.

With a little boy's critical eye, I secretly tended to favor the looks of the town women. But I didn't want Mom or Grandma to know that the ones I thought were the prettiest also wore the heaviest makeup— the ones that Grandma disdainfully called "painted women."

No matter how they were dressed, nearly everybody who was in town on Saturday afternoon had come for the drawing.

Starting February 9, 1946, as Wheaton's merchants became a bit more flush in the postwar economy, the committee in charge of the prize money decided to stop Saturday's 10:00 a.m. drawing and hold only one giveaway at 3:00 p.m.[22] The prize money, it was announced in the *Wheaton Journal*, would be increased, and there would be more cash prizes. To be eligible for a prize, everyone would have to reregister at either the Farmers Exchange (grocery and feed store), Rowland's (clothing store), Frazier-Daniels & Brattin (grocery), Fithians Finer Foods (grocery), or Allman Produce & Feed (grain mill and feed store). At any of those places of business, folks could sign the drawing registry.

This new drawing procedure caused quite a stir. For a few weeks, just about the first thing out of people's mouth was "Have you signed up for the drawing again?" I don't remember any particular rules for eligibility for the event, except that I guess registrants had to be able to write their name and capable of walking up to claim the prize if their name was drawn.

As the clock crept toward three o'clock on those long-ago Saturday afternoons, there was a noticeable increase in the pace of store transactions, because people wanted to complete their purchases in time for them to walk a block or two to the big event. Men leaned on storefronts talking with their neighbors, and friends began to glance to the east down Main Street, snapping their pocketknives shut and shoving their whittling sticks back into their pockets. Women reached for their daughters' hands and began to mosey eastward toward the city park.

Then, at precisely five minutes before three, Roy Dayton "Date" Brattin, lean and on a mission, wearing gray twill trousers supported by suspenders, a matching twill work shirt, and a wide-brimmed straw hat, emerged from Daniels & Brattin's grocery store on the north side of Main Street.[23] Under one arm, he carried an orange metal box about two feet square and a foot and a half deep with a window in one side.

In the box—which, prior to the orange paint, had been a grocery store display box for Junge's cookies—were several hundred large, clear medicine capsules, contributed by a local pharmacist.[24] Each capsule contained a tiny fortune cookie–sized strip of paper, on which was written the name of each person who had registered for the drawing. Also in the box was a small canvas bag containing at least five silver dollars, one crisp five-dollar bill, and more bills totaling the amount of that particular Saturday's grand prize.

Always walking with Date, past Bryan's Barber Shop, past Jerry Guiles's shoe repair store, past the Wheaton Post Office, Walter McAtee's liquor store, and the old city jail, was one of Date's three nearly grown daughters—Helen, Lorene, or Barbara.

The Pied Piper of Hamelin had nothing on Date. The piper's musical pipe lured only the children of medieval Hamelin out of town, but Date's orange box lured people of all ages—men, women, boys, and girls—out of Wheaton's shops and stores. Unlike the children of the Pied Piper legend, the folks who followed Date to the drawing didn't disappear, and Wheaton's merchants counted on people to quickly reappear in their stores after the drawing.

To begin the much-anticipated event, Date and the daughter who was his helper that day would climb a few steps onto a wooden platform about six feet high and four feet square with rails around three sides. Date would set the orange box on a stand. Rolling a cud of chewing tobacco to one side of his mouth, Date would announce with authority, "All right, folks, let's get quiet now." Then he would launch a dart-like shot of tobacco juice against a nearby tree while Helen or Lorene or Barbara reached into the box and stirred the capsules. Persons standing near the platform could hear the capsules rattle against the tin box before Date's daughter drew out a capsule. She would pull it apart, unroll the name, and hand it to Date. The master drawing announcer, his mouth cleared of tobacco juice, would sing out the name. Then the startled and lucky winner would holler, come forward, and collect his or her prize money.

The first five prizes were for one dollar each. If the winner wasn't present, another name would be drawn until five shiny silver dollars were given away. The same rule applied for the next prize category, a crisp five-dollar bill.

Then it was time to draw the name of the winner of the big prize, which started at twenty dollars. If the winner was not present, the grand prize grew by twenty dollars for the next Saturday, increasing by twenty bucks each Saturday until a winner was there to claim the money. A few times, when there was a string of absentees, the grand prize grew to nearly two hundred dollars, a small fortune to lots of folks around Wheaton. I once won eighty dollars when my name was drawn for the big prize. On another Saturday, I won a silver dollar.

As far as I know, Date Brattin was the only person who ever presided over the drawing during my childhood. He was the perfect person to do it, because nearly everyone for miles around knew and trusted him. Date, who was born within a month of my Granddad and Grandma Lamberson in 1883, lived his entire life in western Barry County near Wheaton.

Besides the three daughters who helped him with the drawing, Date and his wife, Cora, had eight sons—Minor, Lillard, Leo, Crawford, Sherman, Ludon, Joseph (Pete), and Roy (Jack).

Like most folks in that part of the country, Date was a farmer, but he had several other valuable skills, one of which was keeping heavy machinery running.

During the first half of the twentieth century, lots of farmers, especially those in the hill country, raised tomatoes. During the late summer, those tomatoes were processed at canning factories where many farm women worked in the late summer to earn extra money by sorting and peeling the red acidic fruit. Canning factories sometimes were open-air affairs under a roof supported by posts, and others were stifling hot warehouse-like buildings. They usually were topped with a tin roof that held the sun's heat while cauldrons of hot water heated by a steam boiler processed the tomatoes and ramped up the temperature to just a few degrees short of Dante's Inferno.

The large boilers had to be operated by someone who knew what he was doing. Date had the skills to keep a boiler going without blowing it up or letting the water get too cool—except for one time. On June 27, 1930, Date, two of his sons, two other men, and a small boy narrowly escaped death or serious injury when a steam engine exploded at a sawmill five miles north of Fairview. The *Wheaton Journal* described the incident in its July 3, 1930, edition:

When the engine exploded, Date and Pharis (Brattin) were about ten feet away getting a drink, and the other four persons were lying in the grass about twenty feet from the engine. The force of the explosion tore the engine into hundreds of pieces and threw huge pieces of iron many feet, some of which were left hanging in nearby trees. The flues of the boiler were twisted around one another like a rope.

It was only a miracle that all the six persons escaped being seriously injured by some of the broken parts of the engine. The only person to receive a scratch was the small son of Pharis Brattin, who received a very small cut on the back of his neck.[25]

Date very likely learned something about servicing boilers because of that explosion. There was never another serious accident involving any boiler he was operating.

Date also knew his way around the moving parts of threshing machines. Until I was nearly grown, most farmers around Wheaton didn't use a combine to harvest their grain. Instead, they harvested their wheat, oats, and barley by using a binder to cut and tie their grain into bundles, and then they pitched the bundles onto a wagon or truck that hauled the grain to a stationary threshing machine. The machine separated the heads of grain from the stems, spitting out the stems into a straw pile and spewing the grain into a truck. Date's ability to keep threshing machines running kept his skills in demand, especially in the summertime during harvesting season.

He had another skill that kept him in the public eye. He could operate a road grader. Before Wheaton's side streets were paved, Date often was paid to operate a grader, sitting tall in the high metal-and-glass-enclosed cab. Occasionally, he was the one who graded the eight-mile stretch of dirt road that ran past our farm, connecting Wheaton and Stella.

Date and his kids had musical skills and often sang and played at local events. A headline in the *Wheaton Journal* of September 18, 1947, read:

WATERMELON FEAST TUESDAY NIGHT

An old time watermelon feast for members of the Ladies Auxiliary and members of their families was held Tuesday evening at the home of Mr. and Mrs. D.G. (Gray) McMillen. Music for the event was furnished by the Brattin string quartet, composed of Date, Leo, Ludon and Pete Brattin. Old time numbers played with the versatility that only the Brattin quartet has, made the evening a most enjoyable one with Date changing from banjo to violin, guitar and finally, piano.

But for me and lots of boys around Wheaton, Date had another talent that was dang near magic. He could take your warts off. The thing was—you couldn't tell your mom you'd asked for Date's services, because his method wasn't exactly sanitary.

You'd just see Date on the street in Wheaton and say, "Date, I've got a wart I'd like you to take off." You'd show it to him, and he'd say, "Got a dime?" His fee was always a dime. You'd give him a dime, and he'd spit on it and then rub the dime over your wart. I didn't care that Date kept the dime; I didn't especially want it after Date's spit bath. A few days after this magic medical procedure, your wart would just kinda begin to disintegrate and disappear.

Quite a few years later, it dawned on me that Date's miraculous wart powers were very likely the result of his nearly always having a chaw of chewing tobacco in his cheek. I can't prove it, but I'm guessing Date's saliva would have dissolved a ball bearing.

Date was a natural showman, and eventually that translated to political skills. In the spring of 1948, he announced his candidacy for judge of the Barry County Court, Western District.[26] Date, a Democrat in a county that leaned Republican, won a narrow victory. In Wheaton, he topped his GOP opponent, Charles England, 262 to 140. In the countywide vote, Date got 2,654 to England's 2,562, winning by 92 votes.[27]

Two years later, Date ran for reelection, but it was a Republican year, and Date lost by 203 votes, countywide.[28] However, he had strong support in Wheaton, getting 239 votes to Roscoe Jackson's 140, the same number who voted for his opponent two years earlier. Apparently, there were 140 Republicans in Wheaton in both 1948 and 1950, or at least 140 who bothered to vote.[29]

That ended Date's political career, but he would continue to preside over Wheaton's Saturday drawing until it ended in 1956, when I was completing my junior year of high school. Date's life would change that year. On Sunday, April 8, 1956, his house in Wheaton burned down, destroying everything in it. Date, his wife, and one of his sons barely escaped, but they were not hurt.[30]

The fire burned all the little slips of paper on which were written the names of persons registered for the drawing, so the April 14, 1956, drawing had to be canceled until people could reregister. The drawing was held as usual on April 21, when seven slightly scorched silver dollars that had survived Date's fire were given away.[31]

Then on April 26, 1956, the Missouri Attorney General and the general counsel of the Missouri Sheriffs' Association warned that the Missouri Supreme Court had ruled that a state law against bingo and other "charity" gambling must be strictly enforced. Any sheriff who failed to enforce the ruling would be kicked out of office.[32]

Two days later, Date presided over Wheaton's last drawing. The first prize was ten dollars, just as it was the day the drawing began in 1932. Date outlived the drawing by almost eight years, dying at age eighty in February 1964 while I was away at college.

Date never knew what an impact he had made during his eighty years in the Wheaton community. Jon Paden grew up half a block north of Main Street in the middle of Wheaton and knew Date well. After he graduated from Wheaton High in 1954, Jon played basketball for the University of Missouri, secured a doctorate in education, and later worked at the prestigious Kettering Foundation. He recalls that Date's name was mentioned once during a scholarly discussion with education experts about what makes a good school. Date knew something about that. After all, he and Cora raised eleven kids.

Date and the drawing made a lifelong favorable impression on Jon and many of us who grew up in or near Wheaton. As Wheaton was planning for its centennial in 2007, Jon suggested that one of the centennial's events should be a reenactment of a drawing in the city park at the end of Main Street. Wheaton's centennial planners liked the idea, and two of Date's surviving children, Barbara and Ludon, agreed to take part.

So on July 7, 2007, Wheaton once again held a drawing. The

grand prize was fifty dollars. Just as she had sixty years earlier, Barbara Brattin Haynes reached into a box and drew out a name, gave it to Date's son Ludon, who took the role of his dad and announced the lucky winner.

Date would have been proud to be remembered that way, but he probably wouldn't have changed expressions. I imagine he would have launched a shot of tobacco juice against the nearest tree and said with his characteristically deadpan demeanor, "There's a lot of fine folks around Wheaton."

5

Rocky Comfort on Sunday

The thing about Rocky Comfort on Sunday was that it looked a lot like Rocky Comfort any other day of the week. The main difference was that on a Sunday there usually weren't as many cars and pickups parked in front of Cecil Shewmake's general store or around Bill Brown's service station.

Rocky Comfort, which the locals shortened to Rocky, has never been an incorporated city, so its boundaries start wherever anyone wants them to. My boundaries for the little town start where Uncle Awk and Aunt Virgie Davidson used to live—in a neat two-story white frame house with a front porch swing located just north of the Rocky Comfort Cemetery. On Sunday mornings in the late 1940s, during my grade school years, I'd often ride to the Rocky Church of Christ with Granddad Earn and Grandma Carrie Lamberson, who was Aunt Virgie's sister.

Until I was a teenager, I had no idea that Uncle Awk's name was Oscar; he was always Uncle Awk to me. Awk Davidson was a lanky, square-jawed man with a very dry sense of humor. Like lots of the old-timers, he generally wore khaki or gray twill pants with suspenders over long-sleeve shirts that he buttoned to the neck. Long before I was born, he had acquired the nickname that was pronounced like the first syllable in the word *awkward*. He was anything but awkward; in fact, he had to be pretty nimble of mind and body to live with Aunt Virgie.

Aunt Virgie was the fussiest woman about her looks that I had ever known at that stage of my life. People in the community who knew her well understood that if they dropped by to visit and knocked on her door in the middle of the day, she typically wouldn't answer for ten minutes. Whenever she heard a knock, instead of going to the door, she would go to the dresser mirror in her bedroom, put on fresh rouge, powder, and lipstick, and comb her hair before she came to the door.

Callers who didn't know this often went away, thinking there was no one home. Aunt Virgie could not bear the horrible possibility that someone might see her at less than her best, or at least at less than the best impression good face paint would convey.

On Sunday mornings, however, Aunt Virgie did not keep us waiting. She knew that Granddad would drive his black 1936 Chevy two-door sedan into her driveway at precisely 9:50 a.m. to pick her up for the five-minute ride to church.

Aunt Virgie, dressed to the nines—gloves; hat, sometimes with veil; dark suit with tailored skirt; hose and heels; head high; chin out; face powdered and rouged—would stride purposefully from the screen door at the back of the house as Grandma got out of the front seat and clambered into the backseat with me. For reasons I never understood, Aunt Virgie often was in a snit about something, so the short ride from there to church was likely to go smoother if Grandma simply ceded the front seat to Virgie so the proud woman wouldn't rumple her outfit and heighten her irritation.

Granddad, as best I can remember, usually never said a word after Aunt Virgie got in the car. He just sat behind the wheel and drove. From the backseat, Grandma would start the conversation carefully.

"Pretty day today" was a line Grandma often used when the weather was reasonably fair.

"Pretty windy" was a typical reply from Aunt Virgie. Or maybe "Pretty chilly. Awk said he froze most of the night, but then he never got up to get another quilt," Aunt Virgie would say stiffly, looking straight ahead through the windshield.

Uncle Awk never went to church. I didn't give it much thought, because instinctively, I knew he regarded Sunday morning as a couple of hours of relief from Aunt Virgie's critical eye. Another reason it didn't bother my youthful religious standards when he stayed home from church is that I knew he was what men in the area called "a good ol' boy."

From time to time, over the years immediately following World War II, he would lend my dad $400–$500 at a time to "trade cattle on," as Dad would say. After the war, as Dad was getting started as a successful cattle trader in that area of southwest Missouri, it often was Awk Davidson, and not the Bank of Wheaton, who supplied the capital that kept Dad in the cattle business.

Uncle Awk always carried himself with an air of dignity, even when he had a cud of chewing tobacco in his mouth and was spitting great splashes of tobacco juice. I liked him, because he treated me as a man, even though I was a little boy.

"Hello, Jimmah," he'd say.

"Uncle Awk," I'd reply as I nodded respectfully.

And then he'd ask me something about the weather or cattle prices or say something about my dad in exactly the same way he talked to the men.

None of his good deeds appeared to impress Aunt Virgie, though. She spent a lot more time complaining to Grandma about Awk's tobacco chewing and spitting than about his admirable qualities. My dad and his cattle-trading partner, Ern Shewmake, occasionally marveled at the way Awk handled, or mostly ignored, Virgie's criticisms.

But one particular Sunday morning when I was about ten years old and riding in the backseat of Granddad's 1936 Chevy on the way to church, Aunt Virgie told Grandma a story that explained to me how Uncle Awk sometimes evened the score with her.

In her most indignant voice, Aunt Virgie began to pour out her tale. It seems that Wallains Goostree, who was married to Grandma and Aunt Virgie's sister, Linna, had come to visit Virgie and Awk the previous week. Uncle Wallains and Uncle Awk were lifelong buddies. Years earlier, Wallains and Linna had moved out west to Marysville, California, where Wallains was a pear farmer.

"We had a good supper," Aunt Virgie said, turning her head from the front passenger seat to speak to Grandma, who was sitting to my left in the backseat. I knew this was going to be a good story, because it wasn't often that she bothered to turn from staring straight ahead through the windshield when she talked to Grandma. I can still hear the agitation in her voice.

"We had corn bread and brown beans and fresh tomatoes and onions out of the garden," Aunt Virgie began. "After supper, Wallains and Awk sat in the porch swing and talked awhile. I decided to go to bed, and after a while, I heard them come up and go to bed."

Grandma and I knew that Awk and Virgie had separate adjoining bedrooms upstairs. Uncle Awk's bedroom had a window to the south, but Aunt Virgie's looked out to the east, and there was a door opening between the two rooms but no door. The breeze must have been blowing from the south, through Awk and Wallains's bedroom that night.

"Well, I could hear them talking for a while, and then they started laughing, and pretty soon, I smelled something just foul," Aunt Virgie said, leaning around to face Grandma and looking like she had just sucked a sour lemon. Granddad, poker faced, didn't react even though I knew he wanted to laugh. He just drove on.

"But that wasn't the worst of it," Aunt Virgie fumed as she described the flatulent pair. "They started to make a game out of it. One of them would let one, and they'd laugh. Then in a minute or two, the other one would let one. And before long, I got to where I could tell by the smell which one of them had done it," she said ruefully. "The breeze from their window was blowing it right through the door to my room, and you can't tell me they didn't know that."

Grandma tried hard to sympathize, but when Aunt Virgie turned back to face the windshield, Grandma gave me a funny little grin that caused us both to squeeze our hands over our mouths to keep from laughing out loud.

About that time, Granddad stopped the car in front of the church house, and Aunt Virgie, hat perched on her head and tilted just so, got out and walked toward the church doors, still looking terribly offended about the acrid odors she had smelled a couple of nights earlier.

Grandma and I followed a few steps behind, barely able to suppress laughter. I thought about Uncle Awk and how much I liked him, and I decided that he and Uncle Wallains would go to heaven, even if they didn't go to church, because God would need someone up there to help him handle Aunt Virgie.

Not every ride to church was as interesting as that one, so I'd amuse myself looking at the sights around Rocky Comfort even though I'd seen them a thousand times by the time I was ten.

On the south side of the cemetery, we'd pass the beautiful old white frame Prosperity Baptist Church, drop down a little grade and cross a culvert that channeled the flow from a trickling spring, and jog to the right toward downtown Rocky, an eighth of a mile to the south.

At that point, we were in bottom land, where in pioneer days several natural springs bubbled up, flowed together, and formed the headwaters of the south fork of Indian Creek. Olin Cartwright, whose family arrived in the 1800s, said he learned from his father, Luther, that in 1900, Rocky was well known for its many mineral springs. When the town staged a celebration to commemorate the new century, more than a thousand people camped out in nearby tents and covered wagons to bathe in area streams and drink the springwater that was thought to be medicinal.

After we crossed the culvert, Granddad would drive across a concrete bridge over a larger stream where Indian Creek began just north of town. Then we'd pass Bill and Gladys Brown's old house with the ornate shutters and double gables and then Bill's all-purpose garage, service station, and appliance store. Gladys, who taught commerce and home economics at Wheaton High School, was known affectionately by Wheaton students as "Ma Brown." She also was a regular at the Rocky Church of Christ on Sunday mornings.

Behind the Browns' house and service station to the west was the ramshackle, tin-roofed canning factory. Twenty years before I was born, the canning factory had been owned and managed by Uncle Awk's brother, Roscoe, known as Ross.

Unlike the flat Wheaton streets two and a half miles to the northeast, Rocky was built on hills. The biggest hill started at the town's primary intersection of Main, the north-south street, and Mill, the east-west street. After we passed Browns' station and continued south on Main to start up the hill, we passed the post office and a second building on the right.

To the left was the croquet court, a drawing place for loafers and croquet sharks. Like Wheaton's croquet court, Rocky's court was made of hard-packed sand with heavy wire wickets set in concrete. So that spectators could view the games, there was a long bench between the court and the back of Cecil Shewmake's general store. The unwritten rules were about the same as the rules in Wheaton: men only, no talking, and no youngsters unless they buttoned their lips and sat quietly on the bench.

Each croquet player had a nickname—a handle. Howard Alexander, the rural mail carrier for the Rocky Comfort Post Office, was known as RFD Howard. Virgil Ford's handle was the same as his nickname, Honk.

Backed up to the croquet court and facing south at the corner of Main and Mill streets was Cecil Shewmake's store—the largest structure in downtown Rocky. To be more precise, Cecil was the proprietor during most, but not all, of my boyhood years. Old-timers like Granddad Lamberson always referred to Cecil as Teedle. I always surmised that he got the nickname when he was very small and couldn't pronounce his name correctly.

Cecil was tall and bald and in later years grew fond of wearing toupees. Although I wouldn't want to be critical of Cecil's toupees, the casual observer would have been capable, from half a block away, of determining that he was wearing a "rug."

Cecil also was fond of Cadillacs, which he traded regularly for the latest model. My dad always thought Cecil was a very able man with a dollar. He was the only person in the area, Dad said, who could make enough money at his store to afford a new Cadillac just about every year through the 1950s. Or maybe he made that extra cash from selling off his beef cattle—Herefords and Angus—which he raised on his farm on old Highway 44, now Highway 76, between Rocky and Wheaton.

Cecil was my friend Dan Shewmake's uncle, and I always felt very comfortable going into his store that stocked everything from groceries to small hardware items to, of course, soda pop, candy bars, and ice cream.

One reason why I always wanted to stop at Cecil's store on the way home from church was to take a close look at Audus Richard "Bill" Buttram. In both actions and looks, Bill always reminded me of Der Captain in the comic strip, *Katzenjammer Kids*—usually scowling and looking like a constipated fellow in need of a laxative.

Bill was a burly old man who apparently hadn't changed clothes for several years, which is why I always tried to stay upwind of him. Set squarely on his head was a black bowler hat. The rest of his outfit was a dark denim jumper worn over a wool knit vest and blue chambray shirt. Under Bill's denim pants, he wore long underwear year round. On his feet were high-top black shoes. His black, bristly moustache twitching, he was always cursing Wheaton, which he claimed he had only visited once and whose merchants hadn't treated him well.

In his semiofficial capacity as the town's night watchman, he wore a badge and a holstered pistol. Bill's duties were semiofficial because Rocky's merchants paid him a small stipend to serve in that capacity even though he was not a sworn peace officer.

For years, my grandparents told me, Bill had lived with his sister, Nannie, and his ailing mother, Mary Eliza Buttram, in a little house up Rocky's big hill. Mary had divorced Bill's father, Bishop "Bish" Pearce Buttram, in 1908. She never remarried.

Unlike her sinister-looking son, Mary Buttram was a pleasant woman who lived in Rocky more than forty years. She was a faithful member of the Methodist Church, according to her obituary in the *Wheaton Journal,* "and leaves scores of friends, who will always remember her sweet, consoling and encouraging words."[33] Mary is buried in the Ottowa Indian Cemetery, Ottowa County, Oklahoma.[34] After she died at age eighty-six in May 1946, my grandparents said, Bill seemed to live most of the time in an unpleasant world that existed only in his mind.

Bill, who was born January 18, 1882, near Pea Ridge, Arkansas, ran a little shoe repair shop with flagstone rock siding next to Cecil's store.[35] He was handy with a sewing machine that could punch through shoe leather.

Who knows how much money he made as a cobbler, because he could be seen seven days a week sitting on a bench in front of his shop or on the wall of the artesian fountain across the street, keeping an eye on any suspicious characters who might be visiting Rocky. To Bill, everyone was suspicious, which meant that every Rocky visitor was subject to his baleful gaze.

Several of Rocky's young women in those days tried to avoid him because they were afraid of him, mostly because of his menacing demeanor coupled with the fact that, as night watchman, he always wore a gun belt with a holstered six-shooter.

One day, Bill walked into Mollie's Café on the southwest corner of Main and Mill Street and saw a sign on the pinball machine. In an effort to discourage teenagers from gambling on the games by requiring players to be at least twenty-one years old, Mollie had posted a sign that read No Minors Allowed.

Ol' Bill stopped, peered closely at the sign, and exclaimed, "No minors allowed? Why, there ain't no miners around here. They're all farmers!"

Everyone in earshot roared with laughter, including J. W. "Dub" Raulsten, who relayed the story to me years later. Bill stayed in character, though. He didn't laugh.

I'm sure Bill was never evaluated by a psychiatrist, because we didn't even know how to spell *psychiatrist* in southwest Missouri in those days, but the consensus among Rocky Comfort residents was that the pinball machine in Bill's head was on "tilt."[36]

However, the old night watchman was present at three of Rocky's most disastrous events, two of which hastened the little village's decline.

The first disaster occurred on April 12, 1932, when a fire of unknown origin broke out between 11:00 p.m. and midnight, according to the *Wheaton Journal.* The blaze "destroyed all the business buildings on the west side of Main Street in the block north of the artesian well ...[37]

"Buttram, the nightwatch, first discovered the fire in the Woodmen's Hall but was unable to get into the hall to extinguish the flames.[38] He gave the alarm but the fire had gained too much headway to be put out," the *Journal* story continued. The alarm system apparently was Bill Buttram's pistol, fired into the air.

However, after Bill awakened the sleeping residents, they quickly gathered "and assisted in saving many dollars worth of property from the post office, barbershops, and the grocery store."[39] But Bill and the other townspeople were powerless to stop the spread of the fire, because there was no town water system or firefighting equipment. Bill was forced to watch his own shoe shop burn down. At the post office, where the old bank vault had been moved, many valuable records were lost, because the door to the vault had been left open.[40]

The 1932 fire began to change the way Rocky Comfort looked. Nearly all of the town's northwest quadrant—roughly one-quarter of the business section—was destroyed. Most of the buildings destroyed in the fire "were two-story buildings and were occupied by the post office, (Grover) Davidson's Barber Shop, Sampson & Ford's grocery store, Harrell's Barber Shop, and Bill Buttram's Shoe Shop," the *Journal* reported. Because the two-story structures that burned were replaced by one-story buildings, Rocky began to look noticeably smaller, Granddad and Grandma Lamberson told me.

Four years later, the town got what should have been a second wake-up call underlining the need for trained volunteers and firefighting equipment that could respond quickly to an alarm. On Sunday, November 22, 1936, a strong wind was blowing from the south about 2:30 in the afternoon when the Church of Christ building caught fire, apparently from a defective flue that vented the wood-burning heating stove in the auditorium.

Townspeople who rushed to the scene found the church building too far gone to save, but by then, the wind had blown sparks and flames across the street to the home of Mrs. Fanny Shelly, who was renting the home to the Charlie Killion family. The people of the community were able to carry out most of Charlie and Evelyn Killion's household belongings and some items that belonged to Mrs. Shelly, but the house was lost, along with the Killions' shepherd dog.

Two barns on the Shelly property also burned down. Windblown sparks set two other residences on fire more than a block to the north, but Rocky's residents managed to save them. If they had burned to the ground, it is likely the north wind would have carried sparks down the hill and into the town's business section, resulting in a repeat of the 1932 disaster.

Still, no action was taken to strengthen Rocky Comfort's firefighting capabilities. The inaction proved to be catastrophic two years later when, once again, Bill Buttram sounded the fire alarm by shooting into the air, just as he had in 1932.

On the night of October 7, 1938, George "Peach" Ford recalled, he was twenty years old and sitting on a bench in front of Rocky's rebuilt post office when he saw a flicker of fire on the second floor of Wid Roberts's hardware store on the east side of Main, just south of the concrete bridge over the Indian Creek headwaters. It was just after 11:00 p.m., George said.[41] George hollered at Buttram, who fired his pistol to arouse the sleeping Rocky residents while George ran to his uncle "Honk" Ford's house to alert him and his wife, Marjorie.

The *Wheaton Journal* told an astounding story of the conflagration, which consumed eight buildings and businesses. Like the stores destroyed in 1932, most of those destroyed in the 1938 fire were two-story structures. Some were never rebuilt at all, and others were rebuilt as one-story buildings.

8 Bldgs. Burn in Rocky Comfort

Eight buildings were destroyed by fire of unknown origin in Rocky Comfort Friday night. According to those who first saw the fire it started in the second story of the Wid Roberts Hardware Building around eleven o'clock and quickly spread to other buildings.

The buildings destroyed by the fire, starting at the north on the east side of Main Street, were: Wid Roberts frame residence building, the Wid Roberts two-story Hardware Building, the two-story building occupied by the Harrell & Lilly drygoods store, the two-story building occupied by the V.T. Ford Restaurant and store and the one-story building on the corner occupied by the Milligan store. On the north side of the street running east from the public artesian well a one-story building belonging to Bill Buttram, a one-story building belonging to Mrs. Josie Montgomery and the Ridenour Blacksmith shop building were destroyed. Stored in Mrs. Montgomery's building were two carloads of newly canned tomatoes belonging to her son, Edgar.

Soon after the fire started, Bill Buttram, nightwatch, noticed it and gave the alarm by firing his gun. In just a very short time the flames were roaring from the buildings. Jim Harrell was sleeping in his building next to where the fire started and was still asleep when Virgil Ford broke into the smoke-filled building and awoke him. Had he been left alone a few more moments he would have burned to death.

In just a short time practically all the residents of Rocky Comfort and many from the surrounding territory were at the scene of the fire helping to carry out merchandise and protect other buildings. Practically nothing was rescued from the Harrell and Ford stores and some of the merchandise was removed from the Milligan store. However, he reports that not much of his high-priced merchandise was saved. Mr. Milligan had the largest stock of goods of any of the firms to burn. The building he occupied also belonged to Mrs. Montgomery and she had no insurance whatsoever on her two buildings. Neither did her son have any insurance on his tomatoes. It is understood some of the other buildings and contents were partially covered by insurance, but not much insurance was carried by many due to the high rate charged by insurance companies.

The garage and filling station belonging to Bill Brown and situated directly across the street from the Wid Roberts Building came very near burning as the wind was blowing the flames directly toward it. A stream of water from Mr. Brown's small water system was all that saved his buildings. A continuous stream of water was applied to the front of his building and gasoline pump and then the paint was burnt from the front of the building, the gasoline pump damaged and "Mooney" Lowe, one of the persons stationed on top of the building to protect it, caught fire.

The filling station equipment belonging to A.E. Elkins in the building across the street to the south from the fire, was removed from the building, but the brick wall next to the street, and the wind blowing from the southeast, saved this building.

It is planned by some to erect new buildings on the sites where the old ones were destroyed.[42]

Bottom line: All the commercial buildings in downtown Rocky, except for the ones that had been rebuilt on the west side of Main and those on the south side of the Main-Mill intersection, were destroyed in 1938's massive fire.

It may have been Bill Buttram's most memorable and most awful moment during all his years as night watchman—he had fired his gun and rousted the town's residents from their beds but still failed to halt an impending disaster. On that Friday night in 1938, Bill again lost his shoe store, which he had rebuilt in a new location after the 1932 fire. Losing his store twice might have been one reason Bill always seemed so out of sorts years later.

Peach Ford, who grew up on Indian Creek near Rocky, recalled that when Bill got sick sometime in the late 1940s or early 1950s, and the aging Doc McCall arrived to examine the stocky old cobbler and night watchman, Doc saw Peach and motioned for him to come and give him a hand. After removing the outer layers of Bill's clothes, they found that his underwear and patches of his blue chambray shirt were imbedded in his skin. Working together and fighting to overcome an awful odor, Peach said, they had to soak Bill in warm water to separate his clothes from his skin before Doc could treat him.

Bill Buttram died on December 30, 1956.[43] He was, undoubtedly, one of the little town's strangest residents. He was buried in the Grand Army of the Republic Cemetery in Miami, Oklahoma, near his father.

The conventional wisdom during the years I was growing up was that Rocky Comfort declined because, in 1907, the M&NA Railroad decided to bypass Rocky and locate a depot and a new town two and a half miles to the northeast—a town that became Wheaton. However, virtually no one seemed to take into account the two disastrous fires that destroyed the bulk of Rocky's business section in the 1930s. If Rocky's residents had chosen to incorporate and had raised the money for a municipal water system, firefighting equipment, and trained volunteers, Rocky's businesses might have survived virtually intact, and the competitive rivalry with Wheaton might have continued for decades longer than it did. Grandma Lamberson got it almost right when she commented ruefully on several occasions that she believed the 1938 fire "was the end of Rocky."

It wasn't quite the end. In the aftermath of the 1938 fire, Clifford Milligan and his father, Alonzo "Lon" Milligan, rebuilt their store on the northeast corner of Main and Mill and sold it to Cecil Shewmake in 1946. But none of the stores on Main to the north toward the lowland springs were ever rebuilt.

In 1952, Cecil leased his store to George "Howdy Howdy" Parrish and his wife, who were living in a structure just east of the store when it burned on June 8, 1954, destroying both the living quarters and the store. Howdy Howdy and his wife barely escaped, losing even their spectacles in the fire.[44]

It also was a close call for much of what was left of Rocky. Wheaton's fire truck and its crew of volunteer firemen responded, but all they could do was protect the post office, Brown's service station and appliance store, and another building across the street on the west side of Main. Cecil rebuilt the store, this time using concrete blocks, and the building stands to this day.

When he rebuilt his store, Cecil made sure that it had a bench in front of it that faced the artesian fountain, just like the old one. In neighboring Wheaton, there were no outdoor benches to sit on, but Rocky had three—the one at the croquet court, the one in front of Cecil's store, and another in front of the post office across the street. All the benches were havens for loafers and gabbers.

Often, Rocky visitors would see a fellow sitting on the bench in front of Cecil's store who held a distinction I envied as a little kid—he was the town loafer. His full name was Marvin Ephron Decker. He was called by his middle name, Ephron—except that nobody, absolutely *nobody* that I ever heard, pronounced *Ephron* correctly. Everyone pronounced it "Eff-ern," with the emphasis on the *Eff.* Often, he was just called Decker.

"Effern" Decker was born in 1905 in the rural community of

Harrel east of the then-thriving town of Rocky Comfort and south of the wheat field that in 1907 would become Wheaton. He graduated from the eighth grade at the rural Harrel school in May 1919. After high school in Rocky Comfort, he worked for a time for the US Postal Service in Kansas City. During World War II, even though he was in the upper reaches of the oldest age bracket for military service, he was drafted into the army and was stationed somewhere in Alaska.

When the war was over, he came back to Rocky Comfort and bought an old house on the west side of Rocky's big hill. From then until his death on February 18, 1983, Decker's only paying job—that I know of—was as a chicken catcher for Stanley Ford. Stanley, the son of one of Rocky's prominent couples, Honk and Marjorie Ford, ran a fleet of chicken trucks.

Chicken catchers worked at night, grabbing roosting half-grown chickens by the legs, holding four or five upside down between the fingers of each hand, and depositing them into coops that were loaded onto trucks and delivered to chicken-processing plants. After a night of exercising his chicken-catching skills, Decker was free to loaf after he arrived home at sunup and got some sleep.

Decker, in fact, was so proficient at loafing that Dan Shewmake and I gave him the prestigious title of Town Loafer for both Rocky *and* Wheaton. We thought that being the star loafer for both towns vaulted him into the status of a world-class loafer. Decker, however, had one trait that never matched up, we thought, with his proficiency for loafing. For someone who took pride in ignoring as much work as possible, he talked very fast, especially for a native of southwest Missouri.

When I was in grade school and often would go to Wheaton with Granddad Lamberson, Decker would buy me an ice cream cone at either Floyd and Anna Lea Hughes's drugstore or Claude and Jewel Shipley's café. But he always extracted a price for my treat. With those clawlike fingers strengthened by years of catching chickens, he would pinch me at least once on the back of my arm or on the back of my leg as I ate the ice cream. Then he would laugh, move on with his loafing, and Granddad would take charge of me again.

When I was ten or twelve years old, Grandma Lamberson came home from church in Rocky Comfort one Sunday totally flummoxed by what the spinster schoolteacher, Miss Ouida Lowe, had asked her. Miss Ouida had asked if Grandma thought it would be okay for her to marry Ephron Decker.

I can still see Grandma throwing up her hands and exclaiming, "My Land-a-Goshen, why would she want to do that?"

Long story short, Miss Ouida didn't marry him, even though Decker undoubtedly did some of his fastest talking to try to persuade her. The possibilities of such a union were fascinating. If they had gotten hitched, and he could have shared her schoolteacher's income, Decker might have been able to retire from chicken catching and devote full time to his primary skill—loafing.

Decker appeared unfazed by Miss Ouida's rejection. For the rest of his life, he continued to maintain a pretty accurate running commentary on people and events in the community for anyone who wanted to listen. From his bench in front of Cecil's store in Rocky—or from Bryan's Barber Shop, the MZ-Dee Café, Claude and Jewel's Coffee Shop, or Floyd and Anna Lea Hughes's drugstore in Wheaton—Decker remained a sharp-tongued pundit.

Aside from chicken catching, Decker steadfastly refused to do anything other than loafing as long as he lived. He became legendary in the annals of loafers when he was approached by his sister, Opal Brown, as he sat on the bench in front of Cecil's store one summer day. She and her husband, Paul, had mowed hay, which was ready to bale and haul in, and it was supposed to rain the next day, which would have damaged or ruined the hay. She desperately needed help in baling and hauling in the hay before it rained. "Would you help?" Opal asked Decker.

"I did not sow that hay, and I will not reap it," Decker answered firmly.

After that declarative statement, Decker got up and strolled across the intersection of Main and Mill for a Coke at Mollie's Café. I have no idea whether the Browns were able to haul the hay in before it got wet or whether it rotted in the field.

Mollie's Café anchored one corner of Rocky's main intersection for many years. The details of Mollie's identity have been lost in the mists of time. I simply know that her last name was Davidson, and her husband was a barber named Grover Davidson.[45] There is no evidence that Grover was kin to my great-uncle Awk and his nine brothers and sisters.

Mollie's Café was the scene of a very early and fond memory for me—my first fountain Coke. When I was a tyke, Uncle Jack, my dad's brother, walked me down the hill from the little house on Main Street where my Lewis grandparents lived for a short time. Uncle Jack sat me on a stool at the counter and ordered a Cherry Coke for me. He showed me how to put a straw in the frosty glass and draw it into my mouth. It was the tastiest thing I had ever experienced in my very early life.[46]

Another refreshing drink was available for free across the street a few feet east of Mollie's Café. It was artesian springwater bubbling from a fountain enclosed on two sides by a three-foot rock wall. Just walk down a couple of steps into the little enclosure, lean over, and open your mouth to get a cool drink. No knob to turn. The water always flowed. However, a few years after World War II, so many deep wells had been drilled near Rocky Comfort that the water table dropped, and the fountain dried up. But in my early years, it was a wonder to me that water could just bubble up out of the ground all the time. As I'd ride south toward church with Granddad and Grandma, I'd always look to make sure water was still coming out of that fountain.

Across the street to the south of Cecil's store and Bill Buttram's third and final shoe repair shop was a small grocery store and service station opened in March 1936 by two brothers, Harry and Earl Clifton.[47] In January 1939, just three months after Rocky's big fire, Harry decided to become the sole proprietor and the main competition for the Milligans and later, for Cecil.

Harry might not have been the best marketer in the world. In the *Journal* article announcing the opening of his new enterprise, Harry wrote that he hoped he would "serve the public better in the future than I have in the past."⁴⁸ He didn't say how he thought he had fallen short in the past, but he said his new store would carry "a staple line of groceries and also handle some dry goods. I buy eggs and chickens at highest market price."

West of Harry's store and station, Rocky's hill began a steep climb. On Sunday mornings, on the way to church, I always liked looking at the row of small houses, most of which had a front porch with a swing—good for visiting with neighbors during warm Ozark summer evenings and catching a breeze, if there was one.

To the south, at the top of Rocky's biggest hill, the land flattened, and to the right was our destination—the Church of Christ. Cattywampus to the northwest, behind the church building, was Rocky's redbrick schoolhouse, home of the Rocky Comfort Greyhounds and their always snappy marching band conducted by a high-school teacher with a well-known name—Henry Ford. Rocky's Henry Ford made music, not cars, and won many honors during the 1940s and '50s.

It was from the top of Rocky's big hill that two boys from Wheaton, D. D. Overton and James Crider, were going north in James's 1941 half convertible one afternoon in July 1952—going north too fast, as it turned out. James's car was a half convertible, because a few weeks earlier, it had been stolen and wrecked by a soldier stationed at Camp Crowder near Neosho, caving in the front part of the roof. So after it was recovered, James solved the problem by cutting off the top of the car from the front seat forward. It might have been the only half convertible in southwest Missouri.

D. D. said James started down the hill at a pretty good clip, thinking they would sail through the intersection of Main and Mill at the bottom and give themselves—and anybody else who happened to be around—a little thrill.

As they neared the bottom of the hill, it was a split second too late that James saw local farmer James Lee Harader's big truck—parked on the right across from Bill Brown's garage—with its front end sticking out into the street. James swerved to miss it, but he didn't; he hit the left front fender and wheel of the truck. The half convertible flipped three times and came to rest in the ditch on all four wheels in front of Brown's.

D. D., riding in the front passenger side, said the next thing he knew, he was sliding on his belly in the chat.[49] James was having a similar experience as the car came to rest in front of Brown's.

When he regained consciousness, D. D. said he saw Ma Brown trotting out. She had heard the crash, and—somewhat panicked—she grabbed a washcloth and a pan of water. D. D. remembers her standing there, bewildered, asking if she could help. D. D. and James, who had chat embedded in their legs and chests, wouldn't let her touch them.

In a few minutes, Dr. James Holmes, who recently had assumed the retired Dr. O. S. McCall's practice in Wheaton, arrived and started to apply alcohol to D. D.'s chest and legs. D. D. stopped him with some colorful language because it hurt too much.

Soon, the Pogue ambulance arrived to take the boys to Wheaton's little hospital. After x-rays showed that they didn't have any broken bones, both boys refused any further treatment, and they were sent home. D. D. said he spent the night and most of the next day with a sharp pocketknife, picking chat out of his legs and chest. He also needed a new shirt and a new pair of jeans, because the ones he was wearing were shredded.

I don't know about James, but D. D. went on to become a long-haul trucker, much of the time transporting munitions—bombs, artillery shells, and other high explosives—for the military services. He probably was never in any more danger than he was when he flew out of James Crider's half convertible at the foot of the Rocky hill in July 1952.

Back at the top of the hill, ninety feet farther south and across the street from the Church of Christ, was the Methodist Church. The Methodist pastor during the immediate postwar years was the Reverend Dr. Earle D. Young. I never heard the Reverend Young preach, but I read his poetry in the *Wheaton Journal*, published under the heading of "The Poet of the Ozarks."

Many newspapers had a strict rule that didn't allow the publication of poems. I once asked Vern Mabry, the veteran night city editor of the *St. Louis Globe-Democrat* when I was there in the mid-1960s, why the paper had such a rule. He answered emphatically, "Because everybody considers himself a poet, and if we allowed everyone who wrote a poem to publish it in our paper, pretty soon, we'd be publishing nothing but bad poetry."

Wally Fox, the editor of the weekly *Wheaton Journal*, obviously didn't share Vern's view about publishing poetry in the paper, and he left any opinions on the quality of the poetry up to the readers. Since Rev. Young's poems continued to be published in the *Journal* from just after World War II until May 1948, the paper's readers obviously gave his poetry a thumbs-up for nearly three years. The poems were discontinued only when the Reverend Young decided to run for the Missouri State House of Representatives, losing in the Republican primary of August 1948. Wally apparently didn't think it was appropriate for a candidate for public office to have a poem featured in each edition.

Rev. Young's poem in the *Wheaton Journal* of September 19, 1946, was called "The Town of, 'I Wish.'"

There's a town we all call "I Wish,"
Over on beyond the hill,
And the easiest way to get there,
Is to take the road, "I Will."

Down the highway known as "Hard Work,"
Up the path of "Try and Try."
Turning right at "Wrong Road" crossing,
Careful past the ditch of "Lie."

You must carefully watch your balance
O'er the bridge of Give and Take,
Detour sharply from the quicksand
On the banks of "Greedy" Lake.

You will see a marsh called "Failure,"
Hurry 'round the bend of "Hate,"
When you cross ravine "Too Late."

As you pass the house "Disaster,"
You will meet old man "Success,"
"I Wish" now is named "Achievement,"
There you'll find true "Happiness."

As the *Wheaton Journal's* subscribers were reading Rev. Young's poems and Rocky Comfort's Methodists were listening to his sermons, members of the Rocky Comfort Church of Christ were listening to a young preacher from Old Hickory, Tennessee. I was in the third grade in the fall of 1947 when they hired John Crosslin.[50]

The congregation of maybe one hundred souls had arranged for the new preacher and his wife, Mildred, to live in a rented farmhouse on a winding dirt road about a mile northwest of Rocky Comfort. It was the old Lee Reed place. Everybody in that part of the country knew the location of the old Reed place except John, as it turned out.

One chilly, gray November day about a month after John had signed on as the preacher, I saw a car sitting in the driveway in front of our farmhouse when I got off the school bus. As I trudged down the narrow gravel lane that led from the main road to our house, I saw that the person in the car was our new preacher, John Crosslin.

Neither my mother nor my dad was home, but John said he knew I'd be getting home from school soon, so he decided to wait. I remember we looked at a couple of flights of geese headed south for the winter, and we talked about how the weather was starting to turn cold before the real reason for John's visit emerged.

He was lost.

John had been driving around for a while looking for a familiar landmark after visiting some member of the far-flung congregation. He'd gotten disoriented as he tried to find the road back to Rocky. He said he finally recognized our house because he'd been there before, and he decided to stop to get directions.

Despite a very country-sounding name, John's hometown of Old Hickory, Tennessee, was a suburb of Nashville, a metropolitan area that had streets and street signs. It was a far cry from the unpaved, unmarked, winding backcountry dirt roads around Wheaton and Rocky Comfort.

From our house, it was fewer than three miles by road to Rocky, and as the crow flies, perhaps two miles. Rocky's schoolhouse was visible from our front yard. But to John on that leaden November afternoon, Rocky Comfort could've been on another continent. So I sat down in the front seat of his car with my third-grade reader clutched in my hand and felt very important explaining to John how he needed to go east to the four-way intersection we always referred to as the Gaston Corner, turn south, and go by Elsie Bufford's house on the left and the Roller place on the right. Keep going past Melvin and Opal Tichenor's place, Curt Long's place, then Aunt Virgie and Uncle Awk Davidson's house, followed by the Rocky Comfort Cemetery and the Prosperity Baptist Church, down the hill, across the little bridge, and into Rocky.

John thought it was marvelous that I could direct him in such detail. I thought it was strange that he didn't know such things.

Then I began to tell him how he could get to his house on the "creek road" if he just wanted to go home without stopping at the church study first. That apparently was too much for him, however, and he said he'd go the way I first described. I remember wondering as he left just what it must have been like to grow up in a city where all the streets had names, and you didn't get to places by counting how many houses or bridges you had crossed or by noting whose place it was before you made a turn.

By the next summer, John finally had learned how to get from Rocky Comfort to Wheaton and Stella and points in between without getting lost. His attention, when he wasn't focused on preparing his sermons and visiting the sick and distressed of the congregation, turned to growing things in the vegetable garden of the farmhouse the church rented for him and Mildred. Because he had been reared in a city, he had never grown much of anything. The old Reed place had a big garden plot where prior owners and renters had planted and grown vegetables and flowers over the years. Stories about their successes fueled John's dreams of a plentiful harvest.

John was proud of his very first garden. Every new bean or tomato was an object of wonder to the young preacher, who was then in his midtwenties. Despite advice that Rocky Comfort's erratic rainfall patterns and uneven soil weren't suited for it, he wanted most of all to grow watermelons. Undeterred, John had planted watermelon seeds that spring. By midsummer, despite his careful weeding and faithful watering of the patch with a garden hose, there were only a few cucumber-sized melons on his plants.

Enter Ern Shewmake—an elder at the Rocky Comfort Church of Christ; father of my best friend, Dan; my dad's cattle-trading partner; and Cecil Shewmake's brother. One hot day that summer, Ern said to Dad, "Let's go to town and buy a big cold watermelon and take it over to John Crosslin's. There's a man with a truckload of Texas melons at Wheaton."

Dad thought that was a good idea, knowing how John enjoyed watermelons. So they drove to Wheaton, bought a big ripe melon that had been in ice water, and headed for Preacher Crosslin's place in Ern's pickup. When they pulled into John's driveway, instead of knocking on the door, Ern started walking toward John's garden, carrying the melon.

When he got to John's anemic melon patch, he took the end of one of John's vines and tied it to the stem of the big cold melon he had just bought. You can guess the rest.

The city preacher was ecstatic when Ern showed him the marvelous melon that had "grown" in his little patch. "It looks ripe," Ern said. "Let's plug it and make sure before we pull it off the vine." He carefully cut a little square plug out of the melon with his pocketknife and gave it to John to taste.

The preacher pronounced it "as perfect as any you'd find in the Garden of Eden"—and never finding it odd that the melon was ice cold—said they should carry it to the kitchen and eat it. The rest of the summer, from the pulpit, John often found a way to brag about that big juicy watermelon he had "grown," while Ern, my dad, and other assorted members of the congregation who knew the story just grinned and sometimes winked at each other.

Like Adam, that episode taught me to be careful about the source of fruit that I ate. Did it come from the Garden of Eden, Texas, or someplace called Rocky Comfort? It certainly wasn't always possible to get the answer to that question when I was listening to a sermon in Rocky on Sunday.

6

The Characters I Met at Church

At the Rocky Comfort Church of Christ on Sunday mornings, the musical part of the worship service revolved around Dudley and Cumi Biggs. Dudley, an elderly, short, thin, wiry man who wore spectacles and often dressed in three-piece suits, was the congregational song leader until I was nine or ten years old. Cumi (pronounced *Q-my*) was a stocky, broad-faced woman who wore her gray hair pulled tightly into a big round bun behind her head. Cumi looked strong enough to break Dudley in two, but apparently she never did. Dudley was mentally sharp and deceptively strong, mowing his lawn the day before he died on April 24, 1952, exactly one month short of his eighty-third birthday.[51]

In the years just after World War I and on into the 1920s, Dudley managed the locally powerful Wheaton Fruit Growers Association that annually sold tons and tons of strawberries, peaches, and apples and shipped them out of Wheaton on the Missouri & North Arkansas Railroad (M&NA).[52] He also was a successful farmer who had sold 118 head of livestock at a sale in 1919. During the Great Depression of the 1930s, Dudley was the proprietor of a general store in Ridgley that went bankrupt. Dudley and Cumi had had their ups and downs, as Grandma used to say.

But I didn't know or care about any of that as a kid. I just knew that Dudley usually would lead the congregational singing at the Rocky Comfort Church of Christ.

At the Church of Christ, all the singing was a cappella, and the entire congregation was invited to sing, although to my young ears, some probably sang even though their ability to carry a tune was questionable, making the quality of the song service unpredictable, depending on how many enthusiastic but tone-deaf persons were in attendance that day.

Nevertheless, Dudley would stand in front of the congregation, strike his tuning fork on the songbook to get the pitch, softly hum the pitch to himself, and begin the song. In my mind's ear, I can still hear him singing an old hymn that began:

"Walking in sunlight, all of my journey, over the mountains, through the deep vale …"

Unfortunately for both Dudley and the rest of the congregation, Cumi always sat in the front pew directly in front of the song leader. She had a voice to match her strong, stocky build, and when she belted out praise to her Lord, she was slightly off key and usually about two beats behind the song leader—even when her husband was leading the singing. Since Cumi was warbling directly into Dudley's face, often the entire congregation would begin to sing slower and lower and Dudley would lose control of both the beat and most of the sharps and flats in the hymns.

When Dudley finally gave up song leading, my dad took over that duty. Every Sunday morning, Dad and I would milk the cows, come to the house, and eat breakfast. Then Dad would sit down in the big rocking chair in the living room, get the songbook we used at church, and start selecting the numbers he would lead that morning at the worship service. He began his song selection with a standard comment: "Let's see now. I'd better start with a fast one. Otherwise, Cumi will drag us down, and pretty soon, the songs will be slower than molasses."

Regardless of Cumi's singing, I always liked her. And Dudley was a cool guy to the end. When I was eleven or twelve, not long before Dudley died in 1952, the little old man saved me from enormous embarrassment. Sometimes the powers that be at the Rocky Church of Christ allowed me to lead the congregational singing, especially at the evening services. On one such winter evening just before services, I was standing among several people at the back of the church auditorium preparing to stride to the front and lead the first song. Dudley was facing me as he stood in front of the stove in the back corner of the auditorium. Without changing expression, Dudley extended his bony index finger directly at me and below my belt. I looked down. My fly was unzipped. I gave him the coolest nod I could muster, stepped behind the stove, and zipped up. Who says old guys ain't sharp?

Dudley and Cumi weren't the only interesting persons who attended the Rocky Comfort Church of Christ.

In 1946, the year after World War II ended, an influx of returning GIs and their families increased the congregation's numbers, and it was decided that the church needed a baptistery so that new converts wouldn't have to be dunked in Indian Creek or Mike's Creek—which was okay in the summer but a frigid experience in the winter. So with volunteer labor from the men of the congregation, a baptistery, three first-floor classrooms, and a second-floor classroom were added.

Our occasional preacher at the time was Murvin Spencer, a self-taught country minister who lived on a farm near Rocky. I don't remember what they paid Murvin to preach, but I'm guessing it wasn't much, because money—especially money contributed to the church—was still in short supply to the local farm families, even in the boom years that followed World War II.

To assist with the family budget and to serve her Lord, Murvin's wife, Geneva, was the church janitor. Geneva was a sturdy, slightly eccentric, and very resourceful woman who spoke with a raspy and occasionally somewhat broken voice in the cadence and pronunciation of the hill people who lived in that part of the country. I still remember her laugh. It would start with a little giggle and build until it was broken at irregular intervals with a yodel-like note.

I think Geneva considered herself a sophisticated woman. And maybe she was, at least for that part of the country. She was fond of wearing hats to church, the kind with just enough feathers and elevation to block your view of the preacher if you were a kid and she sat in the pew in front of you. While that might have been a problem for some of the shorter adults in the congregation, it was just fine with my buddy Dan Shewmake and me, because if the preacher couldn't see us, we were free to whisper more during the sermon.

There was another thing about her appearance that made Geneva noticeable when I first knew her. She had a goiter—a huge growth on her neck under her chin the size of an orange. Later, she had it surgically removed, and it never returned, probably because the medicos had discovered that goiters were due to a lack of iodine in the diet. Presumably, she became not only a convert to the Lord but also a convert to iodized salt. The fact that she had the surgery may have accounted for the raspiness of her voice and her occasionally melodious giggle, but that never occurred to me until I was much older.

One day when the classrooms were almost finished and Geneva was cleaning the church house, my dad, then in his late thirties, went to the church building to fix an electrical connection in the attic over the new second-floor classroom behind the high-ceilinged auditorium. He was carefully walking on the ceiling joists when his foot slipped off one joist. Fortunately, he didn't crash through the ceiling tiles to the floor below, because he landed astraddle one of the joists. Unfortunately, his landing was at considerable expense, he told me later, to the male part of his anatomy.

After straddling the joist in stunned and pained silence for a few minutes, he realized that he had punched out two rectangular pieces of the fiberboard ceiling tile with his feet as he landed on the joist. Both feet were sticking through the ceiling, and one shoe had been separated from his foot and now lay on the floor of the upstairs classroom.

Dad said he realized that turning around in the cramped space of the attic so that he could raise up and walk back to the ladder on the joists would require strength and agility—and retrieval of his lost shoe. Trying to keep his balance on the two-inch ceiling joist with one shoe on and one shoe off, especially with his tender feet, would have been a recipe for disaster, he reasoned. Geneva was his only hope, and he had to get her attention.

Unfortunately for Dad, she was in the auditorium, which was several feet in front of his awkward location over the ceiling of the upstairs classroom. So he drew both legs up, put them carefully on top of the joist, and began to scoot forward until he arrived at a point near the high-ceilinged auditorium. Very deliberately, he said, he reached down, punched out another ceiling tile, and in a voice rendered about an octave higher than normal, hollered weakly, "Miz Spencer! Miz Spencer, could you come up to the classroom and get my shoe and reach up and put it back on my foot so I can get down from here?"

Fortunately for Dad, Geneva heard him, retrieved his shoe, and used the stepladder to climb to a level where she could put his shoe back on as his legs dangled through the holes where the tiles had been. Dad said at first she tried to be serious about it, but when she was fitting his shoe to his foot, she couldn't help but let out one of her melodious giggles.

After that, Dad restricted his repair work at church to whatever could be accomplished at ground level. But for a long time, when he and Geneva said hello, their greeting always included one of Geneva's giggles that recalled their awkward meeting near the ceiling.

Murvin, or more formally, Brother Spencer, may not have had a formal theological education, but he had a certain imposing style in the pulpit. After ascending the two steps to the rostrum and taking his place behind the pulpit, Murvin—a rather portly man—would put on his rimless glasses, open his Bible, step to one side of the pulpit, and read a passage of scripture. Then he would proceed in a very slow—and some said "slightly affected" manner—to tell his audience what the passage meant.

As a kid, the main thing I noticed about Murvin's preaching style was that he had a fondness for spreading his suit coat to each side of his vest, rocking back on his heels and slowly expressing his thoughts by connecting them with a series of *ands*. When he was making a point, his pronunciation of *and* came out more like *ant*.

"Ant we find in Second Timothy 2:15," Murvin would intone, "that the Apostle Paul instructed young Timothy to 'study—to *show*—thyself *approved*—unto *Gawd*—a workman that needeth not to be ashamed—*rightly dividing*—the word of *truth*,'" Murvin would say.

"Ant therein lies the secret," Murvin would explain. "Rightly *dividing*, or correctly *interpreting* the scripture, is the key to the passage. Ant—sometimes we can go badly wrong in the way we divide it."

For a while, during one period in which Murvin preached for several weeks in a row, the congregation seemed to enjoy his sermons. But then my seven-year-old ears began to hear rumblings of dissatisfaction with Murvin's pulpit messages. Several members of the Rocky Comfort congregation began to complain that Murvin had gone badly wrong in *his* interpretation of some of the scriptures. Murvin, they noted, was beginning to hint from the pulpit that despite the church's most cherished doctrine of "speaking where the Bible speaks and being silent where the Bible is silent"—the church wasn't practicing what it preached. It probably was a lot more complicated than that, but that's all my seven-year-old mind could absorb.

The result was that whatever Murvin was preaching contradicted the beliefs of so many members of the congregation that the elders—who included my Granddad Lamberson and Dan's dad, Ernest Shewmake—had a meeting with Murvin to discuss the matter. Another meeting on a Sunday afternoon at Granddad and Grandma's house was long, but it solved nothing. Murvin, in fact, did not back down. Instead, he promised that his sermon the next Sunday would be, and these are my own words, a barn burner.

When the next Sunday rolled around, Dan and I sat on the back pew on the left side of the auditorium and waited until Murvin, in his three-piece blue pinstripe suit, looking a bit puffy faced and peering through his rimless spectacles, mounted the rostrum. Our anticipation was soon rewarded. Although Murvin didn't fit the image of the lean cowboy gunslinger in the movies, he got right to the point just like the buckaroo who shoots first and asks questions later.

Dispensing with his usual deliberate opening, he quickly declared that he differed with a number of his brothers and sisters who believed that there was a very narrowly prescribed road to heaven. As he expounded on that point, out of the corner of my eye, I caught a movement on the far-right side of the auditorium. It was "Uncle" Marion Foster, a lanky and elderly stalwart of the congregation who was well into his seventies, wearing gray twill pants with suspenders and a white shirt and tie. Uncle Marion stood up, moved down the pew to the aisle, slowly walked to the main doors in the back of the auditorium, and exited as all eyes turned from Murvin to him.

As Murvin continued to make his argument, several more of the faithful rose and followed Uncle Marion. Pretty soon, Cumi Biggs, jaws clinched, square face looking neither to the left nor the right, left her usual Sunday morning seat at the front of the auditorium and strode purposefully down the aisle and out the door.

The doctrinal battle then became a rout. Dan and I watched in amazement as our mothers and dads, my grandparents, my great-aunt Virgie Davidson—and every last soul in the auditorium except Cora Ford, Dan, and I—strode out, leaving Murvin preaching to an audience of three. Dan and I stayed because we wanted to see what Murvin would do next. Corie, as we called her, was my grandma's age and lived across the field southeast of us on a farm near Indian Creek. She was pretty feisty and soon started peppering Murvin with questions, which he answered, but not to her satisfaction.

Finally, realizing that the battle was lost, Murvin stopped talking. The portly spiritual maverick had been silenced, at least as far as the Rocky Comfort congregation of the Church of Christ was concerned.

I don't think Murvin ever preached to that congregation again, at least not while I was growing up, but he did manage to preach occasionally at some of the other congregations in the area.

The whole business scared something unmentionable out of me.

If Murvin, who was a preacher, and the rest of the congregation—including my folks—couldn't agree on the clearest path to heaven, how was *I* to know how to get there? It occurred to my youthful mind that maybe I'd better see if I could stand hell.

Not long before that, Dad had remodeled our farmhouse, and in addition to running water in the kitchen, he had added a bathroom with a toilet, sink, and bathtub. For years, I had tried to imagine what it would be like to be tossed into the flames of hell forever without burning up. So I decided that the next time I ran my bathwater, I'd run it a little hotter than usual to get some idea of hell.

That idea didn't work out so well, because as soon as my feet hit the water, I found myself about three feet up in the air and out of the tub. Luckily, I didn't scald myself. But I did firmly decide that I'd better be good, lest I spend eternity in a place hotter than my bathtub water.

Murvin's audience-clearing sermon had been delivered while the new concrete baptistery was under construction at the front of the auditorium behind the pulpit. A burgundy-colored thick velvet curtain concealed the baptistery until someone was being baptized. But when the curtain was pulled, revealing a white plastered wall on the back side of the baptistery, the women of the congregation said that just wouldn't do; there needed to be something prettier than a plain white wall to view as a person was descending "into the watery grave of baptism to rise and walk a new life," as many preachers described the process of conversion.

So after much discussion, Granddad Lamberson and the congregation's other elders decided to enlist the talents of one of the few local artists they knew to paint a scene on the back wall above the baptistery. The artist was Elsie Bufford, who lived about a mile and a half west of Wheaton and south of the Gaston Corner on the road to Rocky Comfort.[53] As a boy of seven, I had passed her house with my parents and grandparents a thousand times. I had heard a little about Elsie, including comments that she was "different" and that she was a talented artist, but I'd never seen her. So Granddad took me with him when he went to ask her if she would be willing to paint a picture behind the new baptistery. Before we left, Grandma said Elsie would be "unusual."

Granddad knocked on her door, and someone with a deep voice said, "Come in." It was Elsie. She was thin with dark hair bobbed almost short enough to be a man's cut, wearing a loose-fitting smock-like dress. When she spoke again, I realized that she probably could sing bass. When I looked at her one way, she seemed like a woman, but when she spoke, she sounded more like a man. In the front room were at least two easels with paint and brushes on nearby stands and two partly finished paintings mounted on the easels.

Granddad asked her if she would be willing to paint an outdoor scene that included a river on the back wall of the baptistery. I don't remember what he said the church would pay for it, but Elsie quickly agreed to the terms and told him when she could start. With that, we said our good-byes, and I left with my curiosity only partly satisfied.

After a few weeks, Elsie had painted a beautiful scene of a flowing river with green trees growing on its banks under a blue sky and white clouds. Everyone I heard talking about the painting agreed that it was pretty and that Elsie had done a good job. As far as I know, the day she finished painting the baptistery was the last time she ever saw it, because she never came to any of the church's services. I never saw her in town or at any public event, either. She seemed to be a virtual hermit who preferred living in seclusion to the scrutiny she would have had to endure if she had ventured out. From then on, every time I looked at that painting behind the baptistery, I felt sorry for Elsie, a talented person who was born—to use a combat term—into a no-man's-land, a no-woman's-land, that excluded her from both.

Elsie was born in October 1890 and died in April 1959. Her obituary said, "She was converted early in life. During the past several months she affirmed her faith and trust in the Lord and spent much time reading her Bible."[54] God bless Elsie.

It was about the time that Elsie was painting the baptistery scene that I regularly saw a kid named Lowell Thomas at church. Lowell had an older sister named Betty and a younger brother named

Ronnie. His parents, Calvin and Faye Thomas, were good singers and often came to our house to sing and visit, so I was well acquainted with the family.

Lowell, who often was called Junior, was towheaded, tall for his age, and had a gift of gab as swift and agile as it was possible for a country boy to possess in the summer of 1946.

One Sunday morning as I sat next to Junior and we squirmed and whispered while Murvin Spencer attempted to inform the congregation that each of us had to be honest and truthful in order to please God and get to heaven, Junior began to try to persuade me to go home with him that afternoon so we could play together until our parents returned for evening services. He said we'd get into his little airplane and fly around his dad and mom's farm. I said I didn't know he had a little plane.

"Yeah," Junior said. "Its wings are about eight feet long, and you just get into the cockpit, start it up, taxi it out to the pasture, and take off. It'll fly higher than the treetops."

"Man!" I said. "Where'd you get it?"

"My dad bought it at Joplin," Junior said.

"When?"

"Just a few days ago," Junior said. "I fly it every day."

"Boy, I want to fly it," I said.

"Yeah, well, you'll get to if you come home with me," Junior promised.

After church that morning, I went to my dad and told him I wanted to go home with Junior so we could play with his airplane. Dad said something like, "Take off," not having any idea that that was exactly what I planned to do.

I was really excited as I rode with Junior's parents and his brother and sister for a couple of miles to their farm on the road to Longview, west of Rocky Comfort.

"Where is it?" I asked as we got out of the car at Junior's house.

"Where's what?" Junior replied.

"Let's go see it," I said.

"Oh, it's out behind the barn. Let's play tag first. I'll be 'it,'" Junior volunteered.

By this time, I was getting irritated. "Let's go see the doggone plane," I said again.

Then Junior said we'd have to eat first. It wasn't long before his mother called us in for Sunday dinner.[55]

After dinner, Junior said we could play catch with his baseball.

"C'mon, man, I want to see the plane *now*!" was my response.

"Well, we had to take it to the garage in Rocky to get some work done on it," Junior said.

"You mean it's not here?" I said in a tone as outraged as it's possible for a seven-year-old to utter.

"Nope," Junior said. "It's in the garage."

"You lied to me," I said. "You never told me it was in the garage."

"Well, it'll be out in a few days," Junior assured me as my visions of flying that afternoon came crashing to earth.

So we did other stuff—cowboys and baseball, mostly, while I occasionally griped to Junior that he'd fibbed to me by not telling me the little plane was in the garage.

That night on the way home with my parents after evening services, I told my dad how Junior had told me a big windy, knowing his plane was in the garage.

Dad grinned one of his big, broad grins. "Son," he said, "I wouldn't count on ever flying that plane."

"Why? Don't you think they'll ever get it fixed?"

"Well, I'm afraid Junior told you an even bigger windy than you guessed."

Now Dad had me going. "What do you mean?" I asked.

"I mean that Junior just has a big imagination," Dad said.

It was only then that it dawned on me. Junior's plane had never flown, and it wasn't because it was at the mechanic's. My imaginary aviation career cratered along with the imaginary plane. I was grounded before my first training flight.

Junior's stories were never as much fun after that, because they no longer caused my imagination to soar.

That was the beginning of my lifelong "little airplane" test whenever I heard a story that I really wanted to believe. I've heard lots of little airplane stories over the last sixty-five or seventy years, but thanks to Junior, when I hear an astounding story from a well-respected businessman, or occasionally by a preacher, I've nearly always been able to figure out whether the "plane" in their stories is behind the barn, in the shop, or just someone's flight of fancy.

Sometimes on Sundays after the end of the war when tires and gasoline weren't rationed anymore, my dad and mom would drive twenty miles into the hill country southwest of Rocky Comfort and Wheaton to visit Grandma Lewis in the tiny town of Jane.

It was at the Jane Church of Christ that I met Palo Stewart, a lifelong bachelor and a brother of Elbert Stewart of Rocky Comfort. I've never figured out whether Palo was a little slow or maybe smart but ignorant of certain basic facts or maybe just eccentric. Unlike Elbert, who worshipped at the Rocky Church of Christ, Palo was virtually a hermit. He didn't own a car. He depended on friends and neighbors to haul him to Mrs. Allison's general store at Jane to buy groceries, to attend church, or to occasionally take him to the county seat at Pineville to buy other necessities. Both brothers were well into their seventies.

Being a practical man, Palo always believed in getting the most out of his possessions, which I guess is the reason he often showed up at church in Jane on Sunday morning wearing his striped pajama tops instead of a regular shirt. Thank God he didn't wear the PJ bottoms, preferring a threadbare pair of dress pants hitched up by suspenders. Many's the time the men of the congregation, with straight faces, would compliment Palo on how good his shirt looked.

Elbert Stewart presented a totally different picture. He always came to church at Rocky dressed to the nines in a suit, crisp white shirt, a straw hat in the summertime and a gray fedora in the winter. Palo was never asked to take a public part in the worship service, but Elbert, being more outgoing, frequently was asked to word the congregational prayer. He would always accept. When it was announced that Brother Stewart would lead the prayer, Dan

Shewmake and I would look at one another in dismay. To us, Elbert had a terribly annoying habit; throughout his lengthy entreaties to the Almighty, he began every sentence with, "Now our dear Heavenly Father …"

"Now our dear Heavenly Father, we want to ask thee to bless all the sick and afflicted in this community," Elbert would pray.

"Now our dear Heavenly Father, we would ask thee to forgive our sins, both of omission and commission, for we know we often make mistakes …

"Now our dear Heavenly Father, we would ask thee to be with the preacher this morning, that he may have a ready recollection of his message for us …" Dan and I always especially agreed with that request, because we didn't want the preacher prolonging his sermon by stumbling around and burning up time while he tried to remember the point he wanted to make.

Despite the fact that there was nothing wrong with anything Elbert requested from Above, the "Now our dear Heavenly Fathers" began to wear on our attempts at pious concentration after a while and instead became a source of entertainment.

One Sunday morning, after years of listening to Brother Stewart's prayers, I bet Dan that Elbert would address the Lord by name thirty times or less in his prayer. If I won, I owed Dan a comic book from Floyd and Anna Lea Hughes's drugstore at Wheaton. Elbert prayed. We counted. I lost. The good Brother Stewart called on "our dear Heavenly Father" forty-seven times.

Despite the fact that neither Elbert nor Palo owned cars, Elbert seemed reasonably comfortable with other twentieth-century conveniences, such as telephones, electricity, and kitchen appliances. Palo was not. One day in the hot summertime during the late 1940s, my cousin Clifford Slinkard went to see Palo. In the kitchen, he saw that Palo had all of his food sitting on the table with an electric fan blowing over it.

"Why do you have the fan blowing on your food and not on you?" Clifford asked.

"Because my icebox is leaking, and I decided to keep my food cool this way," Palo replied without a moment's hesitation.

Later, after Clifford explained to Palo that food preservation depended on a lowering of the temperature instead of the circulation of air, Palo bought a refrigerator to replace his worn icebox. One day, another neighbor stopped by, and Palo was sitting in front of the fridge with the door open. The neighbor asked what he was doing, and Palo said he thought it was a good way to cool off.

One more recollection of Palo—not my recollection, but something recalled by my cousin Clifford's wife, Violet. Occasionally, they used to invite Palo to Sunday dinner at their house. Violet, shaking her head in disbelief, said Palo carried his false teeth in his pocket until mealtime, when he would fish them out and pop them into his mouth. Then when the meal was finished, Palo would remove his dentures—first the lower and then the upper—carefully lick them clean, and put them back in his pocket.

Both Palo and Elbert have long since passed on to their eternal reward, and I sometimes imagine them sitting in a circle with the angels, Palo wearing glowing, multicolor-striped pajama tops, cooling near the open door of a heavenly refrigerator, and Elbert wearing a stylish straw fedora and a natty pinstripe suit, suitcase at his side, thanking his "dear Heavenly Father" for giving him a ride to the pearly gates and a nice place to stay.

Back on earth, Dan Shewmake and I willingly went to church on Sunday mornings and Sunday evenings, telling ourselves that it was what the Lord would want us to do and also reasoning that the Almighty was giving us a "two-fer."[56] Besides pleasing the Lord, we also got to catch up with what the other one was doing at school. Dan attended school at Rocky Comfort, while I was in a one-room country school at Oshkosh until seventh grade, when I went to Wheaton.

Another benefit of church attendance was to see what our friend, J. W. "Dub" Johnson, was doing. Dub was the son of Rocky Comfort's school superintendent, T. L. Johnson. Dub, who was three or four years older than Dan and I, was especially daring and occasionally would dazzle us with his escapades. One Sunday evening during a sparsely attended service—which meant that there weren't many adults sitting close enough to keep an eye on us—Dub produced his pocketknife and attempted to carve the graffiti so popular during World War II and the Korean War—*Kilroy was here*—into the back of a wooden pew. Except that Dub, who was never too good with his spelling, carved *Kickroy* instead of *Kilroy*. Dub's misspelled handiwork stayed on that pew for years.

Except for rare occasions, such as a death in the family or travel with his parents, Dub was always at church services on Sunday mornings and evenings. He had played sick so often trying to avoid church that his mother made him come every Sunday even when he *was* sick.

One Sunday morning when the junior-high and high-school kids were gathered for Bible study in the upstairs classroom, Kate Wright, the teacher, had to go downstairs for teaching material. Dub had had enough. He went to the second-story window, which had no screen, raised it, climbed out, lowered himself as much as possible by hanging onto the bottom of the window sill, and dropped to the soft, grass-covered ground below. We rushed to the window to see if he was hurt, only to see Dub get up, brush himself off, and hightail it around the rear corner of the church building.

When Kate came back up to the class, she asked where Dub was, and we told her he had to leave. We didn't mention *how* he left. Sometime during the following week, the truth emerged to Dub's mother, doubly ensuring his presence at all future church services.

After we were into the fourth or fifth grade, it became customary, though probably not very wise on our parents' part, for the boys at the Rocky Comfort Church of Christ to sit together on a back pew during church services. The practice had two advantages—one for the parents and one for the boys. The parents benefited because they didn't continually have to discipline restless and fidgety boys as the preacher expounded on the finer points of living the Christian life, and the boys benefited because they could whisper to one another about Stan Musial's batting average, whether Joe Louis or Sugar

Ray Robinson or Joey Giardello would win their next boxing match, about the body style of the newest Pontiac or, later on, the body style of two or three of the girls of the congregation.

The arrangement worked fairly well most of the time—as long as the boys didn't create too great a disturbance. On Sunday nights when there were fewer people to keep an eye on us, Dub would educate us about things going on in other parts of the country. I don't know how he knew about such things, but he spent one Sunday evening in the late 1940s filling us in on the Pachuco gangs of Los Angeles and the zoot suits they liked to wear.

On occasion, when the level of whispering or other nonreligious activity reached a decibel level that was annoying to the sincere and faithful souls sitting within earshot, a parent—usually a father—had to be dispatched to sternly warn the pew full of youthful peace disturbers that they had better shape up pronto, or they would be scattered to the four corners of the church house to sit with their *mothers!*

That was a threat too ominous to be ignored. So for a Sunday or two after such a warning, there would be a smidgen of decorum on the boys' pew. Then the warning would fade into the haze of youthful memory and once again pinching, elbowing, whispering, and other such activities would prevail.

One of the more memorable incidents on that back pew occurred when I was about twelve or thirteen, during an evening service as Cleo Blue—a stern, bald-headed, no-nonsense preacher of considerable repute—was delivering a sermon during a revival meeting. The row of back-bench boys that night had swelled to full-pew capacity because of visitors from neighboring congregations.

Brother Blue, who resembled former Soviet president Mikhail Gorbachev except that his forehead bore a deep curved scar instead of Gorbachev's splotchy birthmark, was on a roll.

"And we find in Acts 2:38 that Peter said unto them, 'Repent and be baptized every one of you in the name of Jesus Christ ...'" Just then, Carl Elkins elbowed Dan Shewmake with his left arm and pinched me on the leg with his right hand, causing us to jump and flinch and send a ripple of movement down the row of boys in both directions. We each grabbed Carl to restrain him from repeating his actions, but when we looked up to the pulpit, we realized that Brother Blue had stopped speaking and was looking directly at us with an awful glare.

The auditorium had grown deathly still, and the good preacher's next words cracked like lightning in our ears. "Until the boys on the back row settle down and behave themselves, this sermon will not continue."

About nine boys in unison sat up straight and put their hands in their laps as every adult in the auditorium turned to stare at the offending rowdies. When the staring stopped and the preaching resumed, Dan and I looked at each other from either side of Carl, a kid who was younger than we were but who was built like a tank and outweighed each of us considerably. Both of us knew what we had to do without ever having to talk about it.

We made it through the rest of the sermon without incident. Then when the last amen was said and the crowd started to visit and file out, we each got ol' Carl by an arm and dragged him out the back door of the auditorium. As he protested and tried to break free, we wrestled him to the back, unlit side of the church house and began to pound him, all the while warning him that he'd better never get us in trouble with the preacher again.

Then, sending him dazed and chastened to his parents' car, we went back inside the church house and spotted Dan's mother, Hessie, talking to someone near the preacher. With her looking on, we walked up to Brother Blue, who was still chatting with someone in the front of the auditorium.

"Brother Blue," Dan said, a halo forming over his head, "Jim and I just wanted to apologize for what happened tonight and to make sure you weren't talking about us when you called down the boys on the back row. We're sure sorry about what happened."

Brother Blue looked down at us for a moment and concluded, we guessed, that even though we were at least partially guilty, he would let us off the hook just for having the guts to approach him.

"No, I wasn't referring to just you boys," he said. "I just couldn't preach with all that commotion on the backseat."

"Thank you, Brother Blue," I said, a halo now forming over *my* head. "We've talked to Carl, and I don't think he'll be doing that anymore."

Dan and I then walked back outside and snickered a little at how we'd handled that one. Hessie, we knew, would tell my folks that we'd apologized to Brother Blue, and that would cover me.

As for Carl, we never knew how he explained it to *his* parents, Quannah and Rutholene Elkins. We also never quite figured out how our actions squared with Jesus's teaching to turn the other cheek.

Later in life, I realized that we did to Carl was disgraceful, and if Carl ever reads this, Dan and I offer our sincere apologies for pounding him that night and then acting like good little boys to the preacher.

Now I'd give my life savings to visit with Dudley and Cumi, to stop by Elsie Bufford's and ask her what she was painting, to listen to Elbert Stewart pray to his "dear Heavenly Father," to listen to Geneva Spencer's giggle, to hear Murvin say "ant another thing," to have Junior Thomas tell me another airplane story, to elbow Carl Elkins, and to talk with Dub Johnson about how the St. Louis Cardinals are doing this year. But the best I can do is remember them the way they were and savor the memories of the characters I met at church.

7

O Bury Me Not

On the edge of the hill country about two miles south of Rocky Comfort in the late 1940s, two elderly brothers—lifelong bachelors—lived in an old schoolhouse on a site that had once been known as Buzzard's Glory. Later, the schoolhouse had been renamed Forest Grove, but in the forties, all the children in the area attended school at Rocky Comfort.

As a little boy listening to my parents and grandparents talking about Arch and Brock Cantrell, I came to believe that they had once been cowboys. I concocted a story in my mind that the two old buzzards had left the Missouri Ozarks in their younger days and gone out west where they were ranch hands—cattle wranglers—who had returned to Missouri to live out their days in the land of their birth.

The local items in the *Wheaton Journal* of November 21, 1924, provide a clue that the story I imagined might have at least a grain of truth to it:

> Brock Cantrell, who has been in California for the past six years, arrived in Wheaton on the Thursday morning train. His brother, Arch, who has been in the Northern and Western states for the past eight ...

months, joined him in Colorado ... (and) accompanied him home. They expect to spend the winter here.[57]

There's no doubt that each of the brothers spent time in the West; whether or not they were cowpokes is a matter of speculation. However, when the Cantrell brothers returned to the Wheaton and Rocky Comfort area in 1924, they didn't stay just for the winter; they stayed for the rest of their lives.

Nevertheless, in early 1949, my nine-year-old mind was convinced that sometime in the dim, distant past, the two old duffers had been cowboys on the lone prair-ee. Although they were not regulars at the Sunday morning services of the Rocky Comfort Church of Christ where I attended with my parents and grandparents, they worshiped there often. I also had seen them in Wheaton many times, and I felt I knew them pretty well.

The brothers Cantrell were well into their seventies in the late 1940s. Brock was born in 1870 and Arch in 1874. Both old men were lean and weathered. Arch was loquacious. He was bald except for a band of hair around his sun-darkened pate. Brock was the handsomer of the pair—square faced and with a shock of gray-white hair, but he was the quiet one. After church services on Sunday mornings, Brock seemed content to stand silently while Arch did most of the socializing before they caught a ride home with someone who lived near them.

For a number of years, they had operated a secondhand furniture and household goods store in a little wood-frame building at the east end of Wheaton—across the street from the Calhoon-Putnam lumberyard—that later became "Little Charlie" Keeling's Full Gospel Mission Church.[58] Their store was a junky jumble of dusty tables, chairs, couches, bureaus, and even secondhand mattresses. It was illegal to sell used mattresses without identifying them as such, but it's doubtful that Arch and Brock were into the fine points of the law.

During the years I knew them, neither Arch nor Brock ever owned a car. The Cantrell brothers thumbed rides to make their daily five-mile trip from their house to their store, so their store's opening hour depended on how quickly someone gave them a ride.

Arch was an inveterate hitchhiker who lugged an old, beat-up brown cardboard suitcase everywhere he went—even to church, where he would stow it under a pew during services. I always imagined he kept a change of clothes in it, and he probably did. But I didn't know the half of it. Many years later, I discovered what else he kept in that suitcase, and that knowledge strengthened my youthful conviction that Arch really was a cowboy in his younger days out West.

In that battered suitcase, besides a change of clothes and a few overnight necessities, Arch always carried a long-barreled .38 caliber revolver, and, according to George "Peach" Ford, sometime during the Depression days of the 1930s, Arch had used it. Seems he had won the pot in a poker game with a fellow from Fairview named Labe Stansbury. Labe, the story goes, decided he'd take the money even though he hadn't held the cards, whereupon Arch had reached into his ever-present suitcase, whipped out his trusty .38, and shot a big notch out of one of Labe's ears.[59]

I was a little skeptical of that story, yet later, as I was talking with Floyd Hughes—who, with his wife, Anna Lea, owned and operated a drugstore in Wheaton for many years—I asked him if he knew the story about Arch shooting someone's ear off. "No," Floyd said, "but you know that's funny. There used to be a Stansbury who came into the drugstore, and he just had one ear!"

Moreover, there is a clue as to why Labe might have insisted on taking the money Arch won. Arch and Brock had sold Labe a used table and some other furniture. When Labe started to use the table, the legs gave way, splattering the dishes on the table all over Labe's kitchen. According to Delbert Ely, whose parents were Labe's neighbors in Fairview, Labe had gotten into the poker game intending to win back the money he'd paid the Cantrell brothers for the table and other items. But When Arch held the better cards, Labe lost again. That's when Labe put a move on Arch and lost part of his ear for his trouble. There is no record that any charges were ever filed over the incident.⁶⁰

It was a wonder that Arch hadn't been forced to use his .38 more often. Delbert Ely remembered that his father bought his mother a wood-burning cookstove from Arch and Brock sometime in the 1930s. Delbert's mother fired up the used stove for the first time, excited about baking a loaf of bread in it. But when she opened the oven to check on her baking bread, it was covered with ashes and ruined because the firebox had rusted through.

"I guess you're gonna have to take the stove back to Arch and Brock," she told Delbert's dad.

"Like hell I am," he replied. "They're gonna come and get it." Delbert didn't think they ever did.⁶¹

By the winter of 1949, Arch and Brock had closed their junky store and were simply living out their days in quiet seclusion in the old schoolhouse south of Rocky Comfort, often showing up for Sunday morning services at Rocky's Church of Christ. To me, they were simply a couple of old wranglers who had traded in their hosses and saddles for a roof, a good bed, a stove, and an occasional worship service with their Lord. Sometimes when I saw Arch and Brock, I'd think of a cowboy ditty I'd heard somewhere:

All day on the prairie in the saddle I ride,
Not even a dog, boys, to trot by my side.
My ceiling's the sky, boys, my floor is the grass,
My music's the lowing of herds as they pass.
My books are the rivers, my sermon's the stones,
*My parson's a wolf on his pulpit of bones.*⁶²

In the winter of 1949, a spell of frigid temperatures came on the heels of an ice storm that brought down tree limbs and power lines and left the roads glazed and dangerous. The ice stayed on the ground for days, schools closed, and people were forced to hole up and wait for a thaw.

Delbert Richmond, a neighbor of Arch and Brock, decided to make his way over to their house to check on the two elderly brothers.

The story I heard was that Brock answered the door, and Delbert said, "Thought I'd come over and see how you boys were doing in this ice storm."

"Well, I guess I'm all right," Brock replied. "I've been tryin' to dig a hole in the backyard, but I can't get a shovel in it because the ground's froze."

That caught Delbert a little short. "Well, what in the world do you need to dig a hole for?" he asked.

"For Arch," Brock said, without changing expression. "He died day before yesterday, and I haven't been able to bury him because I can't get a hole dug."

"My Gawd!" Delbert hollered. "Where is he?"

"Oh, I've got him layin' on a bench on the back porch," Brock said.

Sure enough, there was Arch, stiffened no doubt by both cold and rigor mortis, lying in sort of a frozen peace on the bench in the subfreezing temperature of the partially enclosed back porch of their little house right there in Buzzard's Glory.

Delbert, according to all accounts of the incident, had to do some "tall talkin'" to persuade Brock to summon a local undertaker to make his way out on the icy roads to pick up Arch, whose body by then was way past the point where it could be embalmed. I doubt if the county coroner was even notified.

Naturally, funeral services couldn't be delayed. A group of the faithful who could carry a tune was hastily assembled the next day to sing at services for Arch at the Rocky Comfort Church of Christ. At age nine, since school was closed anyway, I was deemed melodious enough to be part of that group.

After we sang "In the Sweet Bye and Bye" and the preacher was delivering his remarks, I had another tune running through my head. I heard a cowboy chorus singing:

Oh bury me not on the lone prair-ee
Where the coyotes howl and the wind blows free.

Oh, dig me a grave, make it six by three,
But bury me not on the lone prair-ee.[63]

And I saw Brock somewhere out on the range, digging a grave with his pick and shovel while Arch lay on the ground with a death grip on his old cardboard suitcase, awaiting his final resting place.

Now Brock has long since joined Arch in repose. Instead of lying in a quickly dug grave in Buzzard's Glory, they rest comfortably side by side among friends and acquaintances in the Muncie Chapel Cemetery north of Wheaton—two old furniture wranglers who died without their boots on.[64]

8

The Buyers, Sellers, and Traders

Sunday, May 9, 1954, dawned cool and clear in Wheaton, Missouri, with not a hint of the heartbreak that was to take place before the day was over.[65] Although I have no memory of that specific morning (I had to check the historic weather records for that day), it's a safe bet to say that I would have risen early, walked to the barn with Dad to milk our cows, finished the chores, and hustled in to get ready for 10:00 a.m. church services at the Rocky Comfort Church of Christ.

In Wheaton, Thelma Smith, the respected, beloved, and "let's get down to brass tacks" English teacher, had gone to Sunday school at the Methodist church.[66] She and her husband, Richard W. "Dick" Smith, returned home to have a midday meal and complete plans for baccalaureate services scheduled for Wheaton's seventeen graduating seniors that evening at the Wheaton High School gymnasium. Thelma was heavily involved with plans for both the baccalaureate services and the graduation ceremony the following Thursday, because she was the class sponsor.[67] But just before noon that Sunday, she collapsed of a stroke, was rushed to the Cassville Community hospital fifteen miles away, and died a short time later. She was only fifty-one years old and a vigorous woman, making the shock even greater.

Losing any teacher in a small district like Wheaton's would have been traumatic, but losing Thelma Smith was more than a traumatic event for the graduating class and the other students she had taught. She was Wheaton aristocracy—or as close to aristocracy as the little town ever had. It wouldn't be an understatement to say that her father, John Silas McQueen—Silas or "Mac" to his friends—was one of Wheaton's founding fathers. He was there in 1907 when the town was little more than two stores, three dwellings, and a plat map laid out by the MONARK Townsite Company to purchase land for the Missouri & North Arkansas Railroad (M&NA). Thelma was four years old.[68]

The McQueen family owned land just south and east of the original plat. Silas became the town's first postmaster, serving until 1914.[69] Many of the old-timers said Silas was responsible for naming the town, which was laid out and built where a Rocky Comfort farmer and livestock dealer, T. L. "Tommy" Shewmake, had a wheat field.[70] When Thelma died on that chilly spring day in 1954, Silas was seventy-seven years old and would live another six years.

Thelma had taught various classes in both Wheaton's grade school and high school for twenty-four years.[71] She was well liked by most of her students and respected by her peers and the community for her teaching skills and her ability to maintain order in the classroom without being overbearing. In her freshman English class that year, I had diagrammed countless sentences; learned the parts of speech backward, forward, and upside down; and gained a feeling for the English language that stuck with me throughout my adult life.

Sometimes, probably realizing that she could look a bit stern, she would say, "If you keep frowning, you'll look just like me."[72] But underneath her serious exterior, she also had the ability to laugh at herself. Her niece, Pat McQueen, the daughter of Thelma's brother, Malloy, used to spend summers in Wheaton with her grandparents, Silas and Letta, who everyone called Lettie. Pat wrote about an incident that showed Thelma had a sense of humor:

> One Shoal Creek summer, Dad's oldest sister, Aunt Thelma, made homemade ice cream. It was

dished up and we all discovered something strange. It had a funny taste—like soap. We were practically blowing bubbles. Somehow Aunt Thelma had gotten powdered soap in (the ice cream) instead of sugar. She was so embarrassed! How could she have done this? We all started laughing, "fit to kill." Aunt Bernie was whooping. Thelma joined in, too. My dad and his sisters had such wonderful laughs and this was a "roll on the floor knee slapper" for sure. We forgot to be disappointed at the inedible ice cream. It was so improbable to mistake powdered soap for sugar, but Aunt T. had done it. This was a never-to-be-forgotten family legend.[73]

I don't remember whether I heard about Thelma's death on Sunday or not until I arrived at school on Monday morning, but I remember the atmosphere when I got there. The entire student body was in mourning. It was a very somber senior class that posed in caps and gowns that Monday for its last photograph—the one that would be in the *Wheaton Journal* Thursday of that week.

Thelma and Dick had been married twenty-seven years. They had one son, Mac, who had graduated from Wheaton High in 1949. For years, Dick had operated a service station on Reasor Street south of Dr. Otis M. Sheridan McCall's Bank of Wheaton and just north of Silas's big two-story house and expansive vegetable garden. Dick had served several terms as a member of the Wheaton School District's Board of Education. Not only was Thelma a respected citizen, but so was her husband.

For Silas, it must have seemed that Thelma's death had closed the curtain in the middle of the last act. Over the next six years before his death on June 5, 1960, he would have a lot to reflect on. I wish I had had the foresight to sit down with him on that big front porch in the heart of Wheaton and quiz him about what he had seen and done since his house in Rocky Comfort burned down on June 21, 1906, before Wheaton existed.[74]

In the half century between Silas's Rocky Comfort fire and Thelma's untimely death, the two little towns—one growing and the other fighting valiantly to hang on—were fueled by an astounding exhibition of entrepreneurship by Silas and a small group of men who shared his love for trade and commerce—for making a deal. Some of them had died in the 1930s before I was born, but I was lucky enough to know quite a few of them—farmers, livestock dealers, and small-town merchants with the steely nerves of gamblers. They were honest but shrewd operators who were willing to trade or buy or sell farms, grocery stores, dry-goods stores, hardware stores, lumberyards, grain mills, horses, cattle, mules, sheep, hogs, empty town lots—anything that wasn't nailed down and some things that were. They were a generation of men my Granddad's age who kept Wheaton and Rocky Comfort humming with commerce for nearly fifty years. They were tough, "country smart," and took life's ups and downs with a stoic disregard for emotions.

In his later years, and when the weather was good, Silas's granddaughter, Pat, recalled that Silas and his third wife, Florence (he had outlived the first two), liked to sit down on the front porch of their big house south of the Bank of Wheaton and "split a beer poured into jelly glasses … for the benefit of Silas's digestion."[75] The beer was poured into jelly glasses, Pat explained, so the neighbors wouldn't know what Silas and Florence were drinking.

Silas was no fool. He was an ordained Methodist preacher, and he lived in a part of the country where drinking fell into two categories—you were either a drunk or a teetotaler. "Social drinking," as many local folks were fond of proclaiming, was simply an excuse that was the first step to becoming a sot.

Nevertheless, if I could, I would go back to Wheaton as it was in the mid-1950s, split a beer in a jelly glass with Silas, rock on his front porch swing, and ask him to tell me what it was like to live there when it was a brand-new town in 1907. I'd ask him to tell me how difficult it was to raise the $10,000 that it took to organize the Bank of Wheaton in 1910. That sum of money in 1910 would be worth nearly $250,000 today—no easy feat in the hardscrabble southwest Missouri farm country just ten years into the twentieth century.[76]

As I was growing up near Wheaton in the 1940s and '50s, I assumed that Doc McCall had always been the principal mover and shaker in the organization of the Bank of Wheaton. That was an erroneous assumption. I don't know exactly when Doc McCall first invested in the bank, but he didn't move his medical practice from Rocky Comfort to Wheaton until 1917. Whether the locally prestigious doctor was an investor before his move is not known, but a list of the original investors shows that Mrs. Silas McQueen— Lettie—was listed as an original investor. Other accounts say Silas himself was the principal investor seven years before Doc arrived on the Wheaton scene.[77]

If I were sitting on his front porch with him, I'd ask Silas about his experiences as Barry County Collector in Cassville before World War I.[78] I'd want to know how he juggled all his business, civic, and political activities in those early years as the town was becoming a shipping center for farm crops and produce. The newly extended M&NA had promoted and publicized the area along its tracks between Neosho, Missouri, and Harrison, Arkansas, as prime country for growing strawberries, tomatoes, peaches, and apples. The idea, obviously, was that the produce would be shipped to market on the M&NA.

Silas and many enterprising farmers, livestock dealers, and merchants who lived in nearby communities, especially Rocky Comfort, got the message. By 1919, immediately after the end of World War I, the *Wheaton Journal* tells us that Silas was a business and civic dynamo, and Lettie was a leader in her own right. In 1919, the *Journal* carried numerous articles listing an astounding array of business and civic activities involving Silas and Lettie:

- Silas and an enterprising, shrewd, and small-statured man named Dudley Biggs from the Rocky Comfort area attended a meeting of the Fruit Growers Association at Monett in April.

- In early May, Silas was appointed to the finance committee of the Good Roads Club in Wheaton. Doc McCall was the chairman.

- Also in May, Silas went to Arkansas "engaging berry pickers" for the Fruit Growers Association.

- A week after that trip, Silas and another Wheaton businessman and carpenter, William J. "Bill" Narrell, went to the M&NA headquarters offices in Harrison, Arkansas, to try to persuade railroad officials to change the train schedule so the Berry Association could ship strawberries out of Wheaton the day they were picked. Apparently, they were successful.

- Thanks to a good growing season and lots of work by Silas, Dudley, and Bill, fifty-three boxcar loads of locally grown strawberries worth more than $130,000 had been sold by mid-June.[79]

- Two weeks later, the *Journal* quoted Silas as saying 1,140 crates of strawberries were picked from his five-acre patch, prompting *Journal* editor Maurice Lamberson to write: "Talk about inconsistency; we have it right here in the Ozarks. Land which yields $1,000 clear profit per acre each year (from strawberries) sells for less than one-tenth of the value of one crop."

- Lettie McQueen also was making her presence felt that year. On September 19, she called a meeting of the "ladies of Wheaton" to organize a Women's Civic Club. She was promptly elected president.

- In October, Silas was one of eight men who quickly raised $22,000 to build a ten-ton ice-and-cold-storage plant in Wheaton—a sum that would be equivalent to more than $310,000 in 2014.[80] The ice-plant stockholders promptly sent Silas and William A. Davidson, the cashier at the Bank of Wheaton, to St. Louis to investigate prices and plans to buy a generator to furnish power for the plant and "various other industries of our town requiring power."[81]

- A week later, Silas sold Doc McCall, who by then was president of the Bank of Wheaton, thirty-five lots in the south part of town.[82]
- The *Journal* of October 31 reported that the Lettie McQueen–led Women's Civic Club met, roll call was answered with quotations from Shakespeare, and a biography of Shakespeare was presented by Mrs. Wallace C. Chenoweth—Sara Geneva, better known as "Neva."[83] Lettie was going to make sure that Wheaton's women were properly cultured.
- On December 5, the *Journal* reported that Silas "attended Putman & Son's big sale of registered sheep at Pea Ridge, Ark., and purchased 10 head of registered imported ewes at a price of $52.50 per head. This will be a valuable addition to his herd of fine sheep which he keeps on his farm near town."

Silas wasn't the only person in the area who was making the economy hum, however. In the months since the armistice of November 11, 1918, the post–World War I flush of victory had sent the price of farms and town property alike shooting up. In the spring of 1919, Wheaton's nearly four hundred citizens were buying and selling houses and lots in flurries.[84] There was another contributor to the euphoria; the deadly influenza epidemic of 1918 had subsided, and people were starting to believe they could live again without the threat of a plague that had killed millions worldwide the previous year. *Journal* editor Maurice Lamberson noted the burst of real estate deals in Wheaton in early 1919 and was moved to write in the April 4, 1919, edition:

When the war ended and the flu ceased to take its daily toll from among our neighbors, the town of Wheaton expected to settle down to a quiet and peaceful life, but about this time along came another epidemic, craze, habit, or whatever you may call it, and again disturbed our peace. This latest activity is in the form of real estate changes. Most any time during the day you could glance out and see a procession of moving vehicles ranging from a wheelbarrow to a ... truck. A few months ago the leading question of the day was about the flu. "Who has it?"

Since then it has developed into a question regarding your neighbor, "Who is he?"

Ninety percent of the following changes have taken place within the last thirty days and few, if any, more than sixty days ago.

The *Journal* article then listed many of the recent transactions:

- Silas McQueen purchased the Jno (John) Davidson property near the bank.

- Jno Davidson purchased the Elbert Davis property two blocks south of the bank.

- J. E. Kelly bought the residence one block south of the hardware from Jim Goostree.

- A. H. Payne bought Jim Marsh's residence near the lumberyard.

- Elbert Davis purchased a residence from Mrs. Lampkins near the mill.

- Dan Flora bought the Allison Kelly property on Main Street and sold it a day or two later to Uncle Charlie Gillman.

- Fred Reece purchased the house and adjoining lots just east of the Baptist Church from Wiley Howard.

- P. A. Boucher of near Exeter purchased the Uncle Charlie Gillman property at the west end of Main Street.

- J. P. Boren traded the building occupied by the light plant and his residence near there for W. A. Hollabaugh's residence on Main Street.

- Albert Miller purchased the Howard property in the northwest part of town.

- J. T. Heard traded for Eli Bodine's residence and store.

- R. D. Pierce bought the Hubbard property west of the lumberyard.

- J. G. Smith of Crane, Mo., bought the F. A. Bible property in the south part of town.

- E. F. Sayles bought the Ed Allman business building on the north side of Main Street and a residence from Jim Goostree just south of the hardware.

- H. G. Goostree bought the residence property formerly occupied by P. S. Potts from Jim Goostree.

- J. A. Duncan purchased the Sam Keeling residence in the south part of town.

- Jess McClure of Exeter traded for the Garrett property near the mill.

- Ezra Cartwright bought four lots from Mrs. J. W. Powell.

- Silas McQueen bought a few lots adjoining his place from Mr. Shrieve.

- Fred McGlothlin bought a residence from Mrs. Hill in the north part of town.

Wheaton was on the move. The *Journal* editor explained that "no fabulous prices were received" in any of the transactions, "yet there was quite an increase in the value of nearly every residence sold, so with this as an index, we feel safe in making the assertion that a better day is in store for Wheaton."

If I were sitting with Silas on his front porch sipping beer from a jelly jar, I'd ask him what he thought Wheaton's future might be when he was living in the twelve-year-old town as all those deals were going down. I'd also ask him to tell me about the Davidson brothers.

Just a couple of miles to the southwest in the Rocky Comfort community, the Davidson brothers were creating quite a stir with their deals. There were lots of Davidsons in the area. Wheaton had John M. Davidson, who was president of the Bank of Wheaton in 1920, and John's son, William A. Davidson, was the bank's cashier. But the Davidsons who would generate a lot of major business transactions around Wheaton and Rocky Comfort in the early twentieth century were five brothers, born near Rocky Comfort. They were, in the order of their birth, Thomas Ozro "Ozzie," born in 1872; Alonzo "Lon," born in 1876; Monroe "Mon," born in 1878; Roscoe "Ross," born in 1880; and Oscar "Awk," born in 1883. Their parents were John and Sarah Brown Davidson, pioneer residents of

Rocky Comfort who had, like many of the early settlers, migrated to southwest Missouri from Tennessee before the Civil War.

All of the Davidson brothers were farmers, and all were resourceful and shrewd. Four of the five were also successful merchants and traders in livestock and real estate.

Ross Davidson focused most of his business activities on Rocky Comfort, where he owned a grain mill and a tomato-canning factory. Ross was the principal owner and manager of the Rocky Comfort Milling Company, which, in 1920, was one of the most active and successful grain mills in the area, competing with the Wheaton Milling & Power Company, managed by Homer Goostree, and Wheaton's Neosho Milling Company, managed by Herman Allman. Ross's partners were his brother Awk and two other prominent local men, W. C. Hill and Hugh Dabbs.

Only Lon, who, like his brothers, was highly respected in the community, confined most of his activities to farming. After Lon died in 1935 at his home one mile west of Wheaton, his widow, the former Irenie May Boswell—who was called Rena—would become the second wife of Silas McQueen after Lettie died in 1943.

Ross died in 1933, six years before I was born, and Ozzie died in 1947 when I was only eight. But my great-uncle Oscar, known as Awk, lived until 1957 and was one of my favorite people. Uncle Awk was married to the former Virgie Kelly, my grandmother Carrie Lamberson's sister.

Mon Davidson also was a man I greatly admired. All men in southwest Missouri wore hats when I was a kid, but I've always remembered the one Mon wore—at least the hat style and the way he wore it. While lots of other men wore their hats at a slightly jaunty angle, Mon wore a high-crowned hat with a narrow center crease and set it squarely on his head, creating a look that always reminded me of a Canadian Mountie. By the time I was six or seven years old, when my dad was occasionally buying cattle from and selling cattle to Mon, I could identify him two blocks away on Wheaton's Main Street by that tall hat he wore. When I was a small boy, Mon and

Uncle Awk treated me just like I was one of them, even though I wasn't tall enough to reach their hats.

As the Davidson brothers got their businesses started in the pre–World War I years, Rocky Comfort was still a flourishing town. Many of its residents and folks on nearby farms regarded Wheaton as an upstart town that wouldn't have existed were it not for the M&NA executives who decided in 1907 to bypass the much older Civil War–era towns of Rocky Comfort, two and a half miles southwest of Wheaton, and Stella, eight miles to the west.

The M&NA management, always cash strapped, concluded that farmers along Indian Creek, which flowed from Rocky toward Stella, wanted too much money for the right-of-way purchases the railroad would have to make to go through those two old towns. Rocky's backers and many surrounding farmers were highly indignant that they were bypassed.

Rocky's supporters believed their town was superior not only in trade and commerce but also in culture. On May 16, 1919, the Rocky Comfort items in the *Wheaton Journal* reported that a play titled *A Daughter of the Desert*, performed in Rocky's Opera House Saturday night by the sophomore class of Rocky Comfort High School, "was well attended, the proceeds being $95."

On June 20, 1919, the *Journal* carried a reprint from the *Pineville Herald*, the paper of the McDonald County seat nearly twenty miles to the southwest of Rocky, that was highly commendatory of Rocky's civic feats:

> Rocky Comfort and surrounding community proved true again for their reputation in putting across noteworthy events. The Fair was attended by more than one thousand people, including the school children. The farm exhibits equaled any displayed at any harvest show. The schools had a very fine display of school exhibits. The community dinner, like the Southwest City Center, is beyond description. Suffice to say that there was enough food to feed more than

one thousand people. Surely such events will make for better community life.—*Pineville Herald.*

But unlike a lot of Rocky Comfort loyalists, the Davidson brothers, Silas McQueen, Doc McCall, Wal Chenoweth, and a few others weren't wedded to the idea of confining their business and trading to Rocky Comfort. It was clear from an item in the June 27, 1919, edition of the *Journal* that Awk Davidson was willing to move to wherever he thought he could make money—including Wheaton.

The *Journal's* Rocky Comfort items on that date reported that one of the Wheaton townsite's original landowners, Tommy Shewmake, purchased a farm from Oscar Davidson "on Saturday of last week. The farm is located about two miles west of town (Rocky Comfort) and Mr. Shewmake's son-in-law, Alfred Land, will move to the farm. Mr. Davidson is thinking of moving to Wheaton but has had difficulty in securing a residence."

It was obvious that in the summer of 1919, Awk Davidson saw Wheaton as a place of opportunity. But he was keeping his options open if other business ventures presented themselves. In September of that year, Awk and his brother Ozzie bought a farm one mile west of Wheaton from Andy Davidson, a relative of theirs. Awk and Virgie planned to move to the farm "in the near future."[85]

Their plans changed. In July 1920, after Awk could find no investment opportunities in Wheaton, he purchased a one-fourth interest in the Rocky Comfort Milling Company owned by his brother Ross. Apparently, vacant lots and houses in Wheaton continued to be scarce. Awk decided to stay in Rocky close to his mill investment, so he purchased property on Rocky's Main Street and moved there on August 2, 1920.[86]

But two of the Davidson brothers, Ozzie and Mon, had started to invest in Wheaton. On January 8, 1920, Ozzie Davidson—referred to as "T. O. Davidson" in the *Wheaton Journal*—bought one-fourth interest in perhaps Wheaton's most successful business—Chenoweth & Frazier's general store.[87]

Wallace Carroll Chenoweth and his partner, Joseph Abner

Frazier, operated a store that, for its day, would be comparable to one of today's department stores that sell a wide variety of products—clothing, housewares, toys, toiletries, paint, and hardware. Wal Chenoweth, who got his start in Rocky Comfort, was one of the area's most capable merchants. His partner, Joe Frazier, also became one of Wheaton's longest-serving store owners. After co-owning the department store, he operated grocery stores well into the 1950s.

Ozzie Davidson also was not a neophyte as a merchant. A *Journal* article of January 9, 1920, disclosed that "Mr. Davidson has had several years' experience in various lines of business and served a few years as general manager of the Rocky Comfort & Wheaton Hardware Co. The firm of Chenoweth & Frazier is conducting one of the best stores to be found in this district and has established a patronage that is seldom equaled in a town the size of Wheaton. We feel safe in predicting a still greater success for the new firm."

The same *Journal* issue carried a separate article announcing that Homer T. Goostree had traded his residence and $4,000 worth of stock in the newly formed Wheaton Lumber Company for William S. Reasor's farm three-fourths of a mile west of town. That transaction was Mon Davidson's opening, and he moved fast. Mon, who had been living in Pea Ridge, Arkansas, purchased $4,000 worth of lumber company stock—$2,000 from Reasor and $1,000 each from A. M. "Mortie" Duncan and Walter O. Brattin. Mon then replaced William Reasor as manager of the lumberyard.[88]

Like his brother Ozzie, Mon Davidson was an experienced merchant. "Mr. Davidson was formerly a member of the Montgomery & Davidson Mercantile firm at Rocky Comfort, but for the past few years has owned a farm near Pea Ridge, Ark.," the *Journal* article said. "His business qualifications assure efficient management of the company's interest while he is in charge."

As two of the Davidson brothers became Wheaton merchants, Silas McQueen maintained his whirlwind pace of business in 1920. He was forty-three years old and in his prime. In February, after Mr. Debusk, the proprietor of Wheaton's Commercial Hotel, served what the *Journal* described as a "light lunch" to Wheaton's merchants, Silas unanimously was elected president of the newly formed Community Club to promote Wheaton's commercial interests. After his election, he delivered a pep talk on the "do things spirit," the *Journal* reported on February 13, 1920.

J. A. Heard, a founding member of the Wheaton Community Club, wrote that its members were "bound together by the ties of common interest. These interests may be trading, marketing, banking, schooling, recreation, advertising our town and surrounding country, or religious worship. To be specific, the mutual relation of the merchant, trader, banker, lawyer, doctor, teacher, pastor, and manufacturer with laborer and farmer creates the community," Heard's civic essay declared. "This relation extends as far out into the country as the automobile, buggy, or wagon that brings customer and client to the common center."[89]

The late winter and early spring of 1920 saw Silas McQueen address representatives of several independent fruit growers' associations that met in Wheaton, where he presented a report on a meeting he had with state road commissioners at the state capital of Jefferson City, two hundred miles to the north. Farm-to-market roads were important to the growers.

On May 21, 1920, Silas and Lettie's seventeen-year-old daughter Thelma, Wheaton High School's future English teacher, left for Springfield where she would take a course in "music and expression" during the summer term at Southwest Missouri State Teachers College, now Missouri State University.[90] Thelma was beginning the college education that would make her such an effective teacher years later. Another seven years would pass before she married Dick Smith.

In late July 1920, the ice and power storage plant that Silas McQueen had helped capitalize the previous October was ready for operation. Reliable electric power had not yet come to Wheaton, but that was about to change.

"For the past two weeks the town has been without lights made necessary by a complete overhauling of the circuits before the connections with the new plant is made," the *Wheaton Journal* reported. "All the machinery has arrived and the management predicts we will have light sometime next week."[91]

Wheaton was still a teenage town in the early 1920s, but Rocky Comfort was a mature town with a corps of active merchants, farmers, and politicians who strove to ensure that Rocky stayed competitive with the upstart burg on the railroad two and a half miles to the northeast.

In 1920, when water still flowed plentifully from underground springs around Rocky, Ross Davidson drilled a 174-foot artesian well that produced fifteen gallons per minute on his twenty-acre farm just west of downtown Rocky. In the *Journal* of September 8, 1922, Ross also was described as "a well-known breeder of thoroughbred Duroc hogs." And in the election of 1922, J. M. "Milt" Long of Rocky Comfort announced that he would seek a third term on the Democratic ticket to represent McDonald County in the Missouri Legislature.

The record is not clear as to exactly when Awk Davidson made his move from Rocky to Wheaton, but sometime in 1921 or early 1922, he bought Wal Chenoweth's share of the Wheaton store that often was advertised as "Barry County's Largest Department Store" and very likely the new town's most successful business. The store that in 1919 had been Chenoweth & Frazier had become Chenoweth Frazier & Davidson after Ozzie Davidson purchased a quarter interest in early 1920. Then when Awk Davidson became a part owner, the store became Frazier & Davidson Brothers. Wal Chenoweth moved twenty-five miles to the northwest to the Newton County seat of Neosho and opened a department store there.

Between 1921 and 1923, a nationwide postwar recession, aggravated in Wheaton by a bitter and sometimes violent strike against the M&NA, slowed train service and affected economic fortunes. (See chapter titled "The 'May Never Arrive.'")

If I could, I'd sit on the porch with Silas and ask him if the railroad strike made him wonder if Wheaton would continue to thrive and if he ever thought that Rocky Comfort might once more become the dominant town in that neck of the woods. But the record shows that Silas remained an optimist—a persistently strong advocate for Wheaton and for the M&NA's capability to ship fresh produce from farm to market on the day it was picked. The result was that in May 1922, despite the strike, the Rocky Comfort Fruit Growers Association decided to build a sixty-foot berry shed in Wheaton along the switch tracks just south of the Wheaton growers' shed.[92]

However, it had been a tough decision. "Rocky Comfort has had several shipping points under consideration, due to the fact that until recently, there has been a 'question' as to the ability of the M&NA to care for the crop," according to a May 12, 1922, *Wheaton Journal* article. Rocky's strawberry growers had been making arrangements to ship from Neosho until the M&NA's local agent, F. E. Vining, persuaded them to ship their berries out of Wheaton.[93] Wheaton had won a round with Rocky, despite the railroad strike.

During the summer of 1922, Silas and Lettie McQueen were, without question, Wheaton's power couple. Their three children, Thelma, Bernice, and Malloy, either already were in college or would be soon. That's when Silas decided that his civic activism, his farming, and his position on the school board were not enough. He would seek another elected office. He started campaigning to become Barry County collector.

In the August primary election, he made a strong showing in Wheaton, garnering seventy-six votes on the Republican ticket, while his nearest Republican rival in the Wheaton voting, W. O. Autry, got fifteen votes.[94] But it wouldn't be enough. In the countywide Republican primary vote, Silas came in sixth with 287 votes. The winner, W. T. Bailey, garnered 667.[95] For the time being, Silas would have to be content with his position on the Wheaton School Board.[96]

If Silas was disappointed by his losing political foray, he didn't let it slow his entrepreneurial drive. In late January 1923, he announced that he planned to build a new tomato-canning factory, capable of processing twelve thousand cans per day, on Mike's Creek at the mouth of Thomas Hollow—a rugged hill country area six and a half miles south of Wheaton.[97] In March, Silas would announce his intention to increase his Wheaton canning factory capacity to thirty thousand cans per day.[98]

The Davidson brothers weren't slowing down, either. On February 9, 1923, a *Journal* article announced that Mon Davidson had sold Walter Brattin, one of the original investors in the Wheaton's lumberyard, his entire interest in the Wheaton Lumberyard that he had purchased three years earlier. Walter became owner and manager of the lumberyard.

Then in May and June 1923, as Dudley Biggs was advertising for a thousand extra pickers to harvest the Wheaton Fruit Growers Association's strawberry crop, a series of spectacular store deals were struck, involving some of Wheaton's most prominent merchants and two other Davidson brothers, Ozzie and Awk.[99]

The *Wheaton Journal* of May 23, 1923, carried the news that Burger & Sons sold their stock of general merchandise in their discount store to Fred Doerge of Diamond, Missouri, and Wallace Chenoweth of Neosho. In the deal, George Burger was to get Wal Chenoweth's residence in Wheaton, a number of shares in Wheaton's Ideal Ice & Power Company, and cash. Mr. and Mrs. Doerge would manage the former Burger & Sons store.

A month later, on June 22, 1923, a *Journal* story announced a three-way blockbuster deal involving more than $100,000 worth of merchandise. In 2014 dollars, it would have been a $1.4 million deal.[100]

In the swap, Joe Frazier and partners Awk and Ozzie Davidson traded their stock of Frazier & Davidson Brothers merchandise for Wal Chenoweth's merchandise in his Neosho store, Chenoweth's Neosho residence, and the stock of merchandise that Fred Doerge recently purchased from Burger & Sons. Ozzie Davidson would move to Neosho and take ownership of Chenoweth's store there. Awk Davidson would take possession of the merchandise owned by Doerge. Chenoweth and Doerge would take ownership of the former Frazier & Davidson Brothers store.

The transactions must have made their customers dizzy.

The result of the switcheroo was that Wal Chenoweth was coming back to his old store in Wheaton with a new partner, Fred Doerge. George Burger and his sons Carl and Oral were, at least temporarily, no longer in business as Wheaton merchants. Awk Davidson, Joe Frazier, and Awk's brother Ozzie would own the Burgers' former discount store in Wheaton. Ozzie, however, would move to Neosho and manage the store that formerly had been Wal Chenoweth's, while Ozzie's partners, Awk Davidson and Joe Frazier, would run the old Burger store under the name Frazier & Davidson Brothers.

Within a few months, Chenoweth & Doerge proved to be just as formidable as merchandisers and competitors as Chenoweth & Frazier had been before the Davidson brothers became part owners of the Wheaton store. In October 1923, a *Journal* ad, no doubt penned by Wal Chenoweth himself—since there was no such thing as an ad agency in Wheaton—explained why his store was doing so well:[101]

> Week after week, we have customers coming to our store from Washburn, Wayne, Exeter, Cassville, Butterfield, Purdy, Pioneer, Fairview, Stark City, Stella, Bethpage, Powell, and even from Monett and Pierce City.
>
> There are perhaps several reasons why they come, but here are some of the main ones:
>
> FIRST—We carry a variety of stock here so that people are reasonably sure before leaving home that they can get what they want here.
>
> SECOND—We try to handle only standard lines of merchandise of proven quality so that our customers will return for more goods of the same kind.
>
> LAST—But not least, we are located in a small town where we have practically no expense compared with the larger towns. This is really our greatest

advantage. We can and do sell merchandise on a margin of profit that stores in larger towns dare not and cannot afford to sell on.

These are the principal reasons why people come here from a long distance and we intend to see to it that they keep coming and that they increase in numbers and come from even greater distances.

"We are located in a town where we can sell cheaper." Chenoweth & Doerge

Not only had Wal Chenoweth explained why *his* store was doing well—he had also explained why Wheaton, which by then boasted a population of 374, was such a thriving little town. In the 1920s and well into the 1940s, driving twenty or thirty miles on muddy, rutted, or dusty, rocky, rough roads could sometimes be a real ordeal; flat tires and other mechanical problems with the cars of the day were a continual nuisance, but Wheaton's businesses had the goods that made such a trip worthwhile. Even folks from the larger towns of Cassville, Monett, and Neosho sometimes drove to Wheaton where they could buy quality products a little cheaper.

By excluding any mention of customers from Rocky Comfort in the ad, Mr. Chenoweth sent a silent signal that Wheaton and Rocky still had a significant rivalry under way.

Chenoweth & Doerge may have been doing a lot of business, but Joe Frazier and Awk Davidson were no pushovers as competitors. Frazier & Davidson Brothers, now in the bargain discount store that had been operated by George Burger and his sons, held a big sale during the first fifteen days of December 1923. Advertised in the *Journal* were those "sensible, serviceable" ladies' Star Brand shoes that George Burger had purchased in bulk before he sold the store. Normally priced at $2.75, the sale price would be $1.95. And ladies' "military boots for wintry weather" that usually cost four dollars would be sold for $2.95. Luna soap was on sale for four cents a bar, and Arbuckle coffee was twenty-five cents a pound.[102]

What's more, the Frazier & Davidson Brothers ad said "the first ten ladies who enter our store on Saturday morning will receive five yards of regular 20-cent (per yard) gingham for 25 cents."

Joe Frazier and the Davidsons were still competitive. Wheaton's business outlook was positive. The M&NA strike was settled in late 1923, and the railroad's freight line was extended from Joplin, Missouri, all the way to Helena, in eastern Arkansas, on the banks of the Mississippi River. The extension, said a *Joplin Globe* article reprinted in the *Wheaton Journal*, "has been responsible for a perceptible increase in business even in so short a time ..."[103]

In the first few days of 1924, with a bright outlook for the year ahead, Joe Frazier and his partners, Awk and Ozzie Davidson, got an offer they couldn't refuse from W. T. Evans, owner of a drugstore and a grocery store in Neosho. Awk and Ozzie sold their Wheaton store to him for a residence in Neosho and a cash difference.[104]

The January 11, 1924, edition of the *Journal* that announced the store sale also carried this item: "Miss Thelma McQueen, who is teaching at Cassville, is spending the week-end at home." Thelma's teaching career was under way.

Frazier & Davidson Brothers didn't stay idle long. Two weeks after they sold their store, the partnership bought a 120-acre farm from the Citizens Bank of Rocky Comfort. Awk Davidson, the item said, "expects to move to the farm in the near future."[105] To Uncle Awk, making the transition between storekeeper and farmer was no big deal. He could manage cattle and crops as well as he could manage store inventory. His new farm near Bethlehem was fewer than five miles southwest of Wheaton and a little more than three miles southwest of Rocky Comfort—just a wide place in the road with a general store and a church.

In late February of 1924, Dudley Biggs resigned as manager of the Wheaton Fruit Growers Association, and to no one's surprise, Silas McQueen was elected to replace him.[106] In April, Silas was reelected chairman of the Commercial Club.[107]

By mid-August 1924, as Silas was preparing his Wheaton canning factory for what promised to be the "largest (tomato crop) ever produced in this section," Awk and Ozzie Davidson were trading the farm they bought near Bethlehem for Roark Brothers general store in Anderson, just over twenty-two miles southwest of Wheaton.[108] The new firm would be managed by former Wheaton merchant George Burger's son, Carl, who was married to Ozzie's daughter, Loris.[109]

After Awk and Ozzie Davidson departed the Wheaton business scene in 1924, store swapping slowed. That fall, Lettie McQueen and her three children, Thelma, Bernice, and Malloy, left for Columbia, Missouri, where the three young McQueens would attend Missouri University.[110] It's a safe bet to say that travel from Wheaton to Columbia by car in those days would have been a difficult journey— approximately 230 miles.

Even a two-and-a-half mile trip from Wheaton to Rocky Comfort could be a challenge, depending on how muddy, rutted, rocky, or dusty the unpaved road was. A *Journal* item of October 3, 1924, informed readers that road work "along the McDonald-Newton County line between here and Rocky Comfort has been progressing nicely the past week. It will soon be possible to travel from here to Rocky Comfort over a graveled road."

To find out more about the Rocky-Wheaton rivalry and local politics in the early twenties, it would be a good time to make a morning visit to Silas McQueen's big house, if I could, and have coffee with him. Silas liked his coffee "saucered and blowed."[111] While he was drinking his cooled coffee, I'd ask him when he seriously began to consider running for the Missouri State House of Representatives. One more thing ... I'd ask Silas about a young fellow named Wally Fox, from the Fox community in the hill country south of Rocky, who showed up in Wheaton in November of 1924 and bought a quarter interest in Maurice Lamberson's weekly *Wheaton Journal*.[112] Wally had completed journalism studies at Kansas State Normal at Pittsburg, Kansas. He was destined to buy the paper outright the next year and would remain the *Journal* editor for the next forty-two years.

The year 1924 closed with an economically damaging event in Rocky. On Saturday night, November 15, the plant of the Rocky Comfort Milling Company, owned by Ross Davidson, was destroyed by fire.[113]

"It was built many years ago and has always played an important part in the industrial and business life of the town and community," the *Journal* article said. "Under the management of Mr. Davidson the mill has been very successful financially and its products enjoyed a popularity and demand such as is seldom found in mills of its size."

It was a blow to Rocky and a portent of the town's fate. (See chapter titled "Rocky Comfort on Sunday.")

For Silas McQueen, life was getting ready to take another leap. In 1926, he again threw his hat into the political ring, this time running for election to the Missouri State House of Representatives. As a Republican, Silas had an advantage. The GOP was the party that enjoyed the approval of most of the nation during the Roaring Twenties. Calvin Coolidge was president, and the economy, generally, was on a roll. Two years after he lost the race for county collector, Barry County's voters sent Silas to the Missouri House of Representatives for his first two-year term as a state legislator.

By the summer of 1928, Silas and Lettie's son, Malloy, had completed his undergraduate degree, studied law, and passed the Missouri bar exam. He also had played three years of varsity baseball for the University of Missouri and was captain of the team in 1927. Scouts for the St. Louis Cardinals, who had defeated the mighty New York Yankees and Babe Ruth in the 1926 World Series, saw Malloy playing baseball in a semipro league in northern Missouri. They took him to meet the Cardinals' president, Branch Rickey, who signed him to a $150-a-month contract to play for a Cardinal farm club. Twenty years later, when Rickey was president and general manager of the Brooklyn Dodgers, he broke the major league color barrier by signing Jackie Robinson.

To begin his professional career, Malloy reported to a minor league training camp in Danville, Illinois, in the spring of 1928 and was sent to the Cardinals' Topeka, Kansas, club in the Class

C Western Association.[114] Then he got bad news. Writing a short history for his great grandson, Malloy described what happened next:

I could field pretty well but as an outfielder I was supposed to hit as well. This I failed to do. I could handle a curve but that "hard one" left me standing with my bat on my shoulder. About six weeks into the season we were at Fort Smith, Arkansas, and Eddie (Eddie Dyer, the Topeka club's manager) called me to his room ... and asked, "Mac, isn't your home near here?" It was, so I replied, "Yes." Eddie then said, "Mr. Rickey thinks you would make a better lawyer than a baseball player," and handed me the "pink slip," which was my release and the end of my pro baseball career. Mr. Rickey was a lawyer and knew that I passed the bar exam just before I came to Danville.[115]

Malloy immediately called his sweetheart, and they were married. The newlyweds finished the summer of 1928 in Macon, Missouri, where Malloy supervised local youth baseball teams.[116]

Meanwhile, in Wheaton, Silas prepared to run for a second two-year term in the Missouri House. He apparently was so confident of winning that he didn't bother to campaign. The crops and the Wheaton area economy were favorable, and that always helped an incumbent officeholder. Eighty railcars with $80,000 worth of strawberries were shipped from Wheaton that summer—779,848 quarts.[117] The local items in the *Journal* of July 19 noted that "Mr. and Mrs. J.S. McQueen left Wednesday for Hudson, Colo., to spend a month with their daughter, Mrs. Richard Smith." Thelma had married Dick Smith a year earlier on Independence Day 1927 in Orchard, Colorado.[118]

In October, Malloy moved to Monett to open a law practice.[119] And in the November general election, Silas easily defeated his Democratic opponent, Minnie Northern, by a margin of 1,917 votes—5,443 to 3,526. Wheaton voters favored their hometown son 242 to 128.[120] Silas garnered the second-highest majority of any Barry County candidate. In the presidential election, Herbert Hoover swept to victory by the greatest electoral majority and the largest popular vote in the history of the United States, receiving 444 electoral votes out of 531.[121]

As 1929 dawned, Silas introduced what undoubtedly was his most widely publicized bill during his years in the Missouri House of Representatives. Chicken thievery had become rampant in rural southwest Missouri. To city folks and people unfamiliar with the economy of that part of the state, chicken stealing might have seemed a trivial matter—even amusing to some. But it was dead serious to farm families.[122]

Silas knew his constituents, and he wanted to respond to their concerns. So in January 1929, fifty-one-year-old Representative McQueen introduced a bill in the Fifty-Fifth General Assembly of the State of Missouri that would require buyers of poultry to keep a complete record of the poultry seller.

Journal editor Wally Fox wrote, "From the way chicken thieves have been operating in this part of the country, the sooner the act's made a law the better." Under the bill, the penalty for failing to properly record a list of required data identifying the seller was a felony, punishable by either two years in the Missouri penitentiary or a year in county jail, or by a fine that wasn't to exceed $500, or both.[123]

Also on the *Journal's* front page in the same issue was a story about—you guessed it—chicken thieves.

Two chicken thieves had raided several chicken houses in the area just three nights earlier, but luckily, they were frightened away by hunters who happened to notice a 'possum hide and a crosscut saw lying at the side of a road near the hill country village of Powell, a dozen miles south of Wheaton. Looking more closely, the hunters discovered several gunnysacks with live chickens in them. The chicken thieves, seeing armed men near their car, hightailed it through the brush and the rocky hills to God knows where. The hunters guarded the car the rest of the night, and the next day, the McDonald County sheriff drove the car to Pineville, the county seat. The owner of the stolen 'possum hide and owners of most of the stolen chickens reclaimed their property, but the owner of several Rhode Island Red hens, which the thieves had stuffed into their car, could not be determined.[124] The story lacked one important detail: it didn't mention how much chicken poop was left in the car.

A week later, a *Journal* article identified the suspected chicken thief as a fellow who "had been a suspected moonshiner and bootlegger, but recently had joined the church and was supposed to be reformed so the McDonald County Court appointed him constable." The constable's wife realized the jig was up for her husband and held a public sale that disposed of their property, provided some cash, and prepared the couple to travel light and flee the area. The sheriff, however, kept her under surveillance, thinking she might lead them to the fugitive constable.[125] There were no more follow-up articles, and whether the disgraced constable was ever caught isn't known, but one thing is certain—he lost his job.

The January 31 article, however, concluded on a happy note. The owner of the Rhode Island Red hens in the chicken thief's car was located, and the hens were reunited with their owner.

In the same edition, a *Journal* article described the final passage of Silas's chicken-thief bill in the Missouri House of Representatives. Most of the afternoon of January 29, 1929, was devoted "to a debate on chicken stealing," the article said. "McQueen explained it was aimed particularly at chicken stealing in the Missouri Ozarks, which, he said 'has become quite an industry.'"[126] The *Journal* described the rest of the story:

This started the debate in which representatives from all sections of the state joined before the measure finally was ordered engrossed.

Representative Proctor of Dade County, in an eloquent plea for the bill, said something of this kind should be done to protect the "poor hill people of the Ozarks," who are being preyed upon by chicken thieves in ever increasing number. The chicken raiders, he declared are "a den of dastardly cowards."

The house engaged in much merriment over the measure and got an extra laugh when Representative Elmer of Dent County, in asking a question, inquired to what class of "chickens" the bill applied—"those that go to bed at 6 at night and get up at 6 in the morning, or those that go to bed at 6 in the morning and get up at 6 that night?"

An amendment by Representative Whitaker of Hickory County to provide the bill would not apply to the purchase or sale of chickens or poultry in carload lots was adopted.

Lettie McQueen also won an honor in January 1929. Members of the Missouri House elected her as the body's postmistress by a vote of 70 to 24. She would be allowed two assistants "and will handle about the same amount of mail that is handled at the post office here," a *Journal* article said.[127]

Lettie, no doubt, had the experience for the job. After all, Silas had been Wheaton's postmaster for the first seven years of the little town's life, and it's virtually certain that Lettie would have been his helper.

Despite his legislative success, Silas was not slowing his business activities in Wheaton. As his chicken thief bill sailed through the Missouri General Assembly in January, he made public his plans to form a joint stock company to raise $5,000 to build a new, modern canning factory in Wheaton to can tomatoes and beans. Interested persons could buy in at $100 per share. The new company would be known as the Quality Canning Company and would be controlled by a five-man board of directors.[128]

Two weeks later, on February 7, the stockholders met and to no one's surprise elected Silas to the board of directors, along with four more of the town's most prominent businessmen—A. M. "Mortie" Duncan, a co-owner of the hardware store; William A. Davidson, the bank cashier; Wal Chenoweth, then of Chenoweth & Doerge, and E. W. Wyatt, a well-known grocer.[129]

Because Silas was keeping a lot of political and business balls in the air, he soon turned to the air to address his need to be in two places at once. A *Journal* article described how he chose to perform that trick. On Sunday afternoon, April 14, the article reported, "a whir of wings and roar of motor and an airplane alighted in the McQueen pasture ... and J.S. himself stepped down. He declared that except for a roaring in his head he felt none the worse from his airplane ride from Jefferson City."[130]

The article didn't say what important piece of business had prompted Silas to fly home and land in his farm's pasture—a risky venture in the days before instrument flying—especially since the single-engine army plane, piloted by a National Guard airman, was enveloped in a heavy fog for several miles between Mount Vernon and Wheaton. The pilot, Captain Wyman, remarked "that since this was McQueen's first flight, he was very 'nervy.'" They had flown in an open-cockpit, single-engine plane for more than two hundred miles.

The story also said, in an unattributed statement, that the pilot "knew his business."

It was a statement that soon proved to be questionable.

Silas stayed in Wheaton a few hours, and at 3:00 p.m., he climbed back into the plane, which took off for the return trip to Jefferson City.

"J.S. may make another trip by plane in several more weeks since he must be home a short time on business and this is a very quick way to travel," the story continued. "Who would have 'thunk' Mack that nervy?" wrote *Journal* editor Wally Fox.

Silas was very nearly too nervy. Between Sunday's flight and the following Thursday's edition of the *Journal*, Silas mailed a letter to editor Wally with shocking news. The plane delivered Silas back to Jefferson City without incident, the letter said, but when it took off again, disaster struck.

The pilot, Captain Wyman, after reaching Jefferson City with Mr. McQueen late Sunday afternoon, secured another passenger and started for St. Louis, but had been in the air only a short time when the motor failed. The plane fell to earth, killing the passenger, a young man, and seriously injuring Wyman.[131]

Nothing in the record indicates that Silas ever tried air travel again.

The remainder of 1929 was relatively uneventful for the McQueen family and for Wheaton. Silas McQueen was appointed Barry County's Commissioner to the State Fair in June and prepared to help the Missouri State Fair Board reach its attendance goal of 333,333 during the eight-day run of the fair in Sedalia.[132] In late July, Silas and Lettie left Wheaton for Hudson, Colorado, for another visit with their daughter Thelma and her husband, Dick Smith.[133]

Wheaton's hardware store was running so well in the summer of 1929 under the tri-ownership of Oscar Garber, Mortie Duncan, and Mon Davidson that Oscar and his wife left to visit relatives in Kansas and Oklahoma. "Mon and Mortie are not expecting them back until late this fall," stated an item in the Local News column of the *Journal*.[134]

The October 24 edition of the *Journal*, under the headline QUALITY CANNING CO. COMPLETES RUN, informed readers that Silas McQueen's new canning factory canned eight (freight) carloads of tomatoes that season and "is one of the best equipped factories in this part of the country." In New York, however, October 24 was a day of disaster for stock traders and for the nation.

October 24, 1929, became known as Black Thursday, which was followed by Black Monday and Black Tuesday, when the bottom fell out of the market. At first, it seemed that it was only people who had lost money in the stock market who would be affected. But by 1930, it was apparent that farmers and merchants all over the country, even around little towns like Wheaton and Rocky Comfort, were going to be hit hard as prices for livestock and grain and produce fell to pre–World War I lows. On September 4, 1930, the *Journal* carried one of the first articles acknowledging that what later became known as the Great Depression was starting to bite, even in southwest Missouri.

FALLING PRICES

This country and the rest of the world have definitely entered a period of falling prices. Just how far they can go down is a question of considerable importance. As usual, the answer is missing. Nine years ago the 1920 World War peak prices have gone down 37 ½ percent. After the Civil War prices continued to decline for 30 years, and turned upward only with new gold discoveries. New gold discoveries are not likely today. Economists, who are supposed to know things, are worried but they have no solution. It looks like we are going to have to get along as best we may.[135]

By the time the November 4 general election rolled around, the country, including southwest Missouri, was falling deeper into the Depression. Voters wanted a change. Silas was not successful in his campaign for a third term in the Missouri House of Representatives. He lost to the Democratic candidate, Monett attorney Fielding P. Sizer Jr., by 243 votes—3,720 to 3,477.[136] But he won a majority of Wheaton's votes, getting 200 votes to Sizer's 138.[137]

In December 1930, farm prices fell to the lowest level in fifteen years.[138]

Wheaton's business activity slowed considerably in 1931. Money was tight. "Because the state last year lost considerable money through bank failures, of which there were ninety-nine in Missouri, 1931 state aid money for consolidated high schools will not be sent in lump sums, but will be sent in installments," said Charles A. Lee, state superintendent of schools, in a *Journal* article of October 1, 1931. In the same issue, Wally Fox reprinted a lengthy article from the *Kansas City Star* analyzing the Depression and concluding that "America needs most of all to get back its nerve." If only it had been that simple.

A week later, Dick Smith showed some nerve, giving Wheaton one of its best business boosts of 1931 when he reported that he was "erecting a new M.F.A. (Missouri Farmers Association) drive-in filling station just south of the Bank of Wheaton building ..."[139] And in Rocky a couple of months earlier, Oscar Schell and his son, Merlie, installed a new hammer mill in the old lumberyard building, finally replacing Ross Davidson's mill that had burned in 1924. The Schells would grind grains and carry a line of feeds, flour, and meal.[140]

The most active of the Davidson brothers in 1931 was Mon, a partner in the hardware store and also Wheaton's mayor. Apparently, Mon was known for his expertise in the timing of the fall and winter farm task of butchering hogs to provide meat for the family for the following year. Lots of farmers consulted *The Old Farmer's Almanac* for advice. Others obviously preferred to consult Mon. The Christmas Eve 1931 edition of the *Journal* reported that "several people in and around Wheaton have been consulting Mayor Mon Davidson the past few days as to when the moon is right for hog killing."

About the time Mayor Mon was advising local farmers about the proper phase of the moon for hog butchering, his brother Ross moved his family from Rocky Comfort to the nearby small town of Fairview.[141]

Despite the downturn in the economy, Silas had not abandoned his political ambitions. Staying active in civic affairs, he represented Wheaton at a truck-permit hearing in Springfield before a member of the Missouri Public Service Commission in early 1932. Silas opposed the application of a Joplin trucking company for an exclusive permit to haul merchandise in and out of Wheaton.[142] Wheaton's leaders didn't want a trucking company to poach business that otherwise would continue to be handled by the M&NA.

A couple of months later, Silas and George Fagan, the city clerk and secretary of the Commercial Club—who was a boarder in Silas and Lettie's big house south of the bank—journeyed to Joplin to oppose another trucking company's application to serve Wheaton.[143] The trip marked the beginning of one of Wheaton's longest bipartisan and cordial relationships—Silas McQueen, the staunch Republican, and George Fagan, one of the town's most active Democrats.

The following week, on March 22, 1932, Silas went to Jefferson City as a representative of the Barry County Taxpayers' League to ask the State Board of Equalization for a 20 percent reduction in taxes.[144] A week later, the Board of Equalization reduced the farm valuation in Barry County by 21 percent. Town real estate was reduced 17 percent.[145] The article commended Silas for his advocacy. He hadn't been reelected, but he was still in the game.

In April, Thelma and Dick moved in with Silas and Lettie, in the big house south of the bank and next door to Dick's MFA service station.[146] Thelma was completing her second year of teaching in Wheaton's public schools.

When Missouri's August primary election rolled around, Silas ran without opposition on the Republican ticket for the right to oppose the incumbent Democrat, Sizer, for the Missouri House. But in November's general election, the economy and the political tide was running not only against Silas but against Hoover and Republicans across the country. Silas lost to Fielding Sizer again, 5,967 votes to 4,674 votes—a margin of 1,293 votes.[147] Silas again won a majority in Wheaton, carrying his hometown 242 to 192.[148] Democrat Franklin D. Roosevelt swept into the White House, carrying forty-two states.

In the late 1930s, Silas would make one more unsuccessful attempt to win a seat in the Missouri House of Representatives. Meanwhile, he kept his hand in the political game by winning a seat on the Barry County Republican Committee throughout the 1930s, as did Lettie.[149]

On February 6, 1933, Silas's father, James Elbert McQueen, died at age seventy-five. J. E. McQueen was born in Lee County, Virginia, and had come to Missouri in 1884. His closest survivors were his sons Silas, Sam, Otis, Boone, and Harrison of Wheaton; Lester, of California; sisters Cora Hensley of Oregon; and Nota Needham, of Joplin.[150]

The remainder of 1933 was a quiet one for Silas and his family. In Wheaton, Fred Doerge sold his interest in the Chenoweth & Doerge store to Wal Chenoweth and Wal's son Carroll.[151]

For the Davidson brothers, 1933 ended with a shocking death in the family. After building a twenty-five-by-forty-foot addition to his Rocky Comfort canning factory in June 1933 and threshing his wheat crop in July, Ross Davidson died of a heart attack on November 12, 1933, at age fifty-three, at his home in Fairview.[152]

Wheaton, like the rest of the country, continued to suffer from the effects of the Depression as 1934 began. There were still no paved streets in Wheaton. On January 11, 1934, a *Journal* article announced that the Civil Works Administration had approved "a project of graveling streets in Wheaton and the work will begin just as soon as weather permits. Seven men with teams (of horses) and three single hands (workers) will be employed on this project. The street, beginning at the H.A. (Herman) Allman hammer mill building and ending near the M.F. Francis home, is to be graveled," the article said. "After this project is completed, Main Street is to be repaired if there are any funds left."

Silas McQueen remained active on the Wheaton civic and business scene throughout the Depression years of the 1930s. He was secretary of the Wheaton Fruit Growers Association in 1933 and managed the association for many more years.[153] He was worshipful master of the local Masonic Lodge in 1934.[154]

In the early and mid-1930s, so many people in rural Missouri were in danger of starving to death that many counties combined with the State Garden Program to establish community gardens and relief canning factories. A half mile northeast of Rocky Comfort, in neighboring McDonald County, T. L. "Tommy" Shewmake managed a two-acre community garden that produced 423 cans of green beans in 1934. The garden was on the farm that his son Ernest L. Shewmake and Ern's wife, Hessie, owned.[155] Twenty-seven years earlier, in 1907, Main Street in Wheaton had been Tommy Shewmake's wheat field.

In the summer and fall of 1934, Ozzie Davidson was managing a relief canning factory in Wheaton that federal, state, and local governments established to can beef for needy families in Barry, McDonald, and Newton counties. The factory was set up with government funds, and workers were paid thirty cents an hour for their work. Needy persons could bring butchered beef to the cannery where 40 percent of the beef would be kept for distribution to other needy persons, and 60 percent of the canned beef would be returned to the person or family that brought it in. The canning was done without charge.

The canning of peaches had different rules, prescribed by the government. In early September, Ozzie reported that peaches would be canned on a 55-45 basis with the government furnishing everything needed for the canning, including sugar. Forty-five percent of the peaches that anyone brought in would be returned to the owner after canning. Fifty-five percent would be retained for distribution to other needy families.

"The factory will can anything you have to can—peaches, apples, carrots, turnip greens, etc … Local relief labor is being used and workmen are being paid at the rate of thirty cents per hour, but if not enough meat, vegetables or fruit is brought in to keep the factory running it will have to be closed down," a *Journal* article warned.[156]

By late summer, Ozzie Davidson's relief canning factory stopped canning beef but was running two shifts a day because it was "covered up" with peaches to can, the *Journal* reported. Ten women peelers and five men, besides the foreman, worked at each shift. Each shift worked fifteen hours a week, so ninety persons were needed to run the double shift for a week. Workers were allowed to work only fifteen hours each week, at thirty cents per hour, which was paid in cash.[157]

Times were desperate for many people.

In McDonald County's rugged hill country southwest of

Wheaton, six thousand persons were on relief, the *Journal* reported on September 13, 1934. That was just under 50 percent of McDonald County's population.[158] My parents, who were married in October 1932, lived deep in McDonald County in an isolated area known as Little Missouri Hollow from the fall of 1932 until sometime in 1934 when they moved to a rented farm three miles west of Wheaton. They counted themselves fortunate to have avoided receiving relief food.

Thievery in those precarious times was widespread. On September 27, 1934, the *Journal* reported that three men were apprehended about midnight one evening during the previous week, attempting to steal apples from the Jim Long orchard, south of Stella—eight or ten miles southwest of Wheaton. Joe Long, a relative of the orchard owner, discovered the theft in progress and alerted three other men who were guarding the orchard. The story provided the details:

> Joe Long discovered a truck parked near the Long orchard about midnight and also heard the thieves shaking apples from the trees. He immediately notified the other three men and with guns started out through the orchard. Tom Payne first discovered two of the thieves under a tree and told them to come out with their hands up. After the second command, the two tried to escape. Mr. Payne fired his gun in the air and one of the thieves immediately stopped and was badly frightened. The other one headed for the truck and ran into Jim Long, Joe Long and (Everett) Utter. He immediately surrendered. One other man was captured at the truck, and was apparently guarding the apples and truck.

> The three thieves were then marched down the road to the Jim Long home and held there until Henry Long, deputy sheriff, arrived. The three thieves were then loaded into cars and taken to Pineville (the

McDonald County seat) where they pleaded guilty and were given jail sentences of thirty days each and the cost.[159]

By early 1935, conditions hadn't improved much. The Missouri Relief and Reconstruction Commission in Jefferson City announced that seeds for subsistence home gardens would be furnished to 114,000 needy Missouri families that year. Fifteen hundred units of seeds, each unit containing eighteen varieties of seeds, were allotted for Barry County. In the previous year, 1934, Missouri's 74,739 relief gardens produced food valued at $1,474,111. Harry Hopkins, President Franklin D. Roosevelt's point man on the program for the federal government, said all families able to do so would be expected to plant gardens.[160]

The economic picture wasn't quite as bleak in sunny California.

On January 21, 1935, J. W. Montgomery of Long Beach, California, wrote a letter to *Journal* editor Wally Fox informing him about life in the Southern California port city. J. W., better known as Walter, accompanied by his brother, Carter, and Carter's wife, Minnie, had moved to Long Beach from Rocky Comfort in 1926.[161] Walter and Carter Montgomery and their father, John L. Montgomery, had operated a general merchandise store, Montgomery Brothers and Co., at the northeast corner of Main and Mill streets in Rocky Comfort throughout the first quarter of the twentieth century.

It was the Montgomery family who gave Wal Chenoweth his start. In 1903, Wal decided to abandon his quest to become a physician, giving up his intention to follow in the footsteps of his late father, Dr. Albert White Chenoweth. Dr. Chenoweth had been ambushed and killed near the McDonald County seat of Pineville in September 1883 when Wal was just shy of two years old. After three trials that resulted in one conviction that was reversed and two hung juries, the accused assassin was shot and killed by an angry mob that broke into the McDonald County jail.[162]

After my great-grandmother Rachael Lamberson died in 1893, my great-grandfather Henry Phelps Lamberson married Dr.

Chenoweth's widow, Laura. Wal Chenoweth became the stepbrother of Phelps and Rachael's seven children, including my granddad, Earnest Lamberson.

In 1903, twenty-two-year-old Wal Chenoweth quit his medical studies at the Methodist Institute in Marionville and instead purchased John L. Montgomery's interest in the Montgomerys' Rocky Comfort store. Wal became the "and Co." part of the Montgomery Bros. and Co. store in Rocky. From there, he moved to Wheaton and established Chenoweth & Frazier general merchandise store with Wheaton merchant Joe Frazier.

In 1926, when the Montgomery brothers moved to Long Beach, the trading of businesses, farms, and livestock was in full bloom in the Rocky Comfort-Wheaton area, prompting Walter Montgomery, in his 1935 letter to *Journal* editor Wally Fox, to write about the days when buyers, sellers, and traders were flourishing.

I expected to visit Missouri last year but on account of the drouth and being rather short on cash I didn't make the trip, but if nothing prevents, I expect to be with the old timers there about August or September (of this year). It has been so long since I made a trade that I am nervous and afraid to trade. But I want those old time traders there to be ready to make some propositions by the time I arrive and if I don't get my nerve back by that time I will go by Albuquerque, N.M. and take Clarence Taylor (another former Rocky Comfort resident) with me to do my trading. In the meantime I have appointed Oscar Davidson as my attorney and business manager, and if any of those old-time traders have any propositions to put up, just tell him about it.

The letter confirmed my suspicions that Uncle Awk Davidson and some of Wheaton and Rocky's older businessmen enjoyed the wheeling and dealing as much for the thrill of it as for whatever profit they made from their buying, selling, and swapping.

When the Montgomery brothers and Carter's daughter, Hazzie, visited Rocky Comfort eight months later on September 1, 1935, Uncle Awk and Aunt Virgie opened their home in Rocky and threw them a surprise dinner attended by 150 relatives and friends—a grand blowout for Depression days. My conclusion is that Uncle Awk must have done very well with his store and farm deals back in the 1920s.

In October 1935, after Uncle Awk and Aunt Virgie held the soiree for the Montgomerys in Rocky, Silas McQueen was elected mayor of Wheaton in a special election, defeating longtime merchant Joe Frazier by a vote of 92 to 81.[163] In April 1936, he was reelected mayor, defeating dentist C. B. "Jerry" McCall 75 to 6.[164] He also was elected to the Wheaton School Board the same day.[165] And for many years, he continued to manage his canning factory.[166]

In August 1936, Silas threw a picnic supper for Lettie at the scenic little village of Pioneer, five miles north of Wheaton.[167] Four months later, on Christmas Eve 1936, Lettie suffered what was referred to in the *Journal* as a "light stroke."

Lettie suffered several more strokes and died on December 19, 1942.[168] Silas was sixty-six years old, and he did not like to live alone. On January 19, 1944, he married Lon Davidson's widow, Rena.[169] Rena was the mother of one of Wheaton's well-known merchants during the 1940s and '50s—Elsie McNeill, co-owner with Eschol Duncan of Duncan & McNeill's department store.

When Rena died on February 22, 1950, Silas was seventy-three. Being a resourceful and practical man, he advertised in the newspaper for wife number three—"for someone who liked to fish and garden."[170] Florence Vineyard, a widow who was reared in the Rocky Comfort and Exeter communities and who was living on a small farm in the Rio Grande Valley of Texas, met those specifications. She and Silas were married on August 11, 1951.

"The newlyweds will make their home in Wheaton for a few weeks, but expect to go to the home of Mrs. McQueen in October to spend the

137

winter. However, they expect to be back in the spring in time for J.S. to put out a garden," said the *Journal* story announcing their wedding.[171]

Silas was married to Florence when his daughter Thelma had her fatal stroke on that Sunday morning in May 1954. It seemed that everyone in town—young and old, schoolkids and the town's citizens—pitched in to prepare for Thelma's funeral, which was scheduled for Tuesday, May 11, only two days after she died.

Several of the senior boys, who would graduate the following Thursday, volunteered to help dig Thelma's grave at the Muncie Chapel Cemetery, a little over a mile and a half north of Wheaton.

Joe Higgs, a sophomore who had a red Ford pickup truck, and James Cantrell, a freshman in my class, were tasked to drive to Wheaton's VFW Hall before the funeral, load as many folding chairs as the pickup could haul, and deliver them to the Methodist church in anticipation of an overflow crowd at Thelma's funeral service. By the time they had finished unloading and placing the chairs in the church auditorium and adjoining classrooms, time for the service was fast approaching.

Joe and James jumped into the pickup and headed back to the Cantrells' house on the south side of town to change into their suits and ties. They stopped to cross East Hurlbut Street, and Joe was suddenly faced with a major dilemma, James said. The funeral procession, led by the McQueen Funeral Home hearse and a long line of cars carrying the McQueen family and close friends, was approaching fast from the east.[172]

Joe and James both knew that if they waited until the procession had passed, they would be late for the funeral. Joe also knew that it was considered very bad manners and disrespectful to pass or pull in front of a funeral procession. He made a quick decision and peeled rubber. Later, both Joe and James decided it had been the right one. No one ever said anything to them about the incident, and they were able to change clothes and make it to the funeral on time. Joe, who became a decorated fighter pilot, flying more than one hundred missions for the US Air Force during the Vietnam War, said he often thought of the moment when Thelma Smith's funeral procession was closing fast on him while he was at the stop sign and counted it one of the most stressful of his life.

At age fourteen, I had attended many funerals in the area and had sung in quartets and choirs at several, but there was something different about Thelma's funeral. Just about every kid in the high school was there, along with many of their parents and members of the Wheaton community. There was standing room only, but I was lucky enough to get there in time to be seated in a pew in the auditorium.

The music was provided by a quartet from the senior class—Kathy Lee, Donna Jean Garrison, Jon Paden, and Mavin "Skip" Stewart Jr. The high-school music teacher, Mrs. Ruth Poor, accompanied them on the piano.

I can't remember anything that Wheaton's Methodist pastor, the Reverend W. P. Richardson, or the church's former pastor, the Reverend Roy Stribling, said that day, but I remember the muffled sobs that could be heard as the preachers read Thelma's obituary and attempted to make comforting remarks. Finally, as was the custom in those days, everyone stood up and began to file by Thelma's open casket for one final good-bye. Before the people in my pew got there, Bill Haynes, a junior who was one of the eleven Haynes kids who had grown up just a half mile from my family's farm, was filing by the casket when grief overcame him. Sobbing uncontrollably, Bill stopped and bent over Thelma's casket. The line of mourners paused, and we waited until Bill could gather himself and file out of the auditorium.

The scene was touching to me, because I had known Bill virtually all my life as a neighbor and schoolmate since I was in the first grade. Bill was tough as nails. Like several of his brothers, he was a great basketball player and a pretty decent baseball pitcher who could break off a good curveball. He was smaller than his brothers, so he had to be a scrapper on the baseball diamond and on the basketball court. I had never seen him this emotional. In my mind, Bill expressed in his grief what the entire town was feeling.

Journal editor Wally Fox must have felt some of the same emotion.

He was moved to pen a tribute to Thelma in the next edition. Under the headline A FRIEND IS GONE, he wrote, "Being no blood kin to me whatever, I figure I lost about as good a friend as I had when Mrs. R.W. Smith passed from this life to the world beyond Sunday afternoon."[173]

Wally praised her for the interest she took in her students. "She knew what an education really means to the youth of today and that all play and no work would not make a smart boy out of Jack. It was her ambition that those whom she taught might get the most out of school and become successful men and women."

Wally, who had been a member of the school board, concluded that Wheaton and the Wheaton School District "owe a lot to Mrs. Thelma Smith, who died as one might say, 'in the harness.'"

Thelma was a dynamo raised by go-getters—Silas and Lettie. I don't know who selected the bulldog as Wheaton High School's mascot, but it certainly fit the McQueen family and most of the tough merchants who owned and bought and sold and traded their businesses, farms, and livestock during the town's first half century.

When Silas McQueen died on June 5, 1960, at age eighty-three, a man who could rightly claim the title of one of Wheaton's "founding fathers" was gone, along with his knowledge of the town's entire history.[174] Just four months earlier, on February 14, his longtime boarder and Masonic brother, George Fagan, had died. George wasn't a Wheaton resident in the beginning like Silas, but since 1930, he had been an integral part of the Wheaton scene.

Seemingly, they were unlikely friends—Silas the Republican and George the Democrat. But they shared a love for Wheaton, for their Masonic organization, and a respect for each other that overcame their political differences.

As one of the founders of the town, Silas had demonstrated for decades that he could work with all kinds of people, and throughout his life, he maintained the same "do things spirit" that highlighted his talk to Wheaton's first Commercial Club four decades earlier. It was an attitude shared by virtually all of the movers and shakers in

Wheaton during its first fifty years, and it was a mind-set that made Wheaton a small-town economic powerhouse.

9

Wheaton's Mystery Man

George Alfred Fagan was just a wisp of a man, maybe five foot seven, and no more than 125 pale pounds topped with neatly trimmed gray hair that once had been sandy. Even his blue eyes were pale. But despite his slight build, George always stood out in any crowd of farm families, cattle traders, store clerks, preachers, auctioneers, salesmen, "shade tree" mechanics, and small-town merchants in Wheaton during the 1940s and '50s.[175] That's because he was one of only three men in town who always wore a dress shirt, tie, and suit. Often, George also wore a vest, and he topped off his outfit with a crisp straw hat in the summer and a blue or gray fedora in the winter. Once in a while, he substituted a snappy sport coat for the suit and vest.

But George's fashion trump card was astounding to a young farm boy like me; he occasionally wore spats—white ones, no less. I remember looking at George's ankle-wear when I was in grade school and wondering just what the heck they were. Then it dawned on me that Jiggs, in the *Bringing Up Father* comic strip that I read religiously in the *Joplin Globe*, also wore spats.[176] Jiggs was a working guy who had struck it rich in the Irish Sweepstakes. I figured that maybe George had struck it rich someplace and was just cooling his heels, or his spats, in Wheaton.

Spats set George apart from Wheaton's other two daily tie wearers, who were his physical opposites—the portly Dr. Otis

Sheridan McCall, who owned the Bank of Wheaton and practiced medicine in an office in the back of the bank building, and the substantially built Wallace Carroll "Wal" Chenoweth, who for many years owned Chenoweth's dry goods store on the north side of Main Street. Although Chenoweth's ads boasted that it was "Barry County's Largest General Store," I don't think you could buy spats there.

Doc and Wal, who were both canny business and professional men, came from families with deep roots in the Wheaton and Rocky Comfort communities, but George was a bachelor with no family that I knew of—at least not around Wheaton. For someone who was well connected and well known in the community, he had no visible means of support. He didn't own a business, and for most of my young life, he didn't hold a job. My parents said he had "retired" from Cecil Daugherty's real estate office on Main Street where he had worked during the 1930s and through most of World War II.

But when I'd ask my parents more questions about George, their usual answer was, "I don't know."

Much later, I found out that in the 1930s, he had been Wheaton city treasurer, Wheaton city clerk, and secretary of the Community Club—the organization of business owners who made Wheaton's big decisions, such as whether the top prize at the Saturday drawing would grow by ten dollars a week or by twenty dollars if no one was present to claim the big money on the previous Saturday.

As a kid growing up near Wheaton, all I knew about George Fagan, with the exception of the way he dressed, was that he rented a room and took many of his meals in Silas McQueen's boardinghouse just south of the bank; that he had notarized the distribution of my great-grandfather George Riley Kelly's will; that he was a prominent member of the Masonic Order (Comfort Lodge No. 533 AF & AM) in Wheaton; that he was one of the serious players at the croquet court at the west end of Main Street; and that my dad and Granddad always spoke to him politely when they saw him.

"How'd do, George," Granddad Lamberson would say when they met on the street in Wheaton.

"Fine, Earn, just fine," George would reply. And despite the fact that he had lived in Wheaton longer than I had been alive, George's means of support was just as mysterious when I graduated from high school in 1957 as when I started first grade.

My curiosity about George and the details of his life lingered. In the 1990s, as I was in Wheaton visiting my old friend Joe Higgs, Joe mentioned that when he graduated from Wheaton High in 1956, George wrote him a letter encouraging him to go out into the world and do great things. Joe said the letter had been a source of inspiration for him as he became an air force officer and one of the nation's elite fighter pilots.

Joe said something else about George that I thought was even more intriguing. Like me, Joe never understood how George supported himself. But Joe said that Leslie Phillips, who was Wheaton's postmaster for nearly two decades, told him that for many years on the same day of every week, a manila envelope with no return address arrived for George Fagan. Leslie speculated that it contained money, but he never knew for sure, Joe told me.

The contents of George's envelopes and the sender's identity are still a mystery, but thanks to George's penchant for keeping records, plus records kept by the US Army and George's writings in the *Wheaton Journal,* a bit more of George's life can be pieced together. According to his obituary, he got off the M&NA passenger train at the Wheaton Depot and walked into Wheaton on January 23, 1930. The Depression had just started, and whether the stock market crash or other misfortune had struck George, no one knows. But Leslie, who remembered George's arrival, told Joe that George was traveling light, carrying only one suitcase as he stepped into Wheaton that day, just a few weeks shy of his forty-fifth birthday.

Other than the fact that he was born in Cherokee County, Kansas, on March 1, 1885, we know little about George Fagan before he joined the US Army at the age of thirty-two, shortly after the country's entry into World War I. Thirty-two was a mature age for a recruit but not without precedent in those days. Harry Truman, a thirty-third degree Mason like George, entered the army for World War I duty when he was thirty-three. Wheaton's physician and bank owner, Dr. Otis Sheridan McCall, volunteered for the army in 1917 at the ripe age, for a soldier, of forty-seven.

George's self-penned obituary said he had been a sergeant in the Forty-Third Ambulance and Field Hospital Company of the Eighth Division of the US Army. The Eighth Division, popularly known as the "Pathfinder Division," was organized in the sunny climes of Camp Fremont near Palo Alto in Northern California on December 17, 1917. Men from across the United States came to Camp Fremont to begin their basic training. There's no record of where George was living when he enlisted in the army or whether he volunteered because he was patriotic or for some other reason.

In late August 1918, approximately five thousand men and one hundred officers were transferred out of the division to the American Expeditionary Force in Siberia to try to bring order to the area during the Russian Revolution. George's company, however, stayed at Camp Fremont to continue training for the war in Europe.

On October 18, 1918, the men of a reconstituted Eighth Division, once again up to full strength, got orders to Camp Mills, Long Island, New York, where they would ship out for the fighting in France. They were to go across country by train. By the end of the month, some of the division's infantry, artillery, and engineering units did sail for France. But George's Forty-Third Ambulance and Field Hospital Company hadn't left when the armistice was signed, so its orders to France were canceled. Instead, they were sent from Camp Mills to Camp Lee, Virginia, where they were discharged in February 1919, following the armistice of November 11, 1918.[177]

We have no record of Sergeant George Fagan's thoughts on the trip across country as his company prepared to ship out, but thanks to an essay written by a soldier in the ammunition unit of George's Eighth Division, we get a pretty good idea of what he experienced. George's company was part of what was referred to at the time as the division's "sanitary train"—the precursor to today's medical battalion.

The three-thousand-mile train trip across the United States was not without peril, according to the ammo soldier, who made the same journey as George but in a different railcar. The ammo soldier wrote:

The trip across the Continent was made during the height of the influenza epidemic, but, due largely to the excellent physical condition of the men and the skill and faithfulness of the surgeons, of which too much cannot be said, only two men were lost through disease out of a total of eleven hundred and fifty-four.[178]

When the troops arrived at Camp Mills on Long Island on October 28, 1918, they discovered that the barracks weren't completed, so the entire division had to pitch tents and sleep on the ground. As they were undergoing medical examinations and receiving their overseas equipment, they got orders to ship out of nearby Hoboken, New Jersey, on November 3.

Then the army did one of its "hurry up and wait" routines. The next day, the troops got fresh orders that delayed their departure until November 4. The day after that, they got an order that again delayed their ship-out date twenty-four hours. On the third day, yet another order made their time of embarkation indefinite. They waited … and waited. On November 11, the armistice was signed.

The Eighth Division troops still waiting at Camp Mills to go "over there," in the words of George M. Cohan's popular song of the day, had extremely mixed feelings, according to the ammo doughboy, who wrote:

> The noise of the celebration in New York twenty miles away failed to find a responding cheer in the entire Train. They were not sorry that war was over, but they felt that all of their efforts and sacrifices had come to nothing, and that they had been denied the opportunity of their lives to share in the greatest work ever given an army or nation to perform.

Sergeant Fagan and the remainder of his disappointed division wouldn't be going to the front in France. Instead, they boarded the transport USS *President Grant* and sailed to Norfolk, Virginia, on November 25. They wore life preservers and were ordered to look out for "undiscovered floating mines," the ammo soldier wrote. Before they left Long Island, however, they had been given "liberal pass privileges," which enabled them "to visit New York City and neighboring points of interest, a privilege they took advantage of to the limit," the ammo soldier reported. George undoubtedly would have been among those soldiers enjoying the sights of the great city before sailing to Virginia's Camp Lee.

"After Camp Mills, with its cold and wind and its tents, dirt floors, and lack of mess halls, Camp Lee, with its barracks, comfortable beds, roomy mess halls, and splendid bathing facilities, seemed the height of perfection," wrote the ammo soldier. George, I'm sure, would have agreed. And he undoubtedly would have shared the disappointment of the ammo doughboy, who wrote:

[T]he great incentive had been taken out of the life of the Train, and while the forms of military courtesy remained intact and there was still much snap and precision in the drill, the spirit was gone, and the one thought of the men was expressed in the popular call, 'I want to go home,' and now the orders for demobilization have come.

George must have felt those same emotions when his Forty-Third Ambulance and Field Hospital Company was mustered out in February 1919.

With one exception, nothing is known about the mysterious little man from Kansas during the eleven years from the end of his World War I service until he arrived in Wheaton in January 1930. In an article published in the *Wheaton Journal* on June 22, 1950, George mentions a conversation with a friend, W. F. "Billy" Kurtz, an assistant postmaster in Columbus, Kansas, in 1923. Columbus is in Cherokee County, where George was born. So during the Roaring Twenties, George may have gone home to Kansas.

We pick up on George on May 29, 1930, four months after he got off the M&NA train and walked into Wheaton. Under "Local News" an item read, "George Fagan spent the weekend in Joplin." Joplin is only twenty-seven miles from George's hometown of Columbus, Kansas, and it was also the northernmost point of the M&NA Railroad, which he took to Wheaton.

Starting with a *Wheaton Journal* article dated April 5, 1934, we begin to get a picture of George Fagan's puckish sense of humor. George describes an election to select a new member of Wheaton's Board of Trustees, the equivalent of a city council. The article begins mysteriously by referring to someone called "Swift."

MACHINE POLITICS

In the City election Tuesday the ticket headed by "Swift" was elected unanimously, the opposition not even having a "look-in." In fact, it more nearly represented a field day than an election, or a big league ball game with "Swift" in the role of pitcher, allowing no hits, no runs and no errors. While the day was singularly free from any riots, which is to be attributed to the good judgment of the citizenry, it is still hard to understand why the forces opposed to the "ticket" did not make a better showing. However, the result proves what a master politician with a good organization can do. If "Swift" can be induced to announce for a county office—he is qualified to administer any of them in a first-class, businesslike manner—he can be assured of the united support of all who know him, regardless of political affiliation, in the general election. He has a head and knows how to use it.

The following were elected as a Board of Trustees at the election Tuesday: M.F. Francis, Dr. J.A. Edmondson, G.M. Turner, A.D. Wiseley and Walter Brattin. Dr. C.W. Poor was slated on the ticket by the retiring Board but as he resides outside the City limits he was disqualified and the person to receive the next highest number of votes was Mr. Brattin. The newly elected Board met Tuesday and organized by electing M.F. Francis chairman and George Fagan secretary.[179]

A week later, the *Journal* carried an article that made it clear that "Swift" was Mayor Maynard F. Francis, who operated a grocery store in Wheaton.

"SWIFT" MEETS THE TRAIN

The special train carrying a delegation of Joplin businessman, their wives and an 18-piece band stopped at Wheaton Wednesday morning on schedule. Mayor Francis had repeatedly stated he did not wish to deliver an address of welcome because the Board of Trustees would not provide him with a silk hat and a frock coat for the occasion. However, he was on hand, his face all wreathed in smiles like a full moon, and in a few well-chosen words, delivered the key to the City to the Joplin Boosters. In accepting the key, Mr. Earl Brown, Secretary of the Joplin Chamber of Commerce, told Mr. Francis he was the best looking Mayor he had seen for many a day and that he had been looking at Mayors a long, long time.

The citizens of Wheaton who were unable to be present will not realize that Mr. Francis is a sure-enough Mayor. He is going to be easy to get along with, but he intends to give Wheaton a business administration. He is a stickler for details and it isn't going to be easy to slip anything over on him.

Just a word of explanation about the hat and coat—the Board may decide later to provide them for him, but they wish to wait and see what kind of an automobile he plans to use in his official capacity. They wish the hat to fit the car and not have to provide a car to fit the hat. It has been claimed that something like that has happened in the past.[180]

Then, in the June 14, 1934, edition of the *Journal*, George got serious, revealing to the readers that he was the author of the "Swift" articles:

GEO. FAGAN ANNOUNCES FOR CIRCUIT CLERK

In announcing for the office of Circuit Clerk of Barry County, subject to the will of the democratic voters August 7, I herewith submit the following information for your consideration. I am qualified for the office by reason of many years experience in clerical work, both in civil life and in The United States Army during the World War. I am engaged in the real estate business at Wheaton, being a member of the Daugherty Realty Company. Owing to financial and other reasons it will be impossible for me to see very many of the voters personally, therefore I am taking this opportunity of asking your support. To those with whom I am not personally acquainted, I refer you to any citizen of Wheaton.

Geo. Fagan

There will be no more "Swift" stories until after the election.

George never explained the "other reasons" that prevented him from seeing "very many" of the voters personally, but there is no evidence George ever owned a car, even though there is evidence that he could drive.

In the August 1934 primary election, George easily carried the City of Wheaton, receiving 143 votes. His nearest competitor, Truman Thompson, received eighteen votes in Wheaton. But when the votes of Democrats from all of Barry County were counted, George fell short. He came in fourth, with 529 votes, while the winner, Otis Cox, got 1,141. It was the high-water mark of George Fagan's attempts to win elected office, but it was not the last of the "Swift" articles.

Two years later, on August 13, 1936, George signed an article thanking the persons who had placed him on the Democratic primary election ticket for the office of Justice of the Peace. The article implied he hadn't been aware he had been placed on the ticket until it was too late for him to remove his name. He said he wasn't qualified for the office, but it was gratifying to know he had tied with "one of the very best men in the county," J. W. Hazel. He and Hazel had each received twenty-two votes, and the winner, Rex Davis, got thirty-one.[181]

George ended his article with one last tongue-in-cheek mention of "Swift:"

I am not qualified for the office of Justice of the Peace either by training, experience or temperament. Should I be elected, it is very likely that I would be entirely too severe in assessing punishment against evil-doers. As an example: If "Swift" was ever brought before me charged with a crime I would give him the limit without taking the trouble to docket the case. So, for the good of the cause and the peace of mind of all concerned, I am asking you to support Mr. J.W. Hazel in the General Election; but I do appreciate your support nevertheless. Geo. Fagan[182]

The record doesn't show whether George, a Democrat, favored Silas McQueen, a Republican, over "Swift" Francis for mayor, but it does show that from time to time, George and Silas journeyed to out-of-town meetings to support Wheaton's opposition to trucking companies that wanted exclusive rights to haul goods and produce in and out of Wheaton. And for many years, George roomed at Silas and Lettie's big house south of the Bank of Wheaton.

As George was withdrawing from the contest for justice of the peace on the Democratic ticket, Silas and Lettie were elected Barry County Committeeman and Committeewoman, respectively, on the Republican ticket.

Whether George actually thought he wasn't qualified to be Justice of the Peace or whether he simply didn't want the job is anybody's guess, but he was considered by the Democratic Party establishment to be qualified for other posts. A year earlier, when the Old Age Assistance portion of the Social Security Act went into effect, he had been appointed a member of the Barry County Board that administered the new law.

George continued to be recognized for his judgment and administrative skills. On December 7, 1941 (ironically, Pearl Harbor Day), he was appointed a member of the Advisory Board of Registrants of the Selective Service System of the United States.

It's likely that if George Fagan's political views had been thoroughly understood by lots of folks around Wheaton, he might have been viewed with more skepticism. On June 22, 1950, just three days before the Communist North Korean army invaded South Korea and started the Korean War, the *Wheaton Journal* published a long, complex article that George had first drafted ten years earlier before the United States was drawn into World War II by the Japanese attack on the US naval base at Pearl Harbor.[183]

George had put the draft article in his desk, where it lay for a decade until he read a newspaper story about a speech that Bernard Baruch, the noted philanthropist, statesman, and advisor to presidents Woodrow Wilson and Franklin D. Roosevelt, delivered at Columbia University in New York in May 1950. Baruch proposed an idea that he had first advocated in the 1920s called a "work or fight" law. The proposal had sometimes been called "universal conscription," meaning that when the United States needed to mobilize in preparation for a war, the federal government could nationalize the banking system, draft men for the military and essential civilian jobs, set prices, and exercise complete control over the economy to restrict war profiteering by industrialists and big business interests.

Baruch's speech, George explained in a letter to *Journal* editor Wally Fox, reminded him of the article he had drafted on September 16, 1940. George's article proposed that when the nation needed to mobilize to fight a war, the federal government should conscript "the entire resources of the nation along with the manpower"—the very same idea Baruch was still advocating in 1950.

George noted that he came up with the notion shortly after he enlisted in the army in 1917 when he saw a number of men in the San Francisco area signing up as ironworkers so they could escape the draft. Ironworkers were draft exempt during World War I. George didn't like that, and he began to think of a way to keep men from dodging the draft.

In 1923, his hometown friend, assistant postmaster Billy Kurtz in Columbus, Kansas, submitted George's universal conscription proposal to the American Legion's national convention, which adopted it as a resolution that was later considered by the US Congress. In 1924, both the Republican and Democratic Party platforms endorsed "universal conscription."

Then in 1940, when President Franklin D. Roosevelt signed a fairly broad conscription act to prepare the country for war, George drafted the article that explained how he got the idea in 1917. But the draft stayed in his desk until 1950. George claimed that in addition to the support of the American Legion and Bernard Baruch, the idea of universal conscription was advocated by no less than the American humorist and social commentator Will Rogers.

It was a radical and controversial idea that was never adopted, despite George's speculation that "statesmen of the caliber of Henry

Clay, Daniel Webster, John C. Calhoun, Abraham Lincoln, and men of their type" probably would agree with him and Bernard Baruch.

Not only was George well liked by the adults around Wheaton; he also enjoyed the friendship of lots of Wheaton's young people. Jo Ann Fox—now Jo Ann Fox Hughes, daughter of *Journal* publishers Wally and Bessie Fox—was seven years old when George entered the Veterans Hospital in Fayetteville, Arkansas, in the summer of 1939 after suffering two heart attacks. Jo Ann liked George and was sorry he was in the hospital, so she took her crayons and red pencil and wrote him a letter. After he recovered, George, in a letter to someone named Margaret, described Jo Ann's letter and commented on how much he enjoyed it:

> Margaret, I had a lot of letters and cards from the folks here, but the prize of them all was from Jo Ann. Jo Ann wrote me a little letter with a red pencil and told me all the news she could think of, closing by saying her daddy was better. Then she drew a line across the page and drew a bed complete with pillow, counterpane, etc., and a patient in it. She indicated that I was the patient. She had a small table with a vase with flowers and a do-dad hanging on the wall with a "I love you" on it. Margaret, I wouldn't take five dollars for that letter and cartoon. But I do intend to attach a note to it with instructions it be returned to her mother or dad in the event of my death and returned to her when she graduates from high school, and if I should live until then I will give it to her myself. That young lady is in a class all by herself and is too young to know it, and I hope she never finds it out.[184]

George observed that his time "from here on out is very uncertain." But he lived another twenty-six years, long enough to see Jo Ann graduate from Wheaton High and honor his promise to return her letter to her. He also lived long enough to write to Joe Higgs when Joe graduated in 1956, but not long enough to know how much his letter inspired Joe throughout his career as an air force fighter pilot.

There were other Wheaton youngsters who George befriended. Bobby Gene Davidson, who grew up in Wheaton in the '30s and '40s, said:

> George Fagan was a special friend. He had an office on Main Street when I was in early grade school ... I used to visit him there as a small boy. We had an arrangement whereby he would pay me for making good grades. It was handled almost like a business agreement. He was always very encouraging. When I graduated from KU (Kansas University) I got a wonderful, encouraging letter from him that I still have.[185]

George not only was a friend to Wheaton's youngsters, he also had a soft spot for his faithful dog, Buck. George was so despondent when Buck barked his last in May 1946 that his friend Bernice Viles—the married daughter of Silas and Lettie McQueen who owned the house where George boarded—wrote a poetic tribute to George's canine pal that was printed in the *Journal*.[186]

"Old Buck"
OLD BUCK—just another dog!
To many who passed his way,
But to the ones who loved him
He was part of every day.

Food and water—a place to rest
Was all he asked of one;
He was so very watchful
Of a stranger who might come.

He protected those he loved,
His eyes alone could tell;
The thanks he gave for kindness
And he was treated well

Each year at hunting season
Old Buck was ready to go;
And when he looked at the hunters
Somehow they couldn't say no.

Buck was ever true to his friends
His eyes gave thanks for every care;
Tho we're told dogs have no Heaven
He must be at rest somewhere.

He didn't suffer as long
As people sometimes do;
But the helplessness of his suffering
Brought grief to those he knew.

So Buck this is my tribute
You were a dog true blue;
I wish that men with souls
Could be just as true as you.

Oh give me ever compassion
For a dog who passes my way.
Let him be to me ever
A part of every day.

(By) Bernice (McQueen) Viles
Dedicated to George Fagan, who was Buck's friend.

Just below Bernice's poem in the *Journal,* George penned a separate tribute to Old Buck that was front-page *Journal* news:

A Tribute to a Friend

Buck, my friend, you were only a dog. I remember you as an awkward, half-grown pup. It never occurred to me that I would develop any particular attachment for you, but as the years passed I came to know and understand you as an unusual fellow.

In addition to being a first-class hunting dog, much in demand during quail season, you assumed duties for yourself for each day of the year. A dozen time a day you escorted those whom you had adopted to and fro as they went about their respective chores. Between these acts of chivalry you had your own activities; carrying bones from the rear of the market to the yard where you could gnaw on them at your leisure, barking at other dogs, guarding the youngsters at play and many other things you considered it your duty to perform. Perhaps you may have incurred the ill will of some, but probably no one seriously criticized you.

Night time and you were at the front door still looking after the welfare of your friends within. When I returned late at night from a tour of studying the planets, you were always at your post to welcome me home.

Also, I shall not forget your last valiant attempt to climb the steps and take your place at the door, but your feeble strength was not equal to the occasion.

You were old and the infirmities of age had taken
their toll.

Bucky boy, you were more than a dog; you were a
friend and companion. If there is a Valhalla for dogs,
you certainly have earned the right to be there.

Geo. Fagan[187]

George loved old Buck, and he also had a passion for one of
Wheaton's foremost "sports." No, it wasn't fishing, basketball, or
baseball. It was croquet.

At the west end of Main Street, there was a fine croquet court of
packed sand with strong metal wickets, six and one-half inches wide
and set in concrete so they couldn't be moved even if they were hit
hard by one of the black, hard rubber croquet balls.[188] Those croquet
balls were apparently hard to come by, so after each session of croquet
games, they were taken home in the custody of Wheaton grocer
Ernest W. Wyatt, who lived nearby.[189] From the Depression days
of the 1930s until a year or two before my high-school graduation
in 1957, croquet was enjoyed by scores of the little town's menfolk.

Croquet was a men-only sport in Wheaton. Women and kids
had to beware if they got too close while a game was under way.
Rocky Comfort had a similar croquet court, and the rules were
the same. On the rare occasion when a boy was allowed near the
court while a game was under way, the rules were: sit on a bench,
sit still, don't talk, don't whittle, don't cough, don't fart, and make
yourself invisible. My experience was limited to a couple of times I
accompanied my great-uncle Earl Lamberson to a game. Based on
my very restricted experience and discussions with some of the town
kids who were my contemporaries, I am under the impression that
a woman never ventured near a game. The word *sexist* had not yet
entered the vocabulary of the Ozarks during the 1930s, '40s, and '50s.

George Fagan was Wheaton's—and occasionally, Rocky's—
croquet reporter. Not every week, but quite often between the

mid-1930s until the mid-1950s, George wrote reports for the *Journal*—"Echoes From the Croquet Court." In his "Echoes" reports before World War II, George sometimes used the competitors' real names, but he used a certain specialized vocabulary to describe the action. In his report of September 14, 1939, George wrote:

> Carroll Chenoweth and Ralph McKinley were the first hunters to rile the skunk's nest after the wickets had been cut down to 6 ½ inches. Charlie Frazier and Oran Cartwright were the birds that applied the skunk oil to these two big boys and they did it in about thirty minutes.

> Quite a number of the players are objecting to the new rules that have been in effect since the grounds have been widened and the wickets narrowed and no doubt they will have the rules changed back so that a player can lay his ball wherever he wishes when he roquets a ball. This is to be regretted as the present rules requiring a player to lay his ball on the line make a more skillful game.

For the uninitiated, if you were "skunked" in a croquet match, your opponent made it all the way through the course of wickets before you ever cleared a wicket with your ball.

By 1946, maybe to avoid embarrassing anyone—but more likely because George enjoyed his reports as kind of an open, but inside joke—every player adopted a "handle" or nickname known only to the regulars who played the game. In an "Echoes" report of November 10, 1949, George wrote:

> Well, it seems that wonders will never cease. There are so many degrees in SWRdom being taken that your humble scribe can't remember them all, but the climax came last Saturday evening when

Texas Leon and Ark Eddie tackled Uncle Joe and Legal Adviser in a fierce game which was to run just 30 minutes, which of course is not a legal game, as 45 minutes is the long-established rule on our court. However, the fans argue that Tex and Ark got skunked as neither made a wicket, Tex not even hitting a ball while Ark only hit one. The game only lasted 25 minutes, but it was illegal, as Tex and Ark say. Draw your own conclusions.

To this day, I don't know what "SWRdom" meant, though I suspect the *S* had something to do with "skunked," but the meaning of the *W* and the *R* are anybody's guess.

There was one other unique quality to Wheaton and Rocky Comfort's croquet players: they made their own mallets.

The process would start with a wooden rolling pin. The ends would be carefully sawed off to shorten the roller, making sure the cut was true and not slanted. Then a hole was bored into the middle of the roller, and a broom or mop handle was glued into the hole. But first the handle was cut to maybe two or two and a half feet in length so that when a ball was struck, the player was bending down close to the ball. To finish the customized short-handled mallet, a piece of thin leather was stretched over both ends of the roller to provide a smooth, flat surface for striking the ball.

Woe to anyone who messed with a player's croquet mallet.

George continued his "Echoes" reports until 1955 or '56, when croquet ceased to hold the interest of the town's menfolk, and the croquet court gave way to a Dairy Haven.

When George Fagan died in 1960, his obituary noted that he was a veteran of World War I and that he was baptized April 20, 1952, in the Methodist church at Wheaton, although he never affiliated with any church.[190] A large crowd of Masons was present for the funeral service. The Reverend Earl D. Young, a local Methodist preacher and fellow Mason, penned an article in the *Journal*:

Words cannot express the irreparable loss this community and the Masonic fraternity has suffered in the loss of our friend and brother, George Fagan, a Christian gentleman, a friend to all, and a man who believed in the Fatherhood of God and the brotherhood of all men.

Geo. Fagan was a self-educated man; his Book of Books, the Holy Bible; his creed, the golden rule; his greatest joy, in doing for others. He loved his friends, his Masonry, and his memories. He thought the "Sermon on the Mount" was the greatest message ever delivered and he read it at least twice each year, always endeavoring to live by its teachings.

Brother Fagan was a perfectionist in everything he did and expected the same in others. He often remarked that anything worth doing was worth doing well.

I'm sure George is doing well now in the great hereafter, but I'd still like to ask him five questions:
1) What was in those manila envelopes?
2) Who sent them?
3) What did you do between 1920 and 1930?
4) Why did you get off the train in Wheaton?
5) And where could I buy a pair of white spats like the ones you wore?

Courtesy of Becky Allman Roskob

Courtesy of Becky Allman Roskob

ABOVE: Wheaton Main Street, 1939

RIGHT: Allman Produce & Feed building

BELOW: The Blue Goose

Courtesy of Fields' Photo Archives

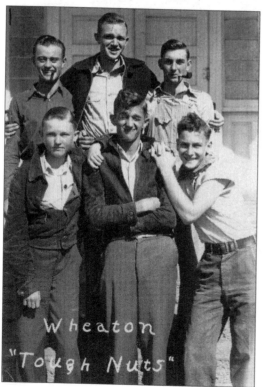

Wheaton
"Tough Nuts"

Courtesy of Becky Allman Roskob

TOP LEFT:
Leonard & Ila Brattin

TOP RIGHT:
Floyd Hughes,
Wheaton Drug proprietor

LEFT:
The Wheaton "Tough Nuts,"
Stratton Allman, front row,
center

163

LEFT: Buck & Marguerite Higgs
RIGHT: Earnest & Carrie Lamberson

From "Wheaton Echoes" Collection

Virgil Paden & Stratton Allman

Courtesy of Becky Allman Roskob

Mom & Dad:
Perry & Velma Lewis,
1932

Three generations: From left, Earn Lamberson, Oscar (Awk) Davidson,
Jimmy Lewis and Perry Lewis

165

Dan & Dick Shewmake

Dayton (Date) Brattin

The Allman crew: From left, Bill Gundell, unidentified, Glenn McTeer, Stratton Allman, Joe McNeill and Olga Lamberson

Rocky
Comfort
Church of
Christ

Church buddies:
From left, Ronnie Thomas,
Lowell (Junior) Thomas
Gale Goostree
and Jimmy Lewis

Rocky Comfort
Methodist Church

Lois Daugherty Fithian, left, and Thelma Smith

Thelma McQueen Smith

Silas McQueen

Mildred & John Crosslin and children

ABOVE: Looking east on Main Street, Wheaton, around 1920

BELOW: Rocky Comfort, early 1900s

LEFT:
Wally & Geneva
Chenoweth

BELOW:
Wal Chenoweth

From "Wheaton Echoes" collection

RIGHT: From left,
Oral Burger,
Wally Fox,
& Ernest Shewmake

Courtesy of Daniel W. Shewmake

TOP: Oscar (Awk) & Virgie Davidson wedding photo, 1906

ABOVE: Awk & Virgie from 50th anniversary *Wheaton Journal* newspaper clipping

LEFT: Back row, Earnest Lamberson & Waillans Goostree; front row, Carrie Lamberson & Linna Goostree, 1906

Courtesy of Daniel W. Shewmake

From left, Hessie Fox Shewmake & friends

Courtesy of Jo Ann Fox Hughes

Jo Ann Fox Hughes with friends
Mildred Burton & Peggy Roller

Courtesy of Daniel W. Shewmake

Dan Shewmake,
Rocky Comfort Greyhounds

Courtesy of Jo Ann Fox Hughes

Bessie & Wally Fox

From "Wheaton Echoes" collection

Wheaton Bulldogs & Coach L.D. Clemons, 1951-52
third place, Missouri state tournament

From "Wheaton Echoes" collection

Wheaton School Board: From left, Wally Fox, Floyd Daniels, Lewis Thomas,
Joe McNeill and Richard (Dick) Smith

Port Potts,
Wheaton blacksmith

From "Wheaton Echoes" collection

Courtesy of Ralph and Betty Higgs Lamberson

The restored Wheaton Depot

ABOVE: Wheaton's
railroad station agent
and violin maker
Walter William Hoyt

LEFT: Betty & Ralph
Lamberson

Rocky Comfort Church of Christ "Dinner on the Ground," October 1945: Among attendees, from left, in hat eating cake, Dudley Biggs; in large circle, Murvin & Geneva Spencer; in gray suit & white hair, Elbert Stewart; woman in hat & dark suit, Virgie Davidson; small circle, Cumi Biggs

Jimmy Lewis, 8th grade graduation

Courtesy of Daniel W. Shewmake

Dan Shewmake, 8th grade graduation

Palo Stewart

"Uncle" Marion Foster

Earl Lamberson
Wheaton postmaster

From left, Clovis & Grace Flaxbeard,
Nina & Grant Robinson

Wheaton flagpole &
concrete barrier

From "Wheaton Echoes" collection

Wheaton girls from left: Virginia Robinson, Jill Paden,
Shirley Birkes & Ann Ruth Burton

Dr. Otis Sheridan &
Linnie McCall

From "Wheaton Echoes" collection

Wheaton Hospital 1937,
built by Dr. McCall in 1924

From "Wheaton Echoes" collection

Barney Bates in his Wheaton jewelry store

Barney Bates & daughter Jeanie
1941

Bates Jewelry grand opening

Barney Bates, outside his
jewelry store

Photos Courtesy of Gary and Maxine Bates and Jeanie Bates Eubanks

Dr. John Ellison

James Cantrell, 7th grade

Henry Lombard's chicken truck

10

The "May Never Arrive"

When the big black steam locomotive pulling the M&A freight train chugged and puffed into Wheaton—metal wheels grinding and squeaking against the rails until it came to a stop under the old round elevated water tank—a railroad fireman would yank the rope that released the spout.[191] Down it would come, and water would pour into the boiler tank.

It wouldn't be long before the boiler popped off steam with a crack that, to my preschool ears, sounded like a stick of dynamite and scared the peewaddin' out of me. Once, when I was in Granddad Lamberson's old Model A Ford parked in front of the Farmers Exchange on Main Street, there were two quick pop-offs. I hopped off the front seat of his car and cowered on the floorboard, covering both of my ears with my hands. Granddad laughed uproariously, contributing to my humiliation.[192]

But watching the train coming in and leaving was fun, especially when it was leaving and picking up speed with chugs that got shorter and faster as it rolled down the tracks. And visiting the depot with Granddad was even more fun. There might be boxcars full of lumber waiting on a sidetrack for the town's two lumberyards to unload and boxes of everything from canned goods for the grocery stores to farm implements for the hardware store waiting for pickup on the loading dock. The depot was like nothing else I had ever seen in the years before I started first grade.

Walter William Hoyt, the station agent, was a kindly, friendly man. Granddad knew him well, and he was nice to me when we visited the depot at the east end of Main Street. I particularly remember that Granddad and Grandma had ordered a new wood heating stove for their farmhouse three miles west of town, and that was the reason for one visit.

A fascinating thing about Mr. Hoyt was that in his spare time as he was waiting for the trains to come in—or when he wasn't tapping out a message on the telegraph key to check on a train schedule—he carved fiddles. A few years later, I learned that he was the grandfather of kids who became my good friends in the seventh grade, Joe and Betty Higgs.

I was too young to even think about asking Granddad how he and Mr. Hoyt became so well acquainted, but I suspect it was during the 1920s when Virgil "Honk" Ford, Granddad, and two of his brothers, Burt and Tan, had grown great quantities of strawberries and shipped them out of Wheaton under the Ford and Lamberson Brothers label.[193] They had begun their strawberry operation in the early 1920s, and they continued to grow and ship berries on the train until after Mr. Hoyt came to Wheaton as station agent for the Missouri & North Arkansas Railroad (M&NA), in 1925.[194] In 1935, the M&NA went bankrupt and was purchased by a Texan, Frank Kell, and renamed the Missouri & Arkansas Railway Company—the M&A.[195] Strikes and labor disputes plagued both the M&NA and the M&A, and after a strike in 1946, the M&A closed, and the last train ran through Wheaton.[196]

Decades would pass before I learned that the early days of the railroad were far more troubled and violent than I ever suspected.

The railroad had its beginnings in Eureka Springs, Arkansas, in the early 1880s when a former Civil War Union Army general and Arkansas governor named Powell Clayton moved to Eureka Springs, a thriving town that was becoming famous as a health resort because of its mineral springs. Clayton and a group of his wealthy friends formed the Eureka Springs Railway and combined it with the Missouri and Arkansas Railroad Company of Missouri to form the Eureka Springs Railway that linked the resort town to the St. Louis and San Francisco (Frisco) line at Seligman, Missouri—a distance of 18.5 miles.[197]

By the late 1890s, however, Eureka Springs' attraction as a health resort was fading at about the same time that interest in lead and zinc mining was increasing fifty miles to the southeast near Harrison, Arkansas, and beyond. Powell and his backers went to work, raised more money, and extended the rail line south to Harrison. On May 25, 1899, the Eureka Springs Railway became the St. Louis and North Arkansas Railroad (SL&NAR).[198] The line was stretched farther to the southeast, reaching Leslie, Arkansas, in 1903.[199]

Then in 1906, the SL&NAR went into receivership, but the owners weren't deterred. They reorganized, poured more money into the venture, and formed the Missouri and North Arkansas Railroad—the M&NA.[200] The M&NA immediately negotiated an agreement to allow it to use the Frisco tracks from Seligman to Woodruff, later to be known as Wayne, about three miles south of Exeter, Missouri. From there, the M&NA would finance the laying of tracks to Neosho, Missouri. At Neosho, the M&NA would use the Kansas City Southern's tracks to connect with Joplin, Missouri. From Joplin, passengers could go on to Kansas City, 160 miles to the north, on the Kansas City Southern line.[201]

By 1909, a passenger could board the train in Kansas City and go as far south as Helena, Arkansas, on the west side of the Mississippi River, seventy-five miles south of West Memphis, Arkansas, and Memphis, Tennessee.[202] But the owners' grand plan to connect with railroads that could take freight and passengers all the way to New Orleans couldn't be completed, because the railroads that could have connected with the M&NA to take passengers farther south already had made other arrangements.[203]

The M&NA was in financial trouble from the git-go. By the time the tracks were laid through Tommy Shewmake's wheat field two and a half miles northeast of Rocky Comfort and Wheaton began to be built in 1907, the newly formed M&NA already was losing money.[204] It wouldn't turn a profit until the year before the US government took over the nation's railroads to support the mobilization for World War I in 1917.[205]

Another concern for the M&NA in the early years it served Wheaton was the lack of dependability that plagued the M&NA's passengers. Trains often were late, and because of that, people started calling the M&NA the "May Never Arrive."[206] Business slackened, and in 1912, the railroad went into receivership.[207] That same year, in an effort to reverse its fortunes and put the railroad into the black, the M&NA purchased two fancy passenger cars. Ed Tolle of Eureka Springs, Arkansas, in his excellent history, *The Eureka Springs Railway: A Short-Line Railroad to a Little Town,* describes what the railcars looked like and how they were powered:

> These all-steel cars were beautiful in many ways, and operated at a fraction of the cost of steam powered locomotives. They were Pullman green in color with gold lettering, had interiors of finished mahogany, plush frizette seats, and could seat up to 85 passengers when fully loaded. Motive power was supplied by twin electric engines that ran on electricity furnished by two gasoline-fueled generators. The gasoline for the generators was stored in overhead tanks that ran almost the entire length of the car.[208]

What were the engineers thinking? Overhead gasoline tanks running the length of the car? The luxurious cars were a death trap. Tolle describes what happened on August 5, 1914, when one of the fancy cars left Joplin "bound for Eureka Springs":

> It had a full load of passengers, with some standing in the aisle. It left Joplin, designated as passenger train #209 while riding the Kansas City Southern tracks, and would have become M&NA #5

once it reached Seligman. Its orders called for it to take a siding at Tipton Ford, 10.8 miles from Joplin.[209] There it should have remained (on a side track) until a northbound freight train cleared that station.

For reasons that were never to be known with any degree of certainty, the passenger train did not stop at Tipton Ford—and ran head-on into the northbound train. A total of 43 people aboard the motor car were killed, none from the freight train. Several of those killed were burned to death by a fire fueled from the motor cars' ruptured gasoline tanks—those still conscious pleading to be released or killed before the flames reached them.

All of the M&NA crew were killed in the accident and the courts were unable to decide definitely just who was at fault. Each line was left to pay for its own expenses, liability and equipment damage. The M&NA assumed by far the greater part of that burden. It never fully recovered from the results of the tragedy.[210]

Legal wrangling related to the crash continued until 1918. A handwriting expert offered the opinion that someone in the Kansas City Southern organization had forged the signature verifying that the M&NA passenger crew had received the Kansas City Southern orders to stop at Tipton Ford until the freight train passed. Eventually, when the case went to trial, a jury awarded the M&NA $190,000. When the Kansas City Southern line appealed, the appellate court decided that the M&NA and the Kansas City Southern should share the liability equally and that each of the rail lines would have to pay for its own property damages. The M&NA came out of the legal wrangle with a pittance—$50,000—but with a moral victory.[211]

Among those who died in the burning wreck were J. R. Patterson, a well-known farmer who lived southwest of Rocky Comfort, and Thomas P. "Little Perry" Duncan, a Fairview barber.[212]

Another problem was brewing for the M&NA. Before World War I, which the United States entered in 1917, the M&NA had paid a wage that was significantly lower than that for trainmen in other parts of the country, because the cost of living was much lower in the Missouri and Arkansas Ozarks.[213] When the Woodrow Wilson administration nationalized the railroads in December 1917 to mobilize for the war effort, every railroad employee in the country got a generous salary increase. Ed Tolle explains what happened to the M&NA when the government stepped in:

> Being brought up to the national (wage) standard, and with a 16 percent raise offered to all railroaders on April 30, 1918, retroactive to January 1 of that year, M&NA employees received what amounted to almost a 100% increase in salary. (While the government also increased freight rates by 25 percent, and raised passenger rates to 3 cents a mile, these increases would not make up for the retroactive part of the pay hike.)[214]

The M&NA's unionized employees were in clover. They got a big pay boost during the war when the government controlled both the pay scale for railroad workers and the level of reimbursement paid to each railroad for operations costs.

But the level of government reimbursement that went to the M&NA for its operational costs was far too low. The reimbursement policy was designed to guarantee railroads the same level of profit that they had enjoyed during each line's last three years of operation, so each railroad was paid based on its average income between 1914 and 1917. The averaging policy hurt the M&NA, because it hadn't started turning a profit until 1916. So the M&NA was reimbursed on a formula that averaged one year of profit and two years of loss at the same time that the government had ordered huge salary increases for its employees.[215] Even with a government policy that was supposed to be generous to the railroads, the M&NA didn't come out ahead.

After the war ended on November 11, 1918, the government eventually relaxed its financial control of the railroads on March 1, 1920, and the rail lines reverted to the management of their private owners. But because of the government-imposed pay raises, the M&NA's payroll for its highly unionized employees was 66 percent greater than it had been before the war.[216]

The stage was set for a labor-management clash. The "lush salary" of M&NA general manager C. A. Phelan enraged the rail line's workers.[217] When management told them they would have to take an immediate cut in wages if the rail line was to stay in business, shop men at M&NA headquarters in Harrison walked off their jobs on February 1, 1921.[218]

The rest of the unionized employees followed the shop men twenty-five days later. Tolle writes:

> The general membership of the unions saw little to be gained by further meetings. At 3:00 P.M., February 26, the engineers, firemen, hostlers, conductors, trainmen, yardmen, agents, telegraphers, train dispatchers, and maintenance men started what was to be one of the longest and bloodiest strikes, both figuratively and literally, in U.S. railroad history.[219]

In Wheaton, as in other small towns along the M&NA rail line in both Missouri and Arkansas, feelings about the strike were running high. Although there was some sympathy for the strikers, the overwhelming sentiment among townspeople, and particularly the merchants, was in favor of the M&NA management.

During the first year of the strike, the citizens of the M&NA headquarters town of Harrison, Arkansas, were "initially sympathetic toward the strikers," according to the Encyclopedia of Arkansas History & Culture's section titled *Harrison Railroad Riot*. "However," the article continued, "that sympathy soon evaporated, especially as the economic hardships of the strike took hold and as striking workers engaged in violence and sabotage, such as attacking 'scabs' and burning railroad bridges." That same pattern of initial sympathy for the strikers, followed by strong opposition to the walkout, occurred in many of the small towns up and down the line.

In July of 1921, it seemed that the strikers had the upper hand. The M&NA went into receivership, and the railroad was shut down until May 1922, when a US District Court in Little Rock, Arkansas, ordered the railroad sold.[220] The company simply reorganized and hired enough nonstriking employees to get the line running again. But it was a risky task because of the violence that was about to erupt all the way from Neosho in Missouri to the end of the line in Helena, Arkansas.

Sympathy for the strikers never did gain a foothold in Wheaton. Wheaton's merchants and most of the area's farmers were outraged by the strike, which was the first time a major labor dispute had ever come to that part of the Ozarks where people had a tradition of gritting their teeth and working harder to accomplish their goals. Striking, as a tool to increase pay or benefits, was regarded as less than honorable by a heavy majority of the citizens in Wheaton and most of the small towns along the line in both Missouri and Arkansas.

Support for the railroad's management, however, was uneven, and there were places where strikers received strong sympathy. One of those places was in neighboring Fairview, only five miles northwest of Wheaton.

Maurice Lamberson, editor of the *Wheaton Journal*, scorched the editor of the *Fairview News Herald* for his critical view of the M&NA in a May 12, 1922, article:[221]

> In commenting upon our new Railway Company, the editor of the *Fairview News Herald* says the following in this week's issue:
>
> It has been thirty days since the sale of the M&NA and no trains have been operated over the line as to

schedule time. A work train has been whistling along the line and a 'hog' train is reported to be operating between Seligman, Mo., and Leslie, Ark. About all that can be expected of 'road-wrecking' managers is a howl for more freight rate and a lower wage scale. The loss of money has been enormous to people living along the line and we are tired of promises—we want real service.

After quoting the *Fairview News Herald* editor, a "Mr. Dougan," Maurice let him have it:

We feel quite sure, Mr. Dougan, that you have misinterpreted the sentiment of the people along the line when you say that they are dissatisfied with the management and the effort that is being made to restore service.

We understand there will be one of your so-called "hog" trains up on this end next week and we don't believe there would be any serious objection to you crawling into the swine department and taking a ride. Your "grunts" wouldn't disturb the rest of the hogs.

The May 12, 1922, *Journal* reported that a "work train, the first to be operated on this end of the line for more than nine months, arrived in Wheaton Sunday afternoon and with only the warning of the whistle a crowd of several hundred people had gathered at the station before its arrival. We'll admit that trains are very commonplace things and all look more or less alike, but put them on a road where you thought perhaps you would never see a train again and they take on an entirely different appearance. They look better—the whistle sounds better, and there's a different feeling among the people who have waited for the past nine months while the fate of the road was all a question."

The article also reported that an M&NA station agent, F. E. Vining, arrived in Wheaton Sunday to take charge of the local station. The M&NA was trying to break the strike, but the next eighteen months would be a war.

By June of 1922, when the strike was sixteen months old, a crowd of Wheaton's citizens gathered and organized a "Citizens Law-Enforcement and Protective League" primarily, the *Journal* article said, "for the purpose of putting an end to the depredations which have been committed against the M&NA since the resumption of service a few weeks ago."[222]

A committee of three prominent Wheaton citizens—Dr. Otis S. McCall, a medical doctor and bank president; Silas McQueen, a business and civic leader; and William A. Davidson, cashier of the Bank of Wheaton—drafted a flaming resolution against the strikers and in favor of M&NA management that was unanimously adopted by Wheaton's assembled citizens. The resolution, among other things, declared the group to be "one hundred percent American" and demanded "a respect for the laws of our country."

It condemned the "depredations" that included "putting acid in the water tanks, disabling pumping stations, throwing off switches, subjecting to insult men in the employ of the company who are satisfied with their work and pay, and firing at trainmen while concealed with the robe of a midnight assassin ..." All those actions were denounced "as Bolshevism in its ugliest form and a menace, not only to our community, but to the nation as a whole." If the resolution had been drafted thirty years later, it is likely that "Bolshevism" would have been replaced by "Communism," but that terminology had not yet evolved.

The resolution declared that the United States Labor Board had investigated the living conditions and earning capacity of the M&NA employees and set the wage scale, so the strikers' effort to "hinder and prevent honest efficient laboring men from operating the road" was "Unamerican." The document also vowed to "hold responsible every member of the organization (presumably, the American Federation of Labor) of said former employees for these dastardly and cowardly deeds unless the organization and its individual members help to bring to justice the person or persons committing such crimes."[223]

The resolution didn't do much to stop the strikers. A week after it was approved by Wheaton's "Citizens Law Enforcement and Protective League," the *Journal* reported that a forty-foot bridge on the Al Hudson farm north of Fairview (about five or six miles northwest of Wheaton) had been discovered in flames the previous Sunday morning. John Armstrong, the M&NA's former station agent at Fairview, and Arthur Skelton, a member of the section crew before the strike, were arrested and taken to the Newton County jail in Neosho.

Later in the week, Wheaton's former postmaster, Elbert H. Davis, who had succeeded Silas McQueen in that post in 1914 and who served until 1921, was arrested and taken to jail at Neosho "on a charge of having put blue vitriol in the water tank at Stark City."[224] Blue vitriol, or copper sulfate, can coat a boiler and damage its ability to produce steam. Davis also had once worked in Wheaton's railway station.[225] The charge against him was dismissed two weeks later as Armstrong requested a change of venue, and a trial date was set for Skelton.[226]

Journal editor Maurice Lamberson seemed to speak for the majority of the Wheaton community when in an editorial of June 30, 1922, he criticized the *Cassville Democrat* and other area newspapers for publishing what he called "glaring accounts" of how persons in other towns had mistreated striking M&NA employees. He wrote, in part:

> Most of the papers describe the bitter feeling existing in this community against those who are committing crimes against the road. To this we plead guilty and we have no apology to offer for it. Almost to a man we are for the road and mean to see that it has a fair opportunity to operate. We're proud of the men who have taken the lead. Likewise, we are

ashamed of the few who, for business reasons or otherwise, are not taking a stand on either side.

We have no mercy for men who wantonly destroy the railroad property; who threaten the welfare of hundreds of thousands of people and jeopardize human life. Such men justly deserve the fate pictured by some of our neighboring papers, but even then it should be done within the law.

In an excellent 1923 book about the strike, the late Rev. Walter F. Bradley of Harrison, Arkansas, described one of the reasons that people along the M&NA route were so opposed to the strike: [227]

Practically every farmer whose land was touched by the right-of-way donated part if not all of the land desired by the company, and in many instances it split their bottom fields "wide open," reducing the acreage of cultivated fields sometimes in half … When the shops and general offices were moved to Harrison, the community "put up" a bonus to the road of $26,000. The gift of thousands of dollars to the road by citizens of this territory both manifested and created a deep interest in the railroad.

While the public through its gifts had not a cent in the enterprise as an investment, yet their gifts coupled with the great necessity which brought the road, made in every citizen a keen sense of personal interest in the road, akin to the feeling of ownership itself.

In early July 1922, an Arkansas judge issued a restraining order against the various labor unions engaged in the strike.[228] Again, the restraining order failed to stop sabotage of the rail line. A railroad bridge was burned near Beaver, Arkansas, in August.[229] And in October, there was an attempt to burn an M&NA bridge near Wheaton.[230]

Between October and the end of 1922, the M&NA's general manager, J. C. Murray, disclosed that "acid was placed in three water tanks for the purpose of damaging the engines and thereby causing additional expense in repairs to the engines as well as causing delay in traffic movement; air hoses have been cut at Heber Springs (Arkansas) and on the night of November 30th, 39 air hoses were cut at Fargo (a tiny town in eastern Arkansas) and emery dust placed in the journals of the (rail) cars. [231] On the night of the 30th, the track was greased from mile 126, just south of Harrison, to mile 130. Spikes were driven between the rail joints within the same mileage and 7 spikes entirely removed in curve on mile 128."[232]

On January 10, 1923, another M&NA bridge was destroyed by fire near Eureka Springs at an estimated replacement cost of $6,000, forcing closure of railroad service between Eureka Springs and Leslie, a distance of ninety-two miles. [233]

On January 12, after two strikers were arrested on charges of bridge burning, William Wenrick, editor of the *Marshall Mountain Wave*, a weekly paper in a small town forty miles southeast of Harrison, published an editorial calling for strikers to be lynched.[234] Three days later, Wenrick got his wish when "approximately 1,000 armed men, many of them prominent citizens, gathered in Harrison to search for explosives and interrogate strikers," says an article published by the *Encyclopedia of Arkansas History & Culture*. The article describes what happened:

> In response to the presence of these vigilantes at his home, striking worker Ed. C. Gregor fired his shotgun to disperse the group. He injured no one, but the vigilantes returned fire, wounding one of their own but later blaming it on Gregor, who was subsequently jailed. Early in the morning on January 16, 1923, a group of men in black masks kidnapped

Gregor from the jail and hanged him from a railroad bridge just outside of Harrison. Other strikers were dragged from their houses and whipped. George W. O'Neal, a former member of the Harrison Protective League, was flogged for his pro-union sympathies. In other parts of the Ozarks affected by the strike, union members were similarly rounded up and beaten. A committee of twelve consisting of prominent citizens from the mob forced the resignation of Harrison's mayor, marshal, and many councilmen—despite lacking any legal authority in the matter. The majority of approximately 200 striking workers in Harrison and their families were rounded up and forced north across the Missouri line.[235]

The *Wheaton Journal* of January 19, 1923, carried the story under the headline OUTRAGED CITIZENS DRIVE STRIKERS FROM HARRISON with a subhead that said STRIKING SHOPMAN HANGED AND OTHERS FLOGGED; TOWN IS AGAIN QUIET.

But the article told a different story of the hanging:

The body of Gregor was found Tuesday hanging from a railway trestle near Harrison. Gregor is said to have resisted attempts of the "Committee of 1,000," an investigating body of citizens, when they sought to question him regarding the identity of persons suspected of carrying on a campaign of sabotage. When called upon to surrender he opened fire upon the committee, wounding one in the hand. His capture by a pursuing posse followed and he was hanged from the trestle.[236]

Regardless of which version is correct, Gregor was dead, and the lynching was under investigation by A. J. Russell, United States deputy marshal of Fort Smith, Arkansas. Russell recommended that a federal guard be placed over the railroad property.[237]

A joint committee of the Arkansas General Assembly opened an investigation into the cause of the violence but decided not to assign blame for it when it issued its report to Governor Thomas C. McRae.[238]

In the same issue of January 19 that described the lynching, *Wheaton Journal* editor Maurice Lamberson wrote an editorial that took issue with the version of the violence that ran in the *Crane Chronicle*, a weekly newspaper from Crane, Missouri, approximately thirty miles northeast of Wheaton. Apparently, some of the strikers who fled Harrison stopped in Crane and told their version of the story. Maurice concluded that their version varied widely from the facts. He closed his fiery editorial by writing:

Rather than see one innocent person lose his life in a train wrecked at the hands of the bridge burners, we would prefer seeing a dozen names added to the list of those hanged if there were proof of their guilt.[239]

Wheaton's Citizens Protective League responded to the violence in Harrison by voting to place guards "at the different bridges in Barry County and a fund was subscribed by those present sufficient to maintain the guard for a few weeks," a *Wheaton Journal* article said. "A reward of $250 was also subscribed and is offered for the arrest and conviction of each and every person committing a felony against the M&NA Railway Company within Barry County."[240]

The January 19, 1923, edition of the *Journal* also carried a short article and a reprint of a *Joplin Globe* editorial announcing that the president of the International Association of Machinists had appealed to Arkansas Governor McRae to punish those guilty of lynching Ed Gregor. In the editorial, the *Globe* denounced the Machinist Union's president, W. H. Johnson, for not also condemning the strikers who had burned railroad bridges and committed other acts of violence against the railroad.

"Good citizens, whether union men or not, are eternally opposed to mob law, to arson and to injustice, no matter where found or when, or under what circumstances," the *Globe* editorial concluded.

A week later, on January 26, 1923, a *Journal* article disclosed that the governor of Arkansas had received a letter postmarked "Springfield, Missouri," threatening that "all towns along the three hundred sixty-five miles of the railway are to be 'blown off the map' by invading airplanes unless the men now in state prison following conviction for bridge burning are released at once and every member of the 'mob' at Harrison is incarcerated in their stead." Governor McRae, the article said, didn't take the threat seriously and said no extra precautions would be taken to protect the towns.

The M&NA strike continued, but the harassment of the nonstriking employees and sabotage of the railroad's facilities slowed. However, there was another unsettling development. On a Sunday morning in late February 1922, the Ku Klux Klan clandestinely papered Wheaton with posters "warning all gamblers, bootleggers, home-breakers and others that law violations must cease."[241] Although the Klan's posters didn't directly mention the railroad strike, the KKK had publicly announced its support for the M&NA management and against the striking railroad workers.[242] The *Journal* article described what happened and the town's reaction:

> It is the general consensus of opinion that an organization exists in Wheaton or the surrounding vicinity, but the identity of the person or persons who posted the signs seems to be a mystery. The night watch says that he didn't see a soul on the streets after the usual hours and it is generally believed that they were posted after he had gone off watch at five o'clock.[243] (5:00 a.m.)

Similar signs were posted in Fairview, about five miles northwest of Wheaton, and Stark City, a dozen miles away. "The posting of the bills and the probable results of the organization, should it exist in this community, has been the chief topic of conversation about town for the past few days," the *Journal* article said. "Comments, both favorable and adverse, can be heard at most any time. Quite a number who declare they are not Knights of the Ku Klux Klan express themselves very favorably toward the organization. There are others who conscientiously condemn it and a few who perhaps object to it because it may interfere with some of their actions."

A week later, the *Journal* reported that members of the International Order of Odd Fellows Lodge in neighboring Rocky Comfort had quickly left the premises after finding KKK members occupying their meeting hall.[244]

As the violence against the M&NA slowly decreased throughout the summer and fall of 1923, the KKK continued to try to gain a foothold in Wheaton. On November 26, 1923, high-ranking KKK members were allowed to give a lecture at the Wheaton High School gymnasium, "explaining the principles for which the Klan stands." The audience, it was reported, "gave good attention to the speakers," who lectured for an hour and a half.[245]

By mid-December 1923, the bitter and violent three-year strike seemed to have run its course. M&NA crews were distributing ties along the tracks north of Wheaton, and another crew was reported to be working south of town. But there were some who had doubts about the long-term future of the railroad. "The people along the line welcome such improvements, not only because they are needed, but because they are a fair indication of stable financial conditions at headquarters—a point which causes the occasional loss of sleep by some of our more skeptical citizens," the *Journal* wrote.[246]

The new year of 1924 began with optimism for the M&NA. The strike had been settled. Business was increasing. And completion of facilities for freight service, as well as passenger service, over the entire line made it possible to get freight and passengers from Joplin, Missouri, to Helena, Arkansas, on the Mississippi River in thirty hours.[247]

The KKK, however, wasn't quite done with Wheaton. On Sunday evening, January 13, 1924, six robed Klansmen filed into the Baptist church where a revival meeting was under way, handed the pastor a letter containing a gift of thirty-one dollars, and quietly filed out.[248] The last mention in the local newspaper of any KKK activity in Wheaton came eight months later when bills were scattered announcing a Klan meeting at night in an open field north of town, "but for some reason the meeting failed to materialize," the article stated.[249]

Although the posters and flyers distributed in Wheaton by the Klan contained no mention of the railroad strike, the Klan had openly used the strike against the M&NA as a recruiting tool in Arkansas and had sided with other railroads against striking railroad unions in neighboring Kansas at the same time that it was making its recruiting pitch in Wheaton.[250] But with the strike over and more prosperous times returning for both the M&NA and the areas along its route, KKK activity in Wheaton faded into the night.

A May 30, 1924, *Journal* article reported that passenger traffic on the M&NA was "the largest in years" and that timber shipments were unprecedented. Freight shipments also were increasing, and poultry, eggs, and dairy shipments were "a big item," as well as "meadow crops, strawberries and other fruits." The M&NA was the exclusive rail line for "approximately 200,000 persons in north Arkansas and to the south."[251] In November, the railroad reported that it had even shipped one carload of goats.

Until 1927, the M&NA seemed to be on the road to prosperity, but the Great Mississippi Flood of 1927 wreaked havoc with many miles of its rail lines, especially in eastern Arkansas. The M&NA again went into receivership. Frank Kell, a multimillionaire of Wichita Falls, Texas, and his associates purchased what the *Journal* called "a large majority of the capital stock of the M&NA just days before the stock market crashed in 1929."[252]

Between 1929 and 1935, several derailments burned or damaged M&NA railcars, but no lives were lost.

In June 1933, as the Depression cut into revenues, the line again was experiencing cash-flow and labor problems. The *Journal* reported that the problems prompted "W. Stephinson, former president and now receiver and general manager" of the line to submit his resignation to a federal judge who was overseeing the M&NA receivership. Employees at the line's Harrison, Arkansas, headquarters, the article said, "marched to the company offices demanding a change of management and charging that many of them had not received their pay regularly during the past five months."[253]

By 1934, the M&NA hadn't paid the taxes it owed Barry County, where Wheaton is located, for four years. Finally, after legal wrangling, the Barry County Court agreed to accept a tax payment of twenty-five cents for every dollar the line owed, canceling the other 75 percent. The M&NA was becoming a deadbeat railroad.[254]

Multimillionaire Kell, who already held $700,000 of the rail line's receivership certificates, bought the M&NA outright for $350,000 in March 1935, reorganized it, and renamed it the Missouri & Arkansas Railway Company (M&A).[255]

The rail line embarked on one last innovation in 1938 when it purchased two gasoline-driven passenger coaches named after two Arkansans—the late Arkansas governor and federal judge, John E. Martineau, and another governor, the late Thomas C. McRae, who was governor during the bitter strike of 1921–23. A *Journal* article of June 23, 1939, announced the purchase of the two coaches at a total cost of $100,000. They were described as "streamlined, 76 feet long, painted in a combination of dark blue and silver, and modernistic in design. The interior of the passenger compartment is green, which with the brown and henna upholstering and cream colored headlining is quite harmonious. They are lighted by dome shaped fixtures along the center line of the car, and arranged on several circuits so that various intensities of light can be achieved. Each car contains seats for 39 passengers, a 30-foot mail compartment and a 10-foot compartment for baggage and express."[256]

The description of the color was a little off. The coaches actually were a bluish gray that faded with age. One coach was used on the northern end of the line—Wheaton's end—and the other was used between Harrison and Helena, Arkansas, on the southern end. The folks in Wheaton, however, had a far more descriptive name for the coach that was used on their section of the line. Wheatonites dubbed it the Blue Goose. My Wheaton High School classmate Betty Higgs Lamberson, writing in *Wheaton Echoes*—which she and her husband, Ralph Lamberson, compiled—knows a lot about the Blue Goose. As a kid, Betty often would hang out at the depot with her station agent granddad, Walter Hoyt. Writing about the Blue Goose coaches, she recalled:

> They were fast. They were powered by a 200 horsepower gasoline engine. As a child I saw them up close when they would stop at Wheaton to pick up passengers. I also remember the quick, quiet "whoosh" they made as they passed, when they did not have to stop at the depot to pick up passengers. They were so quiet compared to the steam locomotives that carried freight and passenger cars. One of the cars was wrecked in 1946 and the other continued to run until the railroad was sold for salvage about 1949.[257]

In the run-up to World War II and during the early war years, freight tonnage increased for the M&A. Camp Crowder, a large US Army training base near Neosho, Missouri, needed lots of supplies, and the M&A was its main supply line. But even then, the M&A seemed snakebit. The rail line's headquarters offices in Harrison were destroyed by fire in December 1941, the same month the Japanese bombed Pearl Harbor and the war started for the United States. M&A shops in Harrison burned a few months later.[258]

The year before the war ended, there was another strike against the M&A, followed in April 1945 by a flood on the White River in Arkansas, a double whammy that spelled the end of the line for the M&A.[259]

On Friday night, September 6, 1946, just a year after World War II ended with victory over Japan, the last passenger train stopped at the Wheaton depot. Two days later, on Sunday afternoon, September 8, a southbound freight was the last train to run through Wheaton.[260]

The M&A's management asked the Interstate Commerce Commission (ICC) for permission to shut down the line. When permission was granted, the line was sold to a consortium of eastern entrepreneurs known as the Salzberg interests, which valued the railroad as a source of scrap metal.[261]

It was a blow to Wheaton's merchants, but it was personal to Walter Hoyt, the loyal station agent in Wheaton—first for the M&NA and then for the M&A—since 1925. His daughter Marguerite, the mother of Joe Higgs and Betty Higgs Lamberson, said, "Papa never missed a day going to work at the depot. The only day he missed was when he accompanied Morris Pogue in the ambulance to a St. Louis hospital with (my mother), Della Hoyt. Many of those months he never got paid!"[262] (Morris Pogue operated a Wheaton mortuary that also provided ambulance service.)

Another Wheaton employee of the M&A who was hit hard by the closure was Rich Powell, who became the town's city marshal and night watchman.

Wheaton's merchants fought hard to save the railroad. For the next three years, committees of leading townspeople went to hearings and meetings in an effort to get the railroad going again. A. E. "Dike" Elkins of Elkins Butane Company; Silas McQueen, who had been active in Wheaton since it became a town in 1907; Stratton Allman, proprietor of the town's grain elevator and feed store, Allman Produce & Feed; and Gordon Kenney, manager of Calhoon-Putnam Lumber Company, were among those who were active in the attempts to revive the railroad.

On January 10, 1949, an Arkansas congressman asked President Harry Truman, a Missourian, to intervene to help save the M&A. Truman was interested, but it was too late; the abandonment had been approved by the ICC.[263] The M&A had run its last train.

Salvage of the rails began in 1949.

M&A DISAPPEARING ONE-HALF MILE EACH DAY read a headline in the June 8, 1950, edition of the *Wheaton Journal*. A crew had started removing the rails and loading them on salvage trucks at Neosho, twenty-five miles northwest of Wheaton, and had worked its way to within a mile and a half of Wheaton, the article said. Rail removal would continue on to Wayne, ten miles to the southeast.

Betty Higgs Lamberson and her brother, Joe Higgs, wrote in the Spring 1998 edition of *Oak Leaves, A Historical Journal of the Missouri & Arkansas Railroad*:

> On the east end of Main Street looms the "DEPOT," a monument to the birth and life of Wheaton, Mo. The birth of Wheaton and the DEPOT are synonymous. In 1908 the M&NA Railroad Depot became the heart and lifeblood of the new city of Wheaton. The trains ran ... and Wheaton grew and prospered. When the trains stopped, there were dire predictions and great fear that Wheaton would die. Through the years, the community struggled to survive. The DEPOT still stands because nobody had the heart to remove the last symbol of prosperity that the railroad had brought. Some feel that the DEPOT is still the symbol that has kept this community alive, and to this day, the DEPOT still stands at the east end of Main Street!

Joe Higgs passed away in 2007, but today, thanks to the hard work of Betty Lamberson, her husband, Ralph, and a group of Wheaton's citizens who formed the Wheaton Historical Society, the sagging old depot has been restored and is now on the National Register of Historic Places.

On July 11, 2009, the Wheaton Depot Museum officially opened. It is filled with railroad artifacts from the days when the M&NA and later M&A trains puffed their way into the depot, took on water, popped off steam, and unloaded feed, farm equipment, groceries, mail, and a thousand items that made the little town and its surrounding farms hum with activity. Shipped out on the M&A were apples, peaches, grapes, freshly picked strawberries, sheep, cattle, horses, mules, hogs, chickens, eggs, wheat, oats, flour, and tons of tomatoes canned by factories in Wheaton and the nearby communities of New Hope, Shoal Creek, Pioneer, Fairview, Rocky Comfort, and Ridgley.[264]

Now the hauling is done by trucks driving on asphalt roads instead of steam locomotives pulling cars running on iron rails.

But for those of us who remember, when we stop at the depot museum and walk up to the ticket window, we still hear Walter Hoyt clacking out a message on the telegraph key asking when the next train will arrive, and in our minds, we hear the rumble and the roar and the grinding of steel wheels on steel rails as the train pulls in. And we are glad we were alive when the M&A was alive.

11

Listening to the Jar Flies

Jiggs was, maybe, the best dog any boy ever had. He was half collie and half shepherd with a coat of beautiful ash-blond fur and a patch of white behind his nose. Just after school was out in May 1947, Uncle Jack told my dad that he wanted to give me a dog. And to my delight, Dad agreed to it, provided I make the standard pledge to feed and care for Jiggs until death do us part.

I was nearly eight years old, and Jiggs was nearly a year old when Uncle Jack brought him up from his hill country farm fifteen miles to the south. The first few days he was with us, we kept him leashed to the maple tree in our front yard, but because Mom and I played with him for hours and served him meat scraps, corn bread, and gravy, Jiggs was soon *my* dog. Granddad Lamberson, who lived half-a-quarter farther down our little dirt country lane, also was quick to make Jiggs his friend.

I often was shirtless on hot summer days, and Jiggs liked to run to me, rear up on his hind legs, and put his front paws on my bare shoulders. I would take a paw in each hand, and we would do a little dance—the kind of dance that only boys and their dogs understand. We always seemed to be in rhythm. Since my folks didn't approve of dancing, I never found another partner who was more in sync with my two left feet until I was in my twenties and away from home.

Jiggs also would shake hands with anyone polite enough to take time to speak to him, but he was far more than a dancer and a glad-hander. He could fetch sticks and balls with the deftness of Marty "Slats" Marion, the lanky all-star shortstop for the St. Louis Cardinals. As good as he was at fetching and dancing, Jiggs had an even greater skill that Uncle Jack had honed to near perfection during his first year of life. Jiggs was a cattle dog, and he was the best one we ever had on our farm.

We milked a few cows by hand in those days—before we built a grade A barn and bought milking machines. Eight-year-old boys usually are not very good at milking cows, but fathers considered them plenty competent to drive cows from the pasture to the barn lot to await milking. Jiggs made that job a whole bunch easier.

By then, Dad had taught me that hollering at cattle was a pretty sure way to spook 'em and send them running—usually in the wrong direction. Besides, it was not good for cows whose udders were loaded with milk to run at all. Because Dad bought and sold a lot of cattle, he nearly always had beef cattle grazing with the milk cows, so driving in the milk cows involved cutting the milkers out of the rest of the herd to avoid driving forty or fifty head of cattle to the barn lot. The goal was to retrieve only six or eight milk cows—all we milked in those days. Jiggs was great at helping me make the "cuts." But even then, there were nearly always one or two independent thinkers that would head for the sassafras patch in the draw below the barn lot. Jiggs took care of getting them turned in the right direction, saving me many foot races with cows.

When Jiggs was working, he kept his head up, continually scanning for cows on either flank that were starting to stray off course. Quick as a silver-blond flash, he would be on the outside edge of the herd, moving the strays back toward the middle. He was amazing, always seeming to read the bovine mind and checkmate any cow that was drifting out of the herd.

When the cows were all in the barn lot and the gate was safely shut on late summer afternoons, I was dismissed—until I was about twelve, when we built the grade A barn and my help was needed every morning and evening as the number of cows we milked increased to about fifty.

In those early days, Dad did all the milking. If there was enough daylight left after we drove in the milk cows, Jiggs and I would trot down the little lane—past our garden with its rows of corn and beans and peas and potatoes and tomatoes and onions and cabbage and carrots, past the two tall bois d'arc trees that dropped yellow hedge apples in the lane, past the field we called our "hog lot," past the big maple tree in Granddad and Grandma's front yard—and around to the back of their house with its old wooden porch.

I'd walk over to the iron pump handle over the dug well a few feet south of their porch and pump fresh water into an old tin pan for Jiggs, which he would drink with great sloppy slurps. Then he would sniff all the interesting odors he detected in the backyard as I talked with Grandma. By then, Granddad, carrying a bucket of milk, would come trudging up the hill from their barn after he had finished milking the one or two cows they kept just to supply them with the milk they needed. He would pour the milk through the strainer and into a milk can sitting in a barrel of cold water.

Usually, even on days when the sun had blazed hotter than Nebuchadnezzar's furnace—turning the humid air into an Ozark steam bath—a light breeze would begin to stir, and the strong scent of honeysuckle would waft across the backyard from the vines growing on the garden fence east of the house.

None of us had much to say because, as the sun sank, we were entertained by a twilight chorus and light show.

The jar flies were the loudest, providing a powerful, low-pitched grinding song from the maple, locust, and walnut trees around the house. Bullfrogs with their bass croaking, tree frogs and toad frogs with their higher-pitched screeching, and katydids and crickets with their chirping provided the rhythm section of the twilight symphony. But it was always the jar flies that were the most strident, sounding like a bad bass fiddle player sawing a grating note.

Granddad would strike a wooden kitchen match off a rock or the bib of his overalls and fire up his pipe. The pipe smoke would blend with the honeysuckle scent and provide the evening aroma. Jiggs would find the coolest spot on the ground, settle down on his tummy, put his head between his extended front legs, and look up at us with his big brown eyes.

As the sunset glowed redder and then began to fade, fireflies would begin their evening light show, filling the backyard with white flashes.

When the darkness deepened, Grandma, wearing a white apron over her print feed sack dress, would open the screen door and step out of the kitchen onto the rickety old back porch to announce to Granddad that supper was ready.

That was the signal. It was time for Jiggs and me to walk back up the lane and have supper with Mom and Dad.

A year later when summer vacation from school rolled around, Jiggs and I were even closer pals. During that summer of 1948, we ran around all over our farm and all over Granddad and Grandma's farm, playing cowboy and soldier and exploring every patch of woods, every ditch and gully. Jiggs helped me flush rabbits and squirrels, which I would occasionally shoot at with my Red Ryder Daisy BB gun. Can't remember ever hitting one.

It was the afternoon of August 11, 1948—just a few days after my ninth birthday—that Mom, Granddad and Grandma Lamberson, Jiggs, and I were sitting in the shade of the big maple tree in my grandparents' front yard when Granddad's brother, my great-uncle "Tan" Lamberson, accompanied by my great-aunt Stella and Mom's cousin Pauline McTeer drove up. All of them lived in Wheaton. They got out of the car looking serious. I knew immediately that something was wrong.

After a round of greetings, Pauline told us that they had received a telephone call from my dad's brother-in-law Noman Slinkard, who lived near Jane, in the hill country twenty miles southwest of our farm. Uncle Noman had tried to call my parents, but no one was home, and Granddad and Grandma had no phone. So they drove the three miles from Wheaton to give us sad news: Uncle Noman and Aunt Bertha Slinkard's son Bill—my cousin—had been killed that morning in a freak accident when an old waterlogged tree had fallen on the cab of his milk truck as he was picking up milk from farms in northern Arkansas.

William Lee Slinkard was not only a relative—he was one of my boyhood heroes. He had been a great basketball player for the White Rock Roosters at White Rock High School in Jane before I was old enough to remember him. Born in 1923, he joined the navy just after high school as World War II raged.

He had trained to be a navigator in a TBF Avenger torpedo plane. But at the completion of his training, the navy finally remembered to measure his height (he was six foot two) and discovered that he would not fit properly into the plane, so he never went overseas. He was transferred from Florida to Memphis, Tennessee, where he met and married a pretty young woman named Willie.

In the summer of 1948, Bill was preparing to enroll in Southwest Missouri State Teachers College, now Missouri State University, in Springfield, Missouri, under the GI Bill.[265] He was twenty-four years old.

Bill and I were buddies. He always answered all the questions I didn't want to ask my folks. The news of his death shocked me so much that I fell backward as I sat on an old wooden chair under the maple tree. My dad, Bill's uncle, was equally shocked by the tragedy. He had watched Bill grow to manhood, and as a little boy, Bill had been his helper with farm chores near Jane.

Jiggs was my main comfort for the rest of the summer.

The holidays that year were tough without Bill. I kept recalling the previous year's Thanksgiving when Bill had met Dad, Mom, and me in our car as we were driving to enjoy the holiday dinner hosted by his parents, Uncle Noman and Aunt Bertha, near Jane. Bill had been waiting for us on a horse at the head of the "holler" where his parents lived and had raced the horse alongside our car for a couple of miles until we got to our destination.

It was hard for me to imagine that I wasn't going to see him again.

So by the next summer—the summer of 1949 after I had finished the fourth grade—I tried to pick up with Jiggs where we had left off the summer before. We did several explorations all over our farm and Granddad's place. I still felt a hollow place in the pit of my stomach when I thought about Bill.

Then one day, Granddad borrowed our Ford tractor and was mowing hay in a field between his house and Indian Creek. Jiggs saw Granddad and ran in front of the tractor, not realizing he was in danger. Granddad tried to stop, but it was too late. The mower sickle slashed one of Jiggs's legs, nearly severing it. Jiggs, mortally wounded, ran down a gully on his three good legs and disappeared.

Granddad stopped his mowing and ran to see if he could find Jiggs, but the wounded dog had vanished. We looked for Jiggs for hours over the next three or four days, but we never found his body.

Now two of my best buddies were gone.

Life went on, and many good things happened, but no one could ever replace Bill—or Jiggs. I didn't get another dog until the eighth grade—a fox terrier named Nippy. Nippy was not a field dog like Jiggs, but he became my good friend.

Years later, I paid a visit to another of my childhood friends and neighbors, Darril Haynes. Darril and his wife, Esther, live on Granddad and Grandma's old place in the house that they've remodeled to look like a log cabin. But the locust trees were still on the east side of the house, and as it was getting late in the afternoon at Darril's, the jar flies began their grinding song from the locust trees. For just a minute or two, I was at Granddad and Grandma's, Jiggs was drinking from his pan of water, and Bill was racing his horse down the "holler."

12

The Blacksmith Shop

In 1946, when I was seven, Dad sold our team of horses, and the Lewis farm shifted from "giddy-up, whoa, gee," and "haw" to a roaring tractor that went where you steered it and consumed gasoline and oil instead of oats, hay, and water.[266]

Actually, the horses had coexisted for some time with a John Deere tractor—a green "poppin' John" that earned its moniker because of the stuttering cadence of its two-cycle engine. After the horses departed the scene, an orange Case tractor took the place of both them and the "poppin' John." And within a year, Dad bought a gray Ford tractor, which was smaller and which I soon learned to drive.

Granddad Lamberson, who lived just "half a quarter" (of a mile) down the lane from us, kept his team of workhorses a few more years, and he occasionally let me drive the team as it pulled his old wagon or his hay rake. I was still pretty small, but like the horses, I learned the difference between "gee" (turn right) and "haw" (turn left), and with great effort, I could get them to go where I wanted them to most of the time.

Occasionally, Granddad's horses would need shoeing, and that was when he would drive the team three miles from his farm to Wheaton where Port Potts and Clarence Rodgers plied their trade at the blacksmith shop. They had been in business there since at least 1930 and probably several years earlier than that. Their shop was in a ramshackle shed very close to the center of town, just north of Main Street between the *Wheaton Journal* building and Virgil and Winnie Paden's house.

The blacksmith shop was a place of fire, red-hot metal, sparks, and puffs of hissing steam that shot up to the tin roof, accompanied by the clash of hammer on iron and the smells of sweaty horses, sweaty men, and horse poop. Despite the fact that many farmers were converting from real horsepower to mechanized horsepower, it was still one of the most important businesses in town in the early and mid-1940s. Farmers for miles around brought their horses for shoeing and their wagons for new iron wheel bands. Port and Clarence occasionally were asked to make new bands for water and pickle barrels when the old bands got loose. In 1933, the two blacksmiths even made a bus body for Rocky Comfort High School.[267] Port and Clarence could fix virtually any metal device that needed heating, pounding, and reshaping. They were the classic village smithies.

The kids who lived in Wheaton got to spend more time around the blacksmith shop than I did. One of them was Bob Davidson, who lived with his mother and brother in an apartment above Roy Robinson's Maytag and Philco appliance store on Main Street.

Bob remembers Port as "a little shorter than the average man, and Clarence as a bit taller than average." I would add that Port was lean and wiry and tolerated no nonsense from either horse or man. Clarence was a strapping man who looked like a blacksmith from head to toe.

Although I can't remember anyone commenting on it, there may never have been a more unlikely pair of blacksmithing partners than Port and Clarence. Port was an outspoken anti-liquor crusader. Clarence was locally famous for his beer drinking.

In the years before World War I, Port had practiced his blacksmithing craft in the tiny village of Jane, Missouri, about twenty miles southwest of Wheaton in the hill country and just a couple of miles north of the Missouri-Arkansas line. He was an outspoken prohibitionist. In Arkansas, a war raged between the "wets," who wanted to retain the right to manufacture, buy, sell, and drink alcoholic beverages, and the "drys," who wanted prohibition. Port was so avidly anti-liquor that unknown persons on the "wet" side dynamited his house in 1913.[268]

The details of the incident remain as murky as Port's thoughts about the drinking habits of his partner. A story about Clarence was told so often that it became legend in the Wheaton community. I first heard the tale from Grandma Lamberson when I was a little boy. I'm guessing that she heard it from Port's wife, Nellie. A few years into the twenty-first century, Bob Davidson repeated the story my Grandma told sixty years earlier, even using the same closing line:

I don't know exactly where he lived, but it was north of town, out toward Muncie Chapel. Clarence walked to work, not on the road, but through the fields. I was told that Clarence would get a paper sack of (bottled) beer when he left work, and drink it on his way home. The story was always told as being the truth, and always ended with the statement: And he was found drunk in the ditch only once.

So the horses of Wheaton and surrounding communities were shoed by a prohibitionist and an avid beer drinker. However, it is believed that not a single horse ever kicked to protest either Port's or Clarence's position on booze.

Bob Davidson paints a vivid picture of what might have been the most fascinating business in Wheaton:

The blacksmith shop was a great place to hang out, especially on Saturday.

That seemed to be the busiest time. Before and during the war (World War II) many farmers used horses in the fields. There really weren't too many tractors around.

I can still remember watching Port or Clarence making the shoes from a strip of steel. They formed the horseshoe shape, folded over the ends to make the cleats, and punched holes for the nails. Of course the steel strip first had to be heated until it glowed red.

I'm trying to remember what the fuel for the forge looked like. As best I can recall, it was coal, but not the big chunks like we used to burn in the stove in our front room to heat our house. I believe the pieces weren't much more than an inch in diameter. They used a hand-cranked blower (bellows) to feed oxygen to the flame to make the coal burn hotter.

When they had the shoe near the shape that their practiced eye told them would fit the particular horse they were shoeing, they plunged the hot shoe into a large tank of water close at hand. That sent a column of steam up to the ceiling.

Most of the time all the doors of the shop were open, not only to help release some of the heat during warm summer days, but also, I suspect, to provide relief from the odor from two or three large horses that were usually tied inside the shop.

Something that always caused me some concern was the preparation of the horse's hoof before being shod. The blacksmith used a very sharp knife with a hooked blade. He would first remove the old shoe, then cut away a portion of the hoof with the knife. I suspect the old shoe became loose with wear and the movement of the shoe, along with the normal hoof growth, would have left an uneven surface, preventing the blacksmith from getting a good fit with the new shoe.

The horse never seemed to suffer any pain as the hoof was being trimmed, but I always expected to see some reaction from the horse. I guess it was like trimming our fingernails.

Once the hoof was prepared, the blacksmith would place the still-hot shoe on the hoof. As smoke and the odor of burning hoof filled the shop, Port and Clarence would look closely at the fit. Usually they wouldn't be satisfied with the initial fit, so they would take the shoe back to the forge, reheat it, and reshape the shoe.

It would have been virtually impossible to raise a large work horse's hoof and hold it while working on it, so they used a steel tripod (I'm sure they built it themselves) to rest the front top of the horse's hoof. Of course, you can't expect a dumb horse to stand there on three legs with one resting on a support while someone worked on it. So the blacksmith would stand with his back to the horse and the horse's leg folded back between the blacksmith's legs. That way he could grip the horse's leg, just above the hoof, between his knees. Finally, satisfied with the fit, the blacksmith would nail the shoe on the horse's hoof.

I wonder how many people today would know what a horseshoe nail looks like. They weren't round like a nail used to join two boards. They were flat, and instead of having a round head, the head was a rectangular shape that blended into the shank, which also was rectangular and not circular like a carpentry nail. The holes in the shoe were also rectangular, larger at the surface of the shoe that contacted the ground.

The shape of the nail head and the shoe hole were such that the nail head rested inside the shoe hole. When the shoe was nailed on, the nails would penetrate the side of the horse's hoof. The blacksmith always bent the nails over and down against the outside of the horse's hoof.[269]

Bob said he imagined "a big docile horse standing there being shod." But he noted that "on occasion, a horse would kick and become ornery." For that, Bob wrote, the horse "often got a big whack with a long file (or rasp) that the blacksmith used to 'fair in' the hoof to the shoe."

It was Port's use of the rasp in 1946 that resulted in a small-town mystery that wasn't solved until sixty years later during a conversation with Jon Paden, whose parents owned the property where the blacksmith shop was located. The intrigue began on May 2, 1946, when an article on the front page of the *Wheaton Journal* reported that the shop would be moved a block to the east to a refurbished building that had long been a chicken house for the Frazier-Daniels & Brattin Grocery & Market. (The grocery sold baby chicks to farmers.)

The *Journal* reported that the property where the old shop was located had been sold, but lots of people thought there must be more to the story than that. Grandma and Granddad Lamberson puzzled and speculated about the reason for the move, but the real reason was known only by the Paden and Potts families, and maybe Clarence Rodgers, for six decades.

The real reason the shop moved, Jon said, was that Port's dog— of mixed heritage that probably included pit bull—and the Padens' family dog, a shepherd named Shep, got into a fight in or near the blacksmith shop. Port whacked Shep over the head with a rasp—a metal tool that resembles a file with teeth—that he used to smooth horses' hoofs before he nailed on a new shoe. Port undoubtedly was too enthusiastic with his application of the rasp, because poor Shep was rendered unconscious for a couple of days, Jon recalled. Shep hovered in that twilight world between earth and dog heaven while Virgil, Winnie, and the Paden children—Jill, Jon, Tommy, and Richard—anxiously awaited the fate of their pet.

Jon's dad, Virgil, was a feed and fertilizer salesman and a pillar of the community. He had been a star athlete in football, basketball, and track for the University of Kansas. Virgil was outraged, partly by the savagery of the act and partly because he and Winnie had four kids who loved Shep. In southwest Missouri in the 1940s, anyone who attacked a family's dog was likely to get a response similar to the United States' response to Japan after Pearl Harbor.

But rather than resort to violence, as many an Ozark resident might have done, Virgil evicted Port and Clarence, and all the parties to the eviction said nothing more about it. It was what the diplomats call "a firm response that sent an unmistakable message." The message, of course, was: "Don't ever hurt my dog again, and you are no longer welcome to do business next door to our home." Shep, by the way, recovered and lived out a full dog's life.

I had one personal connection to the blacksmith shop. Port Potts had a grandson named Bernard, which in Wheaton was pronounced *BER-nerd*. When I was growing up, I knew that Bernard was somehow kin to me by way of Grandma Lamberson, but Bernard was ten or eleven years older than I, so we were never close.

By accident, when I was rummaging through an old box of family photos and mementos that had been stored in my Fair Oaks, California, garage for more than twenty-five years, I found the obituary of Eula Montez Kelly, who was my grandma Cora Caroline "Carrie" Kelly Lamberson's youngest sister. Everyone called her "Montie." She was born August 16, 1897, near Rocky Comfort, and married Port Potts's son, Bert, on June 17, 1917. Montie and Bert had three children—Vera Virginia, Bonna Mae, and Carroll Bernard, so Bernard was Grandma's nephew and my mother's first cousin—a bit of family history that had never been explained to me.

I learned that Montie was only thirty-three years old when she died in Wheaton of a ruptured appendix in 1930. After her death, Bert left Bernard in the care of his grandparents, Port and Nellie Potts, and got work in Tulsa, Oklahoma, as a salesman for Nutrena Feeds.

Bob Davidson remembers an incident that involved his brother, Lindy, Bernard, and a neighbor of the Davidsons who worked for the state highway department:

It seems that he (the neighbor) had some road grader blades that he had placed at the bottom of his fence. I suspect he did that to keep hogs from rooting up the bottom of the fence. People sometimes wired logs or fence posts to the bottom of their fences for that purpose. Anyway, Lindy and Bernard decided that those blades, being steel, would bring a good price from Waddy Jagelski (the local scrap metal buyer), so they "liberated" the blades. Using Bernard's grandad's (Port Potts) horse and buggy (to haul the blades), Lindy and Bernard sold them.

Somehow they got found out and had to make things right. I don't remember exactly how it was done, but I suspect they had to buy the blades back from Waddy. Justice in the country.[270]

I remember Grandma Lamberson telling Mom and me this same story, ending it with, "Bernard's a good boy. He's never been in trouble before." Grandma always stood up for her nephew.

After Port and Clarence moved the blacksmith shop to its new location about a block from the old one, they continued to shoe horses for nearly two more years. Then in January 1948, a horse jerked its leg while Port was shoeing it, throwing Port to the ground. His right leg was fractured when it landed on an iron nail-clenching bar. It was the end of an era. The day before Port broke his leg, Clarence had quit the partnership so he could move a dozen miles to Exeter, where his ailing wife had been living with their daughter.

Wheaton's blacksmith shop closed for good.

When Port died at age eighty-six on March 15, 1962, he had been a blacksmith in Jane, Rocky Comfort, and Wheaton for fifty-seven years.[271] "'Port, the horseshoer,' as he was called by those who knew him, was one of God's choice men," said his obituary. "He was honest, and a man of his word."

There is a postscript to this business. On the flat, dusty lot covered with forge ash behind the blacksmith's shop on the Paden's property, Virgil Paden attached a basketball goal to the back side of the abandoned old shop. Over the next few years, that goal became the site of some of the most ferocious Saturday pickup basketball games in the region.

Though the players came and went throughout the afternoons, the games went on and on. We played until our faces and necks would be covered with gray, soot-laden dust streaked with sweat. For years, there was a great rule that applied to those pickup games. Each team on the court had to allow one little boy to play if younger boys were present. Every kid who wanted to play eventually got chosen to participate in those games that often involved high-school seniors and boys as young as fifth or sixth graders.

While it might be an exaggeration to assign Wheaton High School's later basketball successes to that sooty court behind the old blacksmith shop, there's no doubt in my mind that without it, the Wheaton Bulldogs would have been less likely to develop a series of powerhouse teams that regularly went to state tournaments during the 1950s.

Jon Paden, who was coached on that court by his father, Virgil, went on to play basketball for the University of Missouri. Other college players who were veterans of dusty hours of scrimmage behind the blacksmith shop included Phil Mulkey, University of Wyoming;

J. C. Duncan, Tulsa University; John Howerton, Southwest Missouri State (now Missouri State); Melvin Haynes, Missouri Southern; and Bill Haynes, John Brown University.

There were many more Wheaton boys who racked up several hundred hours on that grimy old court. It would be easy to argue that the blacksmith shop took Wheaton all the way from horseshoes to basketball shoes.

13

Wally Fox, the Wheaton Gym, and Basketball

From 1925 until 1967, James Wallace "Wally" Fox was the eye and ears of Wheaton. I say "eye" because after April 10, 1950, Wally had sight in just one eye.[272] But he saw farther down the road with it than most people with two eyes and a pair of binoculars.

Wally published the *Wheaton Journal* every Thursday with the help of his wife, Bessie, and some very skilled printer's helpers, including Bennie Powell, who was a grade ahead of me. If ill health hadn't forced Wally to sell the paper in 1967, there's no doubt that he'd have stayed on years longer at his old linotype, despite the hard work, long hours, and a tight budget.

The *Journal* did more than merely inform people of the goings-on in Wheaton and a score of surrounding rural communities—Rocky Comfort, Oshkosh, Ridgley, Shoal Creek, Muncie Chapel, among others. Wally was the conscience of Wheaton, never failing to remind readers of their civic duties that included voting in favor of tax levies that funded Wheaton's schools, supporting cleanup drives that spruced up the little town, and contributing to fund-raising campaigns that helped someone in need.

In the 1840s, Wally's Fox ancestors homesteaded a rugged hill country area on Mike's Creek, fewer than nine miles southwest of

Rocky Comfort and a little more than eleven miles southwest of Wheaton. The community that grew around the Fox family's farms, including a church and cemetery, was simply called Fox. Wally's father, Oscar Orin Fox, was a former schoolteacher who "took a great interest in schools and in the upbuilding of the community," said his obituary. When Oscar died at his home on June 30, 1943, he had been clerk of the Fox School District for forty-three years."[273]

Oscar Fox loved his country home in the hills, and that's where his funeral was held on July 4, 1943, at the height of World War II. The music for Oscar's funeral was provided by a quartet composed of Earl Lamberson, Wheaton's postmaster; E. L. Thomas, who operated a livestock feed store in Wheaton at the time; Nina Robinson, our neighbor whose Cooper family was well acquainted with the Fox family; and my dad, Perry Lewis, who had grown up just a few miles from Fox, near the little town of Jane.

Down the rough dirt road a mile or more to the west at Powell, Albert Brumley—the famous gospel songwriter who already had written "I'll Fly Away"—composed a poem in honor of Wally's father. He called it "A Grand Old Man."

As a boy, I always felt comfortable around Wally, partly because he was a cousin of Dan Shewmake's mother, Hessie, and partly because he treated a kid like me just like he treated everyone else— with respect. He would let me watch as he punched out the *Journal* or other printing jobs on the old linotype with its boiling bucket of lead. I particularly remember watching him set "sale bills" (notices of farm or cattle auctions). I was always fascinated by the roiling lead in the "hell box," and the paper folder was, to me, a wondrous machine.

Wally was master of his printing machinery. But his skills went well beyond those of a printer. He also was a good reporter. Wally wasn't as handsome as Clark Kent—he was of medium height, medium weight, and had thinning hair. But like the mild-mannered Kent, he could blend into any crowd. And because he didn't seem too pushy, he was Superman when it came to eliciting information from the very independent and sometimes very private people who read his paper.

I always thought that the reason Wally was so successful in extracting the news from the close-mouthed people of the community was because he grew up among them, and they trusted him. His family was from the same background of tough hill-country folks as most of the people who lived in Wheaton and surrounding communities. During his high-school years, he rode his horse up the Mike's Creek hollow from Fox to Rocky Comfort to attend school during the week, boarded with a family in Rocky, and returned home to the farm on Friday evening.[274]

After high school, Wally took classes in journalism and printing at Kansas State Teachers College of Pittsburg, now Pittsburg State University. After college, he worked a year for *Journal* editor Maurice Lamberson, and he bought the paper from Maurice in 1925.

"Wally can ask more questions than anybody I ever seen," my granddad Earn Lamberson would say, pipe clinched firmly in his teeth. But it never sounded like criticism or disrespect when Granddad said it. It sounded more like a statement of fact and an expression of admiration.

Had it not been for Wally Fox, journalism might never have been a part of my life. I was a freshman in high school when he printed in the *Journal* a little essay I wrote about the futility of going to class during the week Wheaton was hosting a basketball tournament. I was hooked. That eventually led me to journalism school at the University of Missouri and a quarter-century of newspaper reporting and editing.

Wally was the first reporter I ever witnessed in action, up close. And years later, as a rookie reporter for the *St. Louis Globe-Democrat* in the midst of chaos at a bloody prison riot at Menard Penitentiary in Illinois, I stayed calm by remembering how Wally used to gather a lot of information on busy Saturday afternoons in Wheaton. He would mingle with the crowd, engaging in seemingly casual conversations, occasionally scribbling a tidbit of information into a notebook or on a scrap of paper. Often, those scribbles were the basis for articles in next Thursday's *Journal*.

During the prison riot on a cold November night in 1965, as a horde of reporters jostled and shoved to get to the only pay phone after a hastily called press conference inside the prison, I remembered how Wally used to work the Saturday crowds. So instead of joining the jostle, I struck up a conversation with three or four of the guards. I asked one of them if there was another phone somewhere. He led me to a door in a separate area of the prison grounds, knocked on it, and spoke with a woman who I soon learned was the warden's wife. She graciously asked me to come in and use the phone in the warden's quarters to call in my story. The result was a front-page story that contained every detail I had learned about the riot that night. Wally had no idea that he had been such an effective teacher.

His star pupil, though, without question, was Byron "Barney" Calame, the son of Wheaton's Methodist preacher and a classmate of mine in the seventh, eighth, and part of the ninth grade. Barney retired as deputy managing editor of the *Wall Street Journal* in late 2004 and within weeks took a new job as the public editor of the *New York Times*. You could say that Barney's career started with sweeping up Wally's *Journal* office. Later, Barney interned for the *Springfield News Leader* where he reported ball game scores and other local news before he went on to graduate from the University of Missouri Journalism School, as I did a few years later. After forty years as a *Wall Street Journal* reporter and editor and two years as public editor of the *Times*, Barney, the preacher's son from Wheaton—population 394 in the 1950s—is one of the most respected journalists in the nation.

I think that Barney would agree with me that while Wally's grammar was not always flawless, he had a perfect understanding of one very fundamental rule of journalism: people love to see their names in the paper, and both he and his country correspondents filled the *Journal* with names. Page 1 of the January 22, 1948, edition of the *Journal* carried typical name-laden headlines:

ED LANDEN BUYS MORE LAND HERE
MISS ORIVIA PROCTOR ENROLLED IN TENN. COLLEGE
BIRTHDAY DINNER HELD IN CHAS. EDMONDSON HOME

Typical personal items in the local news section of the April 1, 1948, edition of the *Journal* were:

Dr. and Mrs. E.A. Smith, Molly and Blaine and Maxine Roller spent Sunday with friends and relatives in Monett.

Grey McMillen is visiting today with his uncle, H.A. Speight of Houston, Mo., who is a patient in the O'Reilly General Hospital at Springfield. Mr. Speight is a veteran of the Spanish-American War.

But Wally was far more than Wheaton's town crier. In ways both obvious and subtle, he also was the voice of its civic conscience and vision. The fact that he was the *Journal*'s editor and a member of the school board gave him a bully pulpit from which to admonish the citizens of Wheaton to be unselfish in matters concerning their city and their school.

Wally also had another unstated motive for wanting good schools in Wheaton. He and Bessie had a daughter, Jo Ann, who attended school there from first grade until she graduated from high school in 1949—just a year after Wheaton's new gymnasium was built.

On January 8, 1948, Wheaton High School's brand-new gymnasium was almost completed, and Wally's *Journal* article reported that the first games of basketball—against Butterfield, ten miles to the east—had been played in the gym on Friday, January 2, with Wheaton's A team winning 53–27.[275]

Wally's story noted that the two local men who refereed the games, Gene Anderson and Hollis Cox, donated their services, enabling the school district to make a grand profit of eighty dollars from the take at the door, minus federal tax, of course. And the PTA ladies served snacks and drinks and made twenty-six dollars.[276]

Wally closed the story by recounting the amazing community effort that had made it possible to build the Wheaton High gym. The old facility, he reminded readers, was a cracker box basketball court in a small building on Main Street that was used as a community hall in the 1920s and 1930s:

> Considering the bad weather, the first games to be played in the new gym, and incidentally the first basketball games to be played in Wheaton in eight years, were a success. The last matched basketball games played in Wheaton were played in the community hall, which is now occupied by the Wheaton Lumber Company. The community hall was built a little over 20 years ago and a 40 x 60 foot basketball court was made in the building. At that time this was one of the best gyms in (the) country, but as other schools began erecting new school buildings and new and larger gyms, the community hall gym became obsolete and teams from other schools would hardly play in it. Finally it was discontinued and the school used the gymnasium at Rocky Comfort.[277]

What Wally did not say was that because of an intense rivalry between Rocky and Wheaton, it was humiliating for the Wheaton Bulldogs to be forced to use the gymnasium of their most intense rival—the Rocky Comfort Greyhounds—for nearly a decade. The Bulldogs' practice sessions in the Rocky gym had to be after school hours, adding to busing costs and inconveniencing farm families who needed their boys to be home doing evening chores.

A glut of surplus barracks and buildings from World War II military bases in the late 1940s provided a cash-strapped community like Wheaton the opportunity to obtain cheap building materials and regain its dignity. Wally's article went on to say:

> The dream of a new gymnasium, one of the largest and best in this part of the state, was started about a year ago when a delegation of men was sent to Salina, Kan., to inspect a surplus Army recreation

building. Finally, the building, appraised at $32,000, was purchased at 80 percent discount, dismantled and transported to Wheaton.[278]

The surplus building cost Wheaton $6,400, but even at that price, the school district needed more money for a building fund. Wally reported that on May 28, 1947, voters in the Wheaton Consolidated School District approved a tax levy of $5 (per $100 of assessed value) at a special election. It was the second-highest school tax levy in Missouri in 1947.[279]

Six days before the special election, Wally, the school board's vice president, penned a long article urging Wheaton voters to approve the levy.[280] Wally's article explained that board members served without pay and often had to "neglect their own businesses and pay money out of their own pocket to keep the school going."

The four other school board members were no-nonsense, level-headed, down-to-earth leaders who did their best to give Wheaton's youth a good education: E. L. Thomas was owner of Wheaton Lumber Company; Ed McKinley had been Wheaton's postmaster from 1921 until 1934 and a school board member and clerk for nearly three decades; Richard W. "Dick" Smith was operator of Smith's Service Station and husband of Wheaton teacher Thelma (McQueen) Smith; Floyd Daniels was a partner in Daniels & Brattin Food Market; and Joe McNeill was a longtime employee at Stratton Allman's mill and grain elevator, whose wife, Elsie, was the "McNeill" in Duncan & McNeill's clothing store.

But it was Wally Fox who explained the proposed school tax levy issue in words that everyone could grasp. He noted that because state funds failed to cover the school district's operating expenses, the proceeds from an annual local tax levy normally covered the shortfall. However, during the current year, state and local funds weren't enough, and Wheaton's schools had a $3,000 deficit.

Wally continued his plea for the levy by quoting from a recent letter from the Missouri Department of Education.

We are confident that indoor toilets will be provided in the new building, because you realize that your present toilets are very unsanitary. Your school officials and Board of Education have always manifested a cooperative spirit with the State Department of Education.

Wally then inserted the clincher:

According to recent talk, there is to be a re-districting of high schools in the state some time in the future. Small high schools with low attendance will be discontinued, and high schools centralized where there are modern facilities. Wheaton would have no chance without a gym, when and if this time comes.

Wally was prophetic. Over the next fifteen years, various high-school consolidation plans were proposed for districts in the area. Rocky Comfort eventually lost its school, and students are now bused to a much larger school miles away in McDonald County. In the 1960s, a new East Newton School District school absorbed several smaller districts northwest of Wheaton, and new school facilities were built between Wheaton and Neosho. But in 2015, Wheaton still has its school, serving grades K–12.

Informed by Wally's article, Wheaton's voters approved the unusually steep school tax levy by a vote of 234 to 66. Missouri law required two-thirds of the voters to approve a special school levy, and in Wheaton, the levy was approved in a landslide—78 percent to 22 percent.

For the town's banker—the portly, conservative Dr. Otis Sheridan McCall—the vote was a personal defeat. Wally, always a fair editor, had published Doc's screed opposing the tax on the same day that Wally, on behalf of the school board, published the article explaining why the tax was needed. In his vehement opposition, Doc had written that the tax "is for the purpose of building a play house." On election day, only Doc and sixty-five other voters agreed.

Before and after the election, scores of local business owners and nearby residents contributed personal cash to help build the new gym. The donors included Doc McCall's dentist son, C. B. "Jerry" McCall, who gave fifty dollars. Others donated many days of labor.[281]

Work on the new gym started in July 1947. After money from the tax levy was exhausted, the men and women of the community contributed "hundreds of dollars in labor and money" to complete the gym—a generous outpouring from the people in and around Wheaton in 1947. With cash from the donations, more surplus lumber was purchased from the nearby army base at Camp Crowder and hauled to Wheaton to finish the gym.

Ed Landon, an Oklahoma City businessman who owned a farm and one of Wheaton's better homes on Highway 86 just north of town, donated hard-to-get butane ceiling heaters for the gym.[282] A. E. "Dike" Elkins of Elkins Butane supplied a butane tank at cost, and his employees installed the system for no charge.[283]

The outpouring of community support for the gymnasium prompted Wally to write, in a December 18, 1947, article:

Volunteer workmen are continuing to work almost every night at the new gym trying to get it ready for use. As a suitable sanding machine could not be found to rent, the McCormick Construction Company of Joplin was secured to finish the floor. After it is finished, Kenneth Corn (a local sign painter and commercial artist) will paint the lines on the court and it will then be ready for the seal and finish coat.

The entire wiring of the gym is being done by donated labor by Oden Hendrix and his son, with one or two school boys aiding some with the work. Not all the wiring is completed yet, but Mr. Hendrix is putting in the lights as they are needed. Hendrix has also donated day after day of work at the camp.

No attempt will be made to list the names of those who have donated work on the gym, as over 100 men and boys have donated work, not to mention some ladies donating work on the lunches and in other ways. However, the people of Wheaton are indebted to Mr. Hendrix, who does not even reside in the school district, for his untiring efforts to see that Wheaton gets a new gymnasium finished in time to be used this season.

Practically every able-bodied man in Wheaton and some farmers, both in and outside the school district, have donated from one to 15 or 20 days' work. Some businessmen have neglected their places of business to work, and some have made themselves sick by working in bad weather.[284]

Everybody around Wheaton liked Oden "Pappy" Hendrix, and his son Edwin "Edd" Hendrix, who went all out to contribute their special skills to the gym. Lots of people contributed hours of labor, but Pappy and Edd were particularly outstanding. Even casual observers knew that something special was happening as Wheaton's gym was going up. Wally captured that feeling at the end of his December 1947, article:

A man from a neighboring town recently remarked that he didn't believe there was a community anywhere in the country that could get as much donated labor on a public building as Wheaton has already had donated on its gymnasium.

Wally wrote on January 8, 1948:

In dreaming of a new gymnasium for Wheaton, few of those interested in the project a year ago ever dreamed that Wheaton would ever boast of a building as large and as good as the one which it has well on its way to completion.

It is a safe bet that there is not a building contractor in this part of the country who would attempt to erect a building such as this new gym at a figure less than $50,000 or possibly $60,000. As it now stands, it looks as if the building will be entirely completed for a cost to the district not to exceed $20,000, that is, if the good citizens continue to donate in the future as they have in the past.

Exactly three months later, he penned another article that was classic Wally Fox. In the April 8, 1948, *Journal*, under the headline HEAVY VOTE AT SCHOOL ELECTION, Wally reported that "a total of 240 residents of the Wheaton Consolidated School District went to the polls in Tuesday's election for the largest vote to be polled in an annual school election here in years."

Wally wrote that "the interest in the election Tuesday seemed to be centered around the selection of directors and also the levy." The story reported that Coy Holmes and J. W. Fox (Wally) won the school board election, and both the building and incidental fund levies carried by safe margins. Coy, a prominent farmer just west of town, would serve his first term on the board, and Wally had been reelected. Wally got 182 votes, and Coy got 125, nudging out Virgil Paden, an active Wheaton feed and fertilizer salesman, who garnered 108 votes.

But it may have been Wally's article of a week earlier that prompted the "heavy" vote. As he had done in his article a year earlier that had built support for a five-dollar levy, Wally explained why a two-dollar school tax levy was needed for the building fund and for "incidentals." He wrote in the Ozark vernacular that he knew everyone who read the *Journal* would understand:

A certain percent of the people (which is getting smaller year by year) is against any school levy. In other words, they do not have an education, and don't want anyone to get ahead of them. That class of people is very scarce in the Wheaton School District. However, it is possible that there was never a school election held in Wheaton but what there would be at least one or two votes against all levies.

There has never been a school or bond levy defeated in the Wheaton School District, and although some are fighting the levy this year, it is believed by those who are interested in the welfare of youth and the posterity of our country, the levy will carry by a substantial majority.[285]

The line: "*In other words, they do not have an education, and don't want anyone to get ahead of them*" was pure Wally Fox, and anyone who had lived in or near Wheaton knew that Wally had thrown down the gauntlet with that statement. He might as well have said, "Anyone who doesn't vote in favor of this levy is a good-for-nothing, low-down skunk." The straight talk worked. The levy passed.

The gymnasium built by volunteer labor, donated equipment and cash, and lumber from World War II army barracks became the center of Wheaton's civic life for many years. Within three years, Wheaton fielded one of the best basketball teams in the state, winning third place in the state tournament for class B teams at Cape Girardeau.

Throughout my school days and right up to the present, basketball has remained a powerful community force in Wheaton. The basketball teams and games evoked the feverish discussions that still take place in the barbershops, restaurants, feed rooms, and soda fountains. James Cantrell—my friend, classmate, and teammate—captured the importance of basketball and other sports in the little town when he wrote an essay in *Wheaton Echoes*. In pondering the reasons for the extraordinary success of many Wheaton High School graduates, James concluded that involvement in Wheaton's sports played a prominent role:

> I considered many factors that positively influenced my life in Wheaton; but I finally decided that the single most important thing was involvement in sports. And my thought is that involvement in sports certainly included more than just the players on the basketball "A" team. It included virtually everyone in one way or another. There were men's and women's programs, softball, baseball, volleyball, track, basketball "A" and "B" teams. There were grade school, junior high, and high school teams. There were Future Farmers of America (FFA) "A" and "B" teams. There was competition among intramural teams from each class, and pickup games at noon and after school and on weekends. And there were town teams of softball and baseball in the summer. There was significant involvement by more than the players, too.
>
> [There were also] the cheerleaders and cheerleader squads, the super loyal fans, and the merchants who sponsored the sports programs. I firmly believe that it was our total experiences in sports programs that taught us the most important lessons in life.[286]

James wrote that from age seven or eight—that would be from 1946 or '47—until he reached high school in 1952, "the basketball teams had phenomenal success." They won most tournaments, defeated much larger schools, and went to state tournaments several years, he recalled.

I agree with James. Not a week in my life has gone by that I haven't had at least a flash of a play in a basketball or baseball or softball game or in a practice session. I can still hear Doyle Clemons, our coach from my seventh grade year through my sophomore year in high school, yelling, "Bow your neck!" after I would come down with a rebound and attempt to jump back up and score in the middle of a crowd of defenders. It was Mr. Clemons who was coach when J. C. Duncan, Melvin Haynes, Jon Paden, John Howerton, Dewey Brattin, Jack Higgs, James Royer, Bob McTeer, Carrol Lombard, and Sonny Akin were on the great 1951–52 team that won third place in the Missouri state tournament. Several other great teams followed that one.

Later, in my junior and senior years, it was Sam Starkey who guided a team of boys who didn't win as many tournaments as some of our predecessors, but we won a lot of games and learned some of the life lessons James Cantrell wrote about in *Wheaton Echoes*:

> I experienced the total emotional high that comes from winning—being successful. I learned that with really hard work, the right training, planning, and timing you could win in any circumstance and against any odds. In other words, I learned to never think that I could not do something. I learned that I could dream about doing and being anything I wanted. Just as importantly, I also learned that I would not always win. I learned how to handle not winning with dignity—good sportsmanship, how to get over a loss in a short time by immediately planning for the next win in my life. I learned that I would not always be playing for first place in the finals as I live my life. If you do not win first place, it is important to not get down and to go on and try your best to win third place.[287]

Like James and most of the boys who played basketball, baseball, and softball at Wheaton High or for the FFA teams, I value the lessons I learned in sports. I trust that some of those feelings are similar for the young women who played softball or volleyball in those days. Unfortunately, those were the only organized sports offered to the female students of that era.[288]

Without the Wheaton gymnasium, many of these life lessons would not exist. And without Wally Fox, who educated and persuaded the Wheaton community to support the effort to build that gym, Wheaton might well have lost its school long before this writing.

We used to have a saying when I was a newspaper reporter in St. Louis and Sacramento: never argue with anyone who buys ink by the barrel. Wally bought ink by the barrel, and his community benefited.

In 1967, Wally died at age sixty-six, a few months after he and Bessie sold the *Wheaton Journal* and moved to Neosho. My dad, who had sung hymns at Oscar Fox's funeral in the Fox community in 1943, was a member of a gospel quartet that sang at Wally's funeral—two events that Dad said were very difficult because he was close to both men.

Bessie continued to live in Neosho until her death in 2000 at age ninety-five.

Wally and Bessie's daughter, Jo Ann, like her father and grandfather, has had a continuous interest in education since she attended and later taught at Wheaton schools. She graduated from Stephens College in Columbia, taught fourth and fifth grades in Wheaton, and finished her education degree at the University of Missouri. Later, she received her master's degree from Webster University in St. Louis and taught first and second grades in Brentwood, Missouri, for thirty-one years.

Wally and Bessie are buried in the little Fox Cemetery named for Wally's family, in the hill country of McDonald County fewer than a dozen miles south of Wheaton. Only a few feet away lies the great gospel songwriter, Albert Brumley, whose songbooks Wally used to print at the *Journal*. Albert lives on in his songs. Wally lives on in the history of Wheaton and surrounding communities.

I think that today Wally would get a little twinkle in his good eye if he could see Wheaton's children of the twenty-first century still playing basketball and volleyball in the high-school gym and studying in the school he worked so hard to support and guide more than seven decades earlier.

14

Doc McCall—Money and Medicine

Right off the bat, I'll admit that, when I was a little boy, I didn't have a high opinion of Otis M. Sheridan McCall, MD. To me, he was Ol' Doc McCall. The first reason Doc wasn't a guy I wanted to have a fountain Coke with at the drugstore was because of a story Grandma Lamberson used to tell me. She said that long before I was born, she had several cysts on her scalp, so she went to see Doc McCall about them. After examining the offending growths, Doc said he could get rid of them. She expected some kind of medicine, but instead, Doc shaved her head and carved out the growths without administering any anesthetic. Grandma said it really hurt, and there she was, shorn of hair and with a scalp that looked like it had been tenderized with a meat hammer. After she finally healed enough, she wore a wig for months until her hair grew back. Thankfully, though, and to give Doc his due, the cysts never returned. However, Grandma was never very complimentary of the doctor's scalp work.

The second reason I wasn't particularly fond of the old doctor, who was born in 1870, was because as Wheaton's banker, he wouldn't lend my dad enough money to buy and sell cattle, despite the fact that Perry Lewis was a very good cattle trader and made more money as a trader than he did as a farmer. Cattle traders needed a few thousand dollars in cash to trade on, but Doc's banking instincts told him not to lend money for an enterprise he considered as risky as buying and selling cattle for profit. Nevertheless, Dad always kept a small checking account at the Bank of Wheaton. But he did most of his banking at the Barry County Bank in Cassville, which didn't squeeze its lending money as tightly as Doc McCall.

I was a patient of Doc's only a couple of times as a small boy when I had a minor health problem—nothing worse than a sore throat or a heat rash. Most of the time, I went to Doc Ellison, who, most likely, was out of town on one of his pheasant-hunting trips when I visited Doc McCall.

Doc owned controlling interest in the Bank of Wheaton, and his medical office was in the back of the bank building. When Doc left his desk in the southeast corner of the bank to treat a patient in his medical office at the back of the bank, he would shed his blue pinstripe suit jacket and don a white smock. I always supposed the purpose of the smock was to emphasize to the patient that his attention had shifted from money to medicine. Who says that clothes don't make the man!

I remember crawling up onto a table where the bald, wide-faced physician peered at me, poked and prodded me in whatever parts of my anatomy were ailing, listened to my heart, and then stepped back to stroke his considerable chin while uttering thoughtful sounds— "Yeaaah, um-hum, yeesss"—as he pondered my condition. During that time, my eyes would be drawn to the gold chain that lay across the broad blue-pinstriped vest that covered his ample belly and disappeared into the pocket that held his watch.

When his deliberations were complete, he would typically fetch a bottle of medicine, get a label, write instructions on it, stick it on the bottle, and declare that his patient was going to be fine. I remember thinking that I hoped I never needed surgery when Doc Ellison was out of town, because after listening to my grandma's story, I didn't want old Doc McCall to wield a knife on any part of my body.

It's not that Doc hadn't been a successful surgeon. He had, indeed, wielded his knife on many patients during the decades since he began his medical practice in 1895, when he was twenty-five years old. But by the time I came along, Doc was aging. James Leslie Royer, who was four years ahead of me at Wheaton High School, said his parents took him to Doc to have his tonsils removed. However, James Leslie had to have a "do-over" because Doc didn't remove his adenoids the first time, laying him up with the sorest throat he ever had.

Long before I was born, according to Granddad Earn and Grandma Carrie Lamberson, Doc had sawed off some poor fellow's mangled leg in Wheaton's early years under conditions that I imagined were a bit like a Civil War field hospital. The man lived and was grateful that Doc had the skill to complete the surgery under such primitive conditions. In a *Wheaton Journal* article written on the date of the doctor's retirement—January 31, 1952—O. B. Durham, who was then Wheaton superintendent of schools, described the amputation:

> … [A] young man with a badly mangled limb needed medical attention—and bad. The good Doctor, with the assistance of P.S. Potts, who held the feeble light, and in a shack that stood where the Thomas Lumber Company building now stands, successfully amputated the limb. The young man lived in Kansas and is alive today. When he learned that Dr. McCall was retiring, out of gratitude and appreciation, (he) came to Wheaton Monday of this week to again express to Dr. McCall his thanks.[289]

P. S. "Port" Potts was a blacksmith—first in Jane, then in Rocky Comfort, and finally in Wheaton for fifty-seven years. No doubt, he possessed the grit to hold a lantern for Doc in a dilapidated building on Main Street during the gruesome operation. And Doc was, indeed, skilled enough, tough enough, and hygienically careful enough to get the job done in such squalid circumstances. Ever since I first heard that story, it reminded me of the amputation scene in *Gone with the Wind*. I wondered who had to be tougher—Doc, who wielded the saw, or the guy who yielded his leg.

Doc was not a person to be trifled with. "He was an excellent shot with a pistol and always prided himself in having the fastest horse around, which he was known to be ready to prove at any time," wrote Sally Minnehan Kenney, his great-granddaughter.[290] Sally repeated a story Doc's uncle used to tell:

The future physician, at age 19, and his brother, Ulysses S. Grant McCall, went to Arkansas in 1889 to take part in what came to be known as the Oklahoma Land Rush. " ...[T]hey raced their horses and were able to claim a very nice piece of land," Sally wrote. But, she explained, "before going to register it, they stood on that land and looked at each other. One said, 'You know, I really don't want to live in Oklahoma. Do you?' The other one answered, 'No, I really don't.' So they gave up their land and decided to take off for Texas to visit other McCalls who lived there."

On the way, they came to the Red River. There was no bridge, and it was too dangerous to try to swim across, but there were enterprising people with boats who would ferry them across for a fee. "They made a deal with a man who had a small boat and before he landed on the other side he upped the agreed-upon price," Sally wrote. "They tried to negotiate with him, but ended up paying what he demanded."

The story didn't end there. The future doctor and his brother had a surprise for the unscrupulous boatman. "When they were getting off the boat, they turned and shot holes in the bottom," Sally related. She speculated that it is likely they took a different route back to Missouri.

The land rush adventure took place after Otis Sheridan McCall had graduated from the Exeter Academy in the Barry County town of Exeter, a dozen miles from his Rocky Comfort home, and after he attended Presbyterian College at Greenfield, Missouri, for a year. He then enrolled in the University of Connecticut, where he completed a course in business.

But the medical profession was in his blood, and despite his mother's objections—she knew a country doctor would be called from home at all hours of the day and night—Otis decided to follow in the footsteps of his father, Dr. MDL McCall, who practiced in Rocky Comfort. So Otis enrolled in Barnes Medical School in St. Louis, completed his study, and hung out his shingle in Rocky, as the locals called it. His great-granddaughter described how he earned enough money to complete his medical training: "To finance his medical school expenses, young Otis raised mules at his family's farm near Rocky Comfort and sold enough each fall to pay for his next year's medical school expenses. Rocky was famed for its mule trading at that time."

The little town, which was established before the Civil War, thrived until after World War I, but its decline was inevitable after 1907, when the Missouri & North Arkansas railroad bypassed it in favor of putting a depot in a wheat field two and a half miles to the northeast, which became Wheaton.

In 1917, Doc's business instincts and training caused him to relocate his medical practice to the up-and-coming town of Wheaton. That same year, at age forty-seven, he volunteered for the US Army to become a medical officer during World War I. I don't have a clue as to why he volunteered when he was nearly fifty years old; maybe it was patriotism. Maybe it was because he and two of his brothers were named after Civil War generals—all Union men—and Doc wanted to continue the military tradition. Besides Otis M. Sheridan McCall and Ulysses S. Grant McCall, a third brother was named Tecumseh D. Sherman McCall.

The army sent Doc to train at Fort Riley, Kansas, after which he served at Camp Pike in Little Rock and Jefferson Barracks in St. Louis before returning to Wheaton at the end of the war in 1918 to continue his medical practice. After hearing Grandma's story, I always wondered if removing scalp cysts without anesthetic might have been part of his army training.

By 1919, Doc's career really began to take off. That was the year he became president of the Bank of Wheaton, which had been organized in 1910. He was still the bank president thirty-seven years later when he died in 1956. Along the way, he was Wheaton's mayor, president of the school board, and undoubtedly one of the little town's most prominent citizens.

I wasn't around when Doc McCall was in his prime—when he delivered a baby boy to a woman in a covered wagon lit by a smoking lantern in the woods south of Rocky Comfort as the rain fell in torrents. I wasn't there when, eighteen years later, a husky young man appeared in Rocky Comfort, identified himself as the boy born in the wagon, and paid the eighteen-year-old account to honor the request of the young man's dying mother. And I wasn't around when a girl was born to a poor but honest family in the hills south of Wheaton and years later, after the baby girl was grown and married, her father stopped and paid the bill while returning from the Kansas wheat harvest—a bill that the good doctor never sent to the family.

In 1924, Doc built a hospital in Wheaton that contained a reception room, office, laboratory, three rooms for patients, an operating room, sterilizing room, lavatory, and a bathroom. The facility also had a sleeping porch and basement where the doctor and his wife, Lennie, lived. The hospital was used for many years until it grew obsolete sometime in the 1960s.[291]

On the money side of Doc's ledger, to Doc's credit, the Bank of Wheaton did not fail, either through the wild and wooly financial splurges of the Roaring Twenties or the dreadful economy of the Great Depression. The fact that he kept the bank afloat through those dangerous years may have accounted for his very conservative lending policy that irritated my dad years later.

Although I wasn't a witness to Doc's early days, I was around for the last seventeen years of Doc's life—long enough to know that the drummer he marched to was very steady but occasionally a bit out of step with the tune the community was playing.

Because he was at the top of Wheaton's financial and professional circles, Doc occasionally was asked to deliver commencement addresses for Wheaton High School's graduating seniors. As a kid, I didn't understand why Doc spoke in such extravagantly colorful terms. It was like taking a trip back in time, back to the grandiloquent oratorical style of the 1800s, similar to that of Edward Everett, one of the nineteenth century's masters of flowery speech. The day Lincoln delivered his famous two-minute Gettysburg Address, Everett spoke for two hours on the same podium and got more ink in the press than the president.

When I read Edward Everett's Gettysburg speech as an adult, I was suddenly transported back to the Wheaton gymnasium, remembering Doc making a commencement speech in the gym he had bitterly opposed constructing because it required a steep tax levy. I can't quote Doc's phrases all these years later, but reading Everett's opening lines at the dedication of the Gettysburg battlefield gives a close approximation of Doc's speaking style. Everett's words were:

> Standing beneath this serene sky, overlooking these broad fields now reposing from the labors of the waning year, the mighty Alleghenies dimly towering before us, the graves of our brethren beneath our feet, it is with hesitation that I raise my poor voice to break the eloquent silence of God and Nature. But the duty to which you have called me must be performed; grant me, I pray you, your indulgence and your sympathy.[292]

Doc McCall must have read a lot of Edward Everett's speeches, and perhaps he learned to speak in that extravagant style when he was at the Exeter Academy or at Presbyterian College or the University of Connecticut. After all, he was born only seven years after Everett delivered the speech. Regardless of where he had learned it, his speaking style fell with a thud on my young ears. At one commencement event when I was twelve or thirteen, I scooched my way from a seat in the bleachers to the open doorway that led to the side of the stage in Wheaton's new gym and roamed the hallways of the school until his never-ending speech ended.

Speaking style was just another disconnect I felt with Doc. I was always a bit puzzled about Doc's attitude toward the construction of the Wheaton school gymnasium—or at least toward the financing of it.

In the late 1930s, a new high-school building had been completed with money from the Works Progress Administration, but there had not been enough money to build a gymnasium. Then in 1947, despite financial difficulties, the school district decided to build a new gym with money and labor donated by the community.

However, work stopped a few months into the gym project, because donated money had run out. The school board decided that if the district's property owners would approve a steep one-year tax levy of $5 on each $100 of assessed valuation, work could resume, and the gym could be completed.

On Thursday, May 22, 1947, *Wheaton Journal* editor Wally Fox, with the backing of the rest of the school board, penned a lengthy article for the *Journal*'s front page, explaining in great detail the board's reasoning in asking for voter approval of the special levy, which was to be voted on the following Wednesday, May 28.[293] Support for the special tax levy seemed favorable—except for Doc McCall.

Doc, still one of the most powerful men in Wheaton, was in high dudgeon. The proposed levy apparently was too rich for his Scots-Irish blood. In the same edition that Wally's article appeared, Doc wrote his rebuttal:

To the Taxpayers of the Wheaton School District

I want to call your attention to the proposition that is to be voted on by the tax payers of Wheaton School district on Wednesday, May 28, 1947. This proposition, if voted, levies a five-dollar tax on each one hundred dollars valuation of the property, both real and personal, that you own. In other words, this tax would equal one-twentieth of the valuation of your real estate, your cows, your horses, your sheep, your hogs, your chickens, your farm machinery and

your household goods and the money derived from
this tax is for the purpose of building a play house.
Also this tax is in addition to all other state, county,
city, current school tax and tax to pay outstanding
bonds against Wheaton School District. If this is
what you want, vote for the proposition, if it is not
what you want, vote against it.

O.S. McCall[294]

Impassioned as it was, Doc's polemic failed. The special tax levy
was approved by a vote of 234 to 66, "the largest vote cast here in
many years at a school election," according to a *Journal* article of
May 29, 1947.[295] Wally reported the election with a remarkable lack
of bias, resisting what must have been a great temptation to gloat.

With generous contributions from the people of the area, the
gym was completed at a cost of approximately $20,000 to the district.
The first basketball game was played in the new gym in January
1948, and the gym is still being used today.[296]

(For more about Wheaton's school gymnasium, see chapter titled
"Wally Fox, the Wheaton Gym, and Basketball.")

I always imagine that Doc's ruddy complexion and bald head got
a little more flushed than usual the night the votes were counted.
I later learned that Doc's bald head was a source of entertainment
for a couple of local boys I knew who usually attended Sunday
night services at the Wheaton Methodist Church. Doc McCall was
reported to be an outstanding Bible scholar and regularly taught a
large Sunday morning class. He also was a regular at the Sunday
evening services. Lacking air-conditioning during the 1940s and
'50s, Wheaton's Methodists would raise the screenless windows to
allow the breeze—if there was one—to waft into the auditorium on
hot, sticky summer nights.

The breeze wasn't the only thing that wafted. Drawn to the lights,
large brown beetles—June bugs—would fly in through the windows.
Often, according to two witnesses who asked to remain nameless, the
bugs would mistake the light that was reflected off Doc's broad and

perspiring bald head for real light. While I was at the Rocky Comfort Church of Christ with Dan Shewmake counting how many times Elbert "Sleepy" Stewart repeated "Now our Dear Heavenly Father" during his prayers, the boys at the Wheaton Methodist Church were counting how many June bugs dive-bombed off Doc McCall's shiny head.[297] I would venture to guess that both activities were equally lacking in spiritual concentration.

Doc's head may have been shiny, but it was always thinking. Bank security, for example, was an issue that he took seriously. One of the risks of running a small-town bank—especially in the days before the Federal Deposit Insurance Corporation was created to ensure deposits—was that a robbery could leave a bank in serious financial trouble. Doc wasn't about to let that happen. Did he buy an expensive alarm system? Not a frugal Scots-Irishman like Doc. He devised a cheaper system in the 1920s. Every afternoon when the bank closed, he would rig a shotgun at the front door so that if someone tried to break in, the gun would fire. Presumably, Doc entered the bank through a back door, and only he knew how to open it safely.

Herman "Butch" Allman and his sister, Rebecca "Becky" Allman Roskob, whose grandfather, Herman, founded Allman Produce & Feed, said their grandfather had a close call with Doc's homemade alarm.

One morning, probably during the 1930s, the elder Herman went to the bank because it was opening time—9:00 a.m. Herman's watch probably was a little fast that morning, because when he pulled on the front door—*bam!*—the shotgun Doc had rigged went off. Luckily, it missed the mill operator, who continued for many more years to be one of Wheaton's best-known businessmen. After that, Doc changed to a safer security system, undoubtedly more expensive but not as potentially lethal as the shotgun.

It could be argued that Doc's improvised bank security system wasn't as hazardous as his driving, at least in his old age. After World War II, he drove a big black Buick. The Bank of Wheaton fronted on Main Street, at the corner of Main and Reasor in the center of town, and the townsfolk understood that Doc always parked his Buick parallel in the first space on Reasor. The local boys who rode their bicycles around town may have been the first Wheaton residents to learn that you never wanted to be behind Doc's car when he exited the bank to go home at day's end.

That was because Doc drove "by ear." As he aged and his hearing ebbed, he needed to rev up his Buick to be sure it was getting enough gas before he let out the clutch to back out of his parking space. Not always, but often enough to be noticed by folks who were regularly in Wheaton when the bank closed, Doc's roaring car would go shooting backward into Main Street before he could stop it, shift gears, and begin his journey home.

But it was Doc's driving as he left home each morning that may have posed the greater hazard. He and his wife, Lennie, lived in a house on the west side of town that faced Highway 86, a two-lane highway for north-south traffic. Every morning during his later years, he would start his Buick in his garage, floorboard the engine until he could hear that it was running, put it in reverse with an awful "strip the gears" noise, pop the clutch, and lurch backward down his driveway toward the highway. The driveway narrowed to a single lane before it joined the highway, recalled Becky Allman Roskob, who lived nearby. Often, she said, Doc would hit the curb and be forced to pull forward to try again. When he finally cleared the curb and headed for the highway, Doc adopted the technique used by cab drivers worldwide. Instead of hitting the brakes and looking both ways, he leaned on the horn and shot onto the highway, Becky said. As far as I know, there was never a collision, but various witnesses said that brakes occasionally screeched as unwary motorists neared Doc's driveway and failed to hear his horn blaring.

In the evenings, Doc often enjoyed a game of croquet, which was played very competitively by the men of Wheaton on a court made of packed sand near the west end of Main Street. His great-granddaughter Sally wrote that he was "a serious croquet player in his old age. He and his cronies built and maintained a nice, lighted court a little way across the highway from his house. His (croquet) mallet was kept behind the front door and children were not allowed to touch it for any reason," Sally recalled.

"At agreed-upon evenings, these serious players came walking up to the court from all directions and proceeded to quietly play the game. Children were discouraged from attending, but even at a distance it created a quiet, calm scene," Sally remembered.[298]

Becky, Sally's playmate, remembered that Doc usually was chewing on a cigar while he was engrossed in a game. Becky also said that she and Sally had a unique way of addressing Doc. Most residents of the Wheaton-Rocky Comfort area deferentially called him Doctor or Doctor McCall or maybe Doc, if they knew him well. Sally and Becky, however, called him Ha-Ha, because that was the way he laughed when they told him something funny. They were a privileged minority.

It is doubtful that Doc's first- and second-generation descendants would have referred to him as Ha-Ha, partly because he was their family doctor and partly because he demanded respect. Doc took his professional and family obligations seriously, and there was a good and very personal reason for it.

Doc's first wife, the former Vita Hubbard, died due to complications from childbirth. After that, Sally wrote, "He skipped the protocol of not caring for his own family. He delivered his daughter Jewel's children," and his granddaughter Maureen's children, one of whom was Sally.

"I was told, as was the practice at the time," Sally wrote, "that he lined up my mother and her three brothers one morning and proceeded to remove each one's tonsils."[299]

Doc's second wife, Lennie, was a small, spirited woman who the good doctor accommodated every way he could. Because of her short stature, Doc had the kitchen cabinets in their house built lower than the standard height so Lennie could reach the grocery items and the dishes. Their house differed in other ways from some of the others in the community because after their trips to Las Vegas to visit a nephew, they brought back new ideas in home decor. "They were the first and maybe the only people in Wheaton to paint their living room a forest green and their kitchen a deep red," Sally remembered.

Lennie, who was like a mother to Doc's children, enjoyed an evening routine with Doc in their later years. Doc would sit in his favorite living room chair while Lennie, bearing towels and supplies, would skillfully shave his whiskers off while they listened to *One Man's Family*, a daily radio soap opera. "They almost never missed an episode," Sally wrote. "By then they were both a little 'hard of hearing' so we children were on notice not to play just outside their open window in the yard and driveway until their program had finished."[300]

Lennie was very discreet. She smoked Lucky Strike cigarettes, but she didn't want the people of Wheaton to know she smoked. It wouldn't have been a proper image for a prominent Methodist lady whose husband was one of the town's two physicians and the town's banker. To disguise her habit, Lennie would give Becky, Sally, and Sally's younger sister, Jane—when they were still in grade school—money to buy cigarettes for her at one of Wheaton's grocery stores. It was long before there were any laws against selling cigarettes to minors, and Becky said no one ever refused to sell them the Lucky Strikes or questioned who would smoke them.[301]

Doc and Lennie obviously wanted to preserve a clean reputation for the folks of Wheaton and surrounding communities, and Doc was just as fastidious about his hands. Sally recalled that he and Lennie always had a garden and raised cattle and hogs for the beef and pork they produced, "but he never got his hands in the dirt and never did the butchering because he didn't want to take a chance at that time that he couldn't get his hands clean enough to minister to his patients."

Lennie, however, had no such restrictions. By the side of her and Doc's house, Lennie used to grow the most gorgeous hollyhocks in Wheaton. It was no wonder they were so healthy. They were well fertilized, according to a well-informed source who asked to remain nameless. Lennie fertilized, and there's no other way to say this, with Doc's poop. "And to think I used to smell them," the informant said.

Whether he is remembered as Dr. Otis Sheridan McCall, MD, president of the Bank of Wheaton, or Doc McCall or Ha-Ha, the physician was a force in the Wheaton and Rocky Comfort communities during his fifty-seven years of medical practice and the thirty-seven years he headed the bank. He was a member of the Wheaton Masonic Lodge for fifty-one years. He delivered an estimated two thousand babies during his career and treated fifteen to twenty patients nearly every day in his medical office. He doubtless saved many lives and eased much pain.

Dr. McCall died on January 29, 1956. The distinctive old gentleman had lived eighty-five years, first in Rocky Comfort and then in Wheaton.[302]

Doc had made a deal with another of Wheaton's prominent citizens, Silas McQueen: whichever of them died first, the other would preach his funeral. Silas lived four more years after he preached Doc McCall's funeral at the Wheaton Methodist Church.

Wheaton will never see another citizen like Otis Sheridan McCall, MD, who knew how to care for his patients as well as their bank accounts. An article that recounted his life's accomplishments, published in the February 2, 1956, edition of the *Wheaton Journal*—the same day as his obituary—contained a line that many people would like to see in any account of their life's work:

"Good bye, Doctor, glad to have known you."[303]

15

The Crash That Changed Wheaton, or Where Did the Flagpole Go?

About ten o'clock on a quiet Friday night in August 1950, Junior Maness, who was setting type in Wally Fox's *Wheaton Journal* building on Main Street, heard an awful bang and clatter. He looked out to see two young men, both stunned and one bleeding, sitting in a 1940 model Chevy sedan that rested against the sturdy steel flagpole that was positioned smack in the middle of the town's central intersection.[304]

The Chevy had belted the pole pretty hard. It was bent in two places—at the bottom and several feet higher. The car had a sprung bumper and a dented fender. The unfortunate youth in the passenger seat was bleeding from cuts on his forehead caused when the impact with the pole threw him into the windshield.

Junior did what any Good Samaritan would do. He helped the injured boy into his car, drove him down the street to the Wheaton Hospital, and woke Dr. Elburn Smith, who bandaged him up and gave him a bed in the town's hospital for a couple of nights.

The driver and his injured passenger were never identified in the *Journal* article that described the event the following Thursday except to say that both were from Turin, Kansas, and had been on their way to Cassville, Missouri, "on a vacation"—a term that was virtually unknown in Wheaton in 1950. City people took vacations, and occasionally a town merchant or a farmer around Wheaton could get away for a couple of days to go fishing or to take his wife and family for a drive in the hills if someone could be found to milk the cows or mind the store. But "vacations" of longer duration were rare, so two young men "on a vacation" didn't sound quite right to me.

Whatever their reason for being in Wheaton, the driver said he had been blinded by the lights of a car he was meeting, causing him to hit the flagpole, which was planted in concrete poured into the casing of the old city water well. The pole twisted itself around the end of the bumper, smashed into the left fender, and set off a chain reaction that would quickly change the center of Wheaton forever.

A local driver, or probably anyone who had ever driven the length of Main Street in Wheaton, would have steered clear of the pole because he would have known the town's central intersection was hazardous. For years, a four-foot-square concrete "fort" with walls about three or four feet high and six inches thick had stood in the middle of the intersection of Main Street and Reasor Avenue. Local folks were careful to avoid it because a collision with that structure at any speed faster than ten miles an hour would have done more damage to their vehicles than the flagpole did to the Kansas lads' car.

I can still hear Granddad Lamberson, as he drove his 1936 Chevy past the pole with its concrete barrier, muttering one of the Shakespearean bywords that men of his generation used: "I wonder why they built that plagu-ed thing right in the middle of the street."

Just eleven months before the Kansas boys pranged their car into the flagpole, a majority of Wheaton's Board of Aldermen took a position that agreed with Granddad. They ordered the bulky old square concrete structure removed and replaced with a much smaller and less substantial concrete block to protect the flagpole, the *Journal* reported in September 1949.[305]

The aldermen also ordered signs to be placed on the new and much smaller barrier asking drivers to keep to the right. "As it is now," the *Journal* related, "a majority of drivers go to the left of the flag pole when leaving or entering Main Street at this point due to the fact that the 'pen' around the flag pole is so large." Even Wheaton drivers were confused about whether to go to the right or the left around the old concrete "pen" that protected the flagpole.

The original barrier, built decades earlier, had openings in its east and west sides that allowed people to step inside to a hand pump that brought up water from the old city well. In horse-and-buggy days, it was the town's only water system, except for the concrete horse trough that used to sit at the east end of Main. In those earlier days, it made sense to put a water source in the town's central intersection.

Later, after electricity came to Wheaton, an electric motor and pump had been installed beneath the street. When Wheaton got a water tower and ran water lines to businesses and residences shortly before the start of World War II, the pump was removed, but the old concrete barrier remained, protecting nothing but a dry well. The "fort" in the middle of the street was a bit like the useless gun emplacements along the Maginot Line after France had fallen to the Nazis in 1940. During World War II, when I was a very small boy, I imagined the barrier might have been a good place for a machine gun in case the Japanese or the Germans ever made it to Wheaton.

For reasons lost in the sands of time, no US flag flew regularly along Main Street during most of the war years. Certainly, no one doubted the patriotism of Wheaton residents or anyone else in the nearby communities; hundreds of young men from Wheaton and surrounding counties were killed or wounded during World War II, and hundreds of others served in every branch of the military. Women from the area also did everything they could to support the troops, and some served in various branches of the military. But somehow, Wheaton just never got around to flying a flag every day as fighting raged across the globe.

Finally, as the war against Germany was winding down, Wheaton's residents decided to collect public donations to buy a pole and a US flag, which was to be placed at the east end of Main Street near the train depot. A couple of days before Germany surrendered, the pole and flag arrived. A hole would need to be dug and concrete poured to set the flagpole. That's when events overtook procrastination. Necessity, it is said, is the mother of invention. So the day Germany threw in the towel, necessity dictated some kind of a public show of patriotism. Someone suggested that the casing of the old city well, in the center of the little concrete fortress, would provide a ready-made hole for the flagpole. Finally, in 1945, Wheaton's little fort took on a new purpose.

The *Journal* later reported that on VE Day "...the pole was set in the pipe of the old city water well and Old Glory was pulled to its top."[306] After four years of war, Wheaton finally had its flag, and once again the concrete barrier had a purpose.[307]

For a while, the flag flew proudly every day. Then disaster struck. A well-meaning citizen of Wheaton was trying to fly the flag at half-staff for some national day of mourning when the Stars and Stripes got tangled in the hanging light fixture that served as a streetlight in the center of town, and the flag was ripped beyond repair.

Wheaton's central streetlight consisted of a lightbulb mounted into a flat sixteen-inch round reflector suspended on a wire across Main Street about fifteen or twenty feet off the ground, very near the flagpole. The wire was strung between a power pole next to the Chenoweth dry goods building on the north and a power pole on the south side of the street. All it took to tear up the flag was a strong breeze and an inattentive flag hoister.

Wheaton's town fathers knew that poles exclusively for streetlights were expensive, and they also knew that money didn't grow on trees. They reasoned that streetlights could be placed on the already existing electric power poles, or on telephone poles, which would save a lot of money. The exception was the one hanging from a wire over Main Street in the center of town.

By September of 1949, when the Board of Aldermen ordered the old barrier knocked down and a new and much smaller one constructed to protect the flagpole, no US flag had flown for a while.

There may have been another, unstated reason that the town fathers decided to tear down the original sturdy little fort around the flagpole. Bob Davidson and James Ronald Price remember that one Halloween, when each of them was a student at Wheaton High, certain local boys took lawn chairs, planters, and even a porch swing from the yards of Wheaton residents and piled them as high as they could in that fort in the middle of Main and Reasor. Bob recalls that the boys flew a couple of cardboard boxes from the empty flagpole, but James Ronald is pretty sure they also flew the porch swing—not that either one of them had anything to do with it, of course. Young men just have a way of finding out what's happening out on the street.

I later learned that the old concrete fort had another unintended purpose, which the boys who lived in and near Wheaton found very practical. Whenever Bob, James Ronald, Buddy Hayden, Jon Paden, Benny Powell, Lee and Bob McTeer, and, I'm sure, several other boys from Wheaton were cruising on their bicycles near the intersection of Main and Reasor and they saw Doc McCall getting in his Super Eight Buick sedanette to back it from his parallel parking space on Reasor next to the Bank of Wheaton, they would make a quick turn so they would be behind that concrete barrier when Doc's car shot backward into the eastbound traffic on Main Street. Who knows how many lives that old barrier saved over the years?

Then came the aldermen's decision to shrink the barrier, which obviously proved to be too small to protect the flagpole from a Chevy from Kansas. After the collision, the town fathers sprang into action. It wasn't the end of the flagpole, but it was the end of its placement on Main Street and the end of any kind of concreted impediment to traffic in Wheaton.

Fewer than two weeks after the Kansas boys crashed, Mayor Joe Frazier, Tom Post, Bert Corn, and Date Brattin—who was the maintainer for the Wheaton Special Road District—were members of a work crew preparing to knock down the remaining barrier and cover the area with concrete. The sturdy metal pole was cut off at the base of the old well with an acetylene torch.[308] At last, Granddad and everyone who drove down Main Street didn't have to swerve in the center of town.

Despite all the fuss raised by the collision, Wheaton didn't give up on displaying its flag. The damaged flagpole was given to the

Wheaton Veterans of Foreign Wars (VFW) post, who agreed to straighten it and give it a new coat of paint before reerecting it near the VFW building just south of Main Street.[309]

Wally Fox, the *Journal* owner and editor, took the opportunity to chastise Wheaton residents about the casual approach the town had taken to flying the US flag. By August 1950, the Korean War had been raging a couple of months. Already young men from the Wheaton area were in the thick of the fighting, and some had been killed. Wally wrote:

> The VFW boys agreed to at least fly the flag on special occasions, as the pole was given to them. Our nation is again at war, or at least we are fighting and boys are being killed as dead as those who fought in past wars, so maybe Wheaton can again have a pole to fly a flag from by the time the present war has ended.[310]

I don't know whether Wheaton's leaders ever bought another official town flag or not. All I know is that more than sixty years ago, a couple of boys from Kansas accidentally brought down a town landmark and started a discussion about the display of the US flag that got the attention of almost everyone in town. After that, I don't remember that the flag issue was brought up again before I graduated from Wheaton High in 1957. Maybe it's just as well.

As Adlai Stevenson said, "Patriotism is not short, frenzied outbursts of emotion, but the tranquil and steady dedication of a lifetime." That's the way I remember Wheaton residents during my childhood—steady, dedicated, and patriotic, but not given to obvious displays of their feelings.

16

Woodrow Ford—A Soldier Comes Home

I t was the summer of 1951. I was twelve, the Korean War was raging, and I was equipped for battle with the North Koreans—except for combat boots. Over the past year, my buddy Dan Shewmake and I had visited an army surplus store in Joplin where we had bought World War II army helmet liners, backpacks, ammunition belts, canteens, and canteen belts. Armed with our trusty Daisy air rifles and as many BBs as we could afford, we felt we could defend our southwest Missouri farms against any North Korean invaders—or, for that matter, against any German or Japanese force if either nation should again become warlike.

Dan was a bit better equipped, because he had found genuine combat boots that fit him, while I still had to wear my old high-top leather work shoes. Dan and I would go on patrol all over our parents' farms, picking off "North Korean snipers" in the form of everything from sparrows to squirrels. We seldom hit one, but in our imaginations, we were sharpshooters.

Sometimes we fought the Japs (we didn't learn to say *Japanese* until a few years later), especially after seeing John Wayne in *Sands of Iwo Jima* in Cassville a year or so earlier. Crawling on our bellies through the dense South Pacific jungles of the sassafras patches on each of our farms, we were a tough fighting team. Sometimes, when we got into the bigger trees—oaks or the occasional hickory or sycamore—we would fight the Wehrmacht through the Ardennes Forest or the hedgerows of France. We generally defeated whoever we fought, although we were often "wounded," and occasionally we were "killed," always staying dead for at least thirty seconds.

"Boy, I wonder how much it would hurt to get shot or take shrapnel from an artillery shell or a hand grenade?" we'd ask each other. We didn't really consider how much blood was shed on a battlefield, either, probably because the movies we saw didn't show gore in its awful reality.

That summer, my dad decided to build a grade A dairy barn, which had sort of a double meaning. The barn would be a super-duper, whiz-bang, up-to-date barn—an "A" grade barn by any standard—and it would meet very strict State of Missouri specifications so the milk could be classified and sold as Grade A. The floors had to be concrete with drains so they could be washed down. Cement block walls were required to be covered with smooth plaster and painted white. Wooden ceilings were to be painted white, and two heavy wooden doors had to separate the milking parlor from the cooling room. The feed room was sealed from the milk parlor with a heavy door that opened to the concrete trough where the cows ate as they were milked.

Construction of the dairy barn interrupted my battlefield combat. BB-gun warfare against America's enemies was quickly replaced by helping my dad and our neighbor Hub Wright mix concrete for the floor and for the concrete block walls of our new barn.

Occasionally, Dad hired Woody Ford, Hub's brother-in-law, to help. Woodrow Cecil Ford was born in the little house that still sits just a couple of hundred feet north of Indian Creek a half mile southeast of our farm. His mother, Cora (we always called her Corey), lived there and was Grandma Carrie Lamberson's best friend.

Both Woody and his brother George were in the army during World War II and saw lots of action in the South Pacific, so I didn't get to know them very well until the war was over and they came home in late 1945 or early 1946, when I was six years old.

By 1951, I was well acquainted with both of the brothers. Occasionally, George had a bit of an edge to his personality, but Woody was good-natured, easygoing, and given to a fairly steady consumption of cheap fortified wine. That summer, Woody and his wife, Alice, were living in the Rocky Comfort community.

Alice was pregnant, and Carolyn Naramore—who, with her husband, Price, co-owned the IGA store at Wheaton—gave Alice a baby shower. I don't know where our dads were, but our mothers decided that Dan and I had to accompany them to the shower one warm summer night. We didn't like that one dang bit, because a shower in those days was a women-only event, and we would be the only males there.

Price, Carolyn, and their son, Max, lived in a big old steep-roofed, two-story house in Wheaton. Even Max had fled the shower with his dad that night, so when Dan and I arrived with our mothers, who each brought a present for the expected baby and either a cake or a pie for dessert, we didn't bother to go inside. We just stayed outside and chased around doing stuff that boys do to kill time.

Well, at some point in the evening, as a couple of dozen women were enjoying the baby shower, Dan and I stood in the front yard and looked up at the house, which had a front porch supported by porch posts. The porch roof wasn't very steep, but behind it, the roof of the two-story house had steep gables topped by a brick chimney that rose from a small base smack in the middle of the house at the highest point on the roof. We started talking about how cool it would be to shinny up the porch posts, swing ourselves onto the porch roof, crawl up the valley of one of the gables, and sit on the base of the chimney on this warm moonlit night. We proceeded to do just that.

After a while, our mothers started wondering where we were. So as we were sitting happily on the base of the chimney, peering at the rooftops of southeast Wheaton, Hessie Shewmake and Velma Lewis came out the door of the screened-in back porch and started hollering for us.

"Hi, Mom!" each of us yelled back from our lofty perch. Both of our mothers looked up and nearly fainted. For the next few minutes, their tones alternated between sharp commands of "Get down from that roof this minute!" and an apprehensive "Now be careful, and don't get in a hurry."

All I remember about coming down was that it was much harder than climbing up—especially getting off of the porch roof, which required lying flat on our bellies and inching backward to the eave of the roof until we could get our legs locked around the porch posts below and then grabbing the eave until we could lower ourselves enough to get both hands around the porch posts. By this time, some of the other women had come outside, hovering and clucking and watching anxiously. They would have taken great exception to "clucking" as a description of their talking, but that's what it sounded like to Dan and me. When we finally got down, our mothers, despite their relief, gave us a talking to worthy of a drill sergeant (minus the cuss words, because everyone there was a churchgoing woman) that included a lot of stuff about what they were going to do to us when they got us home.

Apparently, hardheads that we were, Dan and I didn't fully get the message that we needed to behave. Later in the evening, while the women were still opening shower presents, we got hungry, so we slipped through the back door and into the kitchen where the cakes and pies sat on a table. We selected a chocolate cake and a table knife and carried them out the back door. I think we knew we were already in such deep trouble that one more offense wouldn't make that much difference.

That was when Woody Ford inadvertently came to our rescue. As Dan and I carried the cake around the house, we saw that Woody had arrived, pulled his pickup off the road, and parked it between two trees in front of Price and Carolyn's house. There were no streetlights, and it was pretty dark out there between the trees, so we carried the cake to the pickup and opened the passenger-side door. Woody was sitting behind the wheel, and as soon as we stuck our heads inside the cab, we could smell the sweet odor of the rotgut wine he drank.

"Hey, Woody," I said. "You want some cake?"

"Yeah, sure, boys," he said. "Get in."

So for the next twenty or thirty minutes, Dan, Woody, and I sat in his pickup, and the three of us consumed at least half of the cake. Woody allowed as how it "sure was a good cake" and thanked us several times for bringing it out to him. It apparently never occurred to him that we might not have had permission to possess a whole cake.

When the charges of stealing the cake were added to scaring our mothers and several of the other women half to death by our roof-climbing adventure, the punishment should have been very severe, but somehow, both Dan and I sensed that telling our folks that Woody was the one who wanted the cake—and that he had been a little drunk and lonely that night—went a long way toward helping us avoid a whipping, and it mitigated our sentences to a week of being grounded and some extra chores.

The little episode with Woody and the cake would not be my last encounter with Woodrow Ford that summer.

One hot day not long after the baby shower, Dad hired Woody to help him lay the blocks for one of the inside walls to our new dairy barn—the wall that would separate the milk parlor from the feed room. Hub, who was a plasterer as well as a farmer, had showed me exactly how many shovels of sand should be added to a precise amount of water and cement to mix the concrete needed to lay the blocks.

As usual, I was mixing the "mud" that day. Then Mom came to tell Dad he had a phone call from somebody who either wanted to buy or sell some cattle, and they wanted Dad to come pronto.

So Dad jumped into his pickup and took off to make a buck, leaving Woody and me to finish the wall that afternoon. Woody was laying the blocks fast enough to keep me pretty busy at the cement mixer until sometime in midafternoon, when he wanted to take a break. I was more than ready. I was a little skinny kid, and that day, I wasn't wearing a shirt—just jeans and my army surplus helmet liner because it had webbing in it like a hard hat that allowed air to circulate and cool your head on a hot day. It looked just like a complete helmet, and I thought it made me look tough.

After getting a big drink of water out of the hose I was using, I reached into my pocket and pulled out little pair of cheap binoculars I'd bought at the five-and-dime in Neosho. Dan and I used them to scan the horizon for enemy troop movements to make sure we weren't walking into an ambush when we were fighting the Japs or the Germans or the North Koreans. Actually, they were little three-power opera glasses, but in our hands, they were army-issue 6X30 field glasses.

I was standing by the cement mixer wearing my army helmet liner and scanning the sassafras patch south of our barn lot for enemy troops when I looked up, and there stood Woody about six feet from me. He had walked back from his pickup where I had seen him taking a few swigs from a bottle that I knew wasn't soda pop. He looked past me, a bit bleary-eyed, and in a soft, kind of a faraway voice, he said, "I was on the beach in a shell hole on Peleliu. The Japs were up in the hills shooting at us. This officer next to me was looking up there with binoculars, and a Jap sniper caught the glint off his binoculars and put a round right through 'em and blew part of his head off."

Whoa! Somehow, if he had said "blew his head off," it wouldn't have affected me as much as when he said, "blew *part of* his head off." That brought my reconnoitering to a halt and gave me a mental image of war that all our playing soldier had not. At first, I didn't know what to say, but I think I said something lame like, "Man, that must've been really tough." I don't remember that Woody said anything else. He just walked back toward the barn, and I walked back to mix him a new batch of mud as we went back to work. Still, I couldn't get the awful picture he had painted out of my mind. I was to learn later that Woody must have seen many, many more horrible scenes on Peleliu.

During the afternoon, Woody made several walks to his pickup— and we knocked off before Dad got home. Dad drove in before dark and walked up to the barn to see how we'd made it without him.

Woody had built the wall up so that it needed about one more course of blocks to finish it.

Dad usually didn't cuss, but I do believe I heard some choice words when he saw the wall, and then he quit talking. Next thing I knew, one of his big old leather work shoes was pressed as high up that wall as he could raise his leg and he began to push that wall down. I stood there with my mouth open and watched him literally kick the wall down. Every time he'd kick, he'd have to jerk his leg back really fast to make sure some of the higher blocks didn't fall on his leg or his foot. I knew that opening my mouth to say anything would be dangerous, so I just stood as still as I could and tried to put on the best poker face a kid of twelve can muster.

Finally, when Dad got the wall down to about the height where it had been when he left that day, he just looked at me and said, "Woody didn't get the blocks level. Was he drinkin'?"

"Well, he went out to his pickup several times," I said, feeling torn between wanting to shield Woody and wanting to avoid my dad's wrath.

"Go get a couple of trowels and help me scrape the mud off these blocks," Dad said. After we had worked awhile, cleaned up the mess, and stacked the cleaned blocks, Dad said, "I'll build it back tomorrow, but Woody won't be helping."

The work on the barn continued all that summer, and it was mainly Dad and Hub, with me as their helper, who did the work. I never did tell Dad or Mom what Woody had told me about Peleliu. But over the years, I did a little research and found out more about Woody and the battle in that South Pacific hellhole.

Woody was born April 1, 1913. He was twenty-nine years old when he was drafted into the army in 1942. He was assigned to the 306th Engineer Combat Battalion that was attached to the Eighty-First Wildcat Army Infantry Division.[311] After training in Alabama, Tennessee, and the Arizona and California deserts, the Eighty-First Division saw its first World War II combat on September 17, 1944, when it made an amphibious landing on the tiny island of Angaur in the Palau Islands, which lie a little more than eight hundred miles east of the Philippines.[312]

It took only four days for the Eighty-First, with the 306th Combat Engineers using bulldozers in creative ways to help the infantry slog through the jungles and swamps, to take Angaur.[313] But nearby on the much larger and more rugged island of Peleliu, the fighting was some of the fiercest of the Pacific war. Shaped like a lobster claw, the southern end of the island is flat and open, but the center was dominated by a series of limestone and coral ridges, which were blanketed by thick jungle. The First, Fifth, and Seventh Marine Divisions, which went in first, had suffered 1,300 dead, 5,450 wounded, and 36 missing when the island finally was secured.[314]

More than eleven thousand Japanese troops were burrowed into caves, tunnels, pillboxes, and defensive positions cut into those ridges, firing down on the three marine divisions that first landed on Peleliu.[315]

By October 15, the marines had taken so many casualties that they requested help from the army's Eighty-First Wildcat Division that had secured nearby Angaur. That's when Woodrow Ford's Company A of the 306th Combat Engineers hit the beach at Peleliu. The island was finally deemed secure on November 27, 1944, but it wasn't until April 22, 1947—nearly two years after the war was over—that a Japanese lieutenant with twenty-six men from an infantry regiment and eight Japanese sailors came out of the hills and surrendered.[316]

The 306th Engineers, Woodrow Ford's unit, formed demolition squads that blew up the openings to caves and sealed the Japanese defenders inside them. With their bulldozers, while under fire, they built a road up the length of Peleliu that allowed the marines and infantry to advance. They rigged a gas pipeline up one of the ridges from a tanker truck down below that allowed a massive flamethrower to be directed against one of the key Japanese cave positions. In his official historical monograph, *The Seizure of Peleliu*, Major Frank O. Hough described it this way:

There seemed to be no limit to the Wildcats' ingenuity, especially that of the engineers. When no amount of labor would suffice to get LVTs (a lightly armored tracked landing vehicle that could be equipped with guns or flamethrowers) into one particularly troublesome area, they rigged up what must stand as one of the most unique flamethrowers in anybody's war: a 300-yard pipe line leading to the target from a fuel truck parked on the West Road, complete with booster pumps to insure pressure and equipped with a nozzle which enabled the operator to play flame on the Japanese positions like water from a hose.

A battery of flood lights was mounted so as to focus on the pond within the Horseshoe which served as the enemy's only stable water source. And near the end the 306th Engineers Battalion built a coral ramp that enabled tanks to get from the floor of Wildcat Bowl to the summit of the rugged China Wall. Some of the conveyor systems developed to get supplies up into the ridges and to evacuate the wounded looked like pure Rube Goldberg.[317]

Near the end of the Peleliu operation, Woody's company built "that remarkable coral ramp from the floor of the Bowl to the crest of the double-pinnacled ridge as a means for bringing flame and armor against the enemy's last and heretofore inaccessible strong points," wrote Major Hough. The ramp played a major role in helping finish off the Japanese resistance.[318]

When the island was finally secured, according to *HyperWar: U.S. Army in WWII*, "approximately 13,600 Japanese were killed on Angaur, Peleliu and other small islands off Peleliu—over 11,000 of them on Peleliu alone." The Eighty-First Infantry Division and attached units suffered over 3,275 battle casualties—542 killed and 2,736 wounded or injured in action.[319]

After Peleliu, Woody saw action in the Philippines and was briefly stationed in Japan after the Japanese surrender. When Woody came home, he was a sergeant.

Civilian life did not go well for Woody, despite the fact that he was one of the most likeable guys I ever knew as a kid. He married Alice Morgan in 1946, not long after he was discharged from the army. He worked as a plumber, a carpenter, and in any other work he could get on farms and in the building trades.[320]

After the baby shower for Alice in 1951, a son, Woody Joe, was born. When Woody Joe was a teenager, he dived or fell into a shallow swimming pool and was permanently paralyzed.

Unfortunately, the American armed services were slow to acknowledge the toll that the trauma of battle took on many soldiers, sailors, and airmen. It was not until 2007 that the army began a teaching program to help soldiers and their families identify symptoms of what came to be known as post-traumatic stress disorder and traumatic brain injury. I have no doubt that Woodrow Ford suffered from the trauma of war.

Throughout the 1960s, Hub and Kate Wright (Woody's sister) continued to live across the field to the east of my parents' farm. Each time I came from California for a visit, I would ask them about Woody, and they would tell me that he was still drinking too much. By the late '60s, he and Alice were living in Joplin, about fifty miles away.

Then in the spring of 1969, I got a letter from Dad. Woody had driven from Joplin to Hub and Kate's farm on a cool, drizzly day in March. They weren't home. Woody sat down on a stump in their barnyard, removed his shoe, placed a shotgun in his mouth, and pulled the trigger with his toe. His obituary in the *Wheaton Journal* of April 3, 1969, said, in part:

He was a lifelong resident of Missouri and a plumber by trade. He served his country in the armed forces during World War II, as sergeant in the 81st Wildcat Army Division. As a member of the 306th Engineer Combat Battalion (he) served overseas in the Hawaiian Islands, Palau Islands, Philippine Islands and Japan. (He) supervised and directed as many as 45 men in the construction of bridges, roads, buildings and wells.

His pleasing personality was enjoyed by all who knew him.[321]

I cried. And I still think about the day Woody told me about the shell hole, the army officer, and the sniper on Peleliu, and I wonder how many other horrific memories haunted him.

17

Doc Ellison

I could never have guessed as I sat in Bryan Wolfenbarger's barber chair in Wheaton on that warm, seemingly ordinary Saturday afternoon that I was about to witness an exhibition of human behavior that I would remember for the rest of my life.

I was almost eight years old and was acquainted with many of the folks in Wheaton and its surrounding communities. After observing them since birth and hearing my parents talk about them, I thought I knew which ones were hard workers and generally honest, which ones were likeable but lazy, which ones casually lied out of habit even when the truth might have served them better, and which ones wanted people to think they were nice but really were meaner than snakes. But that afternoon in May 1947, I was to learn that human behavior is never totally predictable.

As Bryan was snipping away on my hair, we heard the sound of car horns down on the west end of Main Street, a couple of blocks away. As the honking moved closer, sounds of people hollering grew louder. In a minute or so, Bryan—scissors in one hand and cigarette dangling from one side of his mouth—stopped his snipping and walked toward the big front window of the shop. When I turned my half-shorn head to look, I saw what was causing the commotion.

Driving east down Main Street toward us and steering what

navy skippers would describe as a zigzag course was Doc Ellison, one of the town's two physicians. Doc was handsome, sharp tongued, a crack shot honed by years of bird hunting, a collector of American Indian artifacts, and someone who absolutely didn't give a tinker's damn about how he was perceived by anyone in or near Wheaton—as he was to prove once and for all that afternoon.

He was driving his Packard convertible with the top down. Sitting beside him was his pretty nurse, Nelmarie Marney. Together, he and Nelmarie were the best-looking couple I had ever seen outside of a movie theater. John R. Ellison, DO, wasn't just handsome; he was, in the words of a female classmate of mine, "movie-star handsome." With his black hair and moustache, he could have been a half-brother to either Clark Gable or Errol Flynn.

Memories vary on this next detail of that long-ago Saturday; but in *my* memory, Doc was hoisting a clear bottle that even *I* knew contained an adult beverage. Both Doc and Nelmarie also were waving, and Doc was shouting occasional greetings to the crowd on Main Street as the convertible tacked to port and starboard like a destroyer dodging a submarine attack. Not every greeting from Doc would have been printable in a family newspaper. Kids ran for the safety of sidewalks while their dads and moms yelled for them to get out of the way. Drivers in the path of the convertible, including those on the opposite side of the street, pulled as far to the right as possible and stopped their vehicles.

It was obvious to me that Doc, who was one of the most prominent men in Wheaton, had hoisted sail, and the proverbial three sheets were, indeed, in the wind.

And it was obvious that Nelmarie, his "nurse Friday," also had become his nurse Saturday and Sunday and Monday and so on. Doc and Nelmarie proceeded past Bryan's Barber Shop under full sail as they exchanged greetings with the crowd, some of whom Doc had treated in his office or on house calls. It would be one of his last conversations with his Wheaton patients. Doc wheeled his convertible to the east end of Main Street, turned to the right, and disappeared.

Doc left behind his practice and his wife—who I don't recall ever meeting—and Wheaton had lost one of its most colorful, and unpredictable, characters. Although my grandmother, who was a good buddy of Nelmarie's mother, voiced disapproval of Doc and Nelmarie's behavior, that wasn't the way I saw it. Doc could do no wrong in my eyes, even if he *had* left town with his nurse.

My dad had told me many times that in the winter of 1942, when I was two and a half years old, Doc had received one of the first shipments of sulfa drugs available to physicians in rural southwest Missouri. As I appeared to be dying of pneumonia during a blizzard that left deep snowdrifts and a layer of ice on the three miles of road between our farmhouse and Wheaton, Doc prescribed the sulfa drug by phone, and A. E. "Dike" Elkins, Wheaton's butane-propane distributor, drove one of his big tanker trucks to our farm to deliver the drug, which saved my life. Both Doc and Dike were my heroes after I was old enough to appreciate what they had done.

Doc Ellison was always very kind to me. A couple of times, after I had visited his office for minor ailments or checkups as a little boy, he would show me into his office, retrieve his collection of American Indian pipes and arrowheads, tell me what tribe they had come from and how the pipes were smoked in certain kinds of ceremonies. Even the waiting room in Doc's office offered a good exercise in imagination, because the good doctor decorated the floor with a polar bearskin rug that had the bear's head attached, and I always fancied having to run on ice as the bear chased me.

Doc was always a take-charge guy. My classmate Betty Higgs Lamberson wrote about her own birth and how Doc Ellison had transported her mother—then in labor—to the hospital:

> On Saturday afternoon, June 24, 1939, Marguerite Hoyt Higgs, with baby Joe and her mother, Della Hoyt, walked from their house to downtown to go to the Saturday "drawing" (a 3:00 p.m. event).[322] When Marguerite began to have pains of early labor … they walked back to the Hoyt home, which was next

door to (the Wheaton Postmaster) Earl and Marie
Lamberson (home) and the Curt and Frona Price
phone office. Someone either called or went to get
Dr. Ellison. He came to the house and examined
Marguerite, and then he picked her up and carried her
out the backdoor, down the alley past the phone office,
and across Main Street to the Wheaton Hospital.
Betty Higgs made her arrival at the hospital about
6:30 p.m.[323]

Even though he was a very competent physician, there were
people in the community who didn't like Doc as much as I did.
One of those was Jerry Guiles, proprietor of Jerry's Shoe Shop in
Wheaton. George "Peach" Ford told me that Guiles needed some
sort of regularly administered hypodermic injections and received
them from the town's other physician, Dr. O. S. McCall, who also
owned the Bank of Wheaton. Doc McCall charged Guiles one dollar
per shot.

One day when Doc McCall was out of town, Guiles had to rely
on Doc Ellison for his shot, and Ellison charged him five dollars,
according to Peach, who used to hunt quail and pheasant with
Ellison. Guiles was steamed and voiced his outrage at Doc's charge
to everyone who came into his shoe store. A few weeks later, after
Peach and Doc had loaded their dogs into Doc's Packard convertible
and were about to drive out of town on a quail hunting trip, Doc said
he needed to buy some new laces for his hunting boots.

Peach followed Doc into Guiles Shoe Store. Doc reached into a
little bin full of leather laces, put a pair on the counter, and asked
Guiles how much they cost.

"Five dollars," said Guiles.

Never changing expression, Doc reached back into the bin, threw
a second pair on the counter and said, "Well, at that price, I'll just
take two pairs." Peach said that Doc then laid a ten-dollar bill on the
counter and walked out. "I do believe that sumbitch was trying to get
my goat," Doc said with a straight face as he got back into his car.

There also were people in the community who Doc appreciated and who, no doubt, liked Doc. In December 1954, more than seven years after he and Nell left Wheaton, Doc wrote to one of the town's beloved residents, Mary Ann Simmons Hussey, the widow of Ulysses Sherman Hussey, a farmer near Wheaton who had died four years earlier. Mrs. Hussey, who was eighty-two years old when Doc wrote her, was the mother of Bryan Wolfenbarger's barbering partner, George Hussey, and another Wheaton businessman, Everett Hussey.

My Dear Mrs. Hussey:

Throughout the year we think of our many wonderful friends, but at this time of year we think of our special wonderful friends ... so tonight I write you—my one very special friend at Wheaton.

I read the Wheaton Journal and saw the nice things said about you. I could have written a far better invoice of you. I could have told them how warm was your smile, how erect your head, the fire of fine character in your eyes, how unaffected you are by the common fears of most people, of your faith in God and the people about you that has molded your character to the extent that all are happy in your presence. I am so thankful I know you.

A happy Christmas to you.

Respectfully,
Dr. John[324]

Doc may have left Wheaton, but obviously he had not forgotten the people he met there. He had moved to Wheaton from Eldon, Missouri, in January 1937, purchasing Wheaton's hospital, built by Dr. Otis Sheridan McCall in 1924, from Dr. C. W. Poor.[325] Later, he purchased the McCall residence next door to the hospital and joined the two structures, expanding a six-bed hospital to ten beds.[326]

Doc Ellison said he came to Wheaton for its "good fishing." Indeed, Doc was willing to travel a long way for "good fishing." The July 7, 1938, edition of the *Journal* carried an article about a fishing trip he took to Canada with a Cassville doctor:

RETURNS FROM FISHING TRIP TO CANADA

Dr. J. R. Ellison of here and Dr. McDaniels of Cassville returned home Tuesday of this week from Canada with some very nice Brook and Lake Trout. They left here June 23 and drove as far north into Canada as possible and then rode the train to the end of the line. From this point they traveled in a motor boat as far as possible and reached their destination by canoe. They fished in streams that have never been named, and in some of the following streams: Nipigon River, Nipigon Lake, Lioux Lookout, and Vermillion Lake.

Doc also liked to hunt, but it wasn't until years later that I learned about a little quail hunting jaunt he had on Luther Cartwright's property southeast of Wheaton one fall morning in the late 1930s. Olen Cartwright, Luther's son, had seen Doc and his two prize bird dogs driving into Luther's field, so he walked out to meet him. Just as Olen got within earshot, he said he heard Doc cussing his dogs because they couldn't locate two downed quail he had shot near the embankment that supported the M&A Railroad tracks.

"Why, you goddamned worthless mutts," Olen heard him say. "You get back in that car. I'll get a dog that can find a bird." Doc roared off in his car and came back twenty minutes later with his two bird dogs and a little tan cocker spaniel. Ordering the bird dogs to sit, he sent the cocker spaniel for the birds. In a couple of minutes, the little dog trotted back with one of the birds in its mouth. Doc took it and sent the spaniel back after the other one, which it swiftly retrieved.

Then, standing beside the cocker spaniel, with the two bird dogs sitting sheepishly in front of him like two dog-face soldiers caught goofing off while they were supposed to be peeling spuds, Doc proceeded to chew them out one more time before he loaded them all back into his car and drove off.

Doc was generous with the quail he bagged over the years. The *Sedalia Democrat* of November 22, 1940, reported that Doc furnished the quail for a dinner served at a meeting of the State Board of Chiropractic Examiners, which Doc, as an osteopath, attended.[327]

Doc apparently was a perfectionist. As young as I was when he drove down Main Street and left town on that memorable Saturday, I could appreciate that he exited the Wheaton scene with someone who at least *approached* perfection. Nelmarie was flat-out gorgeous to even a little boy like me. So did I have a problem with Doc after that? Nah. I heard people clucking their tongues about it for a while, but in my mind, all of Doc's critics—even my grandma—didn't know what they were talking about. Doc had saved my life, and as a kid of nearly eight, I saw his ride down Main Street with Nelmarie as a great ending to a real-life movie of Doc's life.

Actually, it wouldn't be the end of the movie. Doc and Nelmarie did get married, and he practiced medicine many more years in Thayer, Missouri, 150 miles away.

Further proof that Doc was a take-charge guy was demonstrated in how he took charge of his death. In March 1965, when he was only fifty-eight years old and suffering from poor health, he waited until Nelmarie and his two daughters were away, called the coroner, and asked him to come to his home in Thayer.

"When the coroner arrived, he found Dr. Ellison dead in bed with a bullet wound through the heart," said the article in the March 18, 1965, edition of the *Wheaton Journal*.[328]

If a movie is ever made about Doc Ellison's life, there's only one theme song that would be appropriate—"My Way:"[329]

I traveled each and ev'ry highway
And more, much more than this, I did it my way.

18

The Snake Oil Salesmen

I can't remember exactly when the snake oil salesmen came to Wheaton, but I was in grade school and still small enough and skinny enough to slither my way through crowds of adults, so I was probably somewhere between six and ten.

It was one of those Saturday afternoons when Wheaton's Main Street was so crowded with farm families doing their weekly trading that there was occasional gridlock, not only because of a glut of cars and trucks on the streets but also on the sidewalks as people tried to walk from the Farmers Exchange to Rowland's dry good store or from the IGA grocery to Claude and Jewel Shipley's Café. If you were in a hurry, you were out of luck—just too many people on the streets to walk fast.

In front of stores up and down the two business blocks of Main Street, women in homemade dresses carried groceries, gabbed, and yelled at little boys scurrying through the crowds. Men in Big Smith, Tuf-Nut, and Oshkosh B'Gosh bib overalls, cotton work shirts, straw hats, or striped shop caps were loading their cattle feed and chicken feed, buying several gallons of Dr. Hess spray to keep the flies off their livestock or depositing their milk checks at the bank.[330] The men who already had finished their town business gathered in little bunches on the sidewalk, put one foot against a wall, smoked, whittled, and talked about the weather and the prices of hay and cows and calves and hogs and wheat.

Nearly every Saturday afternoon, Ada Garrison, a devout Jehovah's Witness, stood at the corner by the bank and handed out copies of the *Watchtower,* much to the annoyance of the Baptist, Methodist, Holiness, Church of Christ, and Catholic faithful who had more temporal issues—such as their next purchase—on their minds on Saturday afternoon.[331] One Saturday, I saw a kid accept a tract from Ada, and instead of politely thanking her for it, he hollered, "I don't thank you!" triggering snickers from folks within earshot.

It was getting fairly late in the afternoon on the "snake oil" Saturday when I noticed a lot of people walking toward the east end of Main Street. That sort of mass movement could only mean that something important was about to happen, so I began to head that way, darting through the mass of humanity.

The crowd was gathering at the end of the block in the vacant lot across from Lancelot Bunnell's DX service station. That lot was where itinerant peddlers often set up shop to put on a little show and sell their wares. They didn't need a business permit to hawk their goods in Wheaton.

By the time I got there, the crowd was spilling into the street, and I couldn't see anything through the mass of adults, so I poked and pushed and slid my way through the big people until I had reached the front row. Little did I realize I was about to see something astounding.

From my prime position, I saw two men—strangers to Wheaton—just twelve or fifteen feet from me. They were exhorting the curious farmers and farm wives and kids to stay and watch something they assured us we had never seen before. They were right.

"I'm talking about the wonders of hypnosis," one of the men said. "But I'll need a volunteer."

After a few seconds, a tall, awkward, sunburned stranger stepped forward. He was wearing a gray work shirt and bib overalls. The pitchman asked him if he'd ever been hypnotized. The answer was no. Would he mind being hypnotized? And again the answer was no.

After the volunteer was assured that he wouldn't be injured, the pitchman produced a gold pocket watch on a long chain and told the gangly fellow to stare at it as he began to swing it back and forth, back and forth, a few feet in front of his face. As the stranger stared, the pitchman said something like, "You are going to sleep ... going into a deep sleep ... a deep sleep."

After a couple of minutes, satisfied that his subject was in a trance, the hypnotist told his volunteer that his entire body, from head to toe, was getting rigid as a rock. Then he told the tall fellow that when he woke up, he wouldn't remember a thing that happened.

By then, I had worked my way around until I was no more than six or eight feet from the hypnotist and his subject. The hypnotist's partner quickly moved two sturdy, high-backed wooden chairs—the kind your grandma had at her dinner table—and placed them back to back about six feet apart.

Moving quickly, the hypnotist and his partner picked up the tall, now glassy-eyed volunteer, who was stiff as a bois d'arc corner post. Adjusting the chairs to fit his length, they put the lanky man's heels on top of one of the wooden chair backs and the back of his head on the other. The hypnotized man, face toward the sky, neither grunted nor flinched. There, supported only by his heels and the back of his head, he could have been a log from the Petrified Forest in Arizona.[332]

Then, as we all watched in open-mouthed amazement, the hypnotist's partner picked up a big flat limestone rock, at least four inches thick and about three feet in diameter, and placed it on the volunteer's belly. Before I could draw another breath, the hypnotist grabbed a sledge hammer, and with a mighty roundhouse swing, he shattered the rock on the rigid fellow's belly as the crowd let out a collective gasp.

The hypnotized man didn't buckle, grunt, or moan. I looked down, and shards of the shattered rock lay at my feet. The hypnotist casually brushed the remaining pieces of the rock off of the volunteer's belly. Then the hypnotist and his partner stood the tall, still rigid man on his feet, dangled the watch in front of him, told him he'd feel just fine—again reminding him he'd remember nothing about what had happened—and commanded him to wake up.

The hypnotized volunteer blinked a time or two as they restored him to his normal consciousness. "Are you okay?" the hypnotist asked.

"Yes," nodded the formerly rigid volunteer.

"Do you hurt anywhere?"

"Nope."

"Do you remember anything we just did?"

"Nope."

The hypnotist thanked him for volunteering, and the gangly stranger walked into the still-awed crowd, apparently without a clue as to what had just happened to him.

At the time, it never occurred to me that the volunteer might have been a ringer who was part of the act, and to this day, I don't know for sure.

Of course, by now, the hypnotist and his partner had the crowd right where they wanted them, and they began to address their real objective. They were there to sell their bottles of magic elixir. They assured the crowd their potion would cure gout, the common cold, remove warts, soothe ulcers, and mitigate the pain of arthritis, neuritis, neuralgia, and rheumatism. Not mentioned by the pitchmen was the fact that a whole bottle of their marvelous concoction also was likely to make the partaker a little drunk. I found out later that its main ingredient was alcohol.

I wandered back down the street because I didn't have any money, and besides that, I knew that my parents and grandparents already had a supply of Watkins and Sloan's liniment—both the dark kind and the red kind—and they didn't need any of this potion, I reasoned.

I had no idea that a separate drama was taking place on that lot. Also witnessing the hypnotism and rock-breaking act were a couple of other kids—James Cantrell, who was to become my classmate from the seventh through the twelfth grades, and his sister, Bernadine, who was a year younger than James and me. Like me, they were spellbound.

"I've been around the world and to the eighth grade picnic, and I ain't ever seen anything like that," James told me years later after he retired as a much-decorated colonel in the US Army Medical Service Corps.

The day the snake-oil salesmen performed, I didn't know James and Bernadine, because they lived a couple of miles east of Wheaton and went to a little country school called Oklahoma, whereas I lived three miles west of Wheaton and went to a little one-room country school called Oshkosh.

As James and I swapped memories of that long-ago afternoon, this is what he told me:

I remember that I had a lot of money. It had been a gift from my Grandpa, Vernie Cantrell, probably at Christmas or for picking up walnuts, or something like that. And I think it was fifty cents. In my mind at the time that was a lot of money. More money than I ever had. Half of it was Bernadine's and we had saved it for quite a while ... and it was burning a hole in our pockets that afternoon because we had brought it to town.

For a long time, Mom had hidden it away in a box somewhere. Well, somehow, we talked her into allowing us to take it to town that Saturday and had agreed we would discuss it with her before we made a purchase. But, we stood together and listened to that flim-flam slick talkin' medicine man and hung on every word—and really believed him when he described how it would make any ailment a person had disappear.

With fresh memories of the aches and pains we heard our hard-working folks discuss at the close of each long day working on that little old rocky hard-scrabble farm, we got very excited that we could do something with our money that would help Mom and Dad.

We had a very animated discussion about ... how happy they would be that we had discovered this amazing medicine that would make their hard lives much easier.

So we proudly marched up to the front of the crowd and made the purchase. And I remember actually running through the crowded town searching for Mom to give her the big news. Can't remember being that excited before in my life.

Well ... needless to say, the reception we got from Mother was not what we were expecting. Mom was never someone who resorted to anger ... but she certainly was not happy with our purchase and made it clear that we needed other things much more than this medicine.

She reminded us of our agreement to discuss any purchase with her in advance. She made us feel uncomfortable enough that we learned a lesson. And to the best of my memory, she never mentioned it again the rest of our lives. I am sure she discussed it with our Dad, but I don't remember him ever mentioning it.

Long after it happened, it surprised James and me that we shared such vivid memories of that Saturday afternoon in Wheaton in the late 1940s—the afternoon when two snake oil salesmen shattered a rock and a little bit of the innocence of a country girl and a couple of country boys.

19

Wheaton's Great Banana War

Wheaton's Great Banana War began on the pages of the *Wheaton Journal* on February 5, 1953, and *Journal* grocery ads suggest that it ended on Saturday, June 13, 1953. The winners of this four-month war were the families who bought bananas at Earl Hooten's store, Hooten's Finer Foods; at Price Naramore and Warren Cullers's newly named IGA Foodliner; and, to a lesser extent, the Farmers Exchange, managed by James Woods for the Missouri Farmers Association.

The Great Banana War, like so many wars throughout world history, probably began by accident. Few people on the European continent would have believed that the assassination of an Austrian archduke in June 1914 would light the fuse that exploded into World War I. And when Woods—who, for the prior six years, had proved himself to be a steady and generally unflappable manager of the only store in Wheaton that sold feed, seed, fertilizer, gasoline, *and* groceries—advertised in the February 5, 1953, edition of the *Wheaton Journal* that the Exchange would sell bananas for nine cents a pound, he could never have guessed he was starting a price war for sales of the tasty tropical fruit in Wheaton's grocery stores.

Woods was a navy veteran of World War II who drove a truck for the Exchange until he was appointed manager in 1947. He replaced veteran merchant Joe Frazier, who had been the store's top man since another experienced manager, Bill Baker, resigned to go into business for himself at Cassville. Woods managed the Exchange very ably for twelve and a half years.

Even after the war, the Exchange remained an old-time store in its grocery operation. There were no shopping carts, and grocery customers relied, at least partly, on Exchange clerks to help them fill their orders. Space simply didn't permit the wide aisles and easy access of a modern supermarket.

James Woods's Farmers Exchange ad in the *Journal* of February 5, 1953, looked ordinary enough, except for the surprising price of bananas—nine cents a pound. Bananas were a popular item, and the Exchange's price was a bargain for a farm family. The fruit was considered a treat, because it was fresh, tasty, nutritious, and a bit exotic since you couldn't grow bananas in your backyard in the Ozarks.

The Exchange's ad that week offered weekend specials that included a three-pound package of Crustene shortening for sixty-nine cents; a one-pound jar of MFA coffee for seventy-five cents; six large, fresh grapefruit for twenty-five cents; a two-pound box of Brookfield cheese for seventy-nine cents; three cans of Halman Star peas for thirty-nine cents and ... drumroll please ... bananas for nine cents a pound. The ad also urged customers to visit the Exchange for garden seed, field seeds, and fertilizer.[333]

Although the town's other two grocery stores were competitive, with each regularly advertising Friday and Saturday specials in Thursday's *Journal*, they didn't immediately change their banana prices in response to the Exchange's advertised price.

Then on March 19, Hooten's Finer Foods advertised bananas at three pounds for twenty-nine cents, only two cents higher for three pounds of the yellow fruit than the Exchange had advertised the previous month. The IGA's Naramore and Cullers didn't respond with a lower banana price—possibly because they were preoccupied with the purchase of a much larger store site, located a block to the west in a building they had just purchased from car dealer Bill Hailey, who had moved his business to Cassville.

Earl Hooten knew that competition from the expanded IGA store was about to get a lot stiffer. The April 9 edition of the *Wheaton Journal*, under the headline IGA MOVING TO NEW LOCATION, described the IGA's future digs as "47 feet wide and 90 feet long and contains almost double the amount of floor space which the IGA store now occupies." I suspect that until the Naramores and Cullers moved to the larger Bill Hailey building, their grocery sales were about even with Hooten's Finer Foods, since both stores were of approximately equal size.

Earl also knew that Price would likely respond to his banana price challenge. Like many wars, this one started with minor skirmishes. The following week in his ad for March 26–28, Earl again advertised bananas at twenty-nine cents for three pounds, adding a line that said: "That Is Better Than 15 cents a Pound, Isn't It?"[334] Earl knew that Price would take the bait and lower his banana price.

Now the Banana War was heating up. On April 9, Price's IGA decided to match Earl's March 19 and March 26 banana price by advertising bananas at three pounds for twenty-nine cents.

Two weeks later, advertising for the April 23 sales day specials, Hooten's Finer Foods cut its banana prices with a *Journal* ad offering "three pounds of bananas for twenty-seven cents." A week later Earl again offered bananas at the same reduced price. At the Farmers Exchange, James Woods wasn't taking the bait. He had thrust bananas into the limelight back in February, but now he was taking care of his regular customers and letting Earl and Price peel back Wheaton's banana prices.

In the May 14 *Journal*, the IGA ad announced that Saturday, May 16, would be the last day the store would do business in its present location, and all orders amounting to one dollar or more would get 10 percent off. Business in the new, expanded location would reopen on Friday, May 22, 1953.

In the same edition, Hooten's Finer Foods stepped up its public-relations game with an ad that read:

IT'S NEWS

We've added several NEW items to our stock in the past few weeks. We have also added several NEW Customers.

In consideration of the above we are offering several NEW and LOWER PRICES from day to day. We will have several SPECIAL LOW PRICES FOR FRIDAY AND SATURDAY OF THIS WEEK.

Will also offer at least one SPECIAL EACH DAY NEXT WEEK.

We will be looking for you in order that we might be of service to you and SAVE YOU MONEY.
Hooten's Finer Foods
WHEATON, MISSOURI

A week later, in the May 21, 1953, edition of the *Journal*, Price Naramore won a round in the grocery competition when a news article on page 1 of the *Journal* gushed:

Anyone who has not seen the interior of the former Wheaton Motor Company building since the interior has been remodeled will hardly recognize it. A new floor of red concrete was run over the old floor and a new ceiling installed.

The east wall is painted yellow, the rear wall is painted red, except for the room where the meat cases are located, and that is painted white. The west wall is painted green.

Persons entering the store will turn to the right. First against the east wall is a coin operated pop refrigerator. Then there is (sic) shelves of food and merchandise down the east wall to the two display meat counters and the 'butcher shop.' The large walk-in refrigerator is at the west of the display refrigerators. The refrigerated fruit and vegetable cases, as well as frozen food refrigerators, will be along the west wall.

The southwest corner of the building will contain flour, sugar and other items for baking. There will be two display racks down the center for merchandise and down the two isles on either side of the building will be stacks of canned goods, display racks of candy, fruit, etc.

There will be two check-out counters at the front of the building and both will be used on busy (days).[335]

The newly located IGA store would also have a new name. Instead of the Wheaton Food Market, it would be called the IGA Foodliner.

But Earl Hooten, who physically was a pretty big man, was not going to let his grocery business be caught flat-footed by the smaller, fast-moving Price Naramore. Price and his wife, Carolyn, knew their way around grocery stores. Price could see more with his one good eye than most folks could see with two. He had grown up helping his father, Lawrence, operate grocery stores at various locations in neighboring McDonald County. Carolyn also had grocery experience. Her father, Joe Schell, ran a general store in Powell for many years. Before they bought the small IGA grocery at the east end of Main Street from Mr. and Mrs. H. H. Stacy in January 1950, Price and Carolyn were proprietors of Naramore's Furniture Exchange, a new and used furniture store in Wheaton.

But years earlier, Earl had demonstrated that he was a risk taker

and a quick thinker who was equal to just about any situation. In the
Wheaton Journal of November 2, 1939, a headline read:

BIRD DOG SETS SOW AND LITTER OF PIGS

> Earl Hooten of Wheaton, who teaches at the
> Oklahoma school on Shoal Creek, was training
> a bird dog to set birds Tuesday afternoon in L.O.
> Cartwright's field, south of town. Instead of setting
> a covey of quail the dog set a large white sow and
> a litter of pigs. The pigs flushed and as this was
> something new for the bird dog, it picked up one
> of the pigs and was retrieving it when the old sow
> decided to take some action and started after the dog,
> which was nearing Earl with the pig. Earl jumped
> a fence in order to get in the safety zone. The dog
> released the pig uninjured, but Earl was covered with
> a cold sweat.

Earl may have been covered with a cold sweat when an angry sow
was charging him, but tough grocery competition didn't bother him
a bit. No siree! In the same May 21 *Journal* edition that announced
the new and improved IGA, Hooten's Finer Foods introduced a new
wrinkle of its own:

> We wish to announce that we have become a
> member of the ASSOCIATED GROCERS. With
> the massive buying power of A-G, we are sure we
> can give our customers even better service and as
> competitive prices as can be found in this territory.

Below that announcement was a larger-than-usual list of Hooten's
special sale items. In fact, Earl's ad was larger than the one for Price's
new IGA store.

A week later, on May 28, the Great Banana War escalated, as

war correspondents often say. Price ran a big ad that included golden bananas for ten cents per pound. The smaller ad for Hooten's Finer Foods contained an intriguing line to entice customers:

"There is no telling what we may think of or do for your sake, so come in."

That was equivalent to the US president, when he's talking tough to some country he's upset with, saying, "We're keeping all options on the table."

On June 4, the IGA's full-page ad in the *Journal* urged readers to "Visit our newly remodeled store! Share in these special values," followed by a long list of specials. The ad boasted in capital letters:

MAKE IT POSSIBLE FOR YOU TO ENJOY SHOPPING AT ITS BEST IN THE MODERN MANNER!
PLENTY OF FREE PARKING
NICE WIDE AISLES
EVERY DAY LOW PRICES,
LARGER MEAT DEPARTMENT
NEW MODERN SHELVING
FASTER CHECKING SYSTEM

Hooten's Finer Foods ad that week was routine and far smaller. Earl probably knew there was no way he could match Price's new IGA store ad, so he might as well save advertising money. Knowing that the IGA ad would dominate the *Journal* that week, James Woods didn't even bother to advertise Farmers Exchange grocery items at all. Instead, he advertised MFA liability insurance, which he also sold.

Earl Hooten may not have had the wherewithal to match Price Naramore's store size or grocery inventory, but he was a shrewd reader of people, and he knew Price would respond to a challenge from Hooten's. In the June 11 *Journal,* Earl decided to set an especially low price for bananas on Friday, June 12, and Saturday, June 13.

Earl's ad of that week advertised that Hooten's Finer Foods would sell bananas for *seven cents per pound.* It's very likely that Price got wind that Earl was going to lower banana prices to a ridiculous level that weekend, but it's also likely that he didn't know exactly *how* low Earl would go. So Price kept the price of his "Golden Ripe Bananas" at ten cents per pound, probably thinking that Earl wouldn't go any lower.

It's virtually certain that Saturday, June 13, 1953, was the day that Wheaton's grocery shoppers went bananas. It could be debated that it was another Saturday that summer, but the events of Banana Saturday are more important than the exact date.

I had just completed the eighth grade at Wheaton, and on my family's farm three miles to the west, I was preoccupied with the twice-a-day chore of helping my dad milk about fifty cows, cleaning up the milk parlor, and working in our fields at various tasks on the tractor, so I have only a vague recollection from secondhand accounts of that memorable Saturday.

But two of my classmates, Barney Calame and James Cantrell, were bagging and carrying out groceries in Wheaton that day. Barney was employed at the IGA Foodliner, and James recalls that he "was working at Hooten's and I remember this day very well ..." They agree that Saturday, June 13, was the day the Wheaton's Great Banana War went nuclear.

When the stores opened that Saturday morning, Price Naramore's new, spiffy IGA was selling a pound of bananas for a dime, a bargain even at 1953 prices. But a block to the east, in his older and much smaller store, Earl Hooten was selling a pound of his bananas for seven cents.

Knowing Price Naramore as I did, I strongly suspect that Earl's seven-cent-a-pound bananas presented a challenge that Price was constitutionally incapable of ignoring, especially when some of the customers entering his new store began to ask him why his bananas cost three cents more per pound than Hooten's bananas. So Price did what any competitive grocer would do—he reduced the price. It's very likely that he started by simply matching Earl's seven-cents-per-pound price, although it's possible he went a penny lower.

Since Saturday was typically Wheaton's biggest business day, the town was buzzing. Farm families from a twenty-five-mile radius flocked to Wheaton to do their trading, in the parlance of the day. They had eggs to sell, chicken and cow feed to purchase, trucks and cars to gas up, and, of course, groceries to buy. On a summer Saturday, Wheaton's population of nearly four hundred residents easily could swell to a thousand or more. The sidewalks were full of people, and most of them liked bananas. On this Saturday, they also liked the banana prices.

It didn't take Dick Tracy's two-way wrist radio for the word to spread. Faster than you could peel one of Price's "golden ripe" plantains, Earl heard that the IGA had matched or perhaps undercut his banana price.

Earl did the only thing he could do. He cut his banana price again—whether by one or two cents per pound, no one can remember. The important thing was that after this latest slash in the price of the tropical fruit, Hooten's was selling bananas for five cents a pound, once again leaving Price Naramore's new IGA Foodliner as the higher-priced banana store.

For the rest of that Saturday, prices of the yellow fruit were as slippery as, well, a banana peel.

"From Earl's end, the purpose was never to sell more bananas," James Cantrell recalls. "It was all a big joke."

Back and forth, back and forth, for the rest of the day, first one and then the other competitive grocer reduced the price of bananas. By closing time, bananas at both stores were sold out.

"My memory is that by sundown the price of bananas at the IGA had dropped to two cents a pound," Barney Calame says. "I remember someone—or maybe several guys in a pooled purchase—buying several pounds of bananas and taking them to the movie in a brown grocery sack." The feature movie at Wheaton's Cozy Theatre that night was *The Blazing Forest*. A more appropriate movie for that evening might have been *Top Banana*, starring comedian Phil Silvers, but it wasn't released until the following year—after Wheaton's grocers had signed an armistice in the Great Banana War.

The immediate effect that cut-rate bananas had on the community was that the menu in scores of homes around Wheaton for the next week was banana pudding, banana ice cream, banana creme pie, or just plain bananas.

"Perhaps the reason I remember it," James Cantrell says, "is because my mother fed me so many bananas the next week that I have never liked them since." James says he was paid three dollars for his day's work at Hooten's. Barney's ledger, in which he carefully recorded every payment and expense, shows that he was paid two dollars and ninety cents for his work at the IGA on June 13, 1953. That kind of big money could have kept each of them in bananas until long after the fruit had turned soft and mushy.

The following Friday and Saturday, Hooten's again offered bananas at seven cents per pound, but no one remembers any great run on bananas that week. Whatever their price at the IGA, it wasn't advertised in the *Journal*. Both merchants probably realized that their customers had lost their craving for bananas.

James Woods, the guy whose ad probably started the Banana War, may have attempted to start Banana War II on July 23 when he advertised bananas for ten cents a pound at the Farmers Exchange. If that was his purpose, his competitors didn't take the bait. They very likely guessed that after the sales of the past month, people had not yet regained their appetite for bananas.

Although no formal banana peace treaty was signed, the IGA Foodliner listed no more banana specials in 1953. Hooten's Finer Foods advertised bananas at three pounds for twenty-five cents on August 27, but bananas were not again an ad item until December that year.

Wheaton's grocers had learned that peeling back banana prices was, indeed, a slippery slope.

20

The Day Aunt Jemima Came to Town

As soon as I got home from school, Mom told me the big news. Aunt Jemima—the *real* Aunt Jemima—was coming to town Saturday. She said Wally had written an article about it in the *Wheaton Journal*. Wally Fox, Dan Shewmake's cousin, published the *Journal* with the help of his wife, Bessie. And, except for news from the communities around Wheaton filed by the country correspondents, Wally wrote most of the articles, sold the ads, and set the type for the *Journal*, which was published every Thursday.

Even though I was not quite halfway through the second grade at Oshkosh, the one-room country school five miles west of Wheaton, I could read pretty well, so I grabbed the *Journal* to read about Aunt Jemima. Sure enough, at the top of the front page in the edition of November 16, 1946, was the story:

AUNT JEMIMA TO BE HERE SATURDAY

Aunt Jemima will be in Wheaton Saturday, Nov. 16 and will be the chief center of attraction at the Stacy & Sallee Food Market.

Announcement of her coming is made in a page advertisement appearing in this issue of the Journal, which tells of the fact that "Aunt Jemima" will mix, flip and serve you free those temptin' Aunt Jemima pancakes.

This is a demonstration staged at the Stacy & Sallee Food Store by the Quaker Oats Company through their representative in this territory. The cooked pancakes will be absolutely free to those who visit this store Saturday.

Aunt Jemima is to be here in person. However, there is a legendary story connected with the Aunt Jemima of long ago. It is as follows:

Aunt Jemima was a mammy cook, famous in the Old South in those golden days "befo' de Wah."

They tell us her master was Colonel Higbee, owner of a plantation at Higbee's Landing, Louisiana, on the Mississippi River ...[336]

"Legend has it," the article continued, "that Aunt Jemima was a genius," and that "in a land of excellent cooks, she was supreme."

The achievement she valued the most, the article said, was her secret recipe "for her most famous of delicious dishes—Aunt Jemima Pancakes."

As a seven-year-old, it never occurred to me that Wally got the language about the "legend" from Quaker Oats publicists or that the original "Aunt Jemima" had been a slave. What it told me was that for the first time in my life, I might get to see a black woman up close. My parents had taught me to never to use the N-word. The respectful term in those days was *Negro*. It was years before the terms *black* or *African American* would be commonly used.

I had seen a few black people in Neosho, the Newton County seat twenty-five miles from Wheaton, but I had never spoken a word to any of them, and the closest I'd ever been to them was meeting them on the street. Once in a while, African American men who rode handcars and worked on the Missouri and Arkansas (M&A) Railway had stopped for a drink of water at the depot in Wheaton, but they never stayed long.

In November 1946, the *Journal* article meant one thing to me: I would get to see Aunt Jemima face-to-face—and get a pancake to boot.

When Dad parked his pickup in Wheaton on the Saturday afternoon of Aunt Jemima's appearance, Main Street was packed with people. Outside Stacy & Sallee's grocery store, there was a big crowd. Men and women and kids were lined up, slowly working their way into the store. I finally got close enough to glimpse her through the door. It was Aunt Jemima, all right—plump, pleasant, and wearing the kerchief, apron, and plaid dress she wore in all the pictures advertising her pancake flour.

From a stack of pancakes a little bigger than silver dollars, she used a spatula to place two or three on a paper saucer, pour maple syrup on them, and hand them to the next person in line. Finally, I got close enough to get a better look at her.

I couldn't tell too much about her hair, because it was done up in the kerchief, but it was definitely a different texture than mine and, yes, she *was* black. She was quick and alert and seemed like she was enjoying herself. Occasionally, she would say something—I don't remember what—and it was always friendly and polite. I decided I liked her.

But it still seemed strange to me that anyone could have skin that color. Hers, as best I recall, was a rich brown and a lot darker than mine could become even if I went without a shirt all summer.

She gave me my pancake, and it was good. I drifted away from my parents and walked back outside the store, where there was still a long line of people waiting to get their pancakes. Then I heard some boys talking. I don't remember who it was, but I remember what they were saying.

"She's a fake," one boy declared.

Another boy agreed and added, "Yeah, did you see her hands?"

"Yeah, the palms of her hands are white," said the first kid. "She's just got paint on."

Well, that did it for me. I had to get one more pancake and try to figure this out. I got back in line.

Sure enough, the second time she served me pancakes, I noticed something interesting. The palms of her hands *were* white—not quite as white as mine, but a lot whiter than her face or arms. I looked at my white paper saucer to see if any paint had come off on it, but I couldn't see any smudges.

Still puzzled, I turned to my mother on the drive home. "Mom, I think Aunt Jemima was a fake Negro," I said.

"What do you mean?" my mother asked.

"The palms of her hands were white," I said. "She probably just had paint on."

My mother, though not a great deal more experienced in race relations than I, smiled and said, "No, son, Aunt Jemima is a real Negro."

"Well, what about her hands?" I asked. "The palms of her hands were white."

"Honey, she just comes that way," Mom said. "Maybe it just shows how hard she works."

I thought about that a long time. I still didn't understand it, but I took my mother's word for it.

On the following Thursday, the *Wheaton Journal* carried another front-page story penned by Wally Fox:

LARGE CROWD HERE TO SEE AUNT JEMIMA SAT.

A large crowd was present Saturday at Stacy and Sallee's Food Market to see the one and only Aunt Jemima in person and to eat some of her flapjacks. During the day Aunt Jemima cooked and served 1,000 of her famous flap jacks made from the famous Aunt Jemima ready mixed pancake flour.

Quaker Oat Company officials, who were here and sponsored the appearance of Aunt Jemima, were well pleased with the results of the demonstration. One official related to the Journal that the people attending the demonstration were the best mannered of any demonstration he had taken part in. He also related that Aunt Jemima had an enjoyable time here Saturday and was well pleased with the way people treated her. This commendation speaks well of the people of this territory.[337]

Over the next few days, I heard several adults say that they appreciated Wally's article. "I'm glad people were nice to her," my mother said. I agreed.

Looking back on that Saturday in 1946, from the perspective that nearly seventy years adds, it seems incredible that I could have been so naive.

I was oblivious to the controversy that surrounded the "legend" of Aunt Jemima and only later would recognize civil rights as a major issue. I've wondered many times what happened to the "Aunt Jemima" I met that day. I wish that sometime during my years as a newspaper reporter I could have interviewed her and heard her candid observations about what it was like to play Aunt Jemima for the people in the small towns in that part of the country.

And I would have told her that on November 16, 1946, she began to broaden one ignorant little boy's understanding of, and appreciation for, the diversity of the human race.

21

Dike Elkins, the Forgotten Hero

He was an unlikely hero, but ever since the day Dad told me how Dike Elkins saved my life, he was a hero to me. I thought his name was "Dike," because that's what everybody called him, but Dike was just a nickname. No one I've ever known can say how he got the moniker, but after I read *Hans Brinker, or The Silver Skates* in grade school, I imagined that he plugged a leak in a dike and prevented a flood when he was young, just like the legendary little Dutch boy in the story. When I learned to read, I discovered that the *Wheaton Journal* called him "A.E." Elkins, the initials for Allen Eldridge. Dike's first wife, Montie, always called him "Eldridge," which sounded a bit stiff to a little boy whose ears were used to Ozark nicknames like "Peach" and "Pig" and "Junior."

Dike Elkins didn't look a bit like John Wayne or Clark Gable or any of the movie heroes of the 1940s. Dike was about six feet tall with ample girth, a wide face, and a calm demeanor. I never saw him move fast, but I think his mind was always in high gear, because he built one of Wheaton's most successful businesses from scratch, starting Elkins Butane Company in 1939.

During all the years I knew him, I never heard Dike talk about his family history, but Dad told my mother and me that Dike said he had American Indian ancestors.[338] I never gave it much thought, but he did name his son Quannah. The last great chief of the Comanche tribe was Quanah Parker, pronounced the same way, but spelled differently. Parker became famous in the late 1800s. Quannah Elkins endured some teasing because of his name. Quannah told Dad that when he was in grade school, a new teacher calling the roll on the first day of school said, "Q-Anna Elkins? Who's she?" as most of the rest of the class, who knew the young man, laughed uproariously.

Unlike his substantially built parents, Quannah was slender and wiry. When I saw him working—he was an excellent woodworker and mechanic—I would imagine how he would look if he were dressed as a Native American.

Dike and Montie's other two children were Emma Lane and Mary Helen. All of the Elkins kids were grown by the time I was old enough to start first grade. Dike's brother, Wilbur, worked for him at Elkins Butane and later was cofounder of Elkins Butane's successor—Southwest Gas—after Dike moved on to other things.

Montie was a heavyset lady—a substantial woman. In the 1940s and '50s, her brother Bill Brown ran a service station and garage at the bottom of the hill in the heart of Rocky Comfort, just two and a half miles from Wheaton. Dike and Montie, who were married in 1922, were woven deeply into the Wheaton and Rocky Comfort communities.

Montie and I always laughed about our ages every July when I was a little boy. Montie was born July 25, 1900, and I was born July 25, 1939. So it was easy for me to keep track of Montie's age—and Dike's too—because he was born the same year as Montie, on September 19, 1900. So whatever year it was, that was how old Dike and Montie were on their birthdays, minus 1,900 years.

Dad used to tell me that Dike, Wilbur, and their sister, Grace, grew up "over by McNatt." To me, he might as well have said "up there on the moon." I was a freshman in high school before I ever set foot *near* McNatt. I was never sure you could say "set foot *in* McNatt," because I'm not sure it was even a town. But I played baseball there once. One Sunday morning at the Rocky Comfort Church of Christ, Dale Flaxbeard, who was old enough to drive a car, said he knew a bunch of boys who wanted to play a baseball game that afternoon at McNatt, if Dale could get a team together. So Dan Shewmake and I rode to McNatt with Dale after church that Sunday. Sure enough, there was a baseball diamond, and we played a game against the McNatt boys. But even after I'd been there, I would have said that McNatt was nowhere. Actually, McNatt is roughly fifteen miles west of Wheaton, about halfway between Longview and Goodman, which were "almost nowhere" towns. If McNatt even had a store, I don't remember it, but it might have.

Dike had long since left McNatt by the time I came along in 1939. In 1930, he lived in Oklahoma City, and in 1931, he opened A. E. Elkins Chevrolet Sales and Service in Rocky Comfort—selling Chevys, managing a garage that was part of the business, and selling Crosley Superheterodyne radios and Goodyear tires. Tragically, in May 1932, Dike's garage burned down, wiping out the garage and everything in it—all his tools, tires and tubes, accessories, oil, and a brand-new 1932 Chevy car.[339] Always the entrepreneur, Dike didn't stay out of business long. By July 1932, only two months after the fire, he and his brother-in-law Bill Brown moved to Wheaton and opened Wheaton Motor Company, Chevrolet Sales and Service, and also sold Marathon gas and oil, US tires and USL batteries.[340]

In January 1934, Bill decided to move back to Rocky Comfort and open a filling station and garage there, leaving Dike in sole control of the Chevy agency in Wheaton.[341] What seemed to set Dike Elkins apart from many local business owners was his continual search to sell the public a new, cutting-edge product. In the local items of the April 12, 1934, *Wheaton Journal*, it was reported that the "Wheaton Motor Company sold a new Kelvinator refrigerator to W.C. Chenoweth." Wallace C. "Wal" Chenoweth was one of Wheaton's most successful merchants, operating Chenoweth & Son, which advertised as "Barry County's Largest General Store."

In November 1934, Dike purchased local businessman Oral Burger's insurance agency and began to sell policies insuring town property, farm property, and automobiles.[342] A month later, Dike bought a Marathon gas and oil distributorship and operated it from Wheaton.[343]

Running three operations was too much for even a canny businessman like Dike, so in February 1935, he sold Wheaton Motor Company, his Chevrolet agency, to Wheaton schoolteacher Leslie Fite. Dike decided to concentrate on running his Marathon gas and oil business and his insurance agency. He also began to involve himself in the affairs of the Wheaton School District, winning a three-year term on the school board in April 1935.[344]

In 1936, Dike and a local farmer, Cline Hancock, began to promote the idea of building a better worship facility for members of the Wheaton Church of Christ. They had been meeting in the Farmers Exchange store building where livestock feed and groceries were sold and chickens and eggs were purchased from area farmers. Dike and Cline soon purchased the lot where the current church house is located, and with volunteer labor, the building was completed before the end of 1936.[345]

Dike was content to operate his gas and oil distributorship and his insurance agency until the spring of 1939, when he saw a brand-new business opportunity—something that hadn't been tried in southwest Missouri—a dealership in a new source of heating. Elkins Butane Co. ran its first two ads in the *Wheaton Journal* on March 9, 1939:

Announcement

I wish to announce to the people of this territory that I have moved my insurance office from my home to the Reece Building on the south side of Main Street in Wheaton.

Also I am a distributor for this territory for Butane Gas and Nabuco appliances, and am carrying in stock a complete line of ranges, heaters, hot water heaters, etc.

The Butane gas is similar to natural gas and does not come in pressure tanks as some "bottle gas" and is much cheaper than the "bottled gas" heretofore offered the public.

You are given a cordial welcome to come in and look over these appliances and you will be furnished any information desired.

Let us demonstrate in your home how this new gas works.

A.E. Elkins

The second ad obviously was designed to lure customers into his store, and the coffee and cookies offer provided a hint that Montie was his business partner:

FREE COFFEE AND COOKIES

A.E. Elkins, distributor, for Butane gas and Nabuco appliances, will serve free Coffee and Cookies to every person who visits his store Saturday afternoon, March 11. All you have to do is walk inside and you will be promptly served a cup of coffee prepared on the Magic Chef Butane operated gas stove, and also cookies.

About a month later, Dike scored a prominent customer for his new butane business. He installed a butane system in Wally Fox's *Wheaton Journal* printing plant to heat the lead for Wally's linotype. Wally praised the benefits of the new butane system in the April 20, 1939, edition of the *Journal*. Not only was the article free advertising for Elkins Butane, it also explained some of the mechanical problems faced by a small-town newspaper publisher who operated on a bare-bones budget:

JOURNAL INSTALLS BUTANE GAS EQUIPMENT

The Elkins Butane Gas Co. completed the installation of a Nabuco life-time Butane gas system in The Journal office Saturday. The system was connected to a new gas burner on the Linotype machine, which keeps a uniform heat for melting the metal used in the printing of the Journal and other work.

The burners on Linotype machines can be operated by three methods—gasoline, electricity and natural or artificial natural gas. When the Linotype was installed in The Journal Office several years ago, the cost of the machine was $3100.00, equipped with a gasoline burner, the electric heater being some $200.00 higher, and of course at that time, Wheaton only had electricity part time and the mechanism of the Linotype was operated with a gasoline engine. The gasoline engine was discarded for an electric motor after satisfactory electricity service was established in Wheaton, but due to the cost of the electric heater, the Linotype continued to be heated with the gasoline burner. Unless high test gasoline was used this burner was very unsatisfactory, the temperature of the metal in the machine changing so often that it was almost impossible to run it at times. The price of high test gasoline was increased to 25 cents per gallon, which was too high to burn, and for the past few months the burner has been operated very unsatisfactorily, on the low test white gasoline, as gasoline with lead added could not be used.

With the new system and burner, the metal heat being controlled with a thermostat, about 99 per cent of The Journal's worries over heating the Linotype metal is over.

Without question, Wally went deeply in debt to buy the butane heating system. Southwest Missouri was still mired in the Great Depression in the late 1930s, and Dike Elkins realized a lot of people simply couldn't afford to convert to butane. Even if they could afford the cost of installing a butane tank, they'd have to buy a new butane-burning stove and a water heater, which would put his butane system out of reach financially. A *Journal* ad on April 27, 1939, undoubtedly written by Dike himself, boldly informed potential customers they could get favorable financing through a federal housing plan. His ad ran in boldface type:

SAVE: Time, Money and Your Health Everyday of Every Month of the Year by installing a National Butane gas system in your backyard. That's why we say a baby gas well in every back yard. You will own one some day, why not now, and get that much more use out of it, because it will last a lifetime, and the longer you wait, the more you are cheating yourself. Come in and select the range, hot water heater, floor furnace, circulator or any kind of appliance your friends have in the City—you can have the same wherever you live. We finance your paper through: the Federal Housing Plan, 12 to 36 months to pay. Let us demonstrate this gas in your home.

ELKINS BUTANE GAS CO.
Wheaton, Missouri

Dike wasn't missing any angles. On June 29, 1939, he ran an ad in the *Journal* offering twenty dollars to trade in your old ice box, "regardless of make or condition," toward the purchase of a brand-new SUPERFEX kerosene or butane refrigerator. "Operates anywhere without electricity or running water," said the ad. "Easy monthly plan." Until I read that ad years later, I'd never heard of a kerosene refrigerator.

Dike knew he would need to help his potential customers understand how butane systems worked before they would buy his products. On August 31, 1939, he ran an informative ad in the *Wheaton Journal*:

WHAT IS BUTANE GAS?

A liquefied petroleum gas (butane and propane) are gases refined from natural gas or petroleum refinery gas, and are in a gaseous state in normal atmospheric temperature and pressure, but may be maintained in the liquid state at normal atmospheric temperature by suitable pressure. Advantage of this characteristic is taken by the industry and for convenience the gases are transported and stored under pressure as liquids.

Our Butane is of the highest type and comes to you odorized, so that in the event of carelessness a gas jet is left open the leak may be quickly detected upon entering the room, and windows and doors opened, and the gas driven out before matches are struck …

If you are interested in butane or propane gas to the extent that you may soon become a user—be sure that your dealer is reliable, efficient, and can give you service. Don't let him fill your gas system with a product that is certain to give you trouble.

Elkins Butane Co.
Wheaton, Missouri
Telephone 58

Besides the local newspaper, the next-best way of advertising in a small town like Wheaton is the barbershop. Men waiting to get their "ears lowered"—Ozark vernacular for a haircut—gossip as much as they accuse women of doing at the beauty parlor. Dike knew this. In 1939, Bryan's Barber Shop, operated by bald-headed barber Bryan Wolfenbarger, was located in the *Journal* building. Since Dike had installed a butane system in the *Journal*'s printing plant in April, seven months later, he persuaded Bryan that he needed a butane water heater so he could soften up his customers' beards with warm water when they came in for a shave. On November 9, 1939, the *Journal* reported that the Elkins Butane Gas Co. had installed a new automatic butane gas water heater in Bryan's Barber Shop.

The comfort of a warm, moist towel before and after a shave at the barbershop provided great word-of-mouth advertising for Elkins Butane. This is the way I would describe how word-of-mouth worked in Wheaton in 1939:

A farmer gets a little shaggy. He's tired and needs a break from fixing fence or cleaning out the chicken house. His wife is out of Oxydol washing powder and Clabber Girl baking powder, and she needs some chicken feed for her laying hens. So he gets off his tractor or unhitches his team of horses, takes their harness off, waters them, hops into his old truck, and goes to town for a haircut before he goes to the store. He sits down in the barbershop and talks to whoever's there waiting his turn. Bryan runs some hot water and wraps a steaming towel around the face of the guy in the barber chair, and next thing you know, the guy says that warm towel feels good. So the subject turns to Bryan's new hot water heater—a great promo for Dike's butane gas. This scenario happens a dozen times a day for weeks.

Word about Dike's butane spread quickly throughout southwest Missouri. The same edition of the *Journal* that reported on Bryan's new hot water heater also reported that Dike had sold butane systems to J. W. McGraw of Purdy, a dozen miles from Wheaton; Fred D. Hays of Lamar, some seventy miles to the north; and J. Ray King of Granby, twenty miles to the northwest.

After the United States was thrust into World War II in December 1941, there were shortages of all kinds of consumer products, but Elkins Butane survived. When the war ended in August 1945, sales of butane heating stoves, water heaters, kitchen ranges, and refrigerators shot through the roof as pent-up demand heated up the economy. Dike may have been from McNatt, but he was no country bumpkin. In the butane/propane field, Elkins Butane dominated the southwest Missouri market in the early postwar years.

In 1946, Dike opened a store in Neosho, the county seat of Newton County, twenty-five miles northwest of Wheaton. He also built a big, buff-colored brick building on Highway 86 in Wheaton to house the main company office and to display his Magic Chef ranges, Westinghouse refrigerators, Adams gas heaters, Coleman floor furnaces, and other appliances.

After opening his Neosho store, Dike vastly expanded Elkins Butane's sales territory. He began to sell butane tanks and heating and cooling products to businesses and individuals throughout southwest Missouri. His big trucks with "Elkins Butane" painted on the tanks were common sights on roads all over the area.

One day during my early grade school years, I was riding in the pickup with Dad, and we saw an Elkins Butane truck. That's when Dad told me that if it hadn't been for Dike and one of those trucks, it was very likely that I wouldn't be alive.

In the winter of 1942, Dad said, I got pneumonia. As my breathing became more and more labored, Dad said, he and my mother were frantic to get me to a doctor. But the electricity was off because freezing rain had snapped the power lines, and the road—that stretched three miles from our farm to Wheaton and the nearest doctor—was impassable because of a thick layer of ice and heavy snowdrifts. The telephone lines weren't down, so Dad called Doc Ellison (Dr. John R. Ellison, DO) in Wheaton and explained that I was in bad shape. Doc said he had just received his first shipment of a new medicine called sulfa drug that was supposed to work well against infections such as pneumonia, and he would prepare a bottle of it for me.

However, there seemed to be no way to deliver the medicine to our farm. Ordinary cars and pickups couldn't navigate the snow and ice on the roads. Then Dad remembered Dike's heavy butane tanker truck. He called Dike and asked if he thought his truck could break through the ice and get enough traction to make it to our lane, on the road that ran between Wheaton and Stella. Dike said he'd sure try.

Dike drove his butane truck to Doc Ellison's office on Main Street, picked up the sulfa drug, and headed west toward our farm. The road is straight, but there were dips and hills between Emmett Tichenor's farm and Carl Fehring's farm. Dike steered his big tanker truck down the hills without sliding off the road, and the truck had enough weight to break through the ice and climb the hills. He made it to the end of our lane. Dad trudged through the drifts between our house and the road where Dike waited, picked up the wonder drug, and I lived to tell about it.

The new drug probably saved my life, and so did Doc Ellison, who dispensed it. But neither he nor the medication would have been worth a dime if it hadn't been for Dike's willingness to go out of his way to help. He became one of my childhood heroes.

In 1946, Dike offered Dad a job, and he grabbed it. People around Wheaton were prospering, and lots of them could afford to get rid of their wood or coal heating stoves and their leaky old iceboxes and convert to new and much cleaner butane and propane heating stoves, kitchen ranges, and refrigerators.

Dad always said he got a fair day's pay for a fair day's work at Elkins Butane. I don't ever remember hearing him gripe about Dike as a boss. However, after a year spent crawling under old farmhouses and encountering snakes, spiders, and other inhospitable critters as he installed pipes and copper tubing for butane and propane appliances, he came home one day and said to my mother, in the exaggeratedly hillbilly voice he sometimes adopted when he was trying to be silly, "Vel-me Murl (her name was Velma Muriel), I've quit at Elkins Butane, and if you ever catch me talkin' about goin' to work for anybody else again, as long as I live, I want you to kick my ass." It was a vow he kept. But his relationship with Dike and Montie remained warm.

Elkins Butane was expanding fast, but it wasn't the only appliance game in Wheaton. Roy Robinson, our nearest neighbor on the farm to our north, was selling Maytag washing machines and ironers, Hoover sweepers, Fairbanks Morse water systems, Philco refrigerators, freezers, radios—and a little later, television sets at his Wheaton Maytag store on Main Street.

Wheaton Hardware owners Roy Killion and Floyd "Fat" Flora offered Frigidaire and Crosley Shelvador refrigerators, Crosley radios, Speed Queen and Frigidaire washing machines, and other electric and gas-powered appliances.

At nearby Rocky Comfort, Bill Brown—Dike's brother-in-law and former business partner—was selling Hoover vacuum cleaners, RCA and Phillips radios, Florence butane and electric ranges, and Thor washing machines at his service station and appliance store.

They were worthy competitors, but Dike always seemed to be just a half step ahead of them. At his new building that had an upstairs apartment where he and Montie lived, he was able to display more goods than most of his local competitors. Dike and the merchants of Wheaton and Rocky Comfort knew that people were ready and eager to buy things. During the four years of World War II, no new cars or appliances were manufactured, so for several years after the war, pent-up demand exceeded supply.

Dike knew the public was in a buying mood. He was there to sell them not only what they wanted but also what he could interest them in. He had Westinghouse lamps for better lighting, and Zonolite insulation to make drafty old farmhouses warmer in the winter and cooler in the summer. Realizing that almost every farm family kept a flock of chickens, Dike ran an ad in the January 4, 1946, *Journal* that featured time clocks for the lights in chicken houses. "[T]urns lights on, dim at first, then come on full; goes off the same way, stays dim long enough for poultry to get to their places on the roost before going out."

That early in my life, I knew nothing about Dike's sales strategy; I just knew that I liked to go to Dike and Montie's big new building and look at the merchandise. A lot of it was stuff a farm boy like me had never heard of. One was a "Mexihot sandwich machine," and another was a "Frilator" for deep-fat frying. I think they were mostly for cafés and restaurants. I had never heard of either appliance, but I figured they must be really good, because the sandwich machines cost nearly eighty dollars, and the Frilators cost as much as a milk cow—$189.50.

An Elkins Butane ad in March 1946 closed with a line that showed Dike was a born salesman:

WHAT WE HAVE

We do not have as much merchandise as we want, but sometimes we get to thinking about the things that we do not have, or the things some want, and completely forget the things WE DO HAVE.

We are receiving small shipments of the famous Magic Chef divided top gas range with even control for only $126.25.

We have received 4 Westinghouse refrigerators, 7-ft. size for $179.95. Also have just received two extra large (reach-in type) Westinghouse refrigerators, 30 cubic feet size, each $550.00, plus frt.

Have in stock butane plants. Also gas water heaters (20 and 30 gallon sizes) at $69.50 and up.

Adams gas heaters, Mexihot sandwich machine, $79.50 each; Coleman floor furnaces, $116 each, with thermostat control; famous Frilators for cafes or hotels, deep fat frying saves ½ of grease bill, $189.50; Zonolite home insulation, $1.25 per bag; gasoline, kerosene, heating oils, greases. Yes, we have genuine Westinghouse lamps, also fluorescent lamps in 20 and 40 watts, Maytag oil in 1-quart and 1-gallon glass containers.

Remember good merchandise is NOT CHEAP and cheap merchandise is NOT GOOD.
Elkins Butane Co.
WHEATON, MO.—NEOSHO, MO.

Later in 1946, Elkins Butane was selling bathroom fixtures and pumps for deep and shallow wells. A year later, in September 1947, long before anybody had air-conditioning, Dike was selling swamp coolers with a name that would cool you off before you ever turned it on—"SNO-BREEZE evaporator coolers." He added Servel gas refrigerators, Wear-Ever pressure cookers, electric fans, and steel kitchen cabinets. Toastmaster and Proctor "automatic" toasters were wonders to me. I learned later that "automatic" meant the toast popped up when it was done.

I had never heard of a sunlamp, but Elkins Butane sold them. A Westinghouse "Health Lamp" that usually sold for $39.95 could be yours for only $29.95. I always wanted one, but when Dad asked me why I would want a sunlamp when we already had the sun, I didn't have an answer. Truth was—I just wanted to see if somebody was smart enough to make a lamp that would do what the sun does. It was long before anybody ever thought of opening a tanning salon. But I'll betcha that if Dike were alive today, he'd be thinking about opening one.

Between 1946 and 1951, Elkins Butane thrived and expanded, as did Dike's civic participation. Wheaton was building a new school gymnasium with lumber and building materials salvaged from surplus World War II army barracks and volunteer labor from the people of the community. Ed Landon, a successful Oklahoma City businessman who lived part-time on a farm near Wheaton and who was one of Wheaton's wealthier residents, donated butane ceiling heaters for the new gym. In December 1947, Elkins Butane provided the school district a 2,500-gallon propane tank at cost, and Dike's employees donated the labor needed to install it properly.

In 1948, Huski Garden Tractors were added to the list of items stocked by Elkins Butane. Sales of all merchandise increased. Elkins Butane was going gangbusters, and its territory was exploding. A *Journal* ad in February 1949 listed twenty recent sales of butane or propane equipment. The list showed customers from Cassville, Washburn, Monett, Sarcoxie, Crane, Neosho, and Powell. Only one of the twenty customers, Oval Clymer, was from Wheaton. That same month, Elkins Butane incorporated and boasted a new slogan—"Home of Quality Merchandise."

In midsummer 1949, Dike announced that in addition to his stores in Wheaton and Neosho, he was opening a branch store in Monett, twenty miles to the northeast, giving Elkins Butane an even greater reach into southwest Missouri.[346]

Despite his remarkable salesmanship, Dike was always very low key. When my family visited the Wheaton Church of Christ—which Dike attended—I had to strain to hear him when he made announcements. I can't remember ever hearing him raise his voice, but his humor could sneak up on you, and occasionally it showed up in his newspaper ads, such as the one featuring a hillbilly grandpa that ran on November 3, 1949, in the *Journal*:

MODERN LIVING Westinghouse—Tappan—Coleman—Servel—Magic Chef—Adams. Yes, Even for GRANDAD

Grandad's wife cooked on one of them newfangled wood ranges and het hot water in a tea kettle and wash boiler. She were mighty proud when Paw dug her a cellar for keepin' food cool in. Course the well was fine fer milk and butter and sich like.

Four year after they was married Dick got tard of cuttin' wood for the fireplace and bought Lizzy a new cast iron, wood heatin' stove. It never wore out neither. He sold it when Lizzy died fer more'n he paid for it. The wood range was sold fer junk cause it was all burnt out. Granpaw had boughten Lizzy a new oil range just before she died, and paid upards of $150.00 fer it too. When he sold it though, he didn't get half what he paid.

Now Grandpa is living with his son that has GAS HEATING, COOKING, REFRIGERATION AND AUTOMATIC HOT WATER. He says it really is the Cat's Hair too!

BUTANE OR PROPANE GAS IS CLEAN, ECONOMICAL, CONVENIENT AND COMPLETELY MODERN. (COOK WITH GAS TOMORROW)

Elkins Butane Co.
Wheaton, Mo.-Phone 58 Monett, Mo.-
Phone 124 Neosho, Mo.-Phone 888

The "Grandpa" ad ran just a few days after Halloween in 1949. That was the Halloween when Dad, three other local men, and I pulled a fast one on Quannah Elkins and his wife, Rutholene. It was a night that became a legend in the Lewis household.

I was ten years old and in the fifth grade at Oshkosh, the one-room country school five miles west of Wheaton. A few nights before Halloween, the Oshkosh PTA held a Halloween costume contest. I bought a very real-looking rubber monkey mask, and Mom made a monkey suit from a burlap feed sack. It was a full-body outfit with a piece of rope for a tail, and it was so well done that I won first place in the costume contest.

Dad also had a costume. He was the devil. Mom dyed a pair of long-john underwear bright red, and Dad found a fiendish-looking red rubber devil mask that fit tightly over his head. With slits for his eyes, nose, and mouth, the fiery red mask also had horns. Dad made the whole thing scarier by going to the barn and fetching a real pitchfork to carry. He was a frightful sight. The sudden appearance of a six-foot man wearing a red devil mask and a pair of long red knit underwear and carrying a real pitchfork can make quite an impression on someone who just casually answers a knock at the front door. It was even more bizarre when the devil was accompanied by a chattering little monkey running zigzag circles around him.

On Halloween night, Dad decided he had to have more fun with his costume. He and I picked up our neighbor, Hub Wright, who also put on a mask and drove west to Grant and Nina Robinson's farm. Grant and Nina already had seen our costumes at the Oshkosh PTA contest, so that visit didn't produce the desired effect. At the devil's suggestion, we decided to head east toward Wheaton. We stopped at Dean and Hazel Harter's house, but again, we didn't get much of a reaction, because Dean was such a stoic guy and such a good Baptist that I don't think he would've been scared if the real devil would have knocked on his door. Hazel, a good-natured soul, just thought we were funny.

Then Dad said, "Let's go pick up Price and Leonard and go to Quannah Elkins's house." Price Naramore, who would later own Wheaton's IGA grocery store, operated a furniture store in Wheaton in 1949, and Leonard Brattin was a partner in Daniels and Brattin's grocery store. They were game for Dad's idea, so each of them put on some sort of Halloween mask. But Dad was the scary one in his devil suit, and I was the bizarre one in the monkey suit. We drove to Quannah and Rutholene's house in the south part of Wheaton on Highway 86, walked to the front door, and rang the bell. By this time, it was about 10:00 p.m., a late hour for trick-or-treating and bedtime for most folks in that part of the country.

We expected Quannah to answer the door. Instead, it was Rutholene, a nice lady who wasn't known for her sense of humor. She opened the door to the devil with his pitchfork, the devil's monkey, and three other full-size goblins. "Eeek!" she screamed, and she slammed the door in the devil's face. Quannah, who was in the garage behind the house pouring antifreeze into his car, heard the commotion and came around the side of the house. Rutholene yelled that she was going to call the town's night watchman, Rich Powell. Quannah started calling his dogs. We all took off—the devil, his monkey, and three goblins running up Highway 86 to our vehicles— and laughed all the way home.

Quannah, however, asked around and got a good idea of the culprits' identities, so he decided to tell his version of the story to *Wheaton Journal* editor Wally Fox, who thought it was amusing enough to write an article for the *Journal* the following Thursday.

BARELY ESCAPES ARREST

It has been rumored about town that two prominent businessmen of Wheaton, in company with two well-respected farmers living near Wheaton, were out "kicking up their heels" Halloween night. They are reported to have visited a number of homes, got people out of bed and created considerable disturbances. They narrowly escaped being arrested and charged with vandalism and disturbing the peace.

These four men went to the house of Quannah Elkins about ten o'clock Halloween night and created considerable disturbance. Mrs. Elkins and sons were to bed and Mr. Elkins was out pouring anti-freeze in his automobile when the four came sneaking up. Looking them over, Mr. Elkins decided they were about the worst foursome he had ever laid eyes on and ordered them off his property. They refused to leave and Mr. Elkins attempted to sic his dog on them, but the dog would have nothing to do with them. Finally, Mrs. Elkins was aroused by the commotion and threatened to call the night watch. Fear of being locked in the local hoosegow caused the foursome to flee.

Incidentally, one of the men was dressed in a flaming red (underwear) costume, wearing horns and carrying a pitch fork.[347]

Meanwhile, the late 1940s and the early 1950s saw the Elkins empire reach its peak. Dike was managing three stores and handling hundreds of customers, while Quannah owned and managed Elkins Oil Company, selling lots of oil and gasoline to area residents. Dike also had civic duties. In April 1950, he was reelected alderman in Wheaton's west ward.

In May 1950, Dike and two of his employees attended the State Liquefied Petroleum Gas Association convention in Kansas City, and a *Journal* article noted that Elkins, "founder of the Elkins Butane Company, is one of the leaders of the association and of the state."[348]

Even when I was still in grade school, I knew Dike was a successful businessman, but no matter how busy he was, he always took time to talk to me and make me feel that I was more than just an annoying kid.

In 1950, he and Montie built a large, buff-colored brick home on Highway 86 south of the main part of town. They moved out of their second-floor apartment in the Elkins Butane building. I remember going with my folks to visit Dike and Montie in their new house and thinking that I'd never been in a house that nice—big kitchen, comfortable cushy chairs in the front room, a thick rug that your feet could sink into, and a nice tiled bathroom instead of the cramped bathroom with a linoleum floor and small sink like we had in our farmhouse.

Soon after the Elkinses moved into their new house, my pal Dan Shewmake went with his dad, Ern, to conduct some business in the Barry County Courthouse in Cassville. As they were leaving the County Clerk's office where Margie Land worked, she asked Ern if he was going back to Wheaton. He said he was, and Margie, who was married to Ern's nephew Paul Land, said that A. E. Elkins had left his wallet when he came to the office earlier that day. She asked Ern if he would mind taking it back to Wheaton and returning it to Mr. Elkins. So, with no questions asked, Earn took Dike's wallet, checked, saw that it had a couple of hundred dollars in it, and drove to Dike's house.

Dike walked out of his house and met them in the driveway. Ern put on his best poker face and said, "Say, Dike, I've been pretty down on my luck lately, and I just wondered if maybe you could loan me a couple of hundred dollars. I'll pay you back after my next cattle trade."

With no hesitation, Dike said, "Why, sure, Ern," and reached into his back pocket for his wallet, which, of course, wasn't there. As Dike stood there, looking suddenly alarmed, Ern handed him his wallet. They had a good laugh. But no one involved in the transaction ever questioned the way the return of the wallet was handled or the sincerity of Dike's willingness to lend money to a friend.

Just when it seemed that Dike had the world by the tail, he decided he needed a break. On April 19, 1951, a *Journal* article announced that Dike had sold controlling interest in Elkins Butane to a group of businessmen in Monett. "Due to poor health, Mr. Elkins will retire to his Hereford farm at the south edge of the Wheaton city limits, where he recently completed a nice brick home," the article said.[349]

For the next three years, Dike raised cattle, dabbled in selling portable grain mills, and kept busy in other small enterprises. Then on May 20, 1954, Montie Elkins developed a blocked bowel caused by scar tissue—adhesions—from surgery she had had years earlier. She was taken to the Cassville hospital, where surgery successfully removed the blockage, but hours later, a pulmonary embolism—a blood clot resulting from the surgery—hit her heart, and she died.

Journal editor Wally Fox's article announcing her death summarized Montie's legacy: "Mrs. Elkins was one of the fine women of this community and had reared a family of two daughters and one son."[350]

When Dad came home from Wheaton later that day and told Mom and me that Montie had died, I was stunned. Montie wasn't quite fifty-four years old, and I knew I had lost a friend. That same summer, Dike's brother, Wilbur, and another man from Wheaton, Lafay Decocq, opened a new butane distribution company in Wheaton. They called it Southwest Gas, and it was successful for many years.

Montie's death seemed to motivate Dike to get back into a major business enterprise. The November following Montie's death in May, Dike announced in the *Wheaton Journal* that he and Quannah had purchased the Cassville Tractor and Implement Company and planned to sell Ferguson farm equipment. They built a new building and opened their new Wheaton Tractor Company business in early 1955.[351]

Dike started to live again. In August 1955, he married Cleffa Frances Rogers of Jonesboro, Arkansas—an accomplished woman with a master's degree in education who had taught in the Jonesboro public schools and at Arkansas State College in Jonesboro. Dike met Cleffa through his son-in-law, Delbert Rogers, who was Cleffa's nephew.

Cleffa and Dike seemed happy. Dike and Quannah's farm implement business prospered. Quannah opened a garage and tire business—Elkins Oil Company.

In 1960, life got tougher for Dike and Cleffa. Quannah and a local woman left for parts unknown, at least for a while. Quannah's wife, Rutholene, had no business experience, so Quannah's business— Elkins Oil Company—had no manager. Dike and Cleffa stepped in to help their daughter-in-law, but not before local gossip alleged that they had abandoned Rutholene and left her in debt.

Dike was stunned and outraged, so he and Cleffa did a very gutsy thing. They bought space in the February 2, 1961, edition of the *Wheaton Journal* that laid out, step by step, how they had come to Rutholene's financial aid. They also took a swipe at the folks they called the "whisperers" who were spreading false information:

To Whom It May Concern

In order to clear up any misconception gathered through the "Whispering Campaign" that has been in full swing, concerning the affairs of the Elkins Oil Co., and which should have been only a family affair, we take this opportunity to make the deal clear.

Almost without exception, our many fine friends and customers have remained so, knowing that the disappointment and heartbreak that we have suffered has been enough, but there have been a few "Doubting Thomases" that have made the way rather more difficult for all of us that it should have been.

It has been circulated and believed by a few that we have taken everything from our daughter-in-law, Rutholene, and are putting her "out in the road." We shall use this remaining space to enumerate a few things that have been done for her and her family, with no strings attached.

When this misfortune came upon Rutholene's family, we were the only ones willing and able to come to her aid, personally and financially. Having never had sufficient experience in business, Rutholene could not even under normal circumstances have operated the intricate and complicated affairs of the oil company. Since we had in the past owned and operated this oil business along with our Butane Company, the Small Business Administration and the participating bank who held the mortgage on the company and their home properties selected us as the only acceptable operators. If we had not consented to do so, foreclosure was scheduled within 30 days. Of course, this would have meant that Rutholene would have lost everything, due to the financial status of the company at that time.

Naturally, Rutholene turned to us and her family for assistance, which we were happy to give in whatever way we could. At the personal request of Rutholene, we took over the affairs of the oil company on Aug. 26, 1960, with which we had absolutely no desire to burden ourselves. Since that time we have been able to put the company on a comparatively sound basis with future improvements expected. This has only been done through applying business management and by placing heavy obligations upon ourselves. We have worked six days a week with an average of ten to twelve hours per day since accepting these obligations. There was a noticeable lack of anyone else willing to assume these obligations, so now who dares to criticize! ... [352]

JUST FOR THE RECORD! Anyone of the "Whisperers" that want to put their money where their mouth is, may step in and assume these responsibilities, if the creditors approve them. We will gladly walk out any day, so let's please stop furnishing so much lip service!

TO OUR MANY, MANY FRIENDS AND CUSTOMERS THROUGH THE YEARS, we thank you for your fine patronage and your continued friendship and want you to know that we shall always endeavor to serve you to the utmost of our ability.

Elkins Oil Company
A.E. and Cleffa Elkins

The ad shut down the "whispering campaign," as Dike and Cleffa labeled it, but the situation left Dike with a bitter taste that was hard for him to overcome. However, he accepted it with the stoicism that was part of his heritage.

After a year or two, Quannah and Rutholene reunited. Eventually, they relocated in Webb City about fifty miles from Wheaton, near Joplin. They never lived in Wheaton again.

Wheaton began to change during the 1960s as many of the veteran businessmen and women retired. Dike and Cleffa sold the Wheaton Tractor Company, and in 1969, they sold Elkins Oil Company, which became D&D Oil and Propane. Then, weary after many years in business, Dike and Cleffa left Wheaton and moved to Carlsbad, New Mexico, to retire.

Dike had owned and operated several of Wheaton's most successful businesses for nearly four decades, yet during the 1970s and '80s, when I'd go back to visit old friends and relatives there, I seldom heard his name mentioned. It was as if a name that had helped put Wheaton on the map had vanished while a newer generation of businesspersons carried on, seemingly unaware that there had been a time when Elkins Butane was an economic powerhouse throughout southwest Missouri. Even during the tough Depression years of the 1930s, Dike had operated successful businesses in both Rocky Comfort and Wheaton.

After my mother and dad died in the mid-1970s, I took a batch of their papers and keepsakes to my home in California. Years later, I stumbled upon a letter, postmarked Carlsbad, New Mexico, dated January 27, 1975, and mailed to Mr. Perry Lewis, Wheaton, Missouri—my dad. It was from Dike, and it said:

Dear Perry,

I have been intending to write ever since we received that wonderful Xmas card you sent us. We appreciated it very much. We can truthfully say the same about you. We never dealt with anyone that was as nice and true as you. We will never forget.

How are Jimmy and family getting along? We are not as young as we used to be but God has been good to us. We are busy. Cleffa takes care of the church's library and her work in our home. We have our little rock shop that keeps me busy most of the time. I do a little wood work for ourselves.

If we come up there (to Wheaton) we will see you. We will remember you in our prayers.

Bye Bye, with love, A. E.

For years, I had the *Wheaton Journal* mailed to me in California, just to keep up with what was going on back home. As I was reading the *Journal* in the later summer of 1986, I noticed a short obituary on page two. I almost overlooked it. The headline over the obituary read "Allen Elkins." I wondered who that was. Then I was shocked. It was my old friend and hero, A. E. "Dike" Elkins. No one ever called him "Allen," and the spelling of "Dyke" in the first sentence was unfamiliar:

ALLEN ELKINS

Services for Allen Eldridge "Dyke" Elkins, 85, Carlsbad, N.M., a former Wheaton resident, who died Sunday, Aug. 31, at a hospital in Carlsbad after a long illness, were Wednesday at Denton Mortuary, Carlsbad.

Burial was in Carlsbad Cemetery.

Mr. Elkins was born Sept. 19, 1900, in McDonald County. He was a retired farmer and businessman. He had lived in Wheaton many years before moving to Carlsbad 15 years ago. He was a member of the Church of Christ in Carlsbad and had been an elder at the Church of Christ in Wheaton for many years.

He married Montie Mae Brown May 6, 1922, in McDonald County. She died May 20, 1954. He married Cleffa Frances Rogers Aug. 7, 1955, at Jonesboro, Ark. She survives.

Survivors also include a son, Quannah Elkins, Webb City; two daughters, Lane Elkins, Rogersville, and Mary Rogers, Bellevue, Wash.; a sister, Grace Flaxbeard, Wheaton; four grandchildren; 10 great-grandchildren; and two great-great-grandchildren.

It was a lesson in life to me. No matter how much you achieve, it's likely that you won't be remembered very long. I wish I could do for Dike what the great sportswriter Grantland Rice did for the mythical Casey, who struck out and lost the baseball game for the Mudville Nine in the famous poem "Casey at the Bat," written by Ernest Thayer in 1888. In 1907, Rice wrote another poem under the pen name of James Wilson that he called "Casey's Revenge." In the second poem, it's the season after Casey struck out, and the slumping Mudville team is once again facing the pitcher who had fanned the once-mighty Casey. Casey comes to the plate. The Mudville fans expected Casey to whiff again, just as he did the year before. But Rice penned a different ending in this poem:

> *But fame is fleeting as the wind and glory fades away;*
> *There were no wild and wooly cheers, no glad acclaim this day.*

No roasting for the umpire now—his was an easy lot;
But here the pitcher whirled again—was that a rifle shot?
A whack, a crack, and out through the space the leather pellet flew,
A blot against the distant sky, a speck against the blue.

Above the fence in center field in rapid whirling flight
The sphere sailed on—the blot grew dim and then was lost to sight.
Ten thousand hats were thrown in air, ten thousand threw a fit,
But no one ever found the ball that mighty Casey hit.

O, somewhere in this favored land dark clouds may hide the sun,
And somewhere bands no longer play and children have no fun!
And somewhere over blighted lives there hangs a heavy pall,
But Mudville hearts are happy now, for Casey hit the ball.[353]

If I could, I would resurrect Dike and put him to bat against any of his business competitors. I'd bet on him to hit it out of the park, just as he did with Elkins Butane, and just as he did when he saved my life. An old sportswriter I once knew used to say, when describing a good ballplayer, "He was a good 'un."

Dike Elkins was a "good 'un."

A.E. (Dike) Elkins' Main Street storefront, 1939

Elkins Butane building, 1946

A.E. (Dike) Elkins

Elkins' Butane tanker truck, about 1941

Photos courtesy of Fields' Photo Archives

A.E. (Dike) & Montie Elkins in their appliance store

Elsie McNeill
& Eschol
Duncan in their
Wheaton
drygoods store

Dorothy Cantrell &
Earl Hooten in
Hooten Grocery,
Wheaton, early 1950s

Jimmy Lewis, age 7, and Jiggs

Jimmy Lewis
2nd Grade

Family from left, dog Jiggs, Grandad Earn & Grandma
Carrie Lamberson, Jimmy Lewis &
Velma Lamberson Lewis

Mom & Dad, Velma & Perry Lewis

Courtesy of Daniel W. Shewmake

Dan Shewmake's father, Ern Shewmake,
who suffered from arthritis

Our neighbors, Grant & Nina Robinson

"Uncle" John Robinson

From "Wheaton Echoes" collection

Roy Robinson, with display of antique tools in his Wheaton Maytag store

From left, George (Peach) Ford, Cora Ford, Hazel
Ford Searles, Kate Ford Wright,
Woodrow Ford & Woody Joe

Kate & Herbert (Hub) Wright

Oshkosh basketball team 1951, from left, Melvin Haynes, Leonard Lahman, Bill Haynes,
Melvin Embrey, Jimmie Taylor, Jimmy Lewis, Darril Haynes & Leon Lahman

Jimmie Taylor   Betty Taylor   Jimmy Lewis

1957 senior trip, St. Louis Zoo: From left, James Cantrell, Sharon Kay Stewart, Betty Higgs & Jimmy Lewis

Courtesy of Jaclyn Higgs

Lt.Col. Gary Joe Higgs

Leslie Phillips, Wheaton postmaster

Courtesy of Linda Clymer Stevenson

Oval & Ora Clymer

Courtesy of Daniel W. Shewmake

Jimmy Lewis & Dan Shewmake in
Kansas City in their Sunday finest

Courtesy of Daniel W. Shewmake

Dan & Jim, years later

22

Little Charley and the Unbelievers

Wheaton in the 1940s and '50s had its scheduled entertainment—the Saturday afternoon drawing, movies at Wilbur Ray's Cozy Theatre, and an occasional "street" movie on a warm Saturday night when Abe Green brought his big screen to town to create a drive-in movie at the east end of Main Street. In the spring, the annual junior and senior plays were staged at Wheaton High. Some might argue that the semiannual revival meetings at the Baptist, Methodist, and Church of Christ congregations counted as scheduled entertainment, while others might have counted those events as serious spiritual enlightenment.

But I went to town for the unscheduled entertainment. You just never knew when it might take place or who would be doing the entertaining before it was time to hop into Granddad's black 1936 Chevy or my dad's Ford pickup and head for home to do the milking. One of the best of the unscheduled entertainers was "Little Charley" Keeling—Charles Keeling Jr.

"Little Charley," as contrasted with his father, "Big Charley," was a short, wiry, dark-haired man who was probably in his late twenties and early thirties when I was in grade school. He, like my father, was a farmer and cattle trader. Unlike my father, however, he didn't seem to be very successful at it. I thought maybe he just couldn't focus his mind.

I had heard that he and his wife had been in a horrible car wreck, and she had been killed. As a kid, I was never sure if that report was true, but I always gave Little Charley the benefit of the doubt when he began to behave a little strangely and when, occasionally, I would hear that one of his checks bounced. Whatever the truth of those stories, at some point, Little Charley got religion. Evidently, he got an extra dose, because it wasn't long before he became a preacher who said he could heal people.

In May of 1948, Little Charley's son, Donny, whacked a stray railroad torpedo with a hammer, causing an explosion that injured one of his eyes. Donny was rushed to the Wheaton Hospital, but before he could be treated, Little Charley "came to the hospital and removed the injured youth to his home, refusing to give him medical attention," according to an article in the *Wheaton Journal.*[354] I remember Donny, but I don't remember whether his eye healed properly or not.

Little Charley conducted loud, lengthy, and no doubt theologically enlightened sermons in a little wood-frame building that in an earlier era had been Arch and Brock Cantrell's used furniture store a block east of Main Street across from the Calhoun-Putnam Lumber Company. Little Charley painted it white—as white as the robes of Jesus—and in black block letters over the front door, he painted FULL GOSPEL MISSION.[355] He also painted the name of his church on the door of his pickup truck.

With the sign painting completed, Little Charley set about to convert the sinners of Wheaton and nearby towns, hills, hollows, and flatlands. I guess Little Charley's flock never grew as much as he thought it should, so he began to seek other ways to spread the truth of God's word to the community.

Little Charley was thinking big, so one Saturday—as he was feeling full of the Spirit and perhaps also possessed of a certain sense of countrified public-relations genius—he draped himself in a white sheet in the manner of the robes Jesus always wore in the pictures on the cardboard fans distributed to churches by local funeral homes.[356] Then he mounted a donkey on his farm near Fairview and headed down Highway 86 for the five-mile ride to Wheaton. I heard that drivers on the two-lane highway slowed, swerved, cussed, and marveled at the strange sight of the modern-day prophet; but somehow Little Charley and his donkey made it to Wheaton, just as Jesus made it to Jerusalem on Palm Sunday. Of course, there weren't any palms in Wheaton, and even if there had been, it's not likely that anyone would have thrown palm fronds in Little Charley's path as he rode the three blocks of Main Street proclaiming, "Repent, ye sinners, for the kingdom of Heaven is at hand."

Men stopped their spittin' and whittlin', rose from their squatting positions on the sidewalk, and gawked. Women and kids who had been hurrying to finish their trading froze dead in their tracks. Such expressions as, "Well, I'll swan," could be heard from the women, and "Well, I'll be damned," came from the little knots of men.

"Little Charley's gone plumb off," some said as he admonished what he considered to be the godless throng on both sides of the street. Little Charley, undeterred by any derogatory remarks he might have heard from the unbelievers, rode his donkey at a steady walk to the Full Gospel Mission, dismounted, and went inside. It had been a notable Saturday and one which would be the subject of gossip in the MZ-Dee Café, Bryan's Barber Shop, Elaine's Beauty Parlor, and the feed rooms at Allman's Mill and the Farmers Exchange for weeks.

Little Charley, however, was not done with his evangelizing. Any good public-relations professional knows that one attention-drawing event is not enough. His Jesus-like ride would be a hard act to follow. But it wasn't long before he equaled it, or maybe even topped it, depending on your attitude toward snakes.

Now there were a few people around Wheaton, Rocky Comfort, Fairview, and Ridgley who would tolerate blacksnakes because they ate mice and other pesky rodents. Garter snakes were sometimes allowed to coexist with human beings. But around most farms in that part of the country—home to poisonous copperheads, water moccasins, and timber rattlers—the only good snake was a dead snake. By the time I was twelve, I'd already had occasion to use a garden hoe to chop the head off a half dozen assorted snakes, from blacksnakes that liked to crawl into the chicken house and eat eggs laid by my mother and grandmother's flock to several very scary-looking but nonpoisonous bullsnakes. Bullsnakes could grow to several feet long, and depending on their diet, get quite fat. They had markings that could be mistaken for those of a rattlesnake, and most people wanted nothing to do with them. Enter Little Charley, act 2, on his campaign to save people's souls.

I guess Little Charley, when he became a "holy roller"—the commonly used and somewhat derogatory name that identified those of the Holiness and Pentecostal faith—must have heard about the snake-handling sects that are located mostly in the hills of West Virginia and Kentucky. I was told that they believed if a person had enough faith, he or she could handle poisonous snakes, and God would protect them from harm. I always figured that certainly would have prevented those folks from dozing off during church services.

Anyway, Little Charley was ready for a more dramatic outreach for his church. To demonstrate his faith, he got himself a nice big bullsnake—about four feet long and of husky girth—and began to show up in town with it. At first, a number of the local citizens wanted to get the sheriff to arrest Little Charley, or at least to confiscate the snake, which would slither around on Little Charley's shoulders and arms as he worked his way through the Main Street crowds on Saturday. There would be occasional screams and gasps if an unwary woman or girl found herself on the sidewalk face-to-face with Little Charley and his bullsnake. The men and bigger boys had far too much pride to appear nervous about the snake and tried to act nonchalant as Little Charley asked anyone in earshot if they had faith in the Lord.

"Did you see Little Charley and his snake at town today?" Grandma Lamberson would ask.

"Yeah, Grandma, and I got real close too. That snake sure is a big 'un," I would reply.

"My Land a' Goshen, they oughta lock that feller up! He's half cracked!" Grandma would exclaim.

Apparently, there was no state law or county ordinance against having a nonpoisonous snake on your person in public. As far as I know, Little Charley was never arrested.

He was treading on thin ice, though, the day he decided to do some door-to-door evangelizing with the snake. Little Charley, the story goes, walked up the steps to the front porch of the town barber, Bryan Wolfenbarger, and knocked. Bryan's wife, Delpha, who was home alone, answered. There stood Little Charley, brandishing his snake, and—simultaneous with her scream—he asked, "Do you have the faith?" He never heard her answer—only the sound of the door slamming in his face. I'm not sure what the thoroughly shaken Delpha Wolfenbarger did after that, but I know it wasn't very long until the snake ceased to be part of Little Charley's evangelical outreach. Even the best acts grow stale or become unpopular.

As the fervor of his ministry tapered off and his following dwindled, so did the contributions to the Full Gospel Mission Church. It was about that time that Little Charley developed a modus operandi that left local merchants less than comfortable. At the Calhoun-Putnam Lumber Company, managed by Gordon Kenney, Little Charley scooped ten pounds of eight-penny nails into a bag one day and started to walk out. Gordon, a big man who had a no-nonsense approach to life, said, "Charley, you haven't paid for the nails."

Little Charley, not missing a beat, said, "Charge them to the Lord's account."

Gordon Kenney never blinked. "The Lord hasn't paid up lately. Put the nails back," he reportedly told Little Charley, who did as he was told.

Byron "Barney" Calame sacked groceries at Price and Carolyn Naramore's IGA in Wheaton. He remembers Little Charley's efforts to obtain the staples he needed, free of charge. "The Lord hath need of flour," Charley would say, or "the Lord hath need of sugar." He met with only mixed success using that approach.

I lost track of Little Charley after I left home for college in 1957, but my cousin Ralph Lamberson told me that in 1958 and 1959 when he worked at the lumberyard just across the street from the Full Gospel Mission, he sometimes would peer in the window as Little Charley preached his sermons—to an empty house. After which, Ralph swears, Little Charley passed the collection plate to the empty house. This probably explains why, in Little Charley's mind, that it was the Lord, rather than Charley, who had accounts at several local businesses.

A few years ago, on a visit back to Wheaton, I was told that Little Charley had passed on to his eternal reward. Reflecting a bit, I thought that it was appropriate that he lived to see the beginning of the third millennium, because I had heard that he occasionally spoken of the "end times" in his sermons and, to some, the millennium was thought to be a marker for the "end times." He had lived a long life on his farm near Fairview, possibly the farm where he had begun the donkey ride to Wheaton and kept his bullsnake a half century earlier. If I could talk to him now, I wouldn't question his faith. I would simply thank him for being one of the best entertainers of my childhood.

23

The Tornado That Brought
Barney Bates to Town

O n Halloween Eve, October 30, 1943, as a dark thunderstorm
approached our farmhouse from the southwest, my mother and
I looked out the south window and saw Dad running toward the
house yelling, "Grab Jim and run to the pond bank!"[357] He burst
into the house through the back door and hollered that there was a
tornado coming.

At age four, I never suspected that the events of that day would
affect me years later, starting in the seventh grade. As my mother
and father ran out the front door, my mother carrying me, I couldn't
imagine why they were so excited. I remember looking to the south
as we stopped halfway to the pond bank north of our house and
seeing this black cloud that I thought was smoke moving toward us
in the field south of Granddad and Grandma Lamberson's house.

The "smoke" looked like it was headed straight for their house
and probably ours, which was just an eighth of a mile north of theirs.
But instead, the black funnel veered to the east and followed a gully
between two low hills on Granddad and Grandma's farm. Years later,
I estimated that it missed their house, barn, and chicken house by
maybe two hundred yards.

Grandma, who was in bed with the flu, missed all of the drama, as did Granddad. I don't know what he was doing, but he didn't see it coming, either. They had a storm cellar filled with canned goods and an ax to chop their way out in case a tree fell on the cellar door. We all took refuge in it several times when I was a kid. But if the twister had hit their house that day, my grandparents could have been killed or badly injured, since they didn't go to their cellar.

We watched as the monster roared across the field a quarter of a mile to the southeast of our front yard, keeping to a northeasterly course. When it reached the Gaston Corner, an intersection of country roads about halfway between our house and Wheaton, I remember seeing flashes of fire as it hit the transformers on the power poles, sending the poles tumbling like matchsticks. I had never seen anything like it at age four. I just knew I didn't want to be in its path.

When the tornado was passing ten or twelve miles farther to the northeast, Bert Catron, cashier of the First National Bank of Purdy, watched it from his home near Purdy and said, "It sucked everything up as it passed by, and the dust was thrown out at the top like smoke from an engine. It was long and narrow but had the traditional rat tail which distinguishes the death-dealing and destructive winds."[358]

As I was to learn later, the twister that narrowly missed us was one of the most destructive ever to touch down in that part of the country. It stayed on the ground for about another forty miles, all the way to the town of Marionville.

A few minutes after it went by us, it blew the metal roof off of the Reverend Emmett Tichenor's barn a couple of miles to the east toward Wheaton. I remember clearly that when I was going to town with Dad and Mom a few days later, I saw that Preacher Tichenor's barn had no roof and was sitting crooked on its foundation. Years later, I read an account of the tornado in the *Wheaton Journal*, which reported that the barn was considered a total loss by the insurance adjustors. The house where the Reverend Tichenor and his wife, Ida, lived had clung to its foundation but was heavily damaged, according to the *Journal*.

Practically every window was broken out, part of the roof was blown off, the fireplace chimney and a flue were wrecked, the concrete posts supporting the porch were torn out and plaster was knocked from the walls. The building almost exploded from the inside pressure of air after the storm had sucked the outside air from around the building. The garage roof was blown from off a car, but the car was not damaged. A small barn was wrecked, a large poultry house and other small outbuildings were blown down. The windmill was wrecked, one hog was killed and some others were injured. One cow was in the barn, but she escaped uninjured.

Mrs. Tichenor was just starting to milk the cow when her son, Melvin, and family drove up and honked the horn of their truck. Rev. Tichenor was getting ready to leave for an appointment, and Mrs. Tichenor, thinking that her husband had already gone, left the barn when she heard her son honk his truck, which probably saved her life. The families made a run for the cellar, and Rev. Tichenor and son stood in the door of the cellar and watched the storm until it was almost upon them. It appeared to have three prongs running from the central cone and each was whirling as individual twisters until they merged in the air.[359]

After hitting the Tichenor place, the twister turned north through an orchard and uprooted most of the apple trees in it, and then it veered east toward Wheaton before swerving to the northeast again. When the whirling funnel took its brief turn toward Wheaton, the folks in town scattered fast. The *Wheaton Journal* described the scene:

Saturday shoppers … took to their cars and left
town in all directions. Cellars were soon filled to
capacity. Arch Cantrell and Geo. Burger staged a foot
race to Burger's cellar, but Arch was far in the lead
in a short time. When Geo. reached the cellar it was
so full he had to squeeze in.[360] (George was a short
man, amply built, and it wasn't surprising that Arch
beat him to the cellar.)

But instead of going east all the way to Wheaton, it suddenly
turned north again toward E. L. Thomas's farm near Highway 86.
E. L.—or Lewis, as he was often called—was a former Barry County
assessor and operator of a livestock feed store in Wheaton.[361] He was
driving home after closing his store about 6:00 p.m. when he saw the
whirling plume heading directly for his farm.

The *Cassville Democrat* reported that E. L. "broke all war-time
speeds to rush home with a son, to get Mrs. Thomas, another son
and two men employed on his farm to a cellar. The storm missed the
house and buildings but did move a lot of fencing to hit again at the
highway and do damage at Otto Duncan's."[362]

When the dark funnel reached the Duncan farm, it already
had been on the ground for more than twelve miles. It had first
touched down and destroyed stores, houses, barns, and outbuildings
at Bethpage in McDonald County southwest of Rocky Comfort and
Wheaton, and it wreaked havoc on at least twenty farms before it
crossed Granddad and Grandma's field.

But the tornado had not yet done its most serious damage. It
whirled across the Duncan farm and headed straight for Corsicana,
roughly four miles to the northeast, where it destroyed the little town
that had been established on the banks of Joy's Creek by Jeremiah
Fly in the early 1850s. In the late 1800s, Corsicana boasted a carding
mill, a flour mill, a sawmill, and a cotton gin. "Corsi," as the locals
called it, also sported a racetrack where prize horses showed their
stuff, and it supported a blacksmith shop and general stores that sold
everything from groceries to dry goods to hardware.

By 1943, however, Corsicana had shrunk to one general store, a school, a canning factory, and several farm residences and outbuildings. The general store was owned and operated by Newton L. "Barney" Bates and his wife, Lucile. When the tornado struck, Barney was in the army, far away in Alaska. Lucile and the two Bates daughters, Francis and Norma Jean, were in their home across the street from the store. The *Cassville Democrat* described what happened:

> On the approach of the storm for its destruction of Corsicana, W.E. Smith, who was getting ready to milk at his barn next to the Bates residence, sensing danger, ran from the barn and witnessed the destruction of the school building as it was caught in the swirl of the wind and thrown some distance away, a ruined mass of lumber.

> The Bates store and residence were completely destroyed. At the store the gasoline pumps were torn from their foundation and Mrs. Bates and her two children, Frances, 14, and Norma Jean, 4, were among the flying mass of wreckage and devastation. As the storm left, Mrs. Bates' daughter called her mother's attention to the money drawer and a portion of it was recovered. Their escape from serious injury or death is miraculous. Mr. Bates, a member of the armed forces, is serving in Alaska with other county soldiers.[363]

Norma Jean, who, like me, was four years old when the twister struck, became my classmate at Wheaton when we were in the seventh grade. Jeanie, as we called her, wrote her vivid memories of the storm in *Wheaton Echoes*:

It was raining hard about 6 p.m. and Lucile (Jeanie's mother) had locked the store and walked across the road to our home, putting about $50 in paper money in a kitchen drawer, as she usually did. During the storm, the same money was seen flying through the air, but most of it was found later.

Frances Bates (Jeanie's sister) was in her bedroom looking out the west window when she saw the wind pick up the little school building and smash it down into the trees on the hill. By the time that she ran through the living room into the kitchen where Mother and I were, the roof was jerked off and bricks from the chimney were making deep holes in the floor right in front of our toes. Mother was hit in the top of her head by flying glass, which cut a vein and blood gushed all over her dress and white apron. One wall that we were standing near started to fall with others when a rafter moved and the last wall fell down like the other had. It wasn't our time to go![364]

Years later, writing in third person as if she were a bystander describing the destruction and its aftermath, Jeanie recalled:

[T]he whirling, twisting winds demolished the peaceful little community in only a few seconds, leaving boards and straws driven into the oak trees along the hillsides near the creek and twisted metal everywhere from the canning factory.

It washed sunperch and other fish out of the water and dropped them on the ground to die. It took the barns away from cows waiting to be milked. It picked up the school and scattered it in the trees on the hill. Chickens ran around, if not half dead—scared to death—with feathers blown off …

Barney Bates was in the Army and halfway around the world and received a telegram notifying him there had been a tornado that blew Corsicana away, but he didn't know until later that his family was alive.

The Red Cross moved in soon to help in any way possible and crowds of people came from everywhere to see the damage.

Lucile and the girls stayed with Sophia and Harry Boyce until they bought a home in Wheaton … Barney was discharged in January of 1945.

Corsicana became a thing of the past, never to be the same again.[365]

Largely because the storm destroyed their home and store in Corsicana, Barney and Lucile settled in Wheaton after Barney was discharged from active duty. For more than a year, he worked at Camp Crowder, a World War II army training camp near Neosho, twenty-five miles from Wheaton. But Barney was a clever guy with lots of skills. For several more months, he operated a jewelry repair shop in his home. Then in October 1947, he bought a store that sold electrical supplies, hardware, and home furnishings from Clovis Flaxbeard, who also operated an insurance agency.[366]

An ad for Bates Appliance Store during the holiday season read:

FOR YOUR XMAS SHOPPING

Don't pass up our merchandise consisting of matched Pyrex bowl sets, Dormyer mixers, electric irons, pocket knives, flash lights, waffle irons,

luggage, radios. This is just a few of the items found in
our store. Whether you buy large or small amounts—
your patronage will be appreciated.[367]

Apparently, the Bates Appliance venture didn't work out well for
Barney, and in January 1948, he sold the store to Floyd "Fat" Flora,
former co-owner of the Wheaton Hardware store. Barney got a job
in Wichita, Kansas. By August 1949, however, Barney and his family
were back in Wheaton, where Barney prepared to open a jewelry
store. He had become an expert watch and jewelry repairman. He
built a new store for his jewelry business, described in the *Journal* as
"one of the nicest small business buildings in Wheaton." On Saturday,
August 13, 1949, Barney opened his new store by giving away a set
of matched diamond rings.

Anyone who knew Barney almost immediately sensed that he
was a kind man. His daughter Jeanie, writing in *Wheaton Echoes*,
recalled that "Dad was very good at repairing watches and clocks,
and about anything else that people brought in. When he found out
that companies that sold class rings to schools were making huge
profits, and were keeping some seniors from having one, he started
selling them just a little above cost. I remember several times," Jeanie
wrote, "when a senior couldn't afford a ring; he gave them one and
didn't say a word about it to anyone."[368]

Ila Jean Richter Hazelrigg, a member of the class of 1956, recalled
that when she was a senior at Wheaton High, she "couldn't afford to
buy a senior ring. There was another person who couldn't afford to,
either, but he was on the basketball team and someone else bought
his (ring) for him. Since I was the only one left (without a ring), the
Wheaton jewelry store owner, Barney Bates, bought mine for me.
They gave it to me as a surprise, as my friend got my ring size. I have
always appreciated that act of kindness, and still have the ring."[369]

As Barney's business began to thrive, tragedy struck in his family
yet again. On November 23, 1949, Lucile died at the age of forty-
four, when the couple's youngest child, Gary, was only three years
old. And in an extraordinary show of respect for both Lucile and

Barney, every business in town closed for her funeral on a Saturday afternoon, Wheaton's busiest day.[370]

But Barney stayed on in Wheaton and raised his three children. A year or so later, Barney organized a high-school softball team for Wheaton boys. I was only in the sixth grade and still attending a one-room country school west of Wheaton, but I loved baseball and softball and began to take notice of Barney.

Barney had been a good athlete. He played baseball and basketball for Exeter High School and minor league baseball for the Detroit Tigers organization. He didn't fit my image of a pro baseball player because he was short—only five feet three—but he was strong with quick reflexes.[371]

By the time I was in junior high and going to school in Wheaton, Barney also had organized a baseball team for the younger boys. I played. He was a good manager with good tips for hitting, running the bases, and fielding. I remember Barney counseling me when he was the first base coach in one game:

"Now, that was a good clean single. Just take your lead, watch the pitcher, and if he's not watching you, take off for second."

In the summer of 1953, after I completed the eighth grade, Barney also became scoutmaster for Wheaton's Boy Scout troop. I especially remember a Scout trip to the James River where we earned several merit badges and picked up a lot of chigger bites. Barney knew a lot about the outdoors, and he was a very patient teacher—except that he didn't know how to avoid chiggers.[372]

It was during those middle school years that I claimed Barney's daughter Jeanie as my first girlfriend. I'm not sure she agreed that I was her boyfriend. Because I was too young to drive a car, I didn't have any real dates with her, but I do remember that when milk hauler Mike Patton took Wheaton's seventh- or eighth-grade class—can't remember which—to the movies at Neosho in the back of his milk truck, I managed to get my arm around her. That was the closest to romance I got in my junior high years.

Later, I learned about another of Barney's skills—he was a crack shot. His Model 24 Remington rifle—made between 1922 and 1935—shot only .22 short ammo, commonly used for target practice. In his backyard on Wheaton's north side next to an open field, Barney would throw pennies in the air and with uncanny aim, fire the rifle, and hit virtually every penny. Years later, I was told that he had a contract to stage demonstrations of his marksmanship from time to time.

In 1954, Barney was still running his jewelry store. At the end of the year, he was elected president of the Wheaton Community Club, the organization of business owners that got things done in the little town. Barney also was a member of Wheaton's Masonic Lodge and for a time was commander of Wheaton's chapter of the Veterans of Foreign Wars.[373]

After Jeanie and I graduated from Wheaton High in 1957, Barney closed his jewelry shop and bought the local locker plant where customers brought pork and beef to be cut, wrapped, and placed into cold storage lockers. In addition to his other skills, Barney was an expert meat cutter.

If the tornado of October 30, 1943, had not destroyed the Bates store and home in Corsicana, I might never have known Barney or his family. The storm was devastating to them, but Corsicana's loss was Wheaton's gain—a gain not only for Wheaton's economy but also a personal gain, because every member of the Bates family was an outstanding person.

When Barney died of a brain tumor at age sixty-three in 1968, Wheaton's merchants closed shop again—also on a Saturday afternoon—just as they had for Lucile in 1949.[374] Barney's personal qualities scored a direct hit on everyone's heart.

On our farm west of Wheaton, there was one more lasting effect of the 1943 tornado. At least partly because of that harrowing experience, Mom and Dad would occasionally wake me up on thunderstormy nights during the next thirteen or fourteen years, and we'd run to the pickup and speed down the lane to Granddad and Grandma's cellar until the storm settled down. Dad eventually became more fatalistic, often sleeping through stormy nights while Mom paced the floor near a window trying to catch a glimpse of the clouds when lightning flashed. Dad would say, "Come on back to bed, Velma. You won't blow away any farther in bed than you will in the window."

The tornado of 1943, as destructive as it was, didn't kill anyone. But windstorms, tornado or not, are notoriously quirky. A year and a half after the October 1943 tornado, a severe windstorm that was never officially declared a tornado blew down a barn on Wheaton merchant Wallace C. Chenoweth's farm on Shoal Creek east of town and killed James Fieker, a fourteen-year-old boy whose family rented the farm. The eighteen cows and seven horses in the barn escaped unhurt.[375]

From time to time as I grew up, I would watch small funnel clouds form and pass harmlessly overhead. Fortunately for us, none ever touched down closer than Orba Taylor's barn a couple of miles west of our house. A twister in March 1954 lifted the wood-frame hayloft of Orba's new barn off its concrete block walls and set the loft down gently in a field a few yards away. It ripped off a few blocks, but a wall that otherwise might have collapsed on five calves was held up by a tractor parked in the barn. The tractor sustained heavy damage, but the hayloft didn't lose even a shingle.[376]

Orba repaired the block wall, jacked up the hayloft, and set it back on the repaired block walls, good as new. Sixty years later, the barn is still there.

I never thought to ask Barney, Jeanie, or Gary Bates how they handled thunderstorms and tornado warnings after the storm of October 1943, but all families in southwest Missouri can count on warnings or sightings of tornadoes every spring and summer and, as the 1943 twister taught us, even occasionally in the fall. It simply is the price of living in the Ozarks. However, every cloud has a silver lining, the old saying goes, and the silver lining in the cloud of October 1943 brought the Bates family to Wheaton.

24

My Neighbors, the Robinsons

When I was three or four years old, I would beg my dad to call Roy Robinson on our old party-line crank wall phone. I don't remember how the routine started, but it would go like this: Dad would crank Roy's party line ring of longs and shorts and lift me up to the mouthpiece, and when Roy answered, I'd say, "Roy, you're crazy."

And Roy would say, "Naw, *you're* crazy," and I would laugh, and he would guffaw in that way he had of drawing bursts of air into his throat.

We would repeat these remarks a couple of times, after which my dad would intervene and put an end to this deeply intellectual exchange. But the next day, I would ask Dad if we could call Roy again. I think he was the first person I ever had a phone conversation with—if you'd call those exchanges a conversation.

Roy and Virgie Robinson were my family's closest neighbors. We lived down a gravel lane south of the Wheaton-Stella road, and their house was on the same road and directly north of ours. With just a glance, I could see the front of their house, their driveway, and Roy's pickup truck.

It was Roy and Virgie who drove anxious Granddad and Grandma Lamberson to Cardwell Memorial Hospital in Stella to see my mother and me the day after I was born. My parents didn't have a car, so they borrowed my grandparents' Model A Ford to take Mom to the hospital. Roy and Virgie probably were the first persons, other than my family, to welcome me into the world on that long-ago day in July 1939.

The year before I was born, Roy opened his Wheaton Maytag store, selling Zenith, Philco, and Maytag appliances.[377] At first, Roy's business prospered, but after World War II started, it soon became impossible for Roy to get new appliances, because the nation's resources were diverted to the war effort. So in 1942, Roy closed his store and farmed until the war was over, then reopened the store in 1945.[378]

Sometime during his farming years, probably toward the end of the war in 1945, Roy had cattle to sell, and my dad was interested in buying them. It was a damp, cloudy day. I was about six years old, sitting between Roy and Dad in Roy's pickup as we drove through his pasture looking at the cattle. Roy liked cigars. He lit one. Dad didn't smoke, but Roy handed him a cigar and persuaded him to fire it up.

The concept that exposing children to secondhand smoke was unhealthy had not yet occurred to either the medical community or to Dad and Roy. The air in that pickup was turning blue-gray when Dad, his mouth watering badly, needed to spit. He aimed a big mouthful out the window. But there was a problem. Dad hadn't noticed that the window was rolled up, so his expectoration centered the passenger side window with a mighty splat. Roy and I cracked up, even though I was feeling a little queasy by that time.

After Dad cleaned up the window with his handkerchief, we drove through the field with the windows down. For years after that, Roy and I would laugh about Dad's embarrassing splatter.

Since Roy was in the appliance business, he and Virgie had an electric refrigerator several years before we could afford to get rid of our icebox and buy a refrigerator. When I was small, Virgie, who was one of the kindest women I've ever known, occasionally invited me to her house to eat refrigerator ice cream. For the uninitiated, that's ice cream frozen in an ice cube tray with the cube separators removed. What a treat for a kid whose family had no refrigerator!

From our house, I could always tell when Roy was home. His Chevy pickup, parked in their driveway, was distinctive because above the bed on each side was a wood panel, painted white, with blue letters that read Wheaton Maytag. When Roy was minding his store, his pickup was usually parked in front of his shop on the south side of Main Street, just a few steps east of Floyd and Ann Hughes's drugstore.

Roy knew how to handle his money—frugal is a more refined way to say it. He was a teetotaler, and his only indulgences were his cigars, his collection of antiques, and the prized grandfather clocks that decorated his home.

Roy also was a good salesman. In October 1949, he won a trip to the Maytag factory in Newton, Iowa, because he was one of the top twenty salesmen of Maytag washers in southwest Missouri and northwest Arkansas. Of the more than eighty dealers and salesmen in a selling competition, Roy came in seventeenth. He was low key, always congenial, and inspired great confidence in his customers.[379]

Customers at Wheaton Maytag were immediately reminded of Roy's frugality: the lighting was low, provided mostly by the front window and a few well-placed fluorescent bulbs. Hanging on the wall to the right—above shelves of clocks, lanterns, coffeepots, electric can openers, and other small electric-powered items—was part of his collection of antique hand tools—saws, awls, files, braces and bits, chisels, axes, and more. To the left sat rows of appliances—washers, refrigerators, radios—and in later days, lawn mowers, dryers, deep freezers, and television sets.

The store was long and narrow and smelled faintly of Roy's unlit cigars. Years after Roy gave up smoking cigars, he usually could be found in the back of the shop, sitting in an old-fashioned wooden office chair, gently rolling an unlit stogie between his lips. Behind him was an antique roll-top desk.

"Hello, boys," Roy would say to my dad and me. "What can I do for you today?" We would joke for a few minutes and then casually get around to the business of something we wanted to buy.

Sometime after World War II, we bought a Maytag washing machine from Roy—a gleaming white round one that stood on four legs and had a wringer on an arm above the washer. That washing machine changed my mother's life for the better.

Roy also sold us radios and the most amazing mowing machine I have ever seen. Instead of a blade, it had a round steel plate with holes on the outer edge so that field mower sections could be riveted to it. Thanks to that remarkably sturdy machine, I was able to mow down huge weeds, small saplings, and even an occasional unfortunate snake near our outbuildings. I thanked Roy many times for that mower.

There were other Robinsons who influenced my early life. Roy's brother Grant, his wife, Nina, and their daughters, Wanna Lea and Virginia Nell, lived on the farm next to ours on the west. For a long time, my dad sang in a gospel quartet with Nina, my great-uncle Earl Lamberson, and Clovis Flaxbeard. Before I started to school, the quartet often practiced in the evenings at Grant and Nina's house. While the quartet was learning new songs—often with my mother playing the piano for them—Grant and I were left to entertain ourselves.

The entertainment, for me at least, was simple. I don't think Grant could carry a tune, but he could wiggle his ears; he was blessed with some kind of muscle control that enabled him to move his ears back and forth. I always begged him to wiggle them, and that was the basis of my early bonding with Grant Robinson.

More than I realized, my life and those of my mother and father were intertwined with the Robinson family. It was Roy and Grant's brother Mose who owned the farm we rented on the Wheaton-Stella road when I was born.

Mose and Grant were graduates of Southwest Missouri State College in Springfield, where Grant had played on the SMS basketball team sometime in the 1920s. Basketball was a more stationary game then, with more perimeter passing. A good two-handed set shot was an effective offensive weapon. One afternoon after school, when I was in the fourth or fifth grade at Oshkosh, I was heaving a basketball at the goal on the outdoor dirt court in the schoolyard.

Grant had finished a chore in the schoolhouse that he, too, had attended as a child. He asked me for the ball and sank a long two-handed set shot. He could see that I was having trouble getting the ball to the goal with one hand, so over the next half hour or so, Grant taught me to shoot a two-handed set shot, which was much easier for me to get to the goal. For two or three years, until I was old enough and strong enough to shoot a jump shot, I used the shot Grant taught me.

After SMS, Grant had returned to the farm. Mose went on to earn a master's degree from the University of Missouri—an outstanding accomplishment for a kid from a southwest Missouri farm in the early twentieth century. During the 1920s, Mose taught a year at Oshkosh, and from 1927 to 1931, he was superintendent of the Wheaton School District.

An undated clipping from the *Joplin Globe* records the recollections of Glee Lacy Duncan when she played forward for the undefeated Wheaton High School women's basketball team in 1931—a team coached by Wheaton's then-superintendent, Mose Robinson. Included in the article was the team's rallying song:

> *Wheaton Redbirds will shine tonight*
> *Wheaton Redbirds will shine tonight*
> *Wheaton Redbirds will shine tonight*
> *All down the line*
> *When the whistle blows*
> *And the center jumps*
> *The Redbirds will shine.*

Long before Title IX, the federal civil rights law that prohibits sex discrimination in education, Mose was coaching a women's basketball team at Wheaton High School. By the time I started first grade at Oshkosh in 1945, Mose was Newton County superintendent of schools.

I didn't know Mose as well as I knew Roy and Grant, but I was in awe of him. He was highly respected in the community, and his education had taken him far beyond the farm. Mose's pursuit of higher education was no doubt encouraged by the patriarch of the Robinson family, John Robinson. "Uncle John," as we all called him, and his wife, Martha, lived across the road to the west of Grant and Nina. John and Martha had moved to the Oshkosh community from the Cumberland Gap area near Rose Hill, Virginia, in the early 1900s when Roy, Grant, Mose, their brother Walter, and their sister, Nell, were youngsters.

Uncle John was a successful farmer, a devout Methodist, a strong Republican, and an avid 'coon hunter who always owned several good coonhounds.

Dad liked Uncle John because you always knew where you stood with him. One day, Dad came home amused. He told Mom and me that Uncle John had said to him, "Perry Lewis, you're a pretty good fellow, except that you're a Democrat and a Campbellite [a somewhat unflattering name for members of the Church of Christ]."

But Dad always thought that was funny and enjoyed repeating the story. He liked bantering with Uncle John. One day, as Dad and I were getting the mail from our box at the end of our lane, Uncle John stopped to talk with us.

"What are you doin', John?" Dad asked as Uncle John pulled his car into our lane.

"Well, I'm takin' my radio up to Roy's to see if he can fix it," Uncle John replied.

"What's the matter with it?" Dad asked.

"Every time I turn it on, it starts to squeal, and I can't hear anything," Uncle John explained.

Without a moment's hesitation, my father said with a straight face, "Oh, you don't need to take it to Roy's. Just take it back home, take the back off, and put a few squirts of 3-IN-ONE oil in there, and it'll stop that squeal."

Maybe Dad didn't think Uncle John would follow his advice, but if that's what he thought, he was wrong. Uncle John thanked Dad for his suggestion, got back in his car, turned around, and drove home.

I never did hear Uncle John's account of the matter, but a few days later, Dad went into Wheaton Maytag. He and Roy talked for a while, and then Roy said, "Say, Dad brought his radio in the other day. Took me about half a day to clean the oil out of it. Never could get it to work, so I just sold him a new one." They had a big laugh.

When I was not quite ten years old, Dad took a pickup load of our cattle and a couple of Uncle John's steers to sell at the stockyards in Joplin. Uncle John and I were eating lunch at the little greasy spoon at the stockyards while Dad was outside in the cattle pens with the order buyers from the meatpacking houses. I ordered ice cream for dessert. The waitress was very busy. I needed a spoon, but I couldn't get her attention.

"Well, you'd better just use mine," Uncle John said several times.

I didn't want to use Uncle John's spoon, even though he had licked it pretty clean, so I held out until I got a clean spoon—or at least a spoon as clean as the little joint washed them. I think Uncle John thought I was a little too particular about my tableware.

Like most farmers in southwest Missouri, Dad and Grant enjoyed quail hunting. I was a small boy when each of them got a new shotgun—sixteen-gauge, I think. Grant dropped by, and Dad rushed in and grabbed his new shotgun and several old *Joplin Globe* newspapers.

He and Grant draped the papers over the top of the barbed wire fence north of our house, and pretty soon the *boom, boom* of their shotguns rang out as they cut loose on the newspapers. Dad came to the house to get more papers.

"What're you doin', Dad?" I asked.

"We're settin' the choke on our shotguns, and we want to see what kind of patterns the shot leaves in the papers," he said.

That same week, Dad and Grant went quail hunting. Quail were plentiful in the fencerows of the farms in the Oshkosh community, and I still remember the quail dinners after Dad and Grant's hunting jaunts—always preceded with a warning from Dad to chew lightly just to make sure we didn't chomp down on a stray shotgun pellet.

There was another gun story involving Dad and the Robinsons that didn't turn out quite so well. When I was about ten years old, a big ol' prowling yellow-tabby tomcat began to scare off our barn cats, which Mom fed on a big flat rock in front of our barn. In the summer twilight, after she would put bread scraps and gravy on the rock, the tough old tomcat would show up, run off our barn cats, and get himself a free meal. This happened off and on for a couple of weeks, and Dad decided enough was enough.

For the next several evenings, he kept his .22 rifle handy as he milked. Then one evening at about dark, as he was walking back to the house after the chores were done, there sat the old yellow tomcat on the big bois d'arc corner post of the fence around our vegetable garden. Dad followed the most dangerous code of the West—or of country folks. He shot first and asked questions later. No longer would the yellow tomcat eat our barn cats' meal.

Except that the next night, the danged old yellow tomcat showed up and ran off our cats again. Dad and Mom were dumbfounded.

It was about a week later that Dad saw Roy in Wheaton. "Say, you haven't seen my old yellow tomcat, have you?" Roy asked Dad. "He hasn't been home for several days." It was one of the few times in my life that I ever saw Dad get evasive.

"No, I haven't, Roy," he said. "You say he's yellow?" It may have been convincing to Roy, but it wasn't to me. When Dad got home, he said to my mother, "I think I know why that old tomcat is still showing up. I probably shot the wrong cat."

To my knowledge, my dad never had the courage to tell Roy or Virgie what happened. He could tell them and cause hard feelings, or he could stay quiet and live with his guilty conscience. He chose the latter.

Like their father, Roy and Grant were strong Republicans. The night of the 1948 presidential election, when Truman was thought to have little chance against the Republican candidate, Thomas Dewey, Dad and Mom took me to Grant and Nina's to listen to the election returns on the radio. When we left to go home to bed, Grant was elated, and Dad was dejected. But like Harry Truman, who had gone to bed thinking that he would lose the election, Dad was delighted to discover the next morning that Truman had won.

The next time we saw Grant, he was shaking his head about the election. "Beats all I ever seen," he said disgustedly in his best nasal twang. But their differing politics never came between Dad and the Robinsons.

Over the years, Grant and Nina, Roy and Virgie, and Uncle John were simply a part of my life. They were always there as trusted neighbors, and I guess I thought they always would be. Then Uncle John's wife, Martha, suffered a stroke and died in March 1953. When Uncle John died on December 14, 1956, I was a senior at Wheaton High. He was spending a Friday night at Roy and Virgie's when he suffered a fatal heart attack.

Just two days later, his funeral at the Wheaton Methodist Church, where he had been Sunday school superintendent for decades, involved lots of his neighbors. Roy, Grant, and Mose wanted it that way.

Dad and I joined Fred Allen and Mrs. Maurice Goodrich, also neighbors of Uncle John, to sing hymns at the funeral as yet another neighbor, Mrs. Opal Hailey, played piano. The pallbearers were a mixture of Uncle John's neighbors and men who were well known in the Wheaton community—Norman Dickson, Tom Beal, Tom Stewart, Fred Allen, A. T. Blades, and Montie Forbes.[380]

I graduated from high school the following spring, and the next eight years were spent in college and the navy. When I was married to Jan McNeely in Cassville in the summer of 1965, Roy and Virgie attended our wedding. Grant, whose wife, Nina, had passed away, sent a thoughtful gift.

Roy and Virgie, Grant and Nina, and Uncle John and Martha were the kind of neighbors everyone wishes for—kind, thoughtful, and considerate. How lucky I was to have grown up with a neighbor who I could call "crazy," another who would wiggle his ears for me, and another who didn't get mad when Dad conned him into oiling his radio—and still remain the best of friends.

25

Oshkosh School with Mr. Roller and Miz Sampson

World War II had ended with victory over Japan just days before I started first grade at a one-room country school called Oshkosh. With its classic bell tower and pitched roof, Oshkosh school sat all alone in a flat field on one of the two curves in the eight-mile road between Wheaton and Stella. It was an old school, so old that no one seems to know when the schoolhouse was built. But an elderly woman, Mrs. Hala Sneed, once said she was a pupil there well before the turn of the century—the turn of the *twentieth* century, not the twenty-first.

Francis Roller, a single man with the unlikely nickname of Tiny, was the teacher of all eight grades at Oshkosh in the fall of 1945. I never knew why he had not served in the armed forces, but he may have been a bit too old for the draft, or he might have received some kind of medical deferment.

I can only speculate about how he got the nickname Tiny, since his height and weight was average. He might have been Tiny or Francis to family and friends, but I guarantee you that to the pupils at Oshkosh, he was *Mister* Roller—strict but fair and a thorough master of multiple academic disciplines. From arithmetic to zoology, from English to hygiene to handwriting, Mr. Roller knew his stuff.

Even though he was my teacher for only the first and second grade, I have never learned as much from anyone in such a brief period of time.

The school day at Oshkosh always started with everyone standing for the Pledge of Allegiance. We remained standing for Mr. Roller's personal hygiene inspection, after which, one by one, we could sit down.

The Oshkosh schoolhouse had an enormous floor-to-ceiling panel of windows on the north side of the room that provided good light for studying—and for spotting dirt behind the ears and under the fingernails. It was over near the windows, where the first graders sat, that Mr. Roller began his daily evaluation of his pupils' grooming and general cleanliness.

He'd start by noting whether your hair was combed, looking at your hands with particular attention to fingernails. Then he'd check your ears and your neck to see if you had washed, and finally, he'd pronounce judgment on the cleanliness of your clothes. An older pupil, usually an eighth-grader, would stand in front of a big white cardboard chart on the wall near the front of the room. Every pupil's name was on that chart. If you were totally clean and neat, Mr. Roller would call out "Gold!" Then the helper would select a gold star from a little bin under the chart and stick it across from your name.

A silver star meant you had tried, but maybe your hair needed a little work or you had forgotten to wash behind your ears. A red star meant that maybe you'd better take a bath that night, and a black star ... well, a black one meant you'd better get in the tub and soak and scrub, and do the same to your clothes.

I always took pride in getting a gold star to start the day, and that's why I still remember one morning, after I'd been running late, Mr. Roller completed my inspection by looking in my ears and thundering "Red!" He might as well have hollered, "Here's a dirty kid! He needs to clean up!" You can bet the next day I had scrubbed until my skin had a ruddy glow, and my ears were clean as a whistle.

There were two brothers, who I won't name, who always had a row of black stars after their names. They lived in a rented, dilapidated old farmhouse without indoor plumbing. Their hair was unkempt, their bib overalls so dirty they looked as if they'd been living in a coal pile, and their hands and faces were varying shades of brown and black from lack of washing. I always thought that maybe the next day they'd clean up, but not even a row of black stars that extended across a semester was enough to get them on the business end of a scrub brush or a washcloth. No one wanted to play with them at recess, they struggled with reading, and yet Mr. Roller very patiently would work with them every day to try to make a breakthrough. They moved away before the end of my second grade year, and I have often wondered if life ever improved for those boys and whether they ever had another teacher like Mr. Roller.

But encouraging cleanliness and good grooming was just a tiny fraction of Mr. Roller's job. In the first grade, using *Dick and Jane* reading books, every one of the seven or eight pupils in my class learned to read, although some could read faster than others. We all learned to count and to add and subtract. We had a health class where we were taught the basics of personal hygiene and dietary requirements—eat slowly, chew each bite of food thirty-two times, eat at least a little from each of the basic food groups, drink your milk, and get eight hours of sleep every night.

In the front of the schoolroom, there were a couple of long wooden benches where the kids in each grade went to recite while the rest of the pupils studied. The benefit of that arrangement was that if you weren't too busy working on your lessons, you could tune in to the class that was reciting and learn a lot listening to a class that was several years ahead of you.

Because I had been raised on a farm without a lot of contact with other kids, I came down with colds, scarlatina, measles, and a variety of childhood ailments that caused me to miss about 40 percent of my first year of school. But Mr. Roller was a practical man. If I could do the work and pass the tests, he'd pass me to the second grade. I was promoted.

In the first and second grades, every pupil brought lunch to school in a paper sack or a metal lunch box, often called a "dinner bucket" by persons of my grandmother's generation. If the weather was pleasant, we could eat lunch outside on the steps of the schoolhouse. If it was raining or snowing, we ate lunch at our desks, which Mr. Roller insisted that we clean up after we swallowed our last bite. He taught me to hold my lunch box just below the level of my desk and swipe the crumbs off into it without missing a single crumb—a skill that I still thank Mr. Roller for teaching me.

When we got thirsty, there was a well with a hand pump a few feet from the front steps of the schoolhouse. Getting a drink required at least two persons. As one person worked the pump handle up and down, water bubbled up from two fountains so two thirsty kids could get a drink. If we wanted to pump a bucket of water, a turn of a valve would reroute the water to a spigot instead of the drinking fountains.

Lunch hours and recesses were filled with active games, including basketball on an outdoor dirt court, softball, snowball fights in the winter, and a great game called dare base that was lots of fun for the fleet of foot.

Mr. Roller sometimes used pupils who had mastered a skill to teach the ones who hadn't. One day when I was in the second grade, Mr. Roller walked by my desk and saw me reading a book that was above my grade level. He was skeptical that I was really reading it, so he asked me to read a paragraph out loud to him. I did, and he asked one of the slower readers in my class to come over and sit with me so I could help the other kid with his reading. It worked out pretty well. The other kid's reading improved, and I made a good friend.

One of the tricks of teaching successfully in a one-room school for multiple grades is the ability to keep order in the rest of the room while conducting a class in the front of the room. Mr. Roller was a master of that art, as I found out one day when Jim Taylor and I got into a keep-away fight over a plastic ring. From out of nowhere, a large hand was grasping my hair and yanking me straight up from my desk. On the way to full stand-up position, I glimpsed Mr. Roller's belt buckle, and I knew we'd been nailed. Then I noticed that his other hand was in firm grasp of Jim Taylor's hair.

With a handful of hair in each hand, Mr. Roller marched Jim

and me to the front of the room where we spent the next thirty minutes standing at attention in front of the blackboard while the entire student body stared at us, occasionally snickering. We never did that again.

The Oshkosh School District didn't have a big yellow school bus that delivered its pupils to school. It had a dark-green 1945 Chevrolet panel truck that was sort of an early day sport utility vehicle. It had been outfitted with a bench that wrapped around the inside of the seating area behind the driver, with two or three shorter seats that faced the front in the middle. The driver was Finis Daniels. Finis was a middle-aged, even-tempered man whose brother Floyd was a partner in the Wheaton grocery store of Frazier-Daniels & Brattin. I don't remember that Finis ever had to yell at any of the kids. That could have been because Mr. Roller always rode with him in the passenger seat in the front. Sometimes, in bad weather, Finis would drive the little green bus an eighth of a mile off the highway and down our lane so I wouldn't get wet waiting for the bus.

During the summer between my second and third grades, Mr. Roller got married and took a job as an assistant manager of a lumberyard and hardware store in Springfield, Missouri, more than sixty miles from Oshkosh.

When I arrived at Oshkosh to start third grade in the late summer of 1947, we had a new teacher. Her name was Ruby Sampson. Her husband, Wendell, had died unexpectedly of a heart attack the previous spring. Miz Sampson, as we addressed her, lived in Rocky Comfort. She was an experienced teacher, but she hadn't taught school for several years. However, when she was offered a teaching job at Oshkosh, she accepted because she needed the work.

Miz Sampson picked up with our education right where Mr. Roller had left off. Under her expert tutelage, I memorized the multiplication tables, learned to multiply and divide, and put my commas in the right place—mostly. I also learned longhand writing, a bit of history, and good health practices. When I broke a bone in my foot playing basketball and was on crutches for six weeks, Miz

Sampson sometimes would drive me home after school. As a teacher, she combined effectiveness and kindness.

That school year of 1947/48 was when the National School Lunch Program began, and hot lunches were served to students. To qualify for federal meal funds, a new well was drilled at Oshkosh to replace the old well dug with a pick and shovel that had supplied the school's water for so long. A new electric pump replaced the old hand pump. Water was piped into the new kitchen that was built in the school's entryway area, where the pupils formerly hung their coats.

Some of the best hot lunches in America were served from that new kitchen between 1947 and 1951, when the Oshkosh district was split three ways and consolidated into other school districts. The two cooks I remember were farm women who lived only minutes from Oshkosh, and they had cooked for their hungry farm families all their lives. Lola Hughes, whose grandson Jack was a pupil at Oshkosh, and Wetona "Toni" Taylor—whose children, Betty, Jim, and Evva also were Oshkosh pupils—were the cooks.

From that little kitchen in the schoolhouse foyer, Lola and Toni served up mashed potatoes, slices of meatloaf or beef or pork or chicken, green beans, peas, corn, hominy, lettuce, tomatoes, bread, and milk—a menu that the country boys and girls had eaten all their lives. And cake … I still remember their cinnamon-spiced cake and their cupcakes with the delicious gooey frosting. Plain fare for lots of folks, but it was prepared just the way our mothers made it and served with good humor. I still have fond memories of the school lunch meals at Oshkosh.

Although it might generate controversy today, Oshkosh pupils always decorated a Christmas tree that someone's father would cut and bring to the school. Under Mr. Roller and Miz Sampson's guidance, the pupils also staged a Christmas program for the parents of the district, complete with skits, the singing of carols, and holiday songs. The pupils drew names a week earlier, and the event closed with a gift exchange.

Oshkosh had some very good grade-school basketball players. Our grade-school team managed to defeat several teams from larger schools. Three of the Haynes brothers—Melvin, Bill, and Darril—went on to play basketball for Wheaton High School, as did I. Leonard and Leon Lahman and some of the Embry brothers played for Fairview High.

In 1951, after I had finished the sixth grade and Miz Sampson had completed her fourth year of teaching at this one-room school, the Oshkosh School District was split among three larger districts—Stella, to the west; Fairview, to the north; and Wheaton, to the east. I landed at Wheaton.

After the district was split, the schoolhouse was purchased by Tom Beal, a local farmer who lived near us. The schoolhouse was old but solidly built. Tom moved the building and converted it into a hay barn and machine shed. Years later, the farm was owned by Carl Ellis, who tore down the old schoolhouse and recycled the lumber, which was still of excellent quality.

So was the quality of the education dozens of farm kids received inside the walls of that old schoolhouse, and somewhere behind the ivy-covered halls of academia, there should be a big plaque that reads, "To Francis Roller and Ruby Sampson, two of the finest teachers ever to grace the classrooms of rural America."

26

Good Doughgod

===

Like most small boys in the postwar 1940s, Dan Shewmake and I had lots of cowboy heroes—Roy Rogers, Gene Autry, Hopalong Cassidy, Red Ryder, the Lone Ranger, and others. When we were six or seven years old, the Cozy Theatre in Wheaton ran a movie serial that featured an idealized Wild Bill Hickok who Dan admired so much that our older buddy, J. W. "Dub" Johnson, called Dan "Hick" for years.

My dad used to say that Dan and I had enough cap guns to fill a bushel basket, and we spent hundreds of hours chasing each other through the fields of our farms playing cowboy. Little did either of us realize that in my preschool years, there had been a real live and very authentic cowboy living not more than a half mile from our farm.

He was Grandma Lamberson's cousin James Newton Kelly, a tough old codger who used to go to Oklahoma and bring back mules that he wrangled and cussed and whipped into animals that could be sold to local farmers who still used horses and mules to pull their plows, drills, manure spreaders, and wagon loads of everything from gravel to grain.

I called him Uncle Newt. Lots of old men of generally good repute were addressed as "Uncle" in our neck of the woods, but I sensed that Uncle Newt was special. His standard greeting to me was, "How's that boy?" even though he knew my name. It was clear, my mom said, that despite the difference in our ages, Uncle Newt and I were kindred spirits. Proof that he liked me, I thought, was that he was always telling Dad that he was going to teach me how to cuss.

And cuss he could. When Uncle Newt was working with his mules, he would let go with a string of blue words powerful enough to trigger a hellfire-and-brimstone sermon from every Baptist, Methodist, Holiness, or Church of Christ preacher—or any Catholic priest, any rabbi, or representative of any other religious faith in southwest Missouri, for that matter.

Our neighbor, George "Peach" Ford, a World War II army machine gunner who had seen heavy action in the Philippines, lived on the old dirt road that we called the Creek Road about half a mile south of Uncle Newt's place. Indian Creek was just a good rock throw south of the little house where Peach lived with his mother, Cora. Peach said that in the late 1930s and early 1940s, before he fought in the Pacific, he used to stand on the bank of Indian Creek and watch Newt "educate" mules he had just brought back from Oklahoma. The old man would hitch two mules to a wagon and drive to where the creek was no more than a few inches deep. He'd stop the mules and wagon in the creek close to a gravel bar and shovel so much gravel into the wagon that no average team of horses or mules could have pulled it, Peach recalled.

Then Newt would climb into the wagon seat, crack his whip, and launch into a stream of high-pitched cusswords that greatly expanded my vocabulary of profanities. As a very small boy, I happened to be present with my dad for a couple of those mule-training sessions. Even at my age, I knew the difference between eloquent cursing and purely crude cursing. I knew I'd better never use those words around my folks, but I always marveled at how easily they tumbled out of Uncle Newt's mouth.

Lashed by whip and tongue, the mules would strain until the wagon wheels began to turn—slowly at first as they sank into the creek bed—and gradually pick up speed until they hit the solid ground of the dirt road. Then Newt would give them a fresh dose of oath-laced encouragement, and off they'd go, back up the grade toward his farm as he cracked the whip. When they got back to his place, he'd shovel the gravel into a big pile that he would sell to anyone who needed gravel to mix with cement for a rough concrete job.

Until sometime in the middle of World War II, Newt lived alone in a house that his uncle George Kelly, my great-grandpa, had built where the Wheaton-Stella road met the road down to Indian Creek. His wife, Minnie, had died in September 1941 when I was a toddler. When I was getting acquainted with him, he was "way up in his seventies," as Grandma used to say. She never seemed to be very close to Newt, even though he was her first cousin. About all she ever told me about him was that he had "gone out west" when he was a young man and had spent several years there. But somehow, I never connected him to the swashbuckling movie cowboys who were among my boyhood heroes.

To my surprise, more than sixty years later, I learned that Uncle Newt had fought with—and got the best of—a famous western gunslinger whose life inspired a movie. During the years I knew him as a kid, I just thought of him as a tough old man who really knew how to handle mules.

My dad, a farmer and cattle trader, liked Uncle Newt. Occasionally, during the early World War II years when I was very small, he would come to our house to visit with my folks. He always managed to show up about mealtime so that he got a two-fer—a little visiting to relieve his loneliness and one of my mother's meals that was probably a lot better than anything he could cook. When he would eat something he really liked, he'd say, "That's mighty good doughgod." A big dollop of mashed potatoes with a puddle of Mom's flour gravy in the middle of it was "good doughgod" to Uncle Newt. A piping hot corner piece of Mom's corn bread, split and topped with a knifeload of molasses and butter, was "good doughgod," as was her fried chicken or sweet, fresh, buttery peas straight from our garden.[381]

It was one of those "good doughgod" visits that made Uncle Newt a legend in the Lewis household. I was too small to remember it, but Dad repeated the story many, many times when I was a kid.

Late one chilly, dark afternoon in the winter of 1942, Uncle Newt was lonely. His wife, Minnie, had passed on a few months earlier. He showed up at our front door when Dad was in the barn milking cows. He opened the front door before my mother got there. In the shadowy entryway, he saw his image in the full-length mirror that hung on the wall facing the front door.

As my mother watched with amusement, he stood just inside the front door and, looking sincerely into the mirror a few feet away, reached up and doffed his gray felt broad-brimmed hat politely, and said, "How'd do. Is the lady of the house in?"

After Mom stopped laughing, she stepped to the door and said, "I'm the lady of the house, and I'd like to introduce you to the fellow you just spoke to." She said she quickly determined, after a whiff of his breath, that the old man had quaffed a couple of snorts of liquid corn. Uncle Newt was a little embarrassed by his late-afternoon gaffe, but not too embarrassed to stay for supper. After that, and long after Uncle Newt departed this earth, my dad would often doff his hat and speak to himself when he came in the front door, even when there was no mirror.

By the time Newt died on May 21, 1949, Dan and I were either playing cowboy or fighting World War II virtually every time we got together. As kids, if we had known what I discovered more than sixty years after Newt's death, we would have done a lot of spittin' and whittlin' with the old man just to hear his stories.

The credit for much of the rest of Uncle Newt's story belongs to my cousin George Leon Kelly of Granby, Missouri, who did a ton of research in the 1990s and assembled a thick Kelly family tree notebook. In early 2012, I came across three pages, buried deep in the book, devoted to Newt Kelly. They told an astounding story about the old man who used to eat supper in our house when I was a small boy.

Those three pages revealed that the old mule wrangler had been a real cowboy—and not *just* a cowboy but one who had fought with one of the Old West's most notorious characters and nearly killed him.

Artie Griffis, Newt's daughter, said that Newt and a friend, Jim

Holmes, left their homes near Rocky Comfort, Missouri, for Wyoming when Newt was sixteen years old. That very likely would have been in the spring or summer of 1882. Newt probably accompanied his uncle, John Milton Kelly, who moved from southwest Missouri to Wyoming about that time.

John F. Gooldy, the son of one of the early nonnative settlers in southern Wyoming, recalled:

> My father's cattle, F. C. McCary's cattle, and John Kelley's (sp) cattle were the first domestic stock that was ever in South Fork Park, at the headwaters of the South Fork of the Little Snake River. They ran their cattle two years in that area before there was ever any other cattle there, and it was a number of years before there were many other cattle there.[382]

In 1986, Artie told an interviewer, Janet Oakes Hathaway, that after they left Missouri, her father and Jim Holmes—a pair of Missouri teenagers—ran out of money and joined the army, presumably, in Wyoming, where Indian uprisings still posed occasional problems. But Artie said Newt told her that he and Holmes left camp after three days. It's not clear whether they went AWOL or were simply discharged. But apparently, there was no penalty for leaving the army so soon. After that, "Jim Holmes got homesick and went home," Artie said.

"Newt went on by himself ... to Baggs, Wyoming, and went to work for J. W. Darr, (a prominent rancher) forty miles west of Baggs. He was foreman there until he was thirty-six years old," his daughter said.

In August 1902, Newt turned thirty-six, returned to Missouri, and married Minnie Scott a year later in the Newton County seat of Neosho. But in the summer of 1900, when he was thirty-four and still out west, he more than held his own in a Baggs, Wyoming, knife fight with one of the West's toughest and most notorious characters, the sometimes lawman, sometimes bounty hunter, and sometimes outlaw Tom Horn.

In the Kelly family genealogical notebook, the Kelly researcher wrote:

> There can be no doubt as to the veracity of the story of his (Newt Kelly's) knife fight with the infamous Tom Horn. Tom Horn had been a number of things in the West—miner, deputy sheriff, army scout, etc. During the last years of his life he was a "stock detective," serving large ranch owners to deter rustling, and a bounty hunter. To some he was a paid assassin. One author said of him that when he was drinking, which was quite often, he became loud, caroused the red light districts and saloons, and was filled with braggadocio.[383]

The details of Newt's fight with Tom Horn vary widely according to who is telling the story, but all accounts agree that the fight began after Horn got into some kind of a confrontation with Newt's younger brother, Ed. Chip Carlson of Cheyenne, Wyoming, who researched the life of Tom Horn and wrote, *Tom Horn: Blood on the Moon: Dark History of the Murderous Cattle Detective*, told the Kelly family researcher:

> The account you relate has a familiar ring, and the name, Newt Kelly, does as well ... I have read of Horn getting into a scrape in a saloon in Baggs, when he was on his way back from Brown's Hole in 1900, after the murder of Matt Rash or Isom Dart. The story went that he'd cleared out of the country on his way back to Wyoming, probably Laramie, as he was in the employ of Ora Haley (a prominent cattle rancher) ... He rode into Baggs on a lathered horse, and was covered with the pale, fine dust we are noted

for. He liked his booze, and apparently felt he was out of reach of the law.

> I don't know what happened to spark the knife fight, probably two guys under the influence getting into an argument. I understand he (Horn) was hurt pretty badly, and there was a knife wound on the side of his neck … At any rate, he healed up, probably with the assistance from allies there, and then continued back this way (toward Cheyenne).[384]

In the summer of 1900, when Newt and Tom tangled, Horn had been quietly hired as a range detective by a small group of prominent ranchers that included Haley, a shrewd investor who ran his cattle operations from Denver. Bad blood had developed in Colorado and Wyoming between the wealthy and powerful cattle ranchers and the smaller cattle ranchers and hardscrabble sheep ranchers and homesteaders who were moving into the open-range pasturelands and fencing them off. Another complaint of the cattlemen was that without careful management, sheep eat pasture down to the ground, leaving it unusable for cattle grazing.

Horn reportedly was instructed to scare off cattle rustlers and some of the small homesteaders and sheep growers that interfered with free-range cattle grazing. If he couldn't scare them into hightailing it out of the territory, there was an unspoken understanding that he could take stronger measures. The powerful men who hired Horn had an interest in burnishing his reputation.

Four years before Newt Kelly's death—and about the time Uncle Newt told Dad he was going to teach me to cuss—the author of several books about the Old West, Jay Monaghan, published a book, *Tom Horn: Last of the Bad Men*, which provided two versions of Newt's fight with Horn.

One version of the fight was told by the cattle barons who had hired Horn as a stock detective. The second account was told by the farmers, sheepherders, and other enemies of the well-to-do ranchers.

Even though Newt was foreman for a successful cattle rancher, J. W. Darr, near Baggs, Wyoming, on the southern Wyoming border with Colorado, the fact that he got the best of Horn in a saloon knife fight made him an instant hero with the sheep men and small cattle ranchers.

Each of the two factions had a newspaper in the area that represented its interest, and each paper published its version of the fight that had some details in common but varied wildly in others. The account in the paper sympathetic to the big ranchers was friendlier to Horn.

In that version, an old cowpuncher said Horn rode into Baggs the day after he killed a man named Matt Rash. The fight, according to the big ranchers' version, was at the Four-Ace Beer Hall, which had doors that opened up so that cowpokes could ride into the place and "have a drink in the saddle."

This story says that Horn, however, walked in, threw a silver dollar on the bar, and said, "Give me a pair of overalls," which meant he wanted a bottle of Overholt's whiskey and two glasses. After downing the drinks, Horn walked to a table where a poker game was under way and was challenged by Newt Kelly for drinking alone—provoking a fight.

Newt, this version goes, said he wouldn't fight with fists or pistols—only knives. The two men each put the end of a bandanna handkerchief in their teeth, and the bartender told them when to start fighting. Newt hit Tom in the stomach with his left fist and swiped the knife at his throat, slashing him from the shoulder to the point of his chin. Fortunately for both Tom and Newt, the cut was not fatal, but it was a serious wound.

The cattleman's story says they continued to fight, even though Tom was bleeding, and Tom could have stabbed Newt in the back, but he didn't, according to this account of the story in Monaghan's book.[385]

Tom then wrested Newt's knife from his hand, the bartender tied up Tom's neck, and "wounded as he was, Tom loped sixty miles to Rawlins," Monaghan wrote.

Monaghan's book also tells Newt's side of the knife fight story through the words of an old sheepherder, who started by recalling that the day was so hot that "the lizards carried little boards with them to lay on every little bit so that they could blow on their toes." He then called Tom Horn an "overbearing bully." Even the saloon was different in this version of the tale. Instead of the Four-Ace Beer Hall, the fight took place at the Bull Dog Saloon, the sheepherder said. But the whiskey was the same in each version—a bottle of Overholt's and two glasses for Horn.[386]

The sheepherders' story portrayed Newt's brother as a "freckle-faced kid" who Horn slapped around after he failed to respond quickly enough to Tom's order to take his horse to the livery barn. Horn then walked to the gambling table and asked to play "seven-up" with a man named Jim Davis—the only man in the saloon except the barkeep.

Then in walked Newt. In this version of the story, Tom sees the family resemblance and supposes Newt is there to whip the guy who mistreated his kid brother.

This account, which claimed Newt weighed only 125 pounds, says that he whipped out his pocketknife, jumped on Horn, sliced him from the shoulder to the chin, snatched Tom's gun, ran out of the saloon, and left Horn's gun on a fence post. Horn, this account says, was in bed for six days recuperating from the knife wound.[387]

There probably were elements of truth in each of these stories. Monaghan concluded that it is "certain that Tom Horn had a fight with Newt Kelly and was cut by his opponent's knife. All accounts agree as to the slicing of Tom from shoulder to chin and the rattle of the knife across the floor."[388]

The second version of the story, told by those who didn't like Horn, has a serious flaw. Newt, indeed, had been joined in Wyoming by his younger brother, Ed. Edgar Julian Kelly was born May 14, 1879, and would have been twenty-one years old when Newt fought Tom Horn, according to the Kelly family history. Ed was certainly no kid who ran away from Horn.

Although the details are sketchy as to where Horn went and how long it took him to recuperate from the knife wounds inflicted by Newt, a wildlife photographer and roadhouse operator named A. G. Wallihan saw Horn after the near-fatal scrap and offered an incisive glimpse of Horn's condition and character. Horn was using an alias, calling himself Hicks. Chip Carlson's book, *Tom Horn: Blood on the Moon*, quotes Wallihan's recollection of meeting Horn:

> I know a lot more about the Tom Horn "war" because I saw that. Horn stopped here at my roadhouse on his way to Juniper Springs. He had got cut pretty bad in a fight with Newt Kelly in Baggs, and he thought that the springs might help him. He wasn't a bad-looking fellow, tall. He never looked at you. He always looked down. If you spoke to him he would look at you for a moment then his eyes would fall again ...
>
> My wife had lived all her life on the frontier and she was not afraid of man, God or the devil, but she said that man Hicks is a bad man.[389]

It's likely that the most accurate version of Newt's dustup with Tom Horn is in Carlson's book. Carlson writes that the *Craig* (Colorado) *Empire-Courier* related an account of the fight by Bill Tittsworth, a cowboy who knew Horn by his alias of Hicks:

> About two weeks after Matt Rash was killed (that would be about August 1900) Hicks rides into Baggs and puts his horse up in Bill Penland's stable. Then he heads for Roy Bailey's saloon and proceeds to get drunk. There had been two guys from Missouri around Baggs for some time, Nute [sic] and Ed Kelly. Nute liked to play around with a Colt 45; Ed was very handy with his fists. Ed was tending bar for Roy Bailey. Nute was tending sheep camp. Nute was

in Baggs that day and there were some others in the saloon.

Hicks comes in, don't nobody know Hicks. Hicks gets two or three shots of red eye and he thinks he is a fighting man from Powder River. The thought no more than hits him until Ed's fist connects with his jaw; that slams him up against the bar, then Ed grabs both his arms and pins him to the bar; Nute outs with his knife and slashes his throat; came very near finishing him. They get him over to the hotel and call in Dr. White who sews up his neck.

Bob Meldrum was deputy sheriff and lived at Dixon. Someone got the word to him that Nute Kelly was on the warpath, so Meldrum comes right to Baggs and stands guard over Hicks until he can ride again. Hicks was riding a blue roan horse wearing Ora Haley's heart brand on his left hind leg. [390]

John Gooldy's history of the Little Snake River Valley also contains a brief mention of the knife fight, also misspelling Newt's name:

Knute Kelley, whom I knew and rode with one spring on the roundup, near the headwaters of Savery Creek, and in the Tullis area, cut Tom Horn while in a poker game at Baggs. Knute Kelley was from Southwestern Missouri, on the edge of the Ozark Mountains. [391]

George Leon Kelly, who helped compile the Kelly genealogy, recorded yet another version of the fight, presumably the version that Newt and his brother told:

The family tradition was that Tom and Ed Kelly got into an argument. Tom became abusive and threatened Ed with a knife. Newt stepped in to break up the fight and Tom turned on Newt with his knife. Newt could not reach his pistol quickly enough, so he drew his knife. He slashed Tom in the neck and stomach. Tom was so badly hurt they thought he would die.

Newt and Ed left town and went into the Hole In The Wall area of Wyoming. When they learned that Tom would recover and that no charges were being brought against them, they returned to their jobs in the Baggs area.[392]

It's unclear how long Newt and Ed hid out in the rugged Hole-In-The-Wall area of the Big Horn Mountains about 250 miles northeast of Baggs, but the Kelly family history says that after Newt learned he was not a wanted man, he went back to the Darr Ranch near Baggs and continued his job as foreman for two more years.

In the Kelly history, Bob Oakes, a family friend, reported to another Kelly relative, Dale Dukes, that Newt "got to know" several famous outlaws, probably when he fled Baggs after the knife fight. Who knows what would have happened to Newt if he had killed Horn? Would he have teamed up with the Wild Bunch gang that included Butch Cassidy, whose real name was Robert Leroy Parker; the Sundance Kid, whose name was Harry Alonzo Longabaugh; Bert Charter; and Etta Place? Both Butch and Sundance often hid out with their Wild Bunch gang in Hole-In-the-Wall country.[393]

Oakes said after Newt came back to Missouri and got married in 1903, "he went back to Wyoming twice. Newt went to Wyoming and brought back three boxcar loads of wild mustangs. He went again when Artie was eight, and stayed there three years." Newt's daughter Artie, who was born in 1904 near Rocky Comfort, Missouri, told the Kelly family researcher that Bert Charter gave her a palomino mare when she was a little girl. Charter would have had ample opportunity to send a mare back to Missouri with Newt.

Newt Kelly got a bad rap in Monaghan's book about Tom Horn, probably because Monaghan was not able to locate Newt as he was writing *Tom Horn: Last of the Bad Men*, in 1946. Monaghan wrote:

> The Newt Kelly remembered in later years was, however, no famous knifeman, nor sturdy farmer; he was, instead, a loafing drifter, a little horsejockey of a man with an Irish face, who never worked and seemed welcome without money among the covered-wagon gypsies who camped along Snake River with a bottle and a woman or two for sale.[394]

That description of the post-knife-fight Newt Kelly was dead wrong. The truth is that after Newt returned to southwest Missouri in 1902, married Minnie the next year, and began to raise a family, he became a well-known and successful stockman, mule trainer, horse wrangler, and farmer in the Rocky Comfort and Wheaton communities until his death in 1949.

In 1923, when he was fifty-seven years old, he was judged honest and steady enough to hold a job with the Kansas City, Missouri, police department—another part of his life I knew nothing about until I was searching the back issues of the *Wheaton Journal*. In the *Journal*, Newt was always referred to as "J.N. Kelly." On December 28, 1923, the *Journal's* local items reported:

> Mrs. J.N. Kelly and children left last Saturday night for Kansas City to spend the holidays with J.N. Kelly, who is employed on the police force at that place.

I don't know what Uncle Newt did at the Kansas City Police Department, but you can bet that whatever it was, he did it with the same intensity that he showed when he was breaking in a new team of mules. He certainly was no "loafing drifter," and he was far more than "a little horsejockey." He actually was of average size, not "little," and was one of the hardest working men I've ever known, even when he was well into his seventies.

Tom Horn, on the other hand, lived only three years after his knife fight with Newt. Horn was born November 21, 1860, in Memphis, Scotland County, Missouri. He was hanged November 20, 1903, for the murder of a fourteen-year-old boy, but he was convicted on such questionable evidence that many people, then and now, believe the verdict was wrong.[395]

Horn was famous enough, or infamous enough, that the late great actor Steve McQueen made a movie simply titled *Tom Horn*. It contained no scenes of, or references to, the knife fight. However, one thing is certain: after the knife fight, Tom Horn and Newt Kelly never crossed paths again.

James Newton Kelly was born in 1866, only a year after the end of the Civil War. He would have been thirty-two years old during the Spanish-American War and too old to fight in World War I. He died at age eighty-two on May 21, 1949, in Kansas City, Missouri, where he spent the last few months of his life with his daughter, Mrs. Artie Griffis.

His obituary in the May 26, 1949, edition of the *Wheaton Journal* said that he and his wife, Minnie, had six children, four of whom had preceded him in death. The obituary was complimentary, providing no hint of his colorful past:

> Newt, as he was known by his many friends, was a friend to everyone and always looked on the bright side of life. No matter what his circumstances were or how bad he was feeling, he never complained and when asked how he was getting along, his reply was always "fine."

There was nothing in his obituary about his horse and mule wrangling or his sheep-herding skills, nothing about his knife fight with Tom Horn, and, of course, nothing about his fluency with swear words.

Newt's funeral at the Prosperity Baptist Church at Rocky Comfort on May 24, 1949, was conducted by his lifelong friend and one of Wheaton's most prominent citizens, Silas McQueen, who years earlier had agreed to preside at the old wrangler's last rites.

As was common in *Wheaton Journal* obituaries in those days, Newt's obituary contained a poem:

> *Instead of treasures stowed away*
> *That many long for day by day*
> *It's fine to leave, when we are gone*
> *Rich memories that will linger on.*[396]

Uncle Newt certainly left me with rich memories. He was always good to me, and I always fancied that he and I would have become good buddies if we'd had a little more time together.

As a kid, if I had only known that Uncle Newt had fought one of the most famous men in the West and cut him up in a knife fight, I would've pestered him to tell me stories of his cowboy days. I think he would have told me everything. And I'm pretty certain that he would have supplemented my vocabulary even more with words that I wouldn't have been able to use in polite company. Bustin' mules on the farm in southwest Missouri must've been tame stuff to an old wrangler like Newt.

But a small part of Newt Kelly's legacy lives on in the Lewis family. At the tasty table that my wife, Jan, always sets today, my grown daughters, Angie and Shannon, give Jan her highest compliment for a good dish when they say, as they have since they were little girls, "That's mighty good doughgod, Mom."

27

The Hollow Bull

Cattle trading for a living is a skill and an art form that has nearly disappeared in rural parts of the country, but during the 1940s and 1950s, it was alive and well in southwest Missouri, and my dad was one of the best. Because he was so successful at buying and selling cattle for profit, he made more money that way than he did at farming.

Dad was an excellent judge of bovine quality and weight, whether he was sizing up beef cattle or dairy cattle in any of their variations—cow, calf, heifer, steer, or bull. He could take one look at a dairy cow and determine her weight and propensity for milk production. He was equally good at estimating the weight of cattle to within fifty pounds.

What's more, he could pretty accurately predict how much the younger ones would weigh six months later if they were fed properly. Those skills, coupled with a gifted mathematical mind and the knowledge of what commission companies at the Springfield or Joplin stockyards were paying per pound for different types and grades of cattle, made him a formidable cattle trader.

Dad could walk out into a farmer's pasture, look at twenty head of Hereford steers, estimate each steer's weight, add the weights to a total in his head, and multiply that by the market price per pound, without ever using a pencil. So he knew when the farmer's asking price was too high, or, conversely, when the price would be a bargain.

Sometimes, farmers preferred to sell their cattle by the head instead of by the pound, which simply meant that they would say, "I'll take $175 for that animal and $225 for that one," and so on. It made little difference to Dad, because if he knew he was going to be selling them at the stockyards soon, he went through the price-per-pound calculations to arrive at the price he was willing to pay by the head.

Between the late 1940s and the mid-1950s, Dad's cattle trading partner—and, to some degree, his trading mentor—was a tall, thin, partially bald, straight-faced, dry-humored man named Ern Shewmake. Ernest L. Shewmake was seven years older than my dad, and he had been a reputable and successful cattle trader for many years when they teamed up. Lucky for me, Ern and his wife, Hessie, had a son, Dan, born three months after me, who became my lifelong friend.

As the price of cattle skyrocketed in the late 1940s, it was possible to make "some pretty good money"—as Dad and Ern would say—trading cattle, but it also took more bucks to be able to buy cattle in significant enough numbers to make "cattle jockeying," as I called it, worthwhile. Hence, Dad and Ern pooled their resources and split the profits.

They were a formidable team—Perry Lewis and Ern Shewmake. Unlike a lot of guys who were trying to make their living as cattle jockeys, Dad and Ern didn't spend an inordinate amount of time dickering with the people they were buying from or selling to. They would simply go to the pasture or barn lot or corral where someone had cattle for sale, estimate the weights, and calculate the price they could—or would—pay for the animals. Then they would lean on the barn or pickup truck or sit on the fence and pull out their pocketknives and whittle a bit, while the seller made up his or her mind about whether to accept their offer.

If they knew the seller would try to bargain, their first offer often was deliberately low so they could raise it, make the seller feel good and still make money at the stockyards. If the seller continued to hem and haw, they'd simply say, "Sorry, we can't go any higher," and they were back in their pickup trucks and gone. There wasn't much haggling when you did business with Lewis and Shewmake.

Until I was in the eighth grade or ninth grade, I never heard

Dad or Ern mention that they'd ever been cheated—"skinned," in the vernacular of the day—on a cattle deal, but in the summer of one of those years, the intrepid cattle jockeys heard about a farmer who lived thirty miles north of us, near the town of Mount Vernon, who had a big prize Hereford bull for sale. Beef cattle—Herefords, Angus, Red Polled—were selling well that year, so they called the guy and told him they'd drive up the next day to look at his bull.

I can still see and hear Dad—in his jeans, short-sleeve plaid sport shirt, and snap-brim straw hat, and Ern in his khaki twill wash pants that always slid down around where his hips would have been if he'd had any—describing this bull after they hauled him home that night. "That's the biggest bull I've nearly ever seen," Dad exulted, taking his hat off and running his hand over his sweaty brow. "And he sold him to us cheap. We're gonna take him to Springfield (to the stockyards) in the morning." I could tell that Ern, too, was excited about the big bull and the prospects for his sale. But unlike Dad, Ern never changed expressions except for the gleam in his eye.

The next day, the bull was loaded, along with some other cattle, into a big truck, and off to the stockyards went the bull and the two master traders. I waited patiently all day for Dad to get back. It was about sixty-five miles to Springfield, and he usually didn't get home from a trip to the stockyards until late afternoon.

It was a very different Perry Lewis who returned late that day. He got out of the pickup looking very serious, strode with long steps to the back door, and stopped and tilted his short-brim hat back, exposing a flushed forehead.

"How'd it go with the bull?" I asked.

"Son, do you know that that guy did to us?" Dad said with unexpected bluntness.

"No, what?" I replied.

"He sold us a hollow bull," Dad said with a mixture of incredulity and anger.

"What do you mean, a hollow bull?" I asked.

"Well, he had him in a pen with a water tank and a hose hooked up to a hydrant when we looked at him," Dad said. "But we didn't think anything about it at the time. I guess the ornery pup must have put that hose down his throat and put four or five hundred pounds of water down him. Because when we got him to the stockyard, he had pissed all over the truck, and I saw that he'd pissed a lot last night. By the time we weighed him, he'd lost several hundred pounds!" As the story unfolded further, Dad said he was so mad he wanted to stop at the farmer's place on the way back from Springfield and give the devious bull seller a piece of his mind. But Ern made a shrewd suggestion.

"No, no," Ern said. "Let's not do that. Let's just go back and trade with him next spring when his next bunch of calves and heifers and springer (pregnant) cows are for sale."

Dad took the advice, and for the next nine months, he and Ern would occasionally talk to each other—and no one else—about how they lost money on the "hollow bull" and how they looked forward to trading with the same man next spring.

I won't say that revenge is sweet, but I do remember that they went back the next spring and bought quite a number of cattle from the cunning farmer, who had no idea that they planned to educate him on the finer points of cattle trading. The day Dad got home from the stockyards after selling the second batch of cattle they bought from the Mount Vernon farmer, he was in a much jollier mood than he had been a year earlier when he and Ern took the hollow bull to market.

"How much did you make today, Dad?" I asked.

"We did all right, son," he answered as a broad grin spread across his face. "Ern Shewmake taught me a little lesson in patience, and it sure paid off."

I never did know how much profit they made that spring off the man who sold them the waterlogged bull, and Dad never explained to me the means he and Ern used to make their big profit. However, I did learn the meaning of the old saw, "What goes around comes around."

Some things come around pretty fast, I reckoned, but big things like hollow bulls can take nearly a year.

28

The Gentle Genius

M y first recollection of seeing Albert Brumley in person was at a Sunday afternoon "singing convention" at Union, a little country church on old Highway 44 a few miles north of Powell, Missouri, where Albert lived.[397] I suspect it was in the fall of 1945, just after World War II ended, because we didn't travel much during the war years when gasoline and tires were rationed.

Albert was singing bass in a gospel quartet, whose other three members I have long since forgotten. Even at age six, I already had heard a lot about Albert. My dad used to sing gospel songs in quartets at singing conventions where Albert also performed, and they were acquainted. Dad grew up in the hill country east of Jane, fewer than ten miles from Powell, and everybody knew everybody else in that part of McDonald County.[398]

Dad's brother, my uncle Jack, lived on a farm just a couple of miles south of Albert's place. Uncle Jack had primed me to believe that Albert was someone special. Jack Lewis was the most accomplished musician in my family—not so much because of his singing but because he played the fiddle, banjo, mandolin, and harmonica. He used to visit the Brumleys, tape his stiff crooked finger to one of his good ones, and play up a storm with Albert and his children—five sons and a daughter.

Uncle Jack and my dad used to joke, as we passed the multigabled, one-story Brumley home on our way through Powell, that Albert added a room with a gable every time he and his wife, Goldie, had another child. I never took their comments seriously, because I knew that the Brumleys had six children, and there were fewer than six gables.

Before I heard him sing and play the piano at the Union church, Albert Brumley was a household name all over southwest Missouri, northwest Arkansas, and northeast Oklahoma. He already had written several hundred gospel songs, and others he called his "sentimental" songs, and was well on his way to becoming one of the most—if not *the* most—prolific gospel songwriters in American history. His songs had been sung on the radio, at singing conventions, in churches, and at funerals for at least ten years.

Everyone I knew who could carry a tune sang one or more of Albert's most popular compositions, such as "I'll Fly Away," "I'll Meet You in the Morning," and "There's A Little Pine Log Cabin."

What I remember about Albert that day in 1945 was that he was kind of skinny, baldish, and had a bass voice—not exactly someone who would stand out in a crowd. I already had sung a few of his songs at the top of my voice around our farm, but I had not figured out, at age six, that a man didn't have to look like Clark Gable to have talent.

Albert had a very casual way of sitting at the piano that would have driven conventional piano teachers crazy. After seating himself on the piano bench, he would lean back and drop his arms below the keyboard—exactly what I was told not to do when I was taking piano lessons from my cousin Jim Lamberson. Then Albert would splay his left foot off to the left and pat it to keep time while he worked the pedals with his right foot.

But it wasn't that first brief look at Albert at the singing convention that fixed my lifelong impression of him; it was a second encounter with him three or four years later that imprinted him firmly into my memory. Calvin and Faye Thomas, who lived on a farm between Rocky Comfort and Longview, invited my folks and me to their place to sing one evening. Calvin sang bass, Faye sang alto, and my dad, Perry Lewis, sang tenor or sometimes sang the lead.

Calvin and Faye had also invited Albert and Goldie—and as many of their kids as they wanted to bring. Visiting and homemade ice cream—hand cranked in cracked ice in an old-fashioned wooden ice cream bucket—were on the menu in addition to singing.

I was looking forward to playing with the Thomas boys—Lowell (we called him Junior) and Ronnie—and maybe even Betty Thomas, who was older than I by three or four years. I remember having a great time playing in the yard and in a shed full of baled hay with Junior and Ronnie and with Jack Brumley—the youngest of the five Brumley brothers—who was my age. One of Jack's brothers, Tom, who was eleven or twelve years old, brought his steel guitar and played it for us in the yard. Tom eventually became the steel guitar player for Buck Owens, and later, for Ricky Nelson.

After eating ice cream and visiting, my dad and mom, Albert and Goldie, Calvin and Faye, and Betty Thomas went inside, gathered around the piano, and began singing. I tagged along. Unbeknownst to anyone, I had developed a little boy's crush on Betty, an older woman of probably eleven or twelve. I knew she was an accomplished singer and piano player for her age, so as Faye Thomas and my mother alternated playing piano while the group sang, I saw an opportunity to impress Betty.

The adults and Betty started to sing one of Albert's most famous songs, "Jesus, Hold My Hand." I knew the song by heart and had sung it many times at the top of my voice around our farm, so I walked over into the middle of the singers and began to warble the melody with as much volume as I could muster. I thought I was doing pretty well.

Then I saw Betty, my secret girlfriend, snicker and break into a laugh. She laughed so hard that within a few seconds we had to stop singing. When her mother asked her why she was laughing, Betty pointed at me and proclaimed that I wasn't singing it right. She correctly noted that I wasn't supposed to sing the melody all the way through the chorus. That's because the melody, as Albert wrote the song, shifts from part to part.

I was humiliated, especially when my dad explained that I just sang by ear and didn't read music, so I didn't necessarily sing it the way it was written. I had imagined that I was showing Betty and the song's author just how pretty the song could be sung. It was bad enough that my undeclared girlfriend was not impressed; she also had embarrassed me in front of Albert Brumley himself, who sat not six feet from me. I thought of crawling behind the piano, but there wasn't enough room between it and the wall.

Well, I'll tell you one thing: my crush on Betty Thomas ended right then and there. I glanced at Albert. He looked back at me and gave me a little grin—just enough of a signal to let me know that he wasn't bothered at all by the way I sang his song. In fact, he looked as if he was amused by that little exchange. My pride was salvaged. His quiet grin did more for me than he ever knew. It endeared him and his music to me forever.

As I grew older, the Brumley place at Powell became important to me, not only because of the reputation of the man who lived there but also because a few dozen yards behind the house flowed Mike's Creek and one of the best swimming holes in miles.

The nearest swimming pools from our farm three miles west of Wheaton were the municipal pools at Cassville—fifteen miles to the southeast—and Monett, twenty miles to the northeast. Occasionally, in the summertime, enterprising parents would haul a pickup truckload of youngsters to one of those pools, but such a trip required a lot more organization than it took to get to any of the swimming holes along various creeks in our neck of the woods.

It was possible to swim only a few strokes in a little hole of water on Indian Creek less than a mile south of our farm. Attached to a tree on the bank was a chain with a stick through the lower links so we could swing out over the deep part of the hole and cannonball into it with an enormous splash. But the Indian Creek hole was too small to allow real swimming.

There was another pretty good swimming hole below the

overflow bridge on Mike's Creek in the hill country south of Rocky Comfort. It was hard to get to, though. We had to take a rough and winding dirt road for several miles after turning off of Highway 44.

A few yards below Aunt Bertha and Uncle Noman Slinkard's house on Little Sugar Creek near Jane, there was another good place to swim, but that was twenty miles from home.

There were problems with both the overflow bridge and Little Sugar holes, however. The overflow bridge frequently was crowded on hot Sunday afternoons, and there was a colony of leeches there that nearly always latched onto a swimmer's foot or leg, causing girls to scream and boys to flail around in the water while pulling the pesky critters off and throwing them as far up the creek as possible. You haven't lived until you feel something slick about the size of a penny attaching itself to your leg, and you know it's there to suck as much blood as it can.

The hole on Little Sugar Creek was large enough to do some real swimming, and, in fact, I learned to swim there when I was eight. The problem was that I only got to that hole once every four or five weeks in the summer when we drove into the hill country to visit Grandma Lewis and my aunts, uncles, and cousins.

The best swimming hole in the country, as far as I was concerned, was the one on Mike's Creek behind Albert and Goldie Brumley's house at Powell. The Brumley hole had several advantages. Mike's Creek behind the Brumleys' was clear, deep, and free of leeches. What's more, it was easier to find people willing to take me there on a hot Sunday afternoon. That was partly because Goldie Brumley was a sister of Carolyn Naramore. Carolyn and her husband, Price, ran the IGA store in Wheaton, about fifteen miles from Powell. Dan Shewmake and I also were acquainted with Price and Carolyn's son, Max.

If the Shewmakes weren't going to the Brumley swimming hole, sometimes the Naramores were. And sometimes the Shewmakes were going because several of Dan's Fox family relatives, including his great-aunt Laura Fox, lived a couple of miles up the creek in the community named after her family.

Albert seldom showed up at the creek; he preferred to spend Sunday afternoons in a triangle-shaped area in front of his house where often there was a baseball game under way that involved the Brumley boys. But Goldie was often at the creek with their only daughter, Betty Belle.

One particular Sunday afternoon stands out in my memory of the Brumley swimming hole. On the far side of that hole of water, across the creek and lodged up against the bluff, was a huge flat-topped limestone rock that protruded from the water at about a forty-five degree angle. It was the perfect destination for swimmers, who could glide to it from the deepest part of the hole, scramble up on it, walk to the high end, and dive in. To all the boys and girls who swam there, it was known as "Big Rock."

That afternoon, when I was thirteen or fourteen years old, I learned that even the Brumley hole had at least one flaw. We had been in the water awhile—Dan, Max, and me—having a grand old time while Price, Carolyn, and Goldie Brumley chatted on the creek bank.

I remember thinking how good it felt to go under the cool, clear water without worries about leeches or muddy water or other unpleasant surprises. I was out in the middle of the hole. Dan and Max were on the side closer to the bank. As I came up for air, I heard Price Naramore yelling. For a second, I couldn't make out what he was saying until I got the water out of my ears, but I saw Dan and Max scrambling to get to the bank and running out of the water. "What?" I hollered at Price, whose yelling by then was accompanied by arm-waving. Then I heard him clearly for the first time.

"Snake!" Price was yelling while pointing twenty or thirty feet upstream.

I didn't have to hear it twice, even though Price was repeating it. When there was a snake in the creek in that part of the country, it usually was a water moccasin, poisonous and ornery. I was too far out in the hole of water—and the snake was too close—to try to make shore, so I headed for Big Rock on the far side. I set a world record for the scrambling freestyle. I hit that rock and crawled on all fours to the high end.

From his position across the creek, Price pointed at the intruding reptile and kept up a running commentary on its whereabouts until it was well downstream. I waited a few minutes until we were sure the snake's brothers and sisters weren't following it and then swam back across the creek, ready to call it a day.

From then on, I never was as relaxed in that great old hole of water as I had been before, occasionally glancing upstream to see if a moccasin was approaching, but it never stopped any of us from swimming there. It just reminded us that even paradise had its serpent. That may have been Adam's first lesson in the Garden of Eden, but it took Dan, Max, and me thirteen or fourteen years to learn it.

By the time I was a young adult during the 1960s and '70s, Albert had written even more gospel songs. He had been elected to the Nashville Songwriters Foundation and Hall of Fame, and later, to the Gospel Music Hall of Fame.

Dozens of well-known singers and musical groups recorded his songs, including the Boston Pops Orchestra, Johnny Cash, the Highwaymen, the Ray Charles Singers, Charley Pride, Bill Monroe, the Bill Gaither Trio, Elvis Presley, and many others. The Supremes sang a Brumley song on the Ed Sullivan Show. I was surprised a few years ago to hear Bob Dylan sing "Rank Strangers to Me," a Brumley song, on one of his albums.

Even after his fame grew, Albert never changed. He continued to live in Powell, which consisted mostly of two stores and a church. For years, he had many of his gospel songbooks printed by *Wheaton Journal* editor Wally Fox. When I was visiting my parents near Wheaton in the early 1970s, just a few years before Albert died in 1977, I called Albert to ask his advice about how to credit the writer of a song I cited in a magazine article I had written. As usual, his deep voice sounded eminently reasonable—like a steady old farmer who had just come to the house after feeding the chickens.

To this day, it is hard for me to sing his gospel or sentimental songs without getting a tear in my eye, not only because of the emotions tapped by his songs but also because of the warm memories they bring of Albert and incidents in my childhood.

Not many people can say they sat around a piano with Albert Brumley and sang one of his songs as poorly as I did or that they nearly got snakebit in the creek behind his house.

29

The Best Seat at the Funeral

M y dad was an excellent singer, especially of gospel songs. He had learned to read shape notes at one of the many singing schools in southwest Missouri when he was a youngster.[399] By the time he was a young adult, he was an accomplished congregational song leader. That skill is probably the reason I exist, because he met my mother in 1931 when the Rocky Comfort Church of Christ paid him a small sum to travel the twenty miles or so from the hill country where he lived near Jane, Missouri, to lead the congregational singing for a revival meeting. They were married a year later.

By the time I came along in 1939, my dad had established himself as a quartet singer at "singing conventions," as they were called. Singing conventions usually were held in churches on Sunday afternoons. They were interdenominational and involved performances of two or three gospel songs by each of at least a dozen musical groups, usually accompanied by a pianist. When I was a small boy, my dad sang in a quartet with three Methodists—our friends and neighbors who were some of the best people I have ever known.

The quartet, with Dad singing tenor; Clovis Flaxbeard, bass; Nina Robinson, alto; and my great-uncle Earl Lamberson, the lead, was often asked to provide the music at services for the dearly departed. Singing at funerals became routine for Dad when I was growing up.

However, I do remember one funeral when I was seven or eight years old that was not routine. A prominent man of the Wheaton community had passed unexpectedly, and the funeral was to be held at the Methodist church, home turf for Nina, Clovis, and Earl. I have scoured my brain and asked dozens of people around Wheaton the name of the recently departed soul, but no one remembers who it was. Perhaps it's better that way.

The day dawned hot and sticky, like most summer days in Wheaton, and a huge crowd had gathered in the Methodist church auditorium. In the mid-1940s, air-conditioning in all churches in that part of the country was provided by women and girls wielding cardboard fans that displayed artists' renditions of Jesus or a lovely forest scene on one side and an ad for the local funeral home on the other. The men and boys usually were much too macho to fan themselves, but they didn't hesitate to lean toward the nearest female who was fanning so they would catch a cooling zephyr.

At the front of the auditorium on either side of the casket was a wall of flower sprays sent by the many friends and relatives of the deceased. In those days, unless the departed one had suffered a horrible mutilation, the casket usually was open so that those sitting in the front of the auditorium could easily see the subject of the solemn services sleeping peacefully in eternal repose with hands folded over his or her tummy.

Edith and Boone McQueen, who operated one of the two funeral homes in Wheaton, had left a gap in the flower arrangements so those in attendance could see the quartet sitting at right angles to the audience in the choir seats in the front of the auditorium.

As was the custom on special occasions at the Methodist church, the quartet's singing of such solemn songs as "Abide with Me" and "An Empty Mansion" was to be supplemented with a violin solo by Dave Stump, Wheaton High School's music teacher.

Mr. Stump was an artistic man with, to be charitable, a high forehead and long, white, studiously unkempt hair that grew from the sides and back of his head. Dad always said Mr. Stump's hair resembled the style worn by Albert Einstein.

Since I can't remember whose funeral it was, the account that follows uses a fictitious name.

The service began with the preacher striding to the pulpit and with great solemnity, reading the formal obituary that always started with the name, the date of birth, and the date of death of the dearly departed. "Harley Grover Brown," read the preacher, "was born on November 13th, 1874, and departed this life on ..." At that moment, the quartet in unison saw something that the sporadically sobbing audience could not see. Directly in front of them as they stared across the rostrum, beyond the preacher, and through the open door of a classroom that adjoined the front side of the auditorium, Mr. Stump strolled in holding his violin.

"Mr. Brown," the preacher intoned, "was survived by ..." and the quartet saw Mr. Stump, cradling his violin, sit down in an old cane-bottomed chair in the classroom to await his performance.

"Mr. Brown as a faithful member of the Wheaton Methodist Church," the preacher was saying, just as the bottom went out of Mr. Stump's chair. Still cradling his violin with both hands, both feet shot straight into the air as he sank toward the floor.

All four members of the quartet, being the only witnesses due to the wall of flowers and the angle of their view, snickered. Then, realizing they could be seen by most of the funeral-goers, including the sorrowful family, they caught themselves and put on straight faces. They maintained control for a few seconds until the old music teacher started rocking back and forth to try to free himself from his unfortunate position, and his long hair flopped down over his forehead.

That's when Nina lost it. "Hee, hee, hee," she cackled. Whereupon the entire quartet dissolved into that awful kind of body-shaking laughter that is impossible to contain because it's terribly inappropriate.

Then, with the preacher, the surviving relatives, and most of the mourners staring in shocked disbelief, Earl rose from the quartet's choir seat, strode across the rostrum behind the preacher, walked into the side classroom, and freed the elderly violinist.

Dad said the preacher gamely gathered his poise and proceeded. Mr. Stump performed his solo, and the quartet managed to sing with straight faces. But until the end of the service, no member of the quartet dared look at any of the others because of the imminent danger of explosive laughter.

In telling the story, Dad always said that as far as he could tell, the departed one managed to slide on into heaven, but Saint Peter was laughing when he got there.

30

Joe's Cuban Missile Crisis

The year was 1962, and in October of that year, Second Lieutenant Gary Joe Higgs, US Air Force, was twenty-four years old and on leave in Wheaton visiting his father, Chester O. "Buck" Higgs, and other relatives and friends.

Joe's duty station was Suffolk County Air Force Base on the eastern tip of Long Island, New York. "Our purpose out there was the air defense of New York City," Joe said. "We were under the control of the New York Air Defense Sector, which was a radar facility controlling … the coast around New York City.

"I had been in Wheaton two days when I got a phone call to return immediately to (the base) by the most rapid means possible. I had driven home, so I caught an airplane and went back to Suffolk County. The Cuban thing was starting to rear its head."

The "Cuban thing" Joe mentioned was the Cuban Missile Crisis—one of the most dangerous episodes of the Cold War. On October 14, 1962, a US U-2 reconnaissance aircraft took photographs showing that construction of ballistic missile sites was under way in Cuba. For the next fourteen days, as President John F. Kennedy ordered the US Navy to establish a "quarantine" to stop Soviet ships from delivering "offensive weapons" to Cuba, the Soviet missile sites in Cuba neared operational readiness.[400]

On October 27, a U-2 reconnaissance plane was shot down over Cuba. As the United States prepared to attack Cuba, which risked Soviet retaliation and nuclear war, Kennedy reached a secret diplomatic solution with Soviet premier Nikita Khrushchev. The gist of the agreement was that the United States agreed to remove its ballistic missiles aimed at the Soviet Union from Turkey, and the Soviets agreed to dismantle its missile sites in Cuba, which were aimed at the United States. [401]

The US and Soviet armed forces were on a hair trigger, and the fingers on that trigger in both countries were getting itchy when Joe reported back to Suffolk.

"We were assigned to a new airplane, which was called the 101B ... the Voodoo," Joe said.

The McDonnell F-101B Voodoo's late-production models, which Joe's unit was flying, were outfitted to carry two 1.7-kiloton MB-1/AIR-2 Genie nuclear rockets on one side of its weapons pallet in addition to two infrared-guided missiles with conventional explosives. At thirty-five thousand feet, the Voodoo had a maximum speed of Mach 1.72—1,134 miles per hour. [402]

"The 101 was probably the fastest airplane of its time—a two-seater, kind of a big airplane for a fighter," Joe said. "It was two giant engines wrapped around a pilot [and a radar operator]. We were fighter-interceptors, and this was kind of a new concept because we were night fighters. And that meant we could go into the weather, at night, anywhere. The problem with the 101 was that it took two states to turn it around."

Joe said there were six hangars with double doors that sat just off the runway at Suffolk. Two airplanes were kept on five-minute alert, meaning they could be airborne in five minutes or less "from the time the whistle blew."

One night in late October—Joe didn't remember the exact date—the weather was socked in because of fog and haze. "The clouds went to forty thousand feet, and the ducks walked," Joe said. About midnight—when Joe was part of two F-101 air crews that were on five-minute alert—the claxon went off, signaling that it was a mandatory scramble.

"We ran (and slid) down poles, jumped in our airplanes, and cranked both engines at the same time," Joe said. "The (hangar) doors are opening, and three minutes later we're taxiing out." It was so foggy, Joe recalled, that they couldn't see the runway, so they were forced to follow a yellow line to the end of the runway to position their aircraft for takeoff.

To give the aircraft a faster climbing rate, the plane's afterburners were lit just before takeoff. "You light those two burners—they never lit together—they're big, and the airplane would yaw back and forth on the runway," Joe said. It increased the danger of running off the runway in the fog, but both planes got off the ground safely.

"We got airborne, and they (the New York Air Defense Sector) said, 'We have an unknown.' And that was not uncommon, but we knew it was kind of serious, because we had scrambled on 'mandatory scramble' status," Joe recalled. "So we knew there was something out there that somebody was concerned about.

"I was flying number two (wingman) with a guy I really liked. He was kind of a cowboy and was really a great pilot … and he was squad leader. We're at supersonic air speeds at night in the weather, and we have fairly long (range) radar."

The unidentified aircraft—the "bogey"—was about three hundred miles out over the Atlantic Ocean and flying straight for New York City, Joe said.

He noted that it was fairly routine for the Air Defense Sector to give their fighter pilots some idea of what the bogey might be—an off-course civilian airliner or an overdue aircraft of some kind. But this bogey was different, Joe remembered. It was "messing with our radars," he said, by sending out electronic radiation—interfering with the radar signals attempting to lock onto it, commonly called jamming. When jamming was detected on air force or navy radars, it was called music, and music was what Joe, his flight leader, and the New York Air Defense Sector radar were picking up from this unknown aircraft.

That's when the two young aviators knew the situation wasn't just serious; it was *very* serious. They got word from the NY Air Defense to arm their Genie nuclear-tipped missiles with their 1.7-kiloton warheads. The reason for carrying such potent weaponry, Joe explained, was that military intelligence believed that the Soviets had as many as six thousand long-range heavy bombers. If Soviet leaders ever decided to attack the United States in an all-out nuclear war, our military planners reasoned that they would launch all six thousand at once, Joe explained. To counter that, it was decided to put nuclear warheads on some of our air-to-air missiles. The idea was to fire a Genie into the middle of a swarm of Russian bombers, detonate it, and vaporize a bunch of enemy bombers with one explosion.

Conventional air-to-air Falcon missiles that normally would be used to shoot down a single airplane were useless in fog as heavy as it was that night, Joe explained. Falcon missiles honed in on the heat of the target aircraft's engines in order to find their mark. But on this night, the fog would have diffused the heat, and Falcon missiles would have been unable to find their target. The only effective weapon the interceptors had was the Genie, with its large nuclear blast area.

Joe's plane, as the number-two intercepting aircraft, would be the shooter. In his pocket, he said, was an envelope with a set of codes in it. New York Air Defense ordered him to arm one of the Genies. Joe entered his code, and the green light lit up, meaning that his nuke Genie missile was armed.

Then, as Joe's 101 pulled into shooting position behind the bogey, the job of the lead 101 was to get close enough to identify it and determine if the unknown aircraft was friendly or hostile.

"So we turned in behind him (the bogey), and the pilot of the other Voodoo started driving up toward his tail and slowly tries to get into position, in the murk, about three to five hundred feet behind him. And he has a huge light to find the target," Joe said.

But the clouds were too thick, and the flight leader radioed, "No joy, no joy," meaning he still couldn't see well enough to identify the bogey.

Joe said that at any second, he expected New York Air Defense to order them to break off the attempt to identify the aircraft and shoot it down with the nuclear missile. The problem with carrying out that order, both he and his flight leader knew, was that nuclear explosions are detectable from far away. If there were any Soviet submarines within detection distance of the nuclear blast, they would assume the United States and the Soviets were at war, and they would begin to launch nukes at the United States in retaliation.

"I found myself sitting there (in the shooting position) thinking that a young second lieutenant—a young farm boy from Wheaton, Missouri—is going to launch the first weapon in World War III," Joe said.

Joe knew his flight leader was "pushing it"—that he was determined to close on the bogey until he was close enough to see him. If the aircraft was hostile, Joe had a strong feeling that his flight leader might try to ram the bogey rather than fall back and allow Joe to fire the nuke. Finally, Joe heard, "I got him, I got him, I got him," from his flight leader.

At first, only the tail was visible, but the flight leader pulled to within just a few feet of the bogey and identified it as a KC-135 Stratotanker—a Strategic Air Command (SAC) aircraft used to refuel other aircraft in flight. It had been traveling over the North Pole using a grid navigation system, and it was 650 miles off course, Joe said.

"They thought they were somewhere way up north," Joe said. "All of those tankers have jammers aboard. So the pilot was just sitting there reading a magazine or something ... just playing with us," Joe explained. "As it turned out, he also was not on the correct radio channel."

Once communication was established, the KC-135 was ordered to land somewhere in New York State, and Joe said he heard later that every member of its crew was court-martialed.[403]

Joe went on to fly 158 combat missions over North Vietnam. In 1970, he was assigned to the Office of Air Force Plant Representative at the McDonnell Douglas Corporation in St. Louis. He flew new F-15 Eagles after they rolled off the McDonnell Douglas production line and made sure they were ready for the air force to accept. He logged more than 4,300 hours in various fighter aircraft before he retired and came home to Wheaton. He and his wife, Jackie, bought the Wheaton Tractor Company, operating it for several years before he retired to a farm east of Wheaton to enjoy his remaining years with Jackie, near his parents and his sister, Betty.[404]

In 2007, Joe passed away at age sixty-eight after a short and unexpected illness. He had been my good friend since our junior-high-school days. We were both on the Wheaton High basketball team, and we sang in an award-winning high-school boys' quartet.

It is important to add that both Wheaton and Rocky Comfort produced crack military pilots—Ralph Fehring, a highly acclaimed test pilot for the US Army Air Corps during World War II; Ernest Biggs, who flew more than one hundred missions as an F-51 fighter pilot during the Korean War; and, of course, Joe. Many other young men, and later, women, from that vicinity have either piloted or been part of flight crews and have served in heroic ways since the United States first started using aircraft in its military operations.

But there's only one person from Wheaton or any other small Ozark town who had his finger on the button that could have detonated a nuclear explosion that, very likely, would have started World War III—a war that would have ended civilization as we know it.

Joe, we're glad you didn't have to punch that button.

31

My Last Summer in Wheaton

Oval Clymer was driving the Wheaton Lumber & Supply truck back to Wheaton after we had loaded it with bundles of hardwood tongue-in-groove flooring from the plant at Cassville. It was the summer of 1964.

I was just riding along, daydreaming, as Oval drove north on Highway 37 toward the turnoff onto Highway W toward Wheaton.

Out of nowhere, Oval said, "Do you know what's bad about war?"

I wondered why in the world Oval would just blurt out a question like that.

"No, Oval, what's bad about war?" I replied.

"Snipers," Oval said, with great certainty.

I allowed that he was right. Snipers had picked off many a good man, I said. I remembered the story Woodrow Ford had told me about a Japanese sniper killing the guy with him in the shell hole on Peleliu. Still, snipers had barely crossed my mind since Dan Shewmake and I had fought the Germans, Japanese, North Koreans, and Chinese across our farms with our BB guns when we were eleven or twelve years old. I had finished a four-year hitch in the navy in the fall of '63, and sailors were more likely to be worried about whether there were any girls on the beach than the threat of sniper fire.

I told Oval that no sailor in my navy boot camp company would have been much of a threat as a sniper, either. When my company boarded the bus back to our San Diego barracks after a week of target practice with M1 rifles, the old chief boatswain's mate who was our boot camp company commander said, "Well, you SOBs, if you ever have to use a rifle, the ship's sunk, anyway, so it won't make any difference whether you can hit anything or not."

I passed that piece of sailor's wisdom along to Oval, but he wasn't having any of it. He made the turn onto Highway W and expounded all the way back to Wheaton on the dangers of snipers in a war. All I could say was "Uh-huh" and "yup." I never did figure out what brought on his sniper soliloquy, because the one-way conversation was terminated while we unloaded the flooring back at the lumberyard. He was thirty-five when World War II started, and he was a farmer, so he didn't have to serve in the military. But to this day, when I hear the word *snipers*, I think of my conversation with Oval.

Being back in Wheaton that summer was a time warp for me. The town was still much the same as it had been in 1957 when I graduated from Wheaton High, but I was seeing it through different eyes. Three years of college and four years in the navy that had taken me to California, Japan, Hong Kong, the Philippines, Washington, DC, and Columbia, Missouri, had changed how I saw lots of things. It had been seven years since I had lived with my parents on the farm three miles west of town.

I needed work to help finance my senior year at the University of Missouri, but I couldn't find a steady job near the campus that summer, so I took the job at the lumberyard and enjoyed free housing with my parents back in Wheaton. Luckily, two men I had known most of my life—Leonard Brattin and Price Naramore—needed someone with a strong back and more energy than brains to help Oval at Wheaton Lumber & Supply on Highway 86 just south of town. I was paid the princely sum of $1.25 an hour, ten bucks for an eight-hour day. But looking back on that summer, half a lifetime later, the memories it generated were richer than a piece of your mother's

German chocolate cake topped with a scoop of hand-cranked freezer ice cream.

Like so many folks who lived in Wheaton, lumberyard co-owner Leonard Brattin had an amazing array of skills—farmer, meat cutter, grocery store and lumberyard proprietor, well driller, and plumber. He was born in 1906 and was a couple of years older than my mother and father.

From about the time I was in the first grade, Leonard had a standard greeting for me. I'd go with my dad into Frazier-Daniels & Brattin's grocery store and Leonard, often wearing a white merchant's apron, would walk up and say, "How are you, Jimmy?"

"Fine, Leonard," I'd reply.

"You know what it means when you say you're fine," was his next line. Sticking out his hand, he would tick off on his fingers what *fine* meant. "It means you're fine physically, mentally, morally, and spiritually. You've got to think about each one of those when you say you're fine."

"Okay, Leonard, I will," I'd promise, closing the conversation and trying to figure out if I actually was fine in all those areas. In my mind, I always fell somewhere short of Leonard's definition of fine, but at least he caused me to think about such things.

I remember that on my first day on the job in the summer of '64, Leonard took me to the wide door that opened into the yard of Wheaton Lumber & Supply. The door facing had a smooth, varnished natural wood finish.

"Now, Jimmy, when you're finished with work every day, you just come over here to the door facing and … start up high … you write down the date on the facing here and how many hours you worked that day. That way, we'll have an accurate record," Leonard said.

I did as I was told, and at the end of the summer, I had scrawled three months' of work hours on that door facing—from as high as I could reach all the way down to my knees. I was paid in cash. Mom, bless her heart, usually packed me a sandwich for lunch, minimizing my food costs. Except for soda pop, an occasional ice cream cone from the Dairy Haven, and a few bucks for gas, I spent very little money.

That summer, I came to appreciate another of Leonard's skills—he was a good storyteller. One day at the lumberyard, Leonard shared a yarn with me about Tom Suttles, a country-smart old farmer who lived about three farms west of my parents on the Wheaton-Stella road. Not long ago, Leonard said, Tom decided it was time to stop using an outhouse. He did some remodeling and fashioned a bathroom in his aging farmhouse. After he had dug a septic tank, he came to Wheaton Lumber & Supply to buy a toilet and plumbing supplies.

Leonard got the measurements and sold Tom everything he needed to install his new convenience.

"I showed him how to hook it up," Leonard said. "He said he understood and went on his way."

A couple of weeks later, Tom came into the store, and Leonard asked him how he was getting along with his new toilet.

"Well, pretty good," Tom said. "It works fine. Main problem is that I have a hard time getting on and off of it."

"What do you mean?" Leonard asked.

"It's just hard to get on and off of it," Mr. Suttles said. "Why don't you come out and take a look at it?"

Leonard got into the old pickup that Wheaton Lumber & Supply used for light jobs and drove out to the Suttles' farm. Leonard said that he nearly collapsed laughing when he went into the new bathroom. The problem was easy to diagnose.

"Tom had installed the toilet just fine," Leonard said. "Problem was that he'd installed it backward, with the seat facing the wall. He had to step over it with one leg and sort of straddle it because it was so close to the wall."

Since Tom was a heavyset man who usually wore bib overalls and was not too limber after reaching his seventies, his positioning of the toilet made sitting on the "can" very awkward.

Leonard helped Tom disconnect the toilet, turn it around, and replumb it. He eliminated Tom's plumbing problem and solved Tom's elimination problem in one visit.

Leonard and Price had worked together before they opened Wheaton Lumber & Supply in 1959. Price and his wife, Carolyn, had operated two businesses in Wheaton—a new and used furniture store and then the IGA grocery. While they operated the IGA store, Leonard was, for a time, their meat cutter. Price had been in the grocery business most of his life, helping his father, Lawrence, run country stores in several McDonald County communities southwest of Wheaton.

Price had a sense of humor, but he was a guy who could zero in on a project and temporarily lose sight of the funny side of it.

One afternoon, Price had taken the lumberyard's old Ford pickup a quarter of a mile up the highway to Hayden's garage for repair. Price called Leonard and, in Ozark vernacular, said, "Would you have Oval run up here and pick me up? They're gonna have to keep the old truck awhile."

Leonard told Oval, "Now you drive up there and stop a couple of houses from the garage. You get out and trot into the garage afoot. When Price asks you why you're afoot instead of driving, you huff and puff a little and say, 'Well, you told me to run up here, didn't you?'" Oval did as he was told. Price didn't think it was quite as funny as Leonard and the guys at the garage.

However, Price wasn't devoid of humor. Later that summer, with a twinkle in his good eye, he gave me a slightly X-rated lesson in pipe threading. Price and I were in the supply yard behind the store, near the pipe bins. Someone had bought a batch of two-inch steel pipe for a big project. Oval was making a delivery, so Price and I dragged out a couple of dozen twenty-one-foot lengths of steel pipe and laid them on the ground. They needed to be cut into various lengths and threaded. We set up a couple of metal horses and locked in the first pipe. I fetched an oil can, pipe cutter, and threader.

Price watched as I measured and cut the pipe to the lengths the customer ordered. Then it was time to cut threads into each end. I had helped my dad do that on the farm years before, but Price wanted to demonstrate. He clamped the threader on one end of the pipe, squirted oil into the threader's ratchet, and began to work the handle.

"Now you need to remember that this is the male end of the pipe, Jimmy," he said. "And you know you've got to keep the male end lubricated so the threads will be true and screw into the female fitting," Price said with a sly smile and a wink of his sighted eye.

Obviously pleased with himself, Price handed the tools to me.

"Yeah, I know, Price," I said. "I'll keep lots of oil on it and make sure the pipe will screw straight."

Working alongside Oval Clymer that summer, I was reminded that Oval and his wife, Ora—everyone called her Orie—were a legend of sorts in the community. Though they now lived in Wheaton, in 1939 Oval and Ora were living on a farm about five miles west of Wheaton in the rural community of Waddil.

It was on September 7, 1939, that the *Wheaton Journal* crowned Oval the snake-killing champion of southwest Missouri. We're not talking about killing wimpy nonpoisonous garter snakes or nonvenomous blacksnakes or bullsnakes; we're talking copperheads. A copperhead is one of the most feared snakes in that part of the country. It is extremely venomous and likes to hide in woodpiles and heavy brush and old stumps. Unlike a rattlesnake, a copperhead provides no warning before it strikes. Under an awkward headline, Oval and Ora's achievement was recounted:

Is Champion Snake Killer

Oval Clymer, farmer, living east of Stella, is the champion copperhead snake killer of this territory, and probably the champion of the world, and if anyone can beat the following, The Journal would like to hear from them:

Tuesday afternoon of last week Clymer was splitting wood at the side of his hen house and near where he was splitting wood stood an old tree stump with the center hollow. He decided he could split a few sticks of wood from the old stump and struck it a hard blow with his axe, breaking into the hollow of the stump. He reached down to pick up the piece he had split off and suddenly a copperhead struck at his hand. He took a stick and raked the snake out of the stump and cut its head off with his axe.

After killing the first snake he got a glimpse of two more and killed them. This was all the snakes he saw but something told him there were more in the stump and he started scratching into the rotten wood and debris in the stump and suddenly uncovered a wriggling, squirming mass of copperheads. He called to his wife to bring the hoe and for the next few moments the Clymers and copperheads fought a terrific battle. The snakes lost and when the casualties were counted it was found that 54 copperheads averaging 2 feet long had bit the dust.

This is no snake yarn as Clymer gathered up the 54 snakes and took them to town for proof. Apparently they had congregated in the stump to hibernate for the winter.

About three weeks ago Mr. Clymer killed a copperhead by the side of the cook stove in the Clymer home.

I've always thought the headline should have read CHAMPION SNAKE KILLERS, because Ora was in the fight too. If Oval deserved a serpent-killing award, so did Ora.

Twenty-five years later, when Oval and I were working at the lumberyard, I doubt that Oval had slowed down more than maybe half a step since that September day in 1939. He was still tougher than the sole of a high-top leather work shoe—the kind with leather laces and metal grommets. Matter of fact, those were the kind of shoes he wore. The rest of his standard uniform was blue bib overalls, a long-sleeved work shirt, and a blue-and-white striped engineer's cap.

In 1964, Oval was a couple of months shy of his sixtieth birthday, and the only effect of aging that he admitted to was that he couldn't crawl very well anymore. The result was that when Wheaton Lumber & Supply got shipments of lumber on the train at Exeter, I was the one who had to slither on my belly to the back of a boxcar that was stacked with lumber to about two feet short of its roof.

Crawling into the back of a superheated boxcar on a scorching summer day was a test of the body's cooling system. Inching my way on my belly to the back of the car, I'd slide the lumber out of the car to Oval—two or three boards at a time at first—and he would stack them in Wheaton Lumber & Supply's truck. Outside, on the truck, it was a cool ninety to ninety-five degrees. Who knows how hot it was in the boxcar.

That summer, Oval and I stacked, loaded, and unloaded lumber, dry wall, and just about every other kind of building material on the market in those days. Sand, ceiling tile, flooring, paint … you name it, we moved it.

In August, a guy from McDonald County came to Wheaton Lumber & Supply and bought materials to build a house on top of a tree-covered mountain off State Highway 90, east of the tiny town of Jane.

To make the delivery, Oval and I put one of the heaviest loads of the summer on the big truck. We loaded sand, cement, and concrete blocks into the front nearest the cab. We loaded the lumber last—twelve-foot two-by-twelves and two-by-sixes, and eight-foot two-by-fours—on top of most of the other stuff and in the rear of the truck bed, up against the tailgate. It took a long time to load the truck, so it was midafternoon and hotter than Hades when we left Wheaton.

The truck was so heavily loaded that we couldn't go more than forty miles an hour, but we made steady progress south through

Powell, past gospel songwriter Albert Brumley's place on Mike's Creek, south to Sims store, and west on Highway 90 toward Jane.

Jane is approximately twenty miles southwest of Wheaton, as the crow flies, and deep in the rugged hill country. Grandma Lewis lived in Jane, and I had been in that area many times, but neither Oval nor I had ever been to the site where this guy was building his house. It was soon to become apparent that not very many other people had ever been there, either.

A few miles before we got to Jane, Oval and I finally came to the turnoff, which was a barbed wire gate to a cow pasture. I got out and unfastened the gate that opened to a dusty trail across a flat field where beef cattle were grazing. On the far side of the field was a timber-covered mountain. The top of the mountain was our destination. We drove to the mountain and began a steep climb up a dusty, recently bulldozed trail through the trees and brush.

As we started to climb, Oval kept downshifting to coax the old truck up the grade. The trail soon narrowed so that it was just wide enough to accommodate the truck. A six-inch layer of powdery dust covered the trail that was soft in some places, and then rocky, and then dusty again a few feet farther up.

As the bulldozed trail got steeper, we finally hit a patch where the truck tires were just spinning in the dust—even when Oval put the truck into compound, the lowest gear. Occasionally, as our load shifted toward the back of the truck, the front wheels started coming off the ground.

"Why don't you get out and sit on the hood … give us more weight up front?" Oval said.

I wasn't about to do that.

"Oval, I just weigh 175 pounds, and that's not close to enough weight to do us any good," I retorted. "Besides, what if the truck lurches, and I fall off and you run over me?" I added for good measure.

By this time, it was 5:30 p.m. or later. In our haste to make the delivery, Oval and I had left our water jug back at the lumberyard in Wheaton. We were both getting very thirsty.

Oval finally resorted to backing sideways a few feet to find purchase for the drive wheels. We made a little headway, tacking back and forth like a sailboat going upwind. I thought for a few minutes that we might make it to the top.

Then we heard a crack and a bang, and then a series of bangs, and the truck shuddered a little. We opened the doors and looked. The wooden tailgate of the truck had torn open, and the two-by-fours on top of the load had shot out the back, one on top of the other, creating a slide of boards down the mountain. The twelve-foot two-by-sixes had shot out next, sliding farther down the mountain on top of the two-by-fours. They were followed by all but a few of the twelve-foot two-by-twelves, which now lay cascaded behind us far down the dusty trail. The sand, cement, and concrete blocks were still on the truck.

Oval was a churchgoing man, but between what he and the ex-sailor said in the next few minutes, the air turned at least a pale blue. Oval turned off the motor and found some wire. We went back to the shattered wooden tailgate and wired it to the truck racks the best we could.

Oval stood with his hands on his hips and looked at the boards that extended halfway down the mountain.

"Well," he said, "the truck will be lighter now."

Indeed it was. It was still a struggle for the truck, but we finally made it to the top of the mountain where the builder was living in a little trailer in the clearing where he planned to build his new house.

We unloaded the few two-by-twelves that had stayed on the truck, along with the concrete blocks, the bags of cement, and the sand we had shoveled into heavy bags. We were thirsty before, and now we were desperately thirsty. We had hoped the owner would be home and would have a cold drink of water for us, but the only living creatures in sight were three nanny goats scrambling around the rocks and tree stumps in the clearing. A couple of them had pretty full udders and looked like they needed to be milked.

Oval and I thought we might find something to drink inside the little trailer, and we kept working with the door until we got it open. It could be that we used a screwdriver to help with that task, but I wouldn't cop to that unless I was placed under oath. Once inside, we opened the door of the trailer's little refrigerator and yup, we did find something to drink—goat's milk. We gulped down a few swallows, holding our noses to keep from throwing up.

By then, it was approaching eight o'clock, and the shadows were growing long in the clearing.

We got in the truck with its broken tailgate and headed back down the mountain. Descending in the empty truck was a cakewalk until we got to the place where the lumber had cascaded down the narrow trail. Occasionally, Oval had to stop the truck while I got out and moved a few boards over to the side. We just drove over a few boards, and sometimes there was so much lumber on the trail that we had to drive through the brush.

I looked at Oval. There wasn't a dry thread on the parts of his shirt that I could see outside of his bib overalls. My shirt was equally soaked with sweat. We headed back up Highway 90, looking forward to getting a drink of just about anything wet except goat's milk. I can't remember why we didn't stop at Sims store south of Powell, but Oval just kept driving. We passed through Powell where we knew the general store was already closed and crossed the bridge over Big Sugar Creek, and about a mile later, we saw that the lights were on inside a little store at a wide place in the road known as Beantown.

"Pull it over, Oval," I said. "I've gotta have something to drink."

We got out, staggered into the ramshackle little store, and headed straight for the pop cooler. I pulled out a bottle of Grapette because it didn't have as much carbonation as most cola drinks, and I chugged it down fast. I don't remember what Oval got, but he put some liquid down down his hatch in a hurry too.

I was still thirsty.

"We'd better take another one for the road," I said.

"Yeah, I think so," Oval agreed.

We paid for the drinks and staggered back to the truck, each of us clutching a bottle of pop.

We didn't say much on the way back to Wheaton. When we drove into the lumberyard about an hour later, Oval parked the truck. As we were walking to our cars to go home, it was fully dark. Leonard and Price had long since closed up and gone home.

"You'd better plan on being in before eight in the morning," Oval said. "We're gonna have to go back down there and clean that up."

I went home, drank a lot of water, and strangely, didn't have much to eat. My appetite had vanished sometime after I had chugged down the goat's milk. I took a shower, fell into bed, and got what seemed to be the shortest night's sleep I could remember. The next morning, I hauled myself out of bed and drove to the lumberyard about 7:30 a.m., prepared to go back to the mountain. As I got out of the car, I was overjoyed to see Oval and Leonard driving out of the lumberyard.

It took them most of the day to clean up the mess on the mountain. By the time they finished, they had taken three trips up to the trailer with partial loads of the lumber that had slid out of the truck. Meanwhile, the heaviest item I lifted that day was a sack of nails for a customer as Price and I held down the fort in the building supply store.

I was still thirsty all day, though—for water. And to this day, I can't stand goat's milk.

That summer, Wheaton was only five years into an event that continues to this day—the annual chicken barbeque. The event, which honors the many broiler growers of the area, had grown so popular in 1964 that Wheaton's merchants no longer could afford to provide a meal of half an Ozark-produced broiler, french fries, coffee, bread, and milk free of charge. For the first time, there would be a charge of fifty cents for each plate.

As the Wheaton Community Club was meeting one evening in June to refine its plans for the barbeque, the lights went out in a three-county area, putting a small snag in the planning session. A five-and-a-half-foot bullsnake had crawled into an electric power substation between Wheaton and Rocky Comfort. In the process of frying itself, the snake had shorted out parts of Barry, McDonald, and Newton counties for about an hour, which resulted in the loss of several hundred broilers being raised for market by local growers as the chickens smothered in the summer heat.

Broiler growing could be dicey. Market prices, disease, and many other factors could get in the way of a profit. A power outage caused by a trespassing bullsnake was not likely factored into the hazards of raising broilers.

Despite the interruption, plans for the barbeque proceeded. Tickets were printed, and an appeal was made to the public to buy tickets in advance so the planning committee would have an idea of how many chickens they would need to feed the crowd. Committees were assigned to handle preparation of the grounds, utensils, advertising, entertainment, cooking fuel, parking, sauce mixing, barbecuing, potato peeling, serving, finance, soda-pop concessions, pop coolers, coffee brewing, charcoal supplies, and even delivery to the town's shut-ins.

A list of the volunteers for all those duties appeared in the *Wheaton Journal* of June 4, 1964.[405] Nearly every business in Wheaton was represented.

When I came to work at Wheaton Lumber & Supply on the morning of the barbeque, Price and Leonard volunteered me for duty at the locker plant on Main Street. Since the end of World War II, Wheaton Frozen Food's various proprietors cut and packaged home-butchered meat—usually beef or pork. Customers could rent a box in the plant's big freezer room to store meat, fruits, and vegetables.

I went to the locker plant and reported to the meat-cutting room. Price went with me and showed me a little electric saw with a thin, vertical blade, a big tub of whole, frozen chickens, two smaller empty tubs, a pair of rubber gloves, and a chair.

"Sit down right here, Jimmy," Price said. "Turn on your saw. Just pick 'em up one at a time and saw 'em in two, right down the middle, then let 'em fall into these two tubs."

That day, I didn't saw lumber. I sawed frozen chickens.

I started sawing chickens in half at about 9:00 a.m., because the barbequing crew needed to get a head start on broiling the chickens over a hot charcoal fire, long before serving started at 4:30 that afternoon. I sawed until sometime in the early afternoon, took ten minutes to stuff some food into my mouth, then sawed some more until nearly 4:00.

I don't remember anybody else helping to saw chickens, and I wasn't keeping count of how many I cut in half, but next Thursday's *Wheaton Journal* reported that nearly three thousand meals were served. If each meal included a half-chicken, I must've sawed nearly 1,500 chickens in two that day. It wasn't half as hard as sawing lumber. And besides, eventually, you could eat a barbequed helping of what you had split, which I did about five o'clock that afternoon.

The *Journal* also reported that a few critics complained that the french fries weren't very crisp because they were served too many hours after they'd been fried. I didn't care. After a day of sawing chickens, they could have been cold and soggy and still tasted good to me. I even thought about dropping out of college and asking Leonard to teach me the fine art of meat cutting, but I dropped that idea, because I didn't want a young woman I'd met at MU to get away, so I needed to get back to campus that fall.

One of my last jobs at the lumberyard that summer was loading up the Wheaton Lumber & Supply's old 1940 Ford pickup and delivering a load of concrete blocks and cement to a fellow from Louisiana who was building a house in one of the hollows below Ridgley—Layton Hollow, I think. I didn't have to climb any dusty, newly bulldozed trails to make that delivery, but just as I got to the bottom of a hill, the left rear tire went flat.

I got the jack in place, found the lug wrench behind the seat, and started trying to loosen the lug nuts. By the end of the summer, I thought I was pretty strong, but I couldn't budge a single nut, even by pounding the lug wrench with an old pipe wrench I found under the seat. I didn't understand it. I was trying to turn the nuts counterclockwise to loosen them, which was what I thought was standard procedure.

But it wasn't working. So I started pounding the handle of the lug wrench clockwise. Lo and behold, the stubborn lug nut started to move. That's when I learned that lug nuts, like the nuts you meet in life, don't all act the same way.

Finally, after I changed the tire and got to the place where the Louisiana fellow was building his new house and unloaded the sacks of cement where he wanted them, I began to unload and stack the concrete blocks. "Louisiana" was kind of a friendly guy, and when I'd stacked the last block, he asked me what I was planning to do with my life. I told him I was getting ready to go back to the University of Missouri and finish journalism school.

"Well, with a job like you've got this summer, you oughta be in good shape up there if any of them ol' boys want to fight," Louisiana said.

I said I reckoned so.

On the way back to Wheaton, I thought about what he'd said and hoped I wouldn't have to fight any of "them ol' boys" in order to win Jan McNeely—a girl from the neighboring town of Crane—who I had met at MU that spring. I was fortunate. I didn't have to fight anyone to win her heart. In the spring of 1965, I asked her to marry me, and she accepted. It was the smartest thing I've ever done. Jan and I were married in August of that year. She's a lovely lady, and we're still in love fifty years later.

The $500 I earned at Wheaton Lumber & Supply in the summer of 1964 went a lot further than it would today. The money was important at the time, but the experiences I had and the stories I heard from Leonard and Oval and Price during my last summer in Wheaton made me a rich man for life.

Acknowledgments

Foremost, I want to acknowledge the invaluable assistance of Ralph and Betty Higgs Lamberson, whose *Wheaton Echoes* book laid the cornerstone for this project. Not only was I able to borrow writings of Wheaton and Rocky Comfort residents from *Wheaton Echoes*, Ralph and Betty also graciously provided me a rich supply of photos from the *Wheaton Echoes* collection.

I also owe a great debt to the Wheaton Historical Society and a host of current and former residents of Wheaton whose memories, photos, and records of events in and around Wheaton lent background and rich texture to these stories. Included in this group in no particular order are Byron and Kathryn Calame, James and Linda Cantrell, Jon and Marie Paden, Jo Ann Fox Hughes, Rebecca Allman Roskob, Herman Allman, Jaclyn Higgs, James and Lorene Royer, James and Sue Price, Jill Paden, Doug and Bernadine Cantrell Hobson, Bob and Kay Stewart Lombard, Edna and Bill Haynes, Gary and Maxine Bates, Jeanie Bates Eubanks, Ludon and Helen Brattin, Barbara Brattin Haynes, Bob Davidson, Floyd Hughes, Sally Minnehan Kenney, and Linda Clymer Stevenson.

A number of persons in this group have lent their patient and discerning ears to my stories as I wrote first drafts, read them aloud, and refined them over the years.

For the information and photos about Rocky Comfort, accolades and many thanks to Dan and Janice Kenney Shewmake, Joe and Sue Shewmake Allen, Alvin Ray and Patricia Alexander Mooney, Sue Sappington Seker, and Karl and Helen Wright Kenny.

I also owe a debt of gratitude to my Kelly cousins, George Leon Kelly and Mike Kelly, for without their work and that of other Kelly family members, I would never have discovered the colorful past of the old man I called Uncle Newt. Their work led me to Chip Carlson of Cheyenne, Wyoming, whose excellent book, *Tom Horn: Blood on the Moon*, contains, very likely, the most accurate version of Old West legend Tom Horn's life and also the most accurate account of the knife fight Newt had with Horn.

Ed Tolle of Holiday Island, Arkansas, lent critical detail to the chapter on the Missouri & North Arkansas Railroad with his well-researched book, *The Eureka Springs Railway: A Short-Line Railroad to a Little Town.*

I also must acknowledge the critically important interviews and visits I had with several persons who have passed from this mortal coil: George "Peach" Ford, Leonard Brattin, Wilbur Ray, J.W. Raulsten, Buck Higgs, and Joe Higgs. They knew details about Wheaton and Rocky Comfort and their long-ago residents that few others knew, and they generously shared that knowledge with me.

Fields Photo Archives and the Barry County Museum in Cassville very graciously provided photos of a number of Wheaton residents, plus a prominent Wheaton business structure.

In the Sacramento and Fair Oaks, California, area where I now reside, my friends Bruce and Susan Barstis provided valuable feedback on my stories from the perspective of persons who had never lived in or visited Wheaton and Rocky Comfort, Missouri.

A special category of thanks goes to my friends Kathleen Newton and her husband, Joe Happ, who, as Northwest Media Consultants, digitally processed all of the photos, created the photo pages in the electronic format required by my publisher, took my photo for the back cover, and also spent endless hours listening to my stories and encouraging me to continue this project.

Finally, I owe a mountain of praise to my wife, Jan, who read every version of every draft chapter of *Listening to the Jar Flies*; offered loving and constructive observations, ideas, and criticisms; put up with a sometimes cranky author; and improved this book enormously. Thank you, honey. You're the best.

Endnotes

Preface

1   Jon Paden in *Wheaton Echoes*, edited by Ralph and Betty Lamberson (Wheaton, MO: Wheaton Publishing Company, 2007), 56.

Chapter 1—Around Wheaton, the Way It Was

2   "Practical Christmas Gift," *Wheaton Journal*, December 25, 1947.

3   "New Owners Take Over Food Market," *Wheaton Journal*, September 27, 1951.

4   Chicago Cubs' shortstop Joe Tinker, second baseman Johnny Evers, and first baseman Frank Chance, who played together in 1912.

5   "Linebarger Sells Locker Plant," *Wheaton Journal*, April 29, 1954.

6   Story related to Jim Lewis by Chester "Buck" Higgs several times at unknown dates in the 1960s and 1970s.

7   "Railroad Torpedo Injures Boy's Eye," *Wheaton Journal*, May 27, 1948.

Chapter 2—Feed Room Manners

8   MFA was the acronym for Missouri Farmers Association, a co-op of farmer-owned feed and grocery stores in Missouri.

9   Whereas butter is made from the butterfat of milk, modern margarine is made mainly of refined vegetable oil and water and may also contain milk. In some locales, it is colloquially referred to as "oleo," short for oleomargarine; http://en.wikipedia.org/wiki/Margarine.

10   Hattie Carnegie was a fashion entrepreneur based in New York City from the 1920s to the 1960s. She was born in Vienna, Austria-Hungary as Henrietta Kanengeiser; http://en.wikipedia.org/wiki/Hattie Carnegie.

11   Information researched by Betty Higgs Lamberson, Wheaton, Missouri.

Chapter 3—The Ride with Ol' Mack

12   "Injured by Rolling Log," *Wheaton Journal*, April 10, 1952.

13 The widow put only two copper coins into the temple treasury, but it was all she had. "Calling his disciples to him, Jesus said, 'I tell you the truth, this poor widow has put more into the treasury than all the others. They all gave out of their wealth, but she, out of her poverty, put in everything—all she had to live on.'"—Mark 12:43–44.

14 "An Appeal to the Public," *Wheaton Journal*, May 13, 1954.

15 "Autoette Ordered for Harader," *Wheaton Journal*, August 5, 1954.

16 "Obituary," *Wheaton Journal*, January 22, 1959.

Chapter 4—Wheaton on Saturday

17 "Wheaton Merchants to Give Away $520 This Year," *Wheaton Journal*, January 5, 1933. The article states that Wheaton's merchants agreed to give away the money "at the rate of $10 every Saturday afternoon at three o'clock and will be given away the same as was done the past year." Apparently, the drawing had begun in 1932.

18 A binder was a piece of equipment that cut grain and tied it into bundles. The bundles were then stood upright in the field and stacked into shocks, which protected them from rain and moisture until the grain and stems were separated by a threshing machine.

19 The dictionary says *thresh* is the correct word, but the common pronunciation in the Ozarks was *thrash*.

20 Based on the author's memory and data from the American Petroleum Institute, reported in *Business Statistics*, 1955 edition, US Department of Commerce, Office of Business Economics (Washington, DC: US Government Printing Office, 1955), 171.

21 Related by Rebecca Allman Roscob and her brother, Herman "Butch" Allman, October 8, 2013.

22 "Will Re-Register for Prize Money," *Wheaton Journal*, January 24, 1946.

23 The little grocery had several owners between 1938 and 1959, including Stacy and Sallee, Linebarger and Hooten.

24 The Junge Bread Company made bread and rolls, and the Junge Biscuit Company manufactured cookies and crackers. Both were headquartered in Joplin, Missouri, about fifty miles northwest of Wheaton. The grocery store display boxes for Junge's cookies had an opening in one side that allowed customers to reach inside and pull out a package of cookies.

25 "Six Persons Narrowly Escape Death," *Wheaton Journal*, July 3, 1930.

26 A county judge in those days in Missouri wasn't a judicial judge. He was actually a county commissioner or county supervisor—an elected official who governs a county.

27 "Brattin, Wilson, Ryan And Chastain Winners," *Wheaton Journal*, November 4, 1948.

28 "2 Republicans Win In McDonald County," *Wheaton Journal*, November 16, 1950.

29 "Barry County Goes Republican," *Wheaton Journal*, November 9, 1950.

30 "Fire Destroys House & Contents," *Wheaton Journal*, April 12, 1956.

31 "To Re-register For Drawing Here," *Wheaton Journal*, April 12, 1956.

32 "Town Drawing to Stop After Sat.," *Wheaton Journal*, April 26, 1956.

Chapter 5—Rocky Comfort on Sunday

33 "Oldest R.C. Resident Dies," *Wheaton Journal*, May 23, 1946.

34 Cindy L. Marcell, Jameson, Keeny, Randleman, Stumbo, Pendergraft, & Seamster Family Lines, http://freepages.genealogy.roots.

35 Ibid.

36 The tilt mechanism registers motion applied to a machine; if too much motion is applied this way, the game is said to "tilt," and the player is penalized (losing the ball in play, the bonus points or a combination of both are the most common penalties). Some EM machines void the game of a player when tilted; http://en.wikipedia.org/wiki/Glossary_of_pinball_terms.

37 "Fire Destroys Part of Rocky Comfort," *Wheaton Journal*, April 12, 1932.

38 Woodmen of the World is a fraternal organization that operates an insurance company for its members.

39 "Fire Destroys Part...," *Wheaton Journal*.

40 Ibid.

41 Interview with George "Peach" Ford, November 18, 1998.

42 "8 Bldgs. Burn in Rocky Comfort," *Wheaton Journal*, October 13, 1938.

43 Marcell, "Jameson."

44 "Fire Destroys Grocery Store," *Wheaton Journal*, June 10, 1954.

45 E-mail from Mary Sue (Shewmake) Allen, April 2, 2014.

46 Arvin Hunter "Jack" Lewis and his wife, Ova, lived on a hilly farm two miles south of Powell in McDonald County.

47 Rocky Comfort Items, *Wheaton Journal*, March 19, 1936.

48 "NOTICE, A New Store in Rocky Comfort," *Wheaton Journal*, January 26, 1939.

49 Chat consists of small, sharp-edged pieces of ground limestone rock generated by lead and zinc mining in the tristate area of southwest Missouri, northeast Oklahoma, and northwest Arkansas. Chat is commonly used as a substitute for gravel.

50 "Minister for Rocky Comfort and Wheaton Churches of Christ," *Wheaton Journal*, October 9, 1947.

Chapter 6—The Characters I Met at Church

51 "J.D. Biggs of Rocky Comfort Dies," *Wheaton Journal*, April 24, 1952, and "Obituary," *Wheaton Journal*, May 1, 1952.

52 "Fruit Growers Association Will Meet Saturday August 9," *Wheaton Journal*, July 18, 1919.

53 "R.C. Church of Christ," *Wheaton Journal*, Oct. 17, 1946.

54 Obituary of Elsie Bufford, *Wheaton Journal*, April 23, 1959.

55 *Dinner* was the meal in the middle of the day in southwest Missouri. *Lunch* was seldom used as the name for the midday meal, and the meal at the end of the day was *supper.*

56 Two benefits from one action.

Chapter 7—O Bury Me Not

57 Local Items, *Wheaton Journal*, November 21, 1924.

58 "Railroad Torpedo Injures Boy's Eye," *Wheaton Journal*, May 27, 1948.

59 Interview with George "Peach" Ford, November 18, 1998.

60 Interview with Delbert Ely, July 6, 2007.

61 Ibid.

62 Folk song. Public domain.

63 Ibid.

64 Some details of the story furnished by Leonard Brattin during the summer of 1964.

Chapter 8—The Buyers, Sellers, and Traders

65 At Joplin, the low was forty-five degrees Fahrenheit, the high was fifty-seven degrees, and there was no precipitation; "Weather History for Joplin, MO," http://www.wunderground.com.

66 "A Friend Is Gone," *Wheaton Journal*, May 13, 1954.

67 Muncie Chapel Items, *Wheaton Journal*, May 20, 1954.

68 Wheaton News from *Wheaton Echoes*, 11; quoted from *Cassville Republican*, Thursday, December 19, 1907.

69 "John Silas McQueen" in *Wheaton Echoes*, 441; quoted from *Cassville Republican*, July 14, 1927.

70 "More Questions About Wheaton," *Wheaton Journal*, January 26, 1950.

71 "In Memoriam" in *The Bulldog* (Wheaton, MO: Wheaton High School, 1955).

72 Sandra Holmes Tinsley, "Wheaton School in the 1950's" in *Wheaton Echoes*, 170.

73 Pat McQueen, "Silas McQueen and Shoal Creek Summers" in *Wheaton Echoes*, 445.

74 "30 Years Ago From Richwood Telegram," *Wheaton Journal*, April 16, 1936.

75 McQueen, *Wheaton Echoes*, 443.

76 The US Bureau of Labor Statistics, which started keeping inflation statistics in 1913, says $10,000 in 1913 would be worth $239,466 in 2014, and the website http://m.wolframalpha.com says $10,000 in 1910 would be worth $257,800 in 2014.

77 *Wheaton Echoes*, 21–22.

78 "Obituary of J.S. McQueen," *Wheaton Journal*, June 9, 1960.

79 "Wheaton's Shipment of Strawberries Totals 53 Cars," *Wheaton Journal*, June 13, 1919.

80 http://www.dollartimes.com/inflation/inflation/inflation. php?amount=22000... 1919.

81 "Local Company Will Install Ice Plant and Cold Storage Building," *Wheaton Journal*, October 10, 1919.

82 Local Items, *Wheaton Journal*, October 24, 1919.

83 Neva's husband, a stepbrother of my grandfather Earnest Lamberson, whom Granddad always called "Wal," was co-owner with Joseph Abner Frazier of Chenoweth & Frazier's department store in Wheaton.

84 Wheaton's population was 374 in the 1920 US Census; "Population of Wheaton Decreases, *Wheaton Journal*, May 1, 1930.

85 Local Items, *Wheaton Journal*, September 9, 1919.

86 Rocky Comfort Items, *Wheaton Journal*, July 23, 1920.

87 "T.O. Davidson Buys Interest in Chenoweth & Frazier's Store," *Wheaton Journal*, January 9, 1920.

88 "Lumber Yard Changes Hands," *Wheaton Journal*, January 9, 1920.

89 "Community Club Organized," *Wheaton Journal*, February 13, 1920.

90 Local Items, *Wheaton Journal*, May 21, 1920.

91 "$35,000 Ice Storage and Power Plant Operating," *Wheaton Journal*, July 30, 1920.

92 "Rocky to Build New Berry Shed," *Wheaton Journal*, May 12, 1922.

93 "Harvesting of Berry Crop in Full Swing," *Wheaton Journal*, May 26, 1922; shipping under the Ford & Lamberson Brothers label, Virgil "Honk" Ford, my grandfather, Earn Lamberson, and his brothers Clarence W. "Tan" Lamberson and B. E. "Burt" Lamberson led the Rocky Comfort area in strawberries shipped from Wheaton in 1922.

94 "Vote of Wheaton Township in Primary," *Wheaton Journal*, August 4, 1922.

95 "Official Count Shows Some Close Races," *Wheaton Journal*, August 11, 1922.

96 "Record Enrollment at School Monday," *Wheaton Journal*, September 1, 1922.

97 "Will Build New Canning Factory," *Wheaton Journal*, January 26, 1923.

98 Local Items, *Wheaton Journal*, March 2, 1923.

99 Ad, *Wheaton Journal*, May 11, 1923.

100 The US Bureau of Labor Statistics' inflation calculator says $100,000 in 1923 would have a buying power of $1,386,385 in 2014.

101 "Why They Come," Chenoweth & Doerge ad, *Wheaton Journal*, October 26, 1923.

102 Frazier & Davidson Brothers ad, *Wheaton Journal*, November 23, 1923.

103 "M&NA Looks to 1924 as a Big Year," *Wheaton Journal*, January 4, 1924.

104 "Frazier & Davidson Bros. Trade Store Here to W.T. Evans of Neosho," *Wheaton Journal*, January 11, 1924.

105 Local Items, *Wheaton Journal*, January 25, 1924.

106 "Berry Growers Elect New Manager," *Wheaton Journal*, February 29, 1924.

107 Local Items, *Wheaton Journal*, April 11, 1924.

108 "Canning Factory Will Start Soon," *Wheaton Journal*, August 15, 1924.

109 From obituary of Carl Max Burger (1932–2004), who was Carl Burger's son and George Burger's grandson, and lived in Bentonville, Arkansas; "Find A Grave Memorial# 8486913," http://www.findagrave.com.

110 Local Items, *Wheaton Journal*, September 12, 1924.

111 McQueen, *Wheaton Echoes*, 443.

112 "Wallace Fox Buys Interest in Journal," *Wheaton Journal*, November 14, 1924.

113 "Rocky Comfort Mill Is Destroyed by Fire," *Wheaton Journal*, November 21, 1924.

114 Pat McQueen, "My Dad and the High Hard One" in *Wheaton Echoes*, 245.

115 Ibid, 246.

116 "Supervised Play to Be Staged Here" from the *Macon Chronicle-Herald* reprinted in the *Wheaton Journal*, June 7, 1928.

117 "Strawberry Shipment for 1928 Ended," *Wheaton Journal*, June 14, 1928.

118 "Mrs. R.W. Smith Dies Suddenly," *Wheaton Journal*, May 13, 1954.

119 "Malloy McQueen to Practice Law Here," *Wheaton Journal*, October 18, 1928.

120 "Wheaton Casts Large Vote Tues.," *Wheaton Journal*, November 8, 1928.

121 "Hoover Wins for President," *Wheaton Journal*, November 8, 1928.

122 Farm families in the Missouri Ozarks in those days had only a few ways of generating a steady but often meager flow of income. One of those ways was by milking cows and selling the milk and cream that each cow in the herd produced for approximately ten months of each year. Another way of creating a cash flow was by maintaining a flock of laying hens and selling their eggs every week. Depending on the size of the herd of milk cows and the number of laying hens in each flock, a farm family could depend on a small but steady stream of cash throughout most of each year. Crop production, on the other hand, generated once-a-year income after the crop was harvested.

123 "Chicken Thief Bill Introduced," *Wheaton Journal*, January 24, 1929.

124 "Chicken Thieves Make Raid," *Wheaton Journal*, January 24, 1929.

125 "Chicken Thief Was Constable," *Wheaton Journal*, January 31, 1929.

126 "McQueen's Bill Before House," *Wheaton Journal*, January 31, 1929.

127 "Mrs. J.S. McQueen Postmistress of 55th General Assembly," *Wheaton Journal*, January 24, 1929.

128 "Wheaton to Have a New $5,000 Cannery," *Wheaton Journal*, January 24, 1929.

129 "New Canning Company Held Meeting," *Wheaton Journal*, February 7, 1929.

130 "J.S. McQueen Makes Flying Trip Home," *Wheaton Journal*, April 18, 1929.

131 "Plane McQueen Came to Wheaton In Wrecked," *Wheaton Journal*, April 18, 1929.

132 "J.S. McQueen Appointed Fair Commissioner," *Wheaton Journal*, June 13, 1929.

133 Local Items, *Wheaton Journal*, August 1, 1929.

134 Local Items, *Wheaton Journal*, August 22, 1929.

135 *Wheaton Journal*, September 4, 1930.

136 "Barry Democrats Win Seven Offices," *Wheaton Journal*, November 6, 1930.

137 "339 Votes Cast Here Tuesday," *Wheaton Journal*, November 6, 1930.

138 "Farm Prices Still Lower," *Wheaton Journal*, December 4, 1930.

139 "Erecting New M.F.A. Filling Station," *Wheaton Journal*, October 8, 1931.

140 "New Feed Mill for Rocky Comfort," *Wheaton Journal*, August 27, 1931.

141 "New Year's Party," *Wheaton Journal*, January 7, 1932.

142 "J.S. McQueen Represents Wheaton at Truck Hearing," *Wheaton Journal*, January 28, 1932.

143 "Represents Wheaton at Truck Hearing," *Wheaton Journal*, March 17, 1932.

144 "J.S. McQueen Meets With State Board of Equalization," *Wheaton Journal*, March 24, 1932.

145 "Barry Co. Farm Taxes Reduced 21 Percent," *Wheaton Journal*, March 31, 1932.

146 Local Items, *Wheaton Journal*, April 7, 1932.

147 "Barry County Goes All Democratic," *Wheaton Journal*, November 10, 1932.

148 "Largest Recorded Vote Cast Here Tuesday," *Wheaton Journal*, November 10, 1932.

149 Local Items, *Wheaton Journal*, August 23, 1934.

150 "Prominent Citizen Passes Away," *Wheaton Journal*, February 9, 1933.

151 "Fred Doerge Sells Interest in Store to W.C. Chenoweth & Son," *Wheaton Journal*, April 6, 1933.

152 Rocky Comfort Items, *Wheaton Journal*, June 1, 1933; "Ross Davidson Passes Away," *Wheaton Journal*, November 16, 1933.

153 "Fruit Growers Meeting," *Wheaton Journal*, November 9, 1933; "Will Meet With Strawberry Growers Saturday," *Wheaton Journal*, December 5, 1936.

154 "Attends Grand Lodge," *Wheaton Journal*, September 27, 1934.

155 "Cans 423 Cans of Beans," *Wheaton Journal*, July 5, 1934.

156 "Want More Beef to Can at Factory," *Wheaton Journal*, September 6, 1934.

157 "Canning Factory Running Two Shifts a Day," *Wheaton Journal*, September 20, 1934.

158 USDC, Bureau of the Census, Decennial Census data.

159 "Catch Three Thieves in Apple Orchard," *Wheaton Journal*, September 27, 1934.

160 "Seeds to Be Furnished for Home Gardens," *Wheaton Journal*, February 21, 1935.

161 "Letter from J.W. Montgomery of Long Beach," *Wheaton Journal*, January 31, 1935.

162 See website http://www.chenowethsite.com/chalbert.htm for the story of Dr. Albert White Chenoweth's assassination.

163 "J.S. McQueen Elected Mayor," *Wheaton Journal*, October 3, 1935.

164 "McQueen Elected," *Wheaton Journal*, April 9, 1936.

165 "School Election," *Wheaton Journal*, April 9, 1936.

166 "Tomato Canning About Over," *Wheaton Journal*, September 23, 1937.

167 "Picnic Supper," *Wheaton Journal*, August 27, 1936.

168 Statement, "It was the first of several strokes" from "Silas McQueen and Shoal Creek Summers" in *Wheaton Echoes*, 444. Roots Web for Muncie Chapel Cemetery, Barry County, Missouri entry for McQueen, Lettie Mae (LAMBERT) lists her date of death as 1943, but a research note accompanying the entries by Donna Cooper and Ralph and Betty Lamberson says, "There is a death certificate for Lettie Mae McQueen, who died in Wheaton, Barry County, MO., Dec. 19, 1942, not 1943 as the stone reads."

169 Obituary of Irenie May Boswell McQueen, *Wheaton Journal*, March 2, 1950.

170 "Silas McQueen and Shoal Creek Summers," *Wheaton Echoes*, 443.

171 "Vineyard—McQueen," *Wheaton Journal*, August 16, 1951.

172 The McQueen Funeral Home was owned by Silas McQueen's brother, Boone, and Boone's wife, Edith.

173 "A Friend Is Gone," *Wheaton Journal*, May 13, 1954.

174 "Obituary of J.S. McQueen," *Wheaton Journal*, June 9, 1960.

Chapter 9—Wheaton's Mystery Man

175 A "shade tree" mechanic was a guy with little formal training but with an aptitude for fixing mechanical devices.

176 *Bringing Up Father* was the formal name for the comic strip by George McManus.

177 Historical Section, Army War College; *ORDER OF BATTLE OF THE UNITED STATES LAND FORCES IN THE WORLD WAR*, *American Expeditionary Forces: Divisions, Volume 2*; Washington, D.C.; Center of Military History, United States Army; 107. *Volume 3, Part 3*; 1,458.

178 Author unknown, "The T.N.T., Eighth Ammunition Train, Pathfinder Division, Company 'D,' Camp Lee, Va., 1919."

179 *Wheaton Journal*, April 5, 1934.

180 *Wheaton Journal*, April 12, 1934.

181 "Tuesday's Primary Election," *Wheaton Journal*, August 6, 1936.

182 *Wheaton Journal*, August 13, 1936.

183 "A Reminiscent Moment," *Wheaton Journal*, June 22, 1950.

184 Letter provided by Jo Ann Fox Hughes.

185 E-mail from Bobby Gene Davidson to Jim Lewis, May 31, 2009.

186 *Wheaton Journal*, May 16, 1946.

187 Ibid.

188 *Wheaton Journal*, September 14, 1939.

189 Wally Poor, "A Stroll Down Main Street," *Wheaton Echoes*, 495.

190 George Fagan Obituary, *Wheaton Journal*, February 18, 1960.

Chapter 10—The "May Never Arrive"

191 Missouri & Arkansas Railway Company (M&A), which succeeded the Missouri & North Arkansas Railroad (M&NA) in 1935 after the M&NA went into receivership and was purchased by a Texan, Frank Kell.

192 "Granddad" was Earnest William Lamberson, who lived on a farm a quarter mile south of the Wheaton-Stella road, three miles west of Wheaton. My parents' farm was one-eighth of a mile down the same lane that ended at Granddad's place.

193 Burton E. "Burt" Lamberson and Clarence W. "Tan" Lamberson.

194 "Harvesting of Berry Crop in Full Swing," *Wheaton Journal*, May 26, 1922.

195 "Buys M&NA Railroad," *Wheaton Journal*, March 21, 1935.

196 "No Settlement of M&A Strike," *Wheaton Journal*, September 12, 1946.

197 Edwin R. Tolle, *The Eureka Springs Railway: A Short-Line Railroad to a Little Town* (Eureka Springs, AR: Self-Published, 1992), 13–14; http://books.eurekaspringshistory.com/.

198 Ibid, 23–25.

199 *The Encyclopedia of Arkansas History & Culture, Missouri and North Arkansas Railroad (M&NA)*, Central Arkansas Library System, updated April 15, 2013; http://www.encyclopediaofarkansas.net.

200 Tolle, 25,28.

201 Ibid, 29.

202 *The Encyclopedia of Arkansas History & Culture*.

203 Tolle, 29.

204 "More Questions About Wheaton," *Wheaton Journal*, January 26, 1950.

205 *The Encyclopedia of Arkansas History & Culture*.

206 Ibid.

207 Ibid.

208 Tolle, 32–33.

209 Tipton Ford is just under twenty-six miles northwest of Wheaton, as the crow flies.

210 Tolle, 36.

211 Tolle, 37.

212 "Postcard Recalls Tragic Story of M&NA Accident," *Wheaton Journal*, November 23, 1950; "Article About M&A In Globe," reprinted from *Joplin Globe* in *Wheaton Journal*, November 7, 1963.

213 Tolle, 40.

214 Ibid.

215 Ibid.

216 Tolle, 41.

217 *The Encyclopedia of Arkansas History & Culture*, "Harrison Railroad Riot," updated August 26, 2011.

218 Tolle, 41.

219 Ibid.

220 "M&NA Sold, Reorganized, Resumes Operation," *Wheaton Journal*, May 5, 1922.

221 "Fairview Editor Wants Real Train Service," *Wheaton Journal*, May 12, 1922.

222 "Citizens Organize to Protect Railroad," *Wheaton Journal*, June 16, 1922. *Depredation* as used in the article is defined by Merriam-Webster Online: Dictionary and Thesaurus as "to lay waste; plunder; ravage."

223 Ibid.

224 "Wheaton Services and Businesses—Wheaton Post Office," *Wheaton Echoes*, 54.

225 "Bridge on M&NA Burned Sunday," *Wheaton Journal*, June 23, 1922.

226 "Bound Over to Circuit Court," *Wheaton Journal*, July 7, 1932.

227 *An Industrial War: History of the Missouri and North Arkansas Railroad Strike and a Study of the Tremendous Issues Involved: An Unprecedented Result of a Common Occurrence in American Industry and its Aftermath* (Harrison, AR: Bradley, Walter F. & Russell, 1923).

228 "Court Order Restrains M&NA Strikers," *Wheaton Journal*, July 7, 1932.

229 "New Attempt to Wreck M&NA," *Wheaton Journal*, August 7, 1922.

230 "Attempt to Burn Bridge Near Here," *Wheaton Journal*, October 13, 1922.

231 In locomotives and railroad cars, a journal bearing referred to the plain bearing once used at the ends of the axles of railroad wheels, which were enclosed by journal boxes. If the axle bearing overheated, it became a "hot box" that could start a fire capable of destroying the railroad car and others coupled to it; en.wikipedia.org/wiki/plain bearing.

232 "J.C. Murray Appeals to People Along M&NA," *Wheaton Journal*, December 15, 1922.

233 "M&NA Bridge Burned Near Eureka Tuesday," *Wheaton Journal*, January 12, 1923.

234 *The Encyclopedia of Arkansas History & Culture*, "Harrison Railroad Riot."

235 Ibid.

236 "Enraged Citizens Drive Strikers From Harrison," *Wheaton Journal*, January 19, 1923.

237 Ibid.

238 *The Encyclopedia of Arkansas History & Culture*, "Harrison Railroad Riot."

239 "Exaggerated," Editorial, *Wheaton Journal*, January 19, 1923.

240 "Local Citizens Take Steps to Protect Road in This District," *Wheaton Journal*, January 19, 1923.

241 "Ku Klux Klan Signs Posted Here," *Wheaton Journal*, March 2, 1923.

242 *The Encyclopedia of Arkansas History & Culture*, "Harrison Railroad Riot."

243 "Klan," *Wheaton Journal*, March 2, 1923.

244 Rocky Comfort Item, *Wheaton Journal*, March 9, 1923.

245 "KKK Lecturer," *Wheaton Journal*, November 30, 1923.

246 "M&NA Railway Improving Track," December 14, 1923.

247 "M&NA Looks to 1924 as a Big Year," *Wheaton Journal*, January 4, 1924.

248 "Ku Klux Klan Pay Visit to Revival Meeting," *Wheaton Journal*, January 18, 1924.

249 Local Items, *Wheaton Journal*, September 5, 1924.

250 *The Encyclopedia of Arkansas History & Culture*, "Harrison Railroad Riot"; Charles William Sloan Jr., "Kansas Battles the Invisible Empire, The Legal Ouster of the KKK From Kansas, 1922-1927," *Kansas Historical Quarterly*, http://www.kshs.org/kansapedia/ku-klux-klan-in-kansas/15612.

251 "Rehabilitation of M&NA Progresses," *Wheaton Journal*, May 30, 1924.

252 "Majority of Stock in M&NA Bought," *Wheaton Journal*, October 24, 1929.

253 "M&NA Receiver Resigns," *Wheaton Journal*, June 29, 1933.

254 "M&NA Tax Settlement," *Wheaton Journal*, May 3, 1934.

255 "Buys M&NA Railroad," *Wheaton Journal*, March 21, 1935.

256 "New Train Here Mon., June 7," *Wheaton Journal*, June 23, 1938.

257 "The Blue Goose," *Wheaton Echoes*.

258 *The Encyclopedia of Arkansas History & Culture*.

259 Ibid.

260 "No Settlement of M&A Strike," *Wheaton Journal*, September 12, 1946.

261 Tolle, 43.

262 *Wheaton Echoes*, 46.

263 "Truman Asked to Aid M&A Line," *Wheaton Journal*, January 13, 1949.

264 "Canning Factories Help to Community," *Wheaton Journal*, September 4, 1930.

Chapter 11—Listening to the Jar Flies

265 The Servicemen's Readjustment Act of 1944 (P.L. 78-346, 58 Stat. 284m), known informally as the G.I. Bill, was a law that provided a range of benefits for returning World War II veterans (commonly referred to as G.I.s). Benefits

included low-cost mortgages, low-interest loans to start a business, cash payments of tuition and living expenses to attend university, high school or vocational education, as well as one year of unemployment compensation; en.wikipedia.org/wiki/G.I. Bill.

Chapter 12—The Blacksmith Shop

266 In horse lingo, *giddy-up* means "get moving," *whoa* means "stop," *gee* means "go to the right," and *haw* means "go to the left."

267 Rocky Comfort Items, *Wheaton Journal*, August 14, 1933.

268 "In the Journal 26 Years Ago," *Wheaton Journal*, February 7, 1939. The article reprinted an item from twenty-six years earlier on February 7, 1913, that offered a $900 reward for the arrest and conviction of the person or persons who had dynamited the home of P. S. Potts.

269 Bob Davidson; e-mail messages to Jimmy Lewis; July 29, 1993; September 4, 2000; and December 13, 2000.

270 Ibid.

271 "Services Sunday for P.S. Potts," *Wheaton Journal*, March 15, 1962.

Chapter 13—Wally Fox, the Wheaton Gym, and Basketball

272 "Loses Sight of Right Eye," *Wheaton Journal*, December 14, 1950.

273 "Obituary—O.O. Fox," *Wheaton Journal*, July 8, 1943.

274 Jo Ann Fox Hughes, "The J.W. Fox Family" in *Wheaton Echoes*, 394.

275 "Wheaton Wins 1ˢᵗ Game in New Gym," *Wheaton Journal*, January 8, 1948.

276 Ibid.

277 Ibid.

278 Ibid.

279 "Special Election Levy for Gym Carries 234 to 66," *Wheaton Journal*, May 29, 1947.

280 "Notice to Patrons of Wheaton School District," *Wheaton Journal*, May 22, 1947.

281 "Donations to Date on Gymnasium," *Wheaton Journal*, May 22, 1947.

282 "Ed Landen Plays Santa to Wheaton," *Wheaton Journal*, December 18, 1947.

283 "Gym to Be Heated with Butane Gas," *Wheaton Journal*, December 18, 1947.

284 Ibid.

285 "Voting on $2.00 School Levy Tues.," *Wheaton Journal*, April 1, 1948.

286 James Cantrell, "Reflections on Youth at Wheaton" in *Wheaton Echoes*, 196.

287 Ibid., 197.

288 Wheaton did not play football, partly because the small number of boys in the student body would have made it difficult to field a football team, but more importantly, because during earlier years when there *was* a football team,

a player sustained a serious head injury that caused the school to withdraw from football.

Chapter 14—Doc McCall—Money and Medicine

289 O. B. Durham, "Well Known Wheaton Physician Retiring Today," *Wheaton Journal*, January 31, 1952.

290 Sally B. Kenney, *Memories of Dr. O.S. McCall*, letter written August 2012.

291 "McCall Hospital Is Completed," *Wheaton Journal*, November 14, 1924.

292 "Edward Everett's Gettysburg Address," https://www.gdg.org/Links/everet .html.

293 "Notice to Patrons of Wheaton School District," *Wheaton Journal*, May 22, 1947.

294 "To the Taxpayers of the Wheaton School District," *Wheaton Journal*, May 22, 1947.

295 "Special Election Levy for Gym Carries 234 to 66," *Wheaton Journal*, May 29, 1947.

296 "Wheaton Wins 1st Game in New Gym," *Wheaton Journal*, January 8, 1948.

297 Conversation with Ralph Lamberson, October 2012.

298 Kenney, *Memories*.

299 Ibid.

300 Ibid.

301 Phone interview with Rebecca Allman Roskob, September 27, 2012.

302 "Obituary," *Wheaton Journal*, February 2, 1956.

303 "Dr. O.S. McCall Dies After Three Months Illness," *Wheaton Journal*, February 2, 1956.

Chapter 15—Chapter 15—The Crash That Changed Wheaton, or Where Did the Flagpole Go?

304 "Kansas Boys Run Into Flag Pole," *Wheaton Journal*, August 10, 1950.

305 "Mayor Resigns," *Wheaton Journal*, September 29, 1949. The information about the concrete barrier was contained in the article about Wheaton mayor Bill Wiseman resigning because he was moving to Berryville, Arkansas.

306 "VE Day" was "Victory in Europe Day," May 8, 1945, that marked the formal acceptances by the Allies of World War II of Nazi Germany's unconditional surrender of its armed forces.

307 "Kansas Boys," *Wheaton Journal*, August 10, 1950.

308 "Mayor and Workmen Repairing Streets," *Wheaton Journal*, August 24, 1950.

309 "Kansas Boys," *Wheaton Journal*, August 10, 1950.

310 Ibid.

Chapter 16—Woodrow Ford—A Soldier Comes Home

311 "Obituary—Woodrow Cecil Ford," *Wheaton Journal*, April 3, 1969.

312 Frank O. Hough, *USMC Historical Monograph, The Seizure of Peleliu*, chapter 6, "Third Operational Phase: D-plus8—D-plus 15 (23–30 September)," 106.

313 Ibid., 108.

314 "Bloody Peleliu, The Aftermath," Axis History Forum, http://forum .axishistory.com/vi.

315 Ibid.

316 Hough, 178, for the date Peleliu was secured; Axis History Forum, "Bloody Peleliu, The Aftermath," for the postwar date of the surrender of the last Japanese defenders.

317 Hough, chapter 7, "The Wildcats Take Over (15 October–27 November)," 175.

318 Ibid., 177.

319 Robert Ross Smith, *U.S. Army in World War II, The War in the Pacific, The Approach to the Philippines*, chapter 24, "Peleliu: The Last Resistance," Results of Operations in the Palaus, 573.

320 "Morgan—Ford," *Wheaton Journal*, June 27, 1946.

321 "Obituary—Woodrow Cecil Ford," *Wheaton Journal*, April 3, 1969.

Chapter 17—Doc Ellison

322 Wheaton's weekly event during which names of persons who had registered were drawn from a metal box. If present, those whose names were drawn won a cash prize contributed by local merchants.

323 Betty Lamberson, "Early Ambulance Service in Wheaton" in *Wheaton Echoes*, 79.

324 "Dr. John R. Ellison Writes Mrs. U.S. Hussey," *Wheaton Journal*, December 23, 1954.

325 "New Doctor Coming to Wheaton Saturday," *Wheaton Journal*, January 7, 1937.

326 "Sells Interest In Hospital," *Wheaton Journal*, March 8, 1951.

327 *Sedalia Democrat*, November 22, 1940.

328 "Dr. J.R. Ellison Commits Suicide," *Wheaton Journal*, March 18, 1965.

329 "My Way" lyrics were written by Paul Anka and the music by Claude Francois.

Chapter 18—The Snake Oil Salesmen

330 "Milk checks" were the monthly checks that farmers with dairy cows received from the milk processing companies that purchased the milk, which was poured through a strainer into ten-gallon metal cans that were picked up daily by a milk hauler, who delivered them to a milk plant for processing.

331 If there were persons of other faiths who were in Wheaton on Saturday afternoons in the 1940s and 1950s, it was rare.

332 Petrified Forest National Park is a US national park in Navajo and Apache counties in northeastern Arizona.

Chapter 19—Wheaton's Great Banana War

333 "Weekend Specials Friday & Saturday," Farmers Exchange ad, *Wheaton Journal*, February 5, 1953.

334 "End-of-the-Month Sale" Hooten's Finer Foods ad, *Wheaton Journal*, March 26, 1953.

335 "2 Local Firms Move This Week," *Wheaton Journal*, May 21, 1953.

Chapter 20—The Day Aunt Jemima Came to Town

336 "Aunt Jemima to be Here Saturday," *Wheaton Journal*, November 14, 1946.

337 "Large Crowd Here to See Aunt Jemima Sat.," *Wheaton Journal*, November 21, 1946.

Chapter 21—Dike Elkins, the Forgotten Hero

338 Allen Eldridge Elkins's Native American ancestry is not known, but in *A Special Remembrance: "Let's Not Forget": The Trail of Tears in Barry County, Missouri 1838–1839* is this statement: "Many Cherokee Indians passed through this country and no doubt many of the future residents of Barry County today are descended from those early Indian travelers."

339 "Fire Destroys Garage at Rocky Comfort," *Wheaton Journal*, May 5, 1932.

340 Wheaton Motor Company ad, *Wheaton Journal*, July 7, 1932.

341 Local items disclose Bill Brown's plan to open station in Rocky Comfort, *Wheaton Journal*, January 4, 1934.

342 "A.E. Elkins Buys Insurance Agency," *Wheaton Journal*, November 8, 1934.

343 "Frank Haley Sells Oil Business," *Wheaton Journal*, December 6, 1934.

344 "Stubblefield Carries Wheaton District," *Wheaton Journal*, April 4, 1935.

345 Jeanie Decocq, "Wheaton Church of Christ" in *Wheaton Echoes*, 141–142.

346 "To Open New Store in Monett," *Wheaton Journal*, July 21, 1949.

347 "Barely Escapes Arrest," *Wheaton Journal*, November 3, 1949.

348 "Attends Gas Meet in Kansas City," *Wheaton Journal*, May 25, 1950.

349 "Elkins Sells Butane Business," *Wheaton Journal*, April 19, 1951.

350 "Mrs. A.E. Elkins Dies Suddenly," *Wheaton Journal*, May 20, 1954.

351 "Wheaton Tractor Company to Hold Open House Tues.," *Wheaton Journal*, February 24, 1955.

352 The next paragraph, which is omitted, explained in detail the financial steps Dike and Cleffa took to assist their daughter-in-law and restore the oil

company to solvency. The entire article can be found in the *Wheaton Journal*, February 2, 1961.

353 Grantland Rice, "Casey's Revenge" (1906).

Chapter 22—Little Charlie and the Unbelievers

354 "Railroad Torpedo Injures Boy's Eye," *Wheaton Journal*, May 27, 1948.

355 Ibid.

356 Barney Calame, whose father, Frank, was pastor of the Wheaton Methodist Church, remembers Little Charley's donkey ride as being on a Sunday. I recall that it was on a Saturday, leaving the possibility that Little Charley had two donkey rides through Wheaton.

Chapter 23—The Tornado That Brought Barney Bates to Town

357 Dad apparently thought that lying down behind the pond bank at its lowest point near the water was the next best thing to getting in a storm cellar. Given the ferocity of this twister, it is doubtful that the pond bank would have provided protection if the tornado had come our way.

358 "Storm Does Thousands In Damage Sweep Thru County; None Are Killed," *Cassville Democrat*, November 4, 1943.

359 "Worst Tornado In Years Strikes Here," *Wheaton Journal*, November 4, 1943.

360 "Worst Tornado," *Wheaton Journal*, November 4, 1943.

361 A few years later, E. L. Thomas opened a lumberyard and building supply store on Wheaton's Main Street.

362 "Storm," *Cassville Democrat*, November 4, 1943.

363 Ibid.

364 Jeanie (Bates) Eubanks, "Corsicana," *Wheaton Echoes*, 320.

365 Jeanie (Bates) Eubanks, "On the Banks of Joyce Creek (Corsicana)," *Back to Barry*, compiled by Gloria E. Crosby (Curtis Media Corp., 1989), 4.

366 "Sells Supply Store to N. L. Bates," *Wheaton Journal*, October 30, 1947.

367 *Wheaton Journal*, January 1, 1948.

368 Jeanie (Bates) Eubanks, "Main Street U.S.A.," *Wheaton Echoes*, 491.

369 Ila Jean Richter Hazelrigg, "My Memories of Wheaton," *Wheaton Echoes*, 490.

370 Eubanks, "Main Street," *Wheaton Echoes*, 493.

371 "The Family History of Gary Lee Bates and Norma Jean (Bates) Eubanks," *Wheaton Echoes*, 358.

372 Ann Pietrangelo, "Chiggers: Little Bugs with a Big Bite," http://www .healthline.com/health-slideshow//chigger-bite: "Chiggers are tiny members of the arachnid family. Although they are extremely small in size, their bites pack a powerful punch. They're so tiny that you probably won't notice when they jump from that tall blade of grass onto your skin. You won't feel

it as they hitch a ride right into your home. When you eventually feel them, however, they can make you itch like you've never itched before."

373 "Mothers and Fathers," *Wheaton Journal*, March 25, 1954.

374 "Barney Bates Obituary," *Wheaton Journal*, January 25, 1968.

375 "Boy Killed in Saturday Storm; Barn Is Destroyed But Livestock Not Hurt," *Cassville Republican*, March 29, 1945.

376 "Tornado Does Wide-Spread Damage Wednesday Night," *Wheaton Journal*, March 25, 1954.

Chapter 24—My Neighbors, the Robinsons

377 Maytag ad, *Wheaton Journal*, December 1, 1938. The ad announced sales prices for electric and gas washers, as well as Zenith and RCA Victor radios. Roy Robinson was the proprietor of the Maytag store.

378 "Store Closes After 42 Years in Business," *Wheaton Journal*, June 23, 1983.

379 "Wins Trip to Maytag Factory in Newton, Iowa," *Wheaton Journal*, October 20, 1949.

380 "Obituary (John R. Robinson)," *Wheaton Journal*, December 20, 1956.

Chapter 26—Good Doughgod

381 A corner piece of corn bread had more outside crust and often was regarded as especially desirable.

382 John F. Gooldy, "Early Day History of the Little Snake River Valley," Carbon County Historical Society, April 24, 1960; filed with the American Heritage Center of the University of Wyoming.

383 *Descendants of Judge James Kelly*, a genealogy compiled by Kelly Family members, including George Leon Kelly of Granby, Missouri, 73.

384 Chip Carlson, written comments to Kelly Family researcher, undated, in Kelly Family genealogy, *Descendants of Judge James Kelly*.

385 Jay Monaghan, *Tom Horn: Last of the Bad Men* (Indianapolis, IN: Bobbs-Merrill Company, 1946), 179–183.

386 Ibid.

387 Ibid.

388 Ibid., 183.

389 Chip Carlson, *Tom Horn: Blood on the Moon: Dark History of the Murderous Cattle Detective* (Glendo, WY: High Plains Press, 2001), 117.

390 Ibid., 115.

391 Gooldy, "Early Day History."

392 *Descendants of Judge James Kelly.*

393 Etta Place was a companion of the outlaws—Butch Cassidy, whose real name was Robert Leroy Parker, and Sundance Kid, whose name was Harry Alonzo

Longabaugh. Bert Charter, who owned a ranch near Jackson Hole, also was reported to be a member of the Hole-in-the-Wall gang.

394 Monaghan, *Tom Horn*, 183.

395 Carlson, *Tom Horn*, 307.

396 "Obituary," *Wheaton Journal*, May 26, 1949.

Chapter 28—The Gentle Genius

397 Missouri State Highway 44 is now State Highway 76.

398 "Singing conventions" were gospel songfests, usually held on Sunday afternoons, or sometimes all day, throughout the Ozark Mountains of southwest Missouri, northeast Oklahoma, and northwest Arkansas. Gospel quartets and other small singing ensembles performed.

399 Shape notes rely on the shape of the notes rather than the lines and spaces the notes are on to determine pitch. They were considered easier to sight read than notes on lines and spaces. A shape note scale is recited, "Do, re, mi, fa, sol, la, ti, do," which is equivalent to C, D, E, F, G, A, B, C when notes are written traditionally.

Chapter 30—Joe's Cuban Missile Crisis

400 "The Cuban Missile Crisis, October 1962; Milestones: 1961–1968," US Department of State, Office of the Historian, https://history.state.gov/ milestones /1961-1968/cuban-missile-crisis.

401 Ibid.

402 "McDonnell F-101 Voodoo," Wikipedia, http://en.wikipedia.org/wiki/ McDonnell_F-101_Voodoo.

403 Joe Higgs quotes taken from conversation with him at Roaring River State Park's Emory Melton Lodge, October 2005.

404 "In Celebration of Life," brochure for Gary Joe Higgs, 1938–2007.

Chapter 31—My Last Summer in Wheaton

405 "Committees to Serve at Chicken Barbeque," *Wheaton Journal*, June 4, 1964.

DISCARL

Made in the USA
Lexington, KY
29 June 2015